William Marshal
Earl of Pembroke

Catherine A. Armstrong

Catherine A. Armstrong

June 30, 2008

Text
© Catherine A. Armstrong 2006
Coats-of-Arms & genealogical tables
© W. Greg Armstrong 2006
Interpretations of maps
© W. Greg Armstrong 2006
Interpretations of Pembroke Castle
© George C. Bobo 2006
Layout & Design
Shannon K. Cronin

ISBN   978-1-60530-385-7

ISBN 978-1-60530-385-7

9 781605 303857

90000>

Seneschal Press
P.O. Box 441192 Kennesaw, GA 30160
928 Greenhouse Patio Dr., Kennesaw, GA 30144

Foreword

The life of William Marshal reads like the stuff of medieval legend. Born the younger son of a minor English noble, he rose to become the confidant of kings and one of the most powerful barons of England. Along the way he helped shape the future of the English monarchy and of England itself. After years as a landless knight-errant, earning his living by his skill with arms on the tournament fields of France, Marshal eventually came to the attention of King Henry II, the first ruler of England's Angevin dynasty, and of his queen, Eleanor of Aquitaine. He entered their court as the tutor in arms and chivalry of their eldest son and soon became a trusted member of the royal household. From that point forward, he was the paragon of feudal loyalty through four reigns. He served King Henry steadfastly when his French vassals and then even his own sons rebelled against him. He played a key role in maintaining the stability of the realm during Richard I's long absence on Crusade and helped raise the ransom that released the king from captivity. Though badly mistreated by his sovereign, Marshal stood by King John throughout the baronial rebellion that led to Magna Carta, and at the end of his long life, he served as regent for John's young son Henry III, helping assure both the survival of the dynasty and the guarantees provided to the king's subjects by the Great Charter.

Through royal favor, the once landless knight married Isabelle de Clare, the greatest heiress of her day. She brought her husband the title Earl of Pembroke and claim to extensive holdings in Ireland as well. As earl, Marshal became one of the most important nobles in the Angevin realm, his influence stretching from the Welsh borderlands to Ireland and France. As such, he was potentially both a valued ally to the crown and a possible obstacle to the centralization of royal power in England, Ireland, and the Angevin holdings in France. As Catherine Armstrong rightly asserts, Marshal truly was the "linch pin or the pivot point" in many crucial episodes in the medieval history of England and the rest of the Angevin realm.

The first scholarly biography of William Marshal was published by Sidney Painter in 1933. One of the more recent, George Duby's, <u>William Marshal : the Flower of Chivalry</u>, was published in 1984 in French and translated into English in 1985. Catherine Armstrong's work places William Marshal squarely in the context of his times, inviting us to judge him by the standards of his contemporaries rather than by modern standards, and this makes his achievements all that more astounding. She gives far more attention to Ireland than previous scholars have done, and she deftly guides the reader through the complex web of marriage and kinship connections that were so crucial in gaining and maintaining power, wealth, and status in medieval England. An indefatigable researcher, Armstrong has exhaustively explored the printed sources for Marshal's life, from the contemporary *L'Histoire de Guillaume le Marechal*, the published records of the English chancery and exchequer, and the annals and chronicles of the period to an extensive list of modern monographs and other secondary sources. Her work both updates the older accounts of Marshal's life and career and reveals new information about both the Earl of Pembroke and Isabel de Clare. The end product is a fully realized portrait of one of the most remarkable men of his age or of any other.

Dr. E. Howard Shealy
Chair, Department of History
Kennesaw State University

Front Cover:

Coats-of-arms

William Marshal

Marshal of England

"Per pale or and vert, lion rampant gules"

(Herald's Roll, St. George's Roll, Vermandois Roll, Glover's Roll)

Richard de Clare

Earl of Hertford

"Or three chevrons gules"

(Herald's Roll, The Camden Roll, St. George's Roll

Vermandois Roll, Glover's Roll)

Interpretations by W. Greg Armstrong

Back Cover:

Drawing of Pembroke Castle 20th Century

Interpretation by George Bobo

Preface

This has been a twelve year journey for me, and there are many people to whom I owe debts for their time, assistance, and unstinting support. Sidney Painter and R. Allen Brown brought to life a time period that utterly fascinated me and raised questions that I was determined to answer. So my first debt is owed to two superb writers of history who showed me that history could and should be written so well that it could completely captivate and educate the reader. I also owe a debt to another historian, who prefers to be known as a writer of fiction rather than history. Shelby Foote taught me that any writer, no matter in what genre he or she writes, must learn how to write well. He taught me that a writer writes to learn what he or she does not know and that the success of that written text is in its ability to engage the reader in the writer's exploration of discovery.

I owe a great debt to two professors at Kennesaw State University for teaching me, challenging me, and supporting me in my efforts to write a new biography of William Marshal. Much of what is the best of this text is owed to Dr. Howard Shealy, Chair of the Department of History, and to Dr. Susan Hunter, former Director of the Graduate School of Professional Writing. To Beverly, Rita, Amy, and Michelle of the Inter-Library loan department of the Sturgis Library of Kennesaw State University, I owe a big thank you for struggling through the sometimes complicated Latin names of the books and articles that they so patiently requested and acquired for me over the years. I owe a debt that can never be repaid to Shannon Cronin in KSU's Multimedia Lab for her patience and help over all these years; she is the best, stalwart friend one could ever want.

To Jeff Thomas, webmaster and creator of "The Castles of Wales" Internet web site, I owe the opportunity to publish earlier, condensed versions of my biographical texts of William Marshal, Richard "Strongbow" de Clare, and John fitz Gilbert. My sincere thanks go to two gentlemen from Australia who generously gave of their time and expertise and aided me with any questions about medieval law and the Latin terms used to define them and with the glossary for this book. To Peter Merity, solicitor, and to his father John Patrick Merity, retired magistrate, you have my deepest gratitude for all of your time, your assistance, and your support. Last, but not least, I owe a special thanks to my son, Greg, and to my nephew, George, for their contributions to the final manuscript, for their patience and time, their reading and editing, and their support whenever I needed them.

One editorial note must be explained to preclude any letters to the publisher and/or the author. I have written the word *honour* thus throughout my entire manuscript. Because this word was an essential quality of the man William Marshal and his life, I believed that it was required of me to write it in this manner. Any errors in this book are my responsibility, and any successes are due to that magnificent knight, Earl William Marshal of Pembroke.

Catherine A. Armstrong, 2006

TABLE OF CONTENTS

Introduction   1-2

I. William Marshal's World   3-25

II. John fitz Gilbert, the Marshal   26-49

III. Richard "Strongbow" de Clare   50-82

IV. William Marshal: Knight and Tutor   83-99

V. Marshal as Tourneyer Knight   100-124

VI. William Marshal and King Henry II   125-132

VII. William Marshal and Richard Lionheart   133-165

VIII William Marshal and King John   166-188

IX. Marshal, King John, and Ireland   189-205

X. King John, William de Braose, and Pope   206-218

XI. Road to Rebellion   219-235

XII. Baronial Revolt: John's Last Years   236-242

XIII. William Marshal Regent of England   243-274

XIV. Death of an Earl   275-287

XV. William Marshal's Daughters   288-294

XVI. William Marshal II   295-315

XVII. Richard Marshal   316-345

XVIII. Gilbert, Walter, and Anselm Marshal   346-349

XIX. William Marshal's Legacy   350-354

Abbreviations   355-363

Notations' Bibliography   364-384

Genealogical Tables   385-431

Glossary   432-451

Bibliography   452-505

Index   506-516

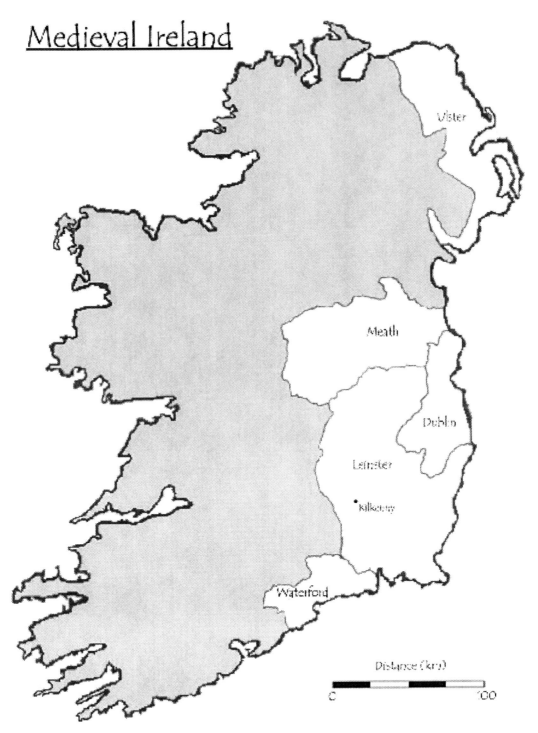

Medieval Ireland

Ulster

Meath

Dublin

Leinster

Kilkenny

Waterford

Distance (km)

0   100

Medieval Wales

William Marshal
Earl of Pembroke

Sometimes in history and in life there is an event or a person that, while

not the main occurrence or the main character, is still a pivotal point in an era.

Without that event's or person's presence the surrounding results could have been

greatly altered. William Marshal was such a pivotal point in the medieval history of

England. Had Marshal not existed and not been the man he was many major events

in late twelfth and early thirteenth-century English history could have been radically

changed. More than once in his life, Marshal was a linch pin, the pivot at the center,

on which the fortunes of others or of a country turned. This is the story of the people and events that played a role in Marshal's life and of Marshal's pivotal role in medieval English history.

The image above is an illustration, a vision, of how a Welsh Marcher castle might have looked in the late twelfth and early thirteenth century. This is the castle of Pembroke in southwest Wales; it was the *caput* of the earldom of Pembroke and held by the man William Marshal in right of his wife Isabel de Clare. The image on the cover is a shadow image of Pembroke today. Though parts of the castle and its outer wall still stand, it is a shadow of the power and influence it once symbolized and embodied. It is an echo of a time that played a part in shaping western civilization. What this castle symbolized and what its lord accomplished are as relevant today as they were in their own time. What follows is the story of both.

I. William Marshal's World

William Marshal (b. c.1147 d.1219) was a medieval knight who rose from the rank of tourneyer to baron, *familiaris Regis,* Earl of Pembroke, and regent of England. This is the story of the life and times of Marshal, of the people and forces that helped to shape the man, and of the family and circumstances that produced Isabel de Clare, the beautiful heiress who married him. An accurate and just evaluation of a person can only be achieved by judging him or her by the standards of his or her own time, not by the standards and values of today's time. Therefore, this story begins with an introduction to William Marshal's world.

To understand William Marshal it is necessary to know the law and customs that ruled medieval man singly and collectively, the expectations of individuals and governments, and the realities that defined his world. The term *feudalism* was not created until well after the time period to which it applies, but it describes the system of customs, practices, and law that defined and governed the world of this time. In 1066, William of Normandy conquered England. As king, William imposed on Britain the feudal system of land possession, of accompanying customs of fealty and homage, and of levels of society based upon the function of individuals. The customs and practices of feudalism formed the basis of rule, law, and society in England and Normandy.

William the Conqueror defined the first parameters of feudalism in England. William as lord and king gave lands (*fiefs*) to the Anglo-Norman men who accompanied him and/or provided resources for taking England. To his most trusted men, William gave large grants of land in England and Wales. These men were responsible for taking and holding their fiefs, for building castles to control the lands and the natives, and for the *enfeoffment* of their own vassals and knights to aid in keeping and developing their own particular fiefs. These grants of land had different economic and social levels.

If a man held his lands directly from the king (i.e. they were granted to him by the king) he was a tenant-in-chief and by definition he was a baron of a higher order than a baron who held his lands from another baron. His lands were called a barony, and each barony had a chief seat or *caput*, which was usually a castle. There were very specific laws regarding a barony because those who held them were usually the most powerful and important men in the land. The caput of a barony could not be alienated (given or sold away from the heir of the baron holding it), granted as dower, or divided among co-heirs. A man could also hold lands at "fee farm," meaning that he lived on and worked the lands; but he did not own them, nor could these lands be automatically inherited by the tenant's heirs. Only the lord who actually did own the lands could dictate who held lands of him as a tenant of a fee farm, and the lord could choose whether to accept the tenant of a prior lord. A man could hold lands that were inherent to the office he held; he could hold by sergeanty or as *seneschal, castellan*, marshal, *justiciar*, or even as bishop or archbishop. These lands were not his; they belonged to the office that he currently held. Unless the man held a hereditary office, his office and lands did not pass down to his son and heir. The lands held as fiefs were the source of a man's survival and the defining factor of his place and power within his world.

To be a knight was to belong to the lowest rung of the upper class; it meant that the man belonged to a professional class, an *ordo equestris*. Matthew Strickland explains that this label denoted a specific function, and that this function clearly carried with it the connotations of a man of martial prowess (War and Chivalry 22-23; 150-53). The function was regarded as that of a warrior and as such recognized as a member of the military elite. The knight had to be fully trained and skilled in the use of all of the equipment required by the medieval knight; he had to be willing and capable of dominating the contemporary battlefield. The Normans had taken and settled England and parts of Wales and Scotland, but they controlled the country through castles and the armed knights, bowmen, and foot soldiers that each baron or lord mustered from his own *caput*. The Anglo-Norman baron or lord could hold fiefs in England, Wales, Normandy, and/or Ireland. He was responsible for the peace and order of his own fiefs. In any wars or actions of his immediate lord, he could be called upon for assistance whether he was knight, baron, earl, or ecclesiastic. This fact made the knight an integral and necessary part of society. A knight might not be a baron or lord, but a baron or lord had to be a knight. You could not survive as a holder of lands if you could not protect and defend your lands and vassals. This was a warrior's world in which the abilities and skills of a man to control and govern his lands and vassals determined his place in society.

Marshal's world was defined by the ties of fealty and homage of lord to vassal whether that lord was king to earl or baron, king to ecclesiastic, king to vassal, earl or baron to vassal, or ecclesiastic to vassal. Feudalism was an organization of society based on the holding of a fief (usually a unit of land) in return for a stipulated honorable service (normally military) with a relationship of homage and fealty existing between grantor and grantee. The ties that bound fief to vassal to lord were the ties of vassalage. The first act of vassalage was the act of homage. The vassal placed his hands between the hands of the man who would be his lord, and the vassal swore fealty, homage, and obedience to his lord. This was a solemn, symbolic, and visual act that carried the hallowed aspect of religious sanction. This act could include the investiture of land, but not always. Knights could swear fealty and homage to a lord and serve in that lord's household without being granted land from him. The relationship of vassalage was a voluntary one between two free men, but it was irrevocable except for the default of obligation on the part of either lord or vassal. If a vassal failed to provide military service or aid to his lord, or if the lord failed to protect and provide maintenance and justice for his vassal, the bond was broken. The greatest crime in medieval England was the crime of *felonie*; this was the crime of breaking one's oath of loyalty to one's lord.

Those men who became knights and vassals were bound to each other by vassalic commendations holding at least part of their lands by knight service or as fiefs. The services due from a vassal to a lord were a fixed number of armed and trained knights for duty during any military contingency, save in rebellion of the king. The vassal also provided men to garrison his lord's castles for a certain amount of time. In the event of his lord being held for ransom, the vassal was required to give a customary aid (money) for the release of his lord. The vassal was expected to contribute a customary set amount of aid on the knighting of his lord's heir and on the first marriage of the lord's eldest daughter.

The other customary aids (*auxiliums*) required of a vassal concerned the inheritance of fiefs. A vassal, should he be the heir to his father's fiefs, was expected to pay a relief for the *seisin* (possession) of his father's lands. The customary relief for a barony was one hundred pounds. The relief was paid to the lord from whom the father had held his lands. If a vassal died with no heir and/or there was a dispute about the right to a fief, the lord could take back the fief as a forfeiture of the vassal. In the case of the Crown the fiefs were *escheated* back to the Crown and placed into royal hands to do with as the king chose. If the vassal died and the heir was under age (under twenty-one), the lord could hold the lands in guardianship until the minor came of age. The custom in this aspect of feudalism was that the guardian had to maintain the estates, but there were no laws to enforce this. With regard to custody of the lands and body of a minor, a lord could sell this custody to another lord or knight. The lord of a vassal had by custom the control of the widow and minor children should the vassal die. The lord decided if and to whom the widow could be remarried, and if and to whom the minor children could be married. These were the customs and practices of feudalism; they fall under the category of patronage and were the powers of a lord over a vassal. Thus the lord could make or break a man by giving or withholding lands, marriage, custody, and *seisin*.

Heirs and heiresses of the king's tenants-in-chief who were minors were held by the king as his prerogative right. The king had the right to hold these children and/or widows in his own hands as overlord, or he could give or sell these wardship rights to one of his barons. A widow could "fine" (offer a payment, an *oblate)* with the king for her right to either not be married again or the right to choose her own second husband with the king's permission and approval. The widow might also fine with the king to have custody and wardship of her own children. The king might grant the widow custody of the children, but the question of the marriage of an heir or heiress and the wardship of that child's lands would usually be held by the king or be given to one of the king's barons. Wardship of the lands could be held until the male heir came of age at twenty-one, or until the heir or heiress was married. The final decision lay with the king when a tenant-in-chief was involved. The inherent problem with wardship was that often a widow might find herself in competition with a baron for control of either her right to remarry or not, or her right to custody and control of the lives of her children.

Wardships and the rights of widows were important economic elements in medieval society. The fines found in the extant records for King Henry II show 2,096 fines offered by widows for their right to remarry or not. The average fine under Henry II was 110 marks. For 3,411 fines made with Richard, the average fine was 131 marks, and for 41,490 fines made with John the average fine was 278 marks (Waugh The Lordship of England p 159, Table 4.4). The fines offered for wardship to these three kings show that of 3,876 fines offered to Henry II, the average fine was 176 marks. Of some 11,579 fines offered to Richard, the average fine was 1,158 marks. For John, of the 49,082 fines offered, the average fine was 3,068 marks (Waugh p 157, Table 4.3). These numbers provide evidence of how economically profitable wardship of heirs and heiresses and rights of widows could be to the king and how costly they could be to the interested parties who wished to obtain those rights.

There was no middle class as such during this time period; a man's identity and place in society was determined by the amount of land he held and the wealth and power it denoted. The men of this time could be individual knights, lesser barons, great barons, and earls. There were never more than twelve earls between 1066 and 1300, and a total of approximately 200 barons who varied greatly in the amount of lands and wealth they possessed. The aristocracy was one of birth rather than merit with the exception of a lesser knight marrying an heiress who brought with her lands, title, and position. It was an aristocracy of inheritance by 1100. The landed elite lived off the resources of their estates that were cultivated by their tenants and paid staffs. The basic components of a baron's income came from rents, the sale of agricultural products, rights in churches and mills, scutage due from subtenants holding by military service, and from towns if they were on the lord's fiefs. The aristocracy was composed of lords and greater barons who were superiors in class and rank. They were expected to take the lead in national politics, advise the king, and direct local government through the power they derived from the lands and men they held and controlled.

The one paramount fact of feudalism was that the oath of fealty given by a knight, baron, or earl to his lord was viewed as the very essence and manifestation of his honour and status as knight. In a world where a man's voluntarily spoken vow of fealty was the visual and symbolic act of feudal commendation, the betrayal of this vow was considered the highest form of treason and one of the most dishonourable acts any man could commit. Their entire world, their system of governance and of life, was based upon the reliability of a man's word, his spoken bond. In the modern world of media, commercialism, and politics, it is almost impossible to conceive of this aspect of early medieval history, to comprehend a world built upon a man's sense of honour and his trustworthiness in keeping his word. Yet, this was William Marshal's world. It functioned, survived, and eventually grew into a world of written laws, rights, and freedoms that would encompass all levels and ranks.

The manifestation of feudalism and power was the castle. The castle was the private fortified residence of a lord; it was the visual *caput* of that lord's power and status. All governance of a lord's fief was conducted in his castle, and that castle served as the center of justice and protection for his vassals. Castles were the visible statement of the relationships among the nobles and barons; the change of ownership or custody of castles was an indication of the political power and status of a given individual A king's ability to rule effectively in medieval time was based upon his ability to appoint custodians loyal to the crown who would not alienate or antagonize the local population and to command the loyalty and support of at least some of the greater tenants-in-chief. One of the main checks on the authority of the English crown was the military power of the baronage, and the key element of that power was the great number of castles controlled by those barons. The castle's importance in warfare lay in its ability to hold during a siege; the longer a castle could withstand a siege the more time, resources, and men it could cost the enemy.

Any castle that was well garrisoned and could control the immediate surrounding area was a base from which revenues could be gathered. The revenues could be custom and were therefore the legal expected revenues to be collected, or they could be irregular such as payment of exceptional taxation, fines for misconduct, or confiscation of rents or produce from the dependent and independent estates tied to that particular castle. Thus castles were not just the manifestation of power; they were seats of actual power and valuable assets to both lord and king.

The castle was a home and a seat of government and justice for the area that surrounded each; castles were somewhat basic in their composition except for the king's castles which were more elaborate than most lords' castles. The castle served as a communication center and a governing center. It was here that the courts of the shire, hundred, and honour met, and it was here that vassals came to pay taxes, answer summons from their lord or king, obtain justice from their overlord, and present themselves for service. Because the castle was the seat of a lord's fief and because a medieval baron might have several fiefs in different parts of England, medieval society was a very peripatetic one. A lord and his family might spend a great deal of their time on horseback and on the move. It was necessary that a lord see and be seen by his vassals as a concerned and interested lord who took the welfare of his lands and his vassals seriously as a duty and an obligation. By necessity, horsemanship became a learned skill by most of the upper class, and though one could travel in a wagon of some sort, the condition of the roads in medieval England would not have made this form of conveyance too desirable or comfortable, particularly in winter.

By the middle of the twelfth century most castles had curtain walls which would surround the main portions of a castle, towers that intersected the walls at strategic points, a bailey, a courtyard, a keep, and often a strongly fortified gatehouse which protected the entrance to the castle. The keep might be a tower keep or a hall keep; these housed the great hall of the castle and would be the focal point for the conduction of all of the lord's business. The great hall was the area used for dining, large gatherings, and for the meeting of the courts: shire, hundred, and honour. The hall could be painted or decorated with tapestries, banners, armour, and trophies from war or the hunt; the stone floor would be covered with rushes or straw which were changed often and scented with herbs. The minor members of the household slept in the hall on pallets or benches. A chapel would be built either within the castle itself, or built as a separate building within the castle walls. This provided for the spiritual welfare of the lord, his family, and his vassals; this was a central part of the lord's household. The solar or bower was a separate room within the castle that served as the withdrawing room for the lord and his family as well as their sleeping area. Heat was provided by fireplaces that were usually built into the wall of the castle to provide adequate ventilation for the smoke. The toilets/latrines were also built into the walls of the castle to allow for chutes down which waste was sent into a cess pit or the moat. Bathing was not unknown during this time, and tubs were not an uncommon piece of furniture. Some tubs might be provided with a canopy or a tent-like covering to provide privacy for the bather. Some lords actually traveled with their tubs, including King John.

Castles and monasteries had fish ponds on their property which provided fresh fish for their table. The lands of both often had orchards of apples, pears, nuts, and sometimes vineyards. If there was no well within the castle walls, a cistern was built to provide a reserve supply of water for general use and in case of war. Other buildings and parts of a castle could include kitchens for preparing meals and workshops for blacksmiths/farriers, carpenters, armourers, barns and stables for their horses, and mews for their hunting birds.

The garrison of a castle would include a castellan, men-at-arms who were both mounted and foot soldiers, crossbowmen and archers, squires who were undergoing training for knighthood, and knights who were part of the lord's household or had not yet been given a fief of their own. Watchmen, porters, engineers, cooks, and servants were all part of the usual household of a castle. The marshal was in charge of providing and maintaining suitable mounts for the lord and his family as well as horses for the garrison's knights (three horses per knight). The marshal was also responsible for transporting the household goods and organizing the departure of the lord from one household to another, for deliveries to and from markets, fairs, and merchants, and for the feed supplies for the horses of the castle. The castle blacksmith forged and sharpened the tools and weapons of the household, maintained them, made the hinges for the doors of the castle, grilles for the windows, and made and maintained all other metal work needed in building and repairing a castle. Carpenters were another essential part of a castle's household for they made the floors and roofs of the buildings and maintained them, the hoardes and brattices of the castle, the siege weapons needed for war, and the furniture and paneling for the rooms of a castle. The butler was responsible for the beer and wine of the castle, the buttery. The porter was responsible for keeping the doors of the castle and seeing that no one left or entered the castle without permission. The seneschal or steward was responsible for the administration of the estate, for routine legal and financial business, and for the management of the household. The chamberlain was responsible for the personal finances of the castle and was keeper of the wardrobe which was in essence the personal finances of the lord. The baronial household might range in size from fifty to one hundred people when the baron was in residence. If the lord was not currently in residence at the castle, the total staff of a castle might range from fifteen to twenty persons.

The diet of medieval society was varied, and it was customary to eat three times a day with a small light breakfast, the main meal eaten between ten and noon, and at sunset a lighter final meal. Mutton, pigs, venison, and cattle were the main sources of meat, but these were supplemented with wild hare, boar, and even bear from the forests. The fowl they ate were poultry, dove, stork, swan, peacock, crane, heron, capon, and even seagulls. When the castle or monstery had its own fish pond, the residents ate fresh trout or carp; sole, haddock, shad, mackerel, and mullet came from the sea. They caught and ate salmon, sturgeon, lobster, white fish, cod, sardines, ray, crab, crayfish, oysters, lamprey eel, seal, porpoise, and salted or wind-dried herrings. They salted pork and beef, stored and ate it, and preserved meats by baking them into pies and stews. Stuffings for meat and birds were made with bread soaked in milk or broth and wine; garlic sauce was a favorite accompaniment to meat dishes. In larger towns and cities one could find pre-cooked food including meat and fish which was served on a plate of bread, an early version of take-out food. Spices and herbs were found in the wild or in the markets supplied by trade. Rue, tansy, mint, sage, marjoram, fennel, and parsley could be found locally; ginger, nutmeg, cloves, and cinnamon were found in the markets. Cheese, bread, and eggs were staple foods; peas, beans, leeks, onions, pumpkin, shallots, celery, radish, garlic, and rhubarb were common vegetables. Figs, dates, raisins, and almonds were imported. For sweets they used dried fruit to make jellies, and made biscuits, tarts, waffles, fritters, gingerbread, and macaroons. They grew apples, pears, cherries, plums, and strawberries. The upper classes had a wide variety of seasonal foods available to them in their daily fare.

A general idea of the costs of some foods common at this time gives a picture of the expense required to feed a household. Using a shilling as equal to twelve pennies: the cost of a gallon of butter was 4 ½ pennies; 120 eggs cost 2 ½ pennies; a pound of pepper cost 9 pennies; and a pound of cloves cost 120 pennies. Since the average baron's yearly income was 200 pounds or so, only the wealthier could afford the imported spices and foodstuffs. Eggs, butter, cheese, and bread were staples to the lower classes. The diet then of the medieval person was not as varied as today's, but they did have more types of food available to them than one would suppose, even with the restrictions of fewer means of preservation and considerably less regard to health and safety precautions.

The family in Marshal's world was an important and complex element. The Normans had introduced hereditary surnames into England, and these names--usually toponymic--attached the family, its history, and its fortunes to the land from which the name came. The importance of the surname or title that a family was given or had chosen cannot be underestimated. The role of the family was to preserve and pass down the name and title to the next generation. If the opportunity came by patronage or inheritance to increase or enhance these, the obligation of the head of the family was to see that this chance was not lost. Because of the bilateral descent of lands in medieval England and because those lands often fell to an heiress instead of an heir, marriage in the baronial class could sometimes bring back together lands that had been lost through marriages or female inheritances. The baronial class as a rule knew their kinship relationships, their genealogy, and definitely knew the lands that had been previously attached to their families. Therefore, marriage alliances were an integral and important part of medieval family life.

Through marriage alliances a family could extend and forge multiple ties of kin, peers, and neighbors. The marriages of this time had wide-ranging political, social, and economic impact on society. Marriage was not only a legal ceremony, but it was also a property transaction that connected the bride's family--mostly the brothers of the bride--to the family of her husband. An actual betrothal involved not only the bride's and groom's families, but also the relations, friends, and dependents of both families. At the higher level of the nobility, it could and did involve the king if one or both parties were tenants-in-chief to the king, or if bride or groom was in wardship due to a deceased parent. With a marriage new ties of family and vassalage could alter the claims and obligations of all involved, not simply the immediate families. Parents therefore sought to betroth their children, particulary their heir, at an early age. Canonical age of consent for marriage was twelve for girls and fourteen for boys, but they were often betrothed at an earlier age.

The actual marriage ceremony of this time was a public ceremony that was begun at the church door. The priest began the ceremony by asking both bride and groom if they consented to the marriage, and if there were any canonical impediments to the union. If the answer to the first question was yes by both parties and the answer to the second question was no, then the lawfulness of the marriage was established. The groom then announced his endowment to his bride, usually giving the bride some coins to symbolize that endowment. The bride's father would then announce his daughter's *maritagium* (dower) and give the bride to the groom.

The dower of a wife was the only recognized transfer of land without the actual transfer of *seisin*, and the only recognized transfer of land from a husband to a wife. The husband might grant his wife specific lands as her endowment at the church door, or the endowment of the bride might be made by contract between the groom's family and the bride's family prior to the marriage. If the groom did not specify the lands of his wife's endowment, the wife was entitled to one-third of all the lands her husband held on the day of the marriage. She would hold her dower as a tenant of her husband's heir as long as she lived and despite any subsequent marriage that she might make. This fact could seriously divide the lands an heir acquired on the death of his father, and made widows an attractive prize in medieval society as the widow could and did bring her dower lands with her to her next marriage. The second marriage of a widow could become even more complicated if the widow was an heiress in her own right because her second husband might claim "the courtesy right" which would entitle him to hold her dower until his own death if she pre-deceased him.

Marriage has always been a means of rising on the social ladder in societies, and it was no different in medieval time. A baron or a king could use daughters to extend his social and economic ties and power. King Henry I used his illegitimate daughters to create ties in England and Normandy. His daughter Sybil was married to Alexander I King of Scotland, Maud to Rotrou count of Perche, Alice to Matthew de Montmorenci constable of France, and Constance to Roscelin de Beaumont viscomte of Maine. However, illegitimate children could not inherit either the titles or the lands of their fathers; their fathers could grant them land from property the father had acquired, but they had no claim on the patrimony of their father or mother. Some bastards were provided for through marriage. Robert of Caen, bastard of King Henry I, was given Mabel, heiress of the earldom of Gloucester and was made earl of Gloucester in right of his wife. Hamelin Plantagenet, bastard of Geoffrey of Anjou, was given Isabel de Warenne, heiress of de Warenne and the earldom of Surrey. William Longespee, bastard of King Henry II, was given Ela, heiress of the earldom of Salisbury. Thus the power of the father or the half-brother could provide for the welfare of illegitimate children, but it was done in the form of a gift not by inheritance. The decision and choice of a marriage partner was never an arbitrary one; regional, political, and family interests always played an important part in any decision regarding the marriage of one's children. The extent to which the bride's or groom's wishes or preferences were considered and valued is not known, but since lands were involved, particularly with the upper baronial class, once a contract for marriage had been made it was to the interest of all that the marriage succeed.

John Gillingham writes that in the late twelfth century love became a more important factor in marriages of the upper class of society. This was due to two factors; a new canon law which stated that what constituted a valid marriage was the freely given consent of both parties (no longer the consent of parents or guardian), and the role greater heiresses played in this time Period ("Love, Marriage and Politics" 294). These factors produced a greater degree of free choice in regard to a spouse and a stronger bond between a husband and wife when that wife was an heiress. Since daughters, as sole heiresses, were allowed to succeed to the possessions of their parents, they could carry the power of their fathers (Gillingham 295). When the future wife was an heiress, the man whom she married became in effect the ruler of her domains. Her husband held her lands, castles, knights/vassals, and titles only as her husband. They did not belong to him; he held them only "in right of his wife" as long as he was married to her. Therefore, this type of marriage was politically crucial in a feudalistic society where fiefs determined power.

If there was no consideration of the personal feelings of the intended spouses, the survival of the marriage could be in jeopardy along with the chaotic results of the dissolution of such a marriage. One has only to look at the results of the separation of Eleanor of Aquitaine and Louis VII; Eleanor took all that she possessed as heiress of her father with her to her marriage to Henry II. Henry II, however, did not divorce her when she rebelled with their sons. No male would easily repudiate marriage to an heiress.

These were the secular reasons for the realization that love was an important factor to consider in marriage. The church also placed a high value on love and sexual compatibility in marriage (Gillingham 297). Medical knowledge at that time believed that a woman's pleasure was an essential element to procreation; both church and secular powers had to take into account the emotions of both future wife and husband (Gillingham 298).

Two other factors are mentioned as influencing the change of attitudes regarding love in the context of marriage. There was a greater awareness of sex and all of its attending nuances and a growing sense of the value of individual freedom and of choice. Gillingham considers that the courtly love songs of this period were extolling the virtues of love in marriage and as the precursor to marriage as much as any illicit type of love (300). During the late twelfth and early thirteenth centuries, any male who would consider love and/or the consummation of love with a lady of a higher status or the wife of that man's lord had to be mentally deficient or suicidal. While a young lady might dream of such a love by a young knight who was not her husband, young knights who were second or third sons having to make their own way in the world by serving in a lord's household knew that this would lead to ruin. Neither custom nor law would tolerate this.

The main purpose of marriage was the creation of heirs that would continue the family line and preserve and protect the family inheritance. Since there were no birth certificates at this time, it was important to mark the birth of a child by other means. The parents would create some situation that would make the birth of a child memorable. They might give presents on the birth of their child or have the child baptised on a Saint's Day or at the time of some noteworthy celebration. The birth of a child was usually attended by a midwife, ladies of the household, and often a doctor. The baby would be baptized either the day of its birth or shortly thereafter. The godparents for the child would be chosen from the notables, either ecclesiastical or lay, or from the lord's *familiares*. The role of godparent was a serious obligation during this time, and the parents would make a careful selection of a godparent. The godparent could be the person who would be responsible for the training of a male child for knighthood or the person who provided the child with the entrance to a higher level of society. The position of godparent was considered so important that the law prohibited marriage between a godson and a godmother and also between the godson and his godmother's daughter (The History of English Law ii 389).

While discussing the customs and laws of society in Marshal's time it is important to recognize the Church's position with regard to the pregnant mother. Once a woman became pregnant she was not allowed inside the Church until after the birth of her child and after her cleansing ceremony. The pregnant woman was considered unclean. If the woman died in childbirth without the blessing and cleansing of her person, she was condemned to burial in unconsecrated ground. If a child died before it was baptized, it could not be buried in consecrated land. If the woman had a male child, she had to wait thirty-three days before she could receive the blessing and cleansing ceremony and then return to the Church. If she had a female child, she had to wait sixty-six days before the ceremony and her return to the Church. Considering that the female was responsible for the childbearing and that without her there would be no heirs, it is illuminating to know the Church's position regarding the pregnant female in medieval society and the burdens that she carried along with a child.

Once children were born the responsibility for their care and education was first with their parents, attending wet-nurses, nurses, clerics, and/or priests. Boys were usually sent to another lord, relative, or godparent for their training as squires and then knights. The male child was sent usually to another lord's household at the age of seven or eight to begin his training as a page. The household chosen for the young boy would be one noted for its quality of knights trained or its position in medieval society that allowed the young man's introduction to a wider range of opportunities. As a page the young boy would be taught manners and the behavior expected of a young noble; he would begin his training in horsemanship, archery, and small weapons. At the age of fourteen, the young man would begin his training as a squire. This was the time that was used to build his strength and stamina, especially with regard to his shoulders and upper body for wielding a sword and lance and his legs so that he could control a warhorse without the use of reins. The squire was trained to ride and control a warhorse, to wear and fight in armour, and to skillfully use all the weapons of a knight. As a squire he would be required to clean and keep the stables, care for the knights' horses, and clean and maintain the knights' armour and weapons. A squire was not allowed to fight except in his training classes; only after the squire was knighted and recognized as a knight could the young man engage in actual tournaments or war. A young man was not considered ready for knighthood until he could mount his warhorse without the use of stirrups while he was dressed in full armour and carrying his weapons on his person. This feat required a great deal of physical strength and coordination as well as skill and took years of training on the part of a young adult. The time, expense, and training necessary to create a knight in this time period made it a profession that could be achieved only by the wealthier baronial class. If a man had more than two sons, it was possible that the heir was trained as a knight in the most important household that the father could place him; the second son would be expected to train in an important household that would provide the best training for a young man who would have to make his own way in the world once he was knighted. Any other sons might be placed in an ecclesiastic household or a monastery to train for a church or clerical profession. Only the king or the very wealthiest of the baronial class could afford to train three or more sons for knighthood.

Young girls might be trained by their own mothers or sent to other noble households for training and education in household management. If there were a number of daughters, one or more might be entered into a nunnery where she could reach a position of power and influence as an abbess. Of course this could also reduce the amount of the drain on the patrimony of the family because the endowment of a daughter entering a nunnery would be much less than the dower required of a woman who was to be married.

By the time of Marshal, the nobility and the knightly class were bilingual or trilingual. Vernacular English was learned without conscious effort by the vast majority of children because it was spoken by those who cared for them and worked in the household which surrounded them. French and Latin were learned languages, and Anglo-Norman French was the language of administration and lordship. It was the language of the king's court and of the upper classes. By Henry II's reign, holding any government position required a man to be literate in Latin. There were three levels of literacy: the professional who was a man of letters; the amateur who had been taught his letters in an ecclesiastic setting but was not a churchman;

and the functional who was able to handle simple Latin needed for government tasks (Turner "Miles Literatus" 931). The men who served as *familiares* of the Angevin government, and those who served as sheriffs, custodians of castles, barons of the Exchequer, itinerant justices, ambassadors abroad, and even military commanders were pragmatic readers in Latin and proficient in Anglo-Norman French by necessity. Any layman who served in an office that demanded the use of written records was literate in simple Latin used for the writs, plea rolls, fine rolls, and other government documents. By the mid-twelfth century letters became an essential skill of the knightly class and was learned in the courts of the king, in a bishop's household, or in an aristocratic household which had an ecclesiastic tutor (Turner 941-42). Those of the knightly class or above were skilled in Anglo-Norman French, vernacular English, and in simple Latin. They may not have written, as in penmanship, these languages well for they had clerks to do the actual writing itself, but they were definitely not illiterate as is defined today.

When one speaks of knights during the period of King Henry II or later, one is not talking of mere physically strong males. The young men of the baronial class had to be in excellent physical condition because of the requirements of being a fighting knight, whether in tournament or war. But, the knight was not simply a fighting weapon; the knights of Marshal's class and time were also required to function in their whole world. Henry II used his knightly class for government offices and duties as castellans, sheriffs, itinerant justices, counselors, and ambassadors. This world had no place for a knightly warrior who could not also serve as an intelligent and literate man of his lord or king. Mercenaries were used for the job of simple fighting tools, but much more was expected of the knights of the baronial class. This was the world that Marshal would enter as a young man, and a world in which he would not only survive, but one in which he would excel.

This story of Marshal's life begins with the known story of John fitz Gilbert, the marshal. This was the man who sired William and provided the foundation stones on which William would build his own life.

II. John fitz Gilbert, the Marshal

The story of William Marshal's life begins with the extant records of his father, John fitz Gilbert. John was the son of Gilbert, the marshal of Henry I's royal household. There are no known records of John's mother or of the origins of the family. It is reasonable to assume that the father, Gilbert, came from Normandy either with William I or shortly thereafter. On his maternal side, John fitz Gilbert was cousin to William de Tancarville, hereditary Chamberlain of Normandy to the Dukes of Normandy (Crouch Image of Aristocracy 131).

The office of marshal of the royal household that both Gilbert and John held was an *ex officio* of the *Curia*. It was both an office and an honour; an office in that the marshal was the Marshal of England (*Marcellus Angliae*), and it was an honour in that it became earl marshal (*Comes Marecallus*). He was marshal of the king's army in war and in the king's court in peace. As marshal he would have a deputy in the Exchequer, the King's Bench, and the Court of the Marshalea. The responsibilities of the office of marshal included everything connected with the horses, hounds, and hawks of the royal household. The marshal was responsible for keeping the tallies and vouchers for any payments made from the royal Treasury and Chamber, for maintaining peace and order in the royal household, for guarding the door to the king's hall, for arranging billeting of the members of the court, for keeping rolls and accounts of all who performed military service in the royal household and court, and for the imprisonment of debtors. The *Constitutio Domus Regis* gives the duties and responsibilities of the royal marshal for King Henry I.

If the office of marshal was not hereditary prior to Gilbert holding the office, it became so during his tenure. Sometime prior to 1130 Gilbert and John are found on the king's rolls maintaining their right to the office of marshal against William de Hastings and Robert de Venoiz (PR 31 Henry I 46b). They probably defended their right to this office by a trial by battle in which the victorious knight won the disputed issue. At some point during 1130 Gilbert died, and John fitz Gilbert succeeded his father by paying 22 pounds and 13 shillings for *seisin* of his father's lands and *ministerium* and paying 40 marks for the office of marshal (PR 31 Henry I 18, 23). Also during this same year, John fitz Gilbert married Adeliza (Aline) Pipard, daughter and heiress of a minor Wiltshire landholder, Walter Pipard (*Reg Anglo-Norm* ii #339).

From the records and charter witness lists, it appears that John served King Henry I loyally and well, witnessing at least twelve royal acts between 1129 and 1135 (Hollister, "Henry I and the Anglo-Norman Magnates" 174-88; Farrer *Itin HenryI* 128, 129, 135, 136, 138). On the death of King Henry I and the assumption by Stephen of Blois of the crown of England in 1135, John retained his office and lands. John accompanied Stephen to Normandy in 1137 and witnessed several charters of Stephen's during the early years of Stephen's reign (Cal. Doc. France #570; *Reg Anglo-Norm* #288, #384-85, #868, #954).

When Stephen of Blois took the crown of England in 1135, he assumed the title as nephew of King Henry I and second son of Henry I's sister Adela. Henry I's daughter, the Empress Matilda, had not only the closer blood right to the crown, but her father before his death had required all barons of England and Normandy to swear to uphold the Empress' right to the Crown on Henry I's death. Had King Henry I spent a little more time and energy with his wife Matilda and insured that there was a least one extra legitimate male heir instead of propagating some twenty or more bastards, the drowning of Henry's only legitimate male heir, William, in The White Ship in 1120 would not have resulted in the devastating years of civil war that followed Henry I's death (Given-Wilson Royal Bastards 60).

Stephen's seizing of the crown of England created a problem that would grow into civil war in both England and Normandy. Most of the greater barons had sworn to defend Matilda's right to the crown, and most held lands in both England and Normandy. Matilda's second husband was Geoffrey Plantagenet, count of Anjou, which gave her a power base in Normandy. Her natural half-brother was Earl Robert of Gloucester, the most powerful baron in England, and her uncle was David King of Scotland. Two factors enabled Stephen to rather easily assume the crown and rule of England in the first years after Henry's death. The first was the fact that primogeniture was not yet a law or even a universally accepted custom, and the second factor was that a man was definitely preferred as ruler to a woman. According to the chronicles and records, the Empress Matilda was certainly her father's daughter and possessed the ambition, determination, and ego to fight for what she considered her birthright. She believed that Stephen was a usurper of her crown, and she was not going to allow Stephen to take her crown or displace her son, Henry II, from his rightful succession to that crown.

Stephen's acquiring the crown of England inevitably led to civil war in England and on the continent, and the years between 1138 and 1154 saw sporadic battles in both places between those that supported Stephen and those that supported the Empress. England paid the greater price for these battles because most of the battles were fought across her lands without much regard to person, place, or current allegiance. With barons holding lands on both or only one side of the channel, any given self-interested man could switch his allegiance if the circumstances warranted such a move. An ordinary man, a common farmer or villein, could witness his crops and home destroyed with no chance of reparation when barons on one side decided to attack and destroy the resources of barons on the other side. Even ecclesiastical lands and persons were not immune should a baron decide to take a church for a stronghold or the church's goods for his own benefit. One wonders how the average person managed to survive the insanity that seemed to rage across England's lands for those years.

With the loss of Henry I, the barons and magnates of both England and Normandy had lost their strong government. What they wanted in 1135 was a strong overlord and a single place to look to for order and peace in the kingdoms (King "King Stephen and the Anglo-Norman Aristocracy" 192). Under Henry I they had learned to live with a strong king, to accept his peace, order, and rule, and to adapt their strategies to his power. When Stephen became king, his position was insecure, and he had to try to placate and entice the powerful barons in order to strengthen his position. Stephen disrupted and weakened much of the power and order Henry I had created. Some of the first men that Stephen sought to gain to his side were Robert earl of Gloucester, the Beaumont twins, Robert earl of Leicester and Waleran count of Meulan, and Miles of Gloucester. Miles was sheriff of Gloucester and had power, lands, and vassals in the south Welsh Marches. Stephen needed someone to counter

the power of Robert of Gloucester in that part of England in the event that Robert

abandoned Stephen for his half-sister, the Empress.

Miles served Stephen well and faithfully for over three years, but in 1139 the

Empress Matilda came to England to fight for her right to the throne which changed

the dynamics of power in England (*Reg Anglo-Norm* iii #134, #347-50, #383,

#386-8, #395). Miles of Gloucester met the Empress at Bristol, and then, or shortly

thereafter, Miles became her man by swearing fealty and homage to her as rightful

heir. As the Empress' vassal, Miles received the fiefs of St. Briavel's castle and the

forest of Dean (*Reg Anglo-Norm* iii #391). Miles did not change sides because of

the prospect of acquiring lands, castles, or titles, as some barons did during the civil

wars. Miles changed sides to preserve what he already held. With the Empress in

England and with her natural brother Robert of Gloucester now at her side, Miles

knew that he could lose everything he had. King Stephen could not protect Miles in

south Wales where the Angevins were strong; so Miles chose the side that had the

power to preserve what he held in fiefs, castles, and vassals (King "King Stephen

and the Anglo-Norman Aristocracy" 185).

Once the Empress Matilda landed on the English shore, the barons faced an

entirely new situation. There were now two sources of lordship, of power, and of

legitimate authority. Both Stephen and Matilda claimed authority over England,

but each had effective control over only limited and constantly fluctuating areas.

The barons who would survive this chaos were the ones who kept their options

opened and whose allegiance might inevitably follow the events and changes in their particular situations. These powerful men were not "kingmakers"; they sought stability in their lands and protection of their right to those lands, castles, and titles. Barons who had the ability and temperament to mould their own futures did their best to exercise skill and sagacity to achieve their ends. In the contemporary records of this time, John fitz Gilbert comes to life as a man as shrewd, opportunistic, and far-seeing as any man. The world of fitz Gilbert's time was one of constantly changing power bases and control, a world that demanded that an ambitious man be quick and sure about where and when he stood. The actions of fitz Gilbert during this period provide an excellent example of some of the means necessary to not only hold onto what one possessed but choose the right side to support as claimant to the throne.

The year 1138 saw John fitz Gilbert take possession of the castles of Marlborough and Lugershall in Wiltshire for Stephen and strengthened and fortified both of them because of the civil war being fought between the supporters of Stephen and those of the Empress Matilda (*Ann Mon* ii 51). This was not war as we know it; it was a series of attacks (sorties) against the men, castles, and lands on the opposite side. Instead of besieging an opponent's castle, a group of knights might simply ravage the land around it that supplied the majority of the provisions for that castle. Because fitz Gilbert was known as a skilled military captain and was a man with a charismatic personality, he attracted a large number of knights to his service. These knights were sworn to fitz Gilbert as his vassals; they were men who owed fealty and service only to fitz Gilbert as their lord and would follow him wherever he led (Painter Marshal 5).

Between 1135 and 1139, the contemporary chronicles and records reveal fitz Gilbert as an opportunistic warrior who increased the knights bound to him, generously gave to them of the spoils of battle, repaired and strengthened those castles that he held, and kept a sharp eye on the ebb and flow of the fortunes of both sides in the civil war. John fitz Gilbert was not idle; this was a time when any baron who had enough loyal knights could attack and ravage another's lands, manors, or castles without being too particular about what side that other baron supported. An opportunistic baron could carry off the spoils of provisions, horses, and armour from his sorties, and he could hold those he defeated for ransom and increase his own wealth. According to Henry of Huntingdon:

> John, also, that child of hell and root of all evil, lord of Marlborough Castle was indefatigable in his efforts to create disturbances. He built castles of strong masonry on spots he thought advantageous, he got into his power the lands and possessions of the monasteries, compelling the monks of every order; and when the sword of ecclesiastical discipline was unsheathed, he was in no wise deterred, but became still more hardened. He even compelled the monks of the highest order to come to his castle in a body on certain fixed days, when, assuming episcopal power, he issued irreversible decrees for the payment of taxes or for compulsory labor. (Henry of Huntingdon, 400-09; *Gesta Regis Henrici* 107-08; 168-69).

John's actions even attracted the attention of the Pope. Pope Eugenius wrote a letter to four English prelates at this time naming fitz Gilbert, William Martel, Hugh de Bolbec, William de Beauchamp, and others who had plundered the lands of

Abingdon and exacted forced labor for castle building (*Chronicon Monasterii de Abingdon* ii 200). The man that appears from the contemporary records is a man who was a very skilled and opportunistic warrior. John fitz Gilbert was a generous lord who succeeded as a leader because he was ruthless, ambitious, shrewd, and successful. Not unlike many of his contemporaries, fitz Gilbert saw the opportunity to increase his holdings, vassals, wealth, and power during this civil war, and he took full advantage of that opportunity. In the actions of John fitz Gilbert during the war between King Stephen and the Empress Matilda, one can perceive a clear picture of the Norman knight before the ideas of chivalry made their appearance in history. This was the pure military fighting knight who could and did venture into his world willing and able to fight, take, and hold what he could by his superb skill and ability as a fighting knight and as a man who possessed a loyal retinue of military men. Machiavelli would have recognized fitz Gilbert as a man who acquired lands and goods by his own ability and arms, as a man who took every opportunity to shape his own fortune and future.

The fall of 1139 the Empress Matilda landed in England and went to Arundel Castle. King Stephen was besieging John fitz Gilbert at Marlborough Castle at that moment trying to remove fitz Gilbert from the castle and his position as castellan. Apparently Stephen had either had enough of fitz Gilbert's free-wheeling attacks on everyone's lands in Wiltshire, or he believed that fitz Gilbert had switched from Stephen's side to the side of the Empress Matilda. Without succeeding in his purpose at Marlborough, Stephen broke off his attack and moved his army to Arundel Castle to try to capture and defeat the Empress (<u>William of Malmesbury</u>

35; Bradbury <u>Stephen and Matilda</u> 73). It does not seem that John fitz Gilbert had actually changed sides at this time; the chronicles and records merely show a man fighting for his own side and furthering his own ends, not a man fighting Stephen's or the Empress' war.

One example from 1140 shows fitz Gilbert's attitude and approach to the civil war in England. Robert fitz Hubert, a sometime Flemish mercenary of Stephen's, proposed a bargain with fitz Gilbert. The bargain proposed was that fitz Hubert and fitz Gilbert attack and seize the lands of men in Wiltshire from both sides and split the spoils (Davis <u>Mediaeval England</u> 81). John did not accept the bargain, but merely bided his time. When fitz Hubert seized Devizes Castle in March 1140, planning to garrison the castle with a large body of his own Flemish men, John saw his opportunity and laid a trap (<u>The Church Historians of England</u> "Chronicle of Florence of Worcester" ii 366). Apparently fitz Gilbert saw Devizes castle as a plum that only he had the right to pluck. John invited fitz Hubert to his castle at Marlborough to discuss the proposed bargain. After fitz Hubert arrived, John threw him in prison and held him there until John decided that it would be profitable to sell fitz Hubert to Robert of Gloucester, leader of the Empress's party, for 500 marks (*Gesta Regis Henrici* 65-67). However, according to another source, John the Marshal actually hung fitz Hubert. According to this chronicle, fitz Gilbert had actively encouraged the garrison in Devizes to refuse to surrender to him promising no harm to fitz Hubert. When the garrison did refuse, fitz Gilbert had cause to hang fitz Hubert, which he did (<u>William of Malmesbury</u> 563-64). John fitz Gilbert was obviously a man who was using the chaos of civil war in England to his own advantage; he was not the only baron to do this. To his credit, fitz Gilbert switched his allegiance from King Stephen to the Empress only once in this war and thereafter never changed sides.

At the battle of Lincoln in February 1141, King Stephen was captured and taken prisoner by Robert of Gloucester. This seems to have been the turning point for fitz Gilbert. From this point on, fitz Gilbert was actively fighting and supporting the cause of the Empress and her son Henry. John was with the Empress at Reading in May and with her at Oxford in July 1141. August 1141 the Empress attacked the bishop of Winchester's castle. Henry of Blois was not only bishop of Winchester, but also King Stephen's brother. Henry had tried early in 1140 at Bath to arrange a truce between Stephen and Matilda and again late in 1141 (King Medieval England 189). King Stephen had refused both attempts to reach a settlement and stop the civil war.

With the capture of King Stephen by the Empress' army in 1141, the Empress had quickly appeared at the gates of Winchester to try and take the castle and see of Henry bishop of Winchester. Henry decided that the time had come to recognize the Empress' right to the throne providing that the Empress confirmed Henry's unwritten primacy of England, and she granted King Stephen's sons' rights to their father's inheritance (King 189). Henry summoned a council to Winchester to recognize the Empress' right to the throne. However, this reversal of Henry of Blois' allegiance and his plan to end the wars came to nothing. Within three months, the Empress had negated all of Henry's efforts by alienating the citizens of London by her demands to the point that they drove her from the city. When King Stephen's wife, Matilda, gathered an army on the south bank of the Thames across from London and the

Empress Matilda refused to concede any of Stephen's inheritance to Stephen's sons,

Henry of Blois switched sides back to his brother Stephen (<u>William of Malmesbury</u>

45-58, Reg Anglo-Norm iii # 790; Gesta Stephani 83). Henry of Blois then joined

Stephen's wife Matilda and gathered an army to retake Winchester and relieve the

siege of his palace (*Gesta Stephani* 79-80; <u>Church Historians of England,</u> "Chronicle

of Florence of Worcester" ii 133-35).

On September the 14, 1141, at Winchester those of the Empress' army

decided that the Empress must be removed to safety while her brother Robert

of Gloucester maintained the battle against Stephen's forces (Bradbury <u>Stephen</u>

<u>and Matilda</u> 97-100). John fitz Gilbert would escort the Empress to his castle of

Lugershall along with Brian fitz Count, lord of Wallingford. When the party reached

the village of Wherwell, fitz Gilbert, according to *L'Histoire*, decided that they were

making too slow a progress. John had the audacity to insist that the Empress ride

astride instead of sidesaddle and proceed with Brian fitz Count with all due speed

to Lugershall. John would remain at the river Test with some of his knights and

protect their retreat. John and his men fought King Stephen's forces commanded

by William of Ypres at the river; overwhelmed by the number of men attacking,

fitz Gilbert and his knights were forced to take refuge in the Abbey of Wherwell.

William of Ypres' men set the Abbey on fire in an attempt to force fitz Gilbert and

his men out. When the fury of the fire caused John and one of his knights to retreat

to the Tower of the Abbey, the knight, apparently not wishing to be burned alive,

suggested they surrender. John fitz Gilbert reacted as one would have predicted;

fitz Gilbert threatened to kill the knight right there, and this ended any talk of surrender. William of Ypres left with his army thinking that the men had died in the fire, but they had survived. John fitz Gilbert lost the sight in one eye from the lead melting from the roof of the Tower, but he made it back to his castle of Marlborough (William of Malmesbury 60; *Gesta Stephani* 130-33; *Hist* 187-99; Painter "The Rout of Winchester" 70-75).

The battle at Winchester cost fitz Gilbert an eye, and it also resulted in the capture of Robert of Gloucester by Stephen's supporters. Before the end of 1141, King Stephen was exchanged for Robert of Gloucester, and everything was back almost to the prior status quo with no one side having the advantage. The Angevins were still predominant in Wales, the southwestern shires, and in the south midlands with particular strength in Oxfordshire, Berkshire, Wiltshire, and Devonshire. Stephen still held most of the rest of England firm.

After the events of 1141, John fitz Gilbert was plundering and attacking the lands of Stephen's supporters in Wiltshire once again from his castles of Lugershall and Marlborough. One of fitz Gilbert's frequent victims was Patrick, constable of Salisbury.

Patrick was a supporter of Stephen and a great landholder in Wiltshire. Patrick had a large retinue of his own knights, and he apparently decided that he had had enough of fitz Gilbert's raids. The time had come to rid the shire of John fitz Gilbert. From Winchester, Patrick sent word to fitz Gilbert at Lugershall that if fitz Gilbert would wait for him the next day, Patrick and his men would attack him there. Underestimating his foe, Patrick and his men departed Winchester the next morning without wearing their helmets and hauberks, obviously thinking that fitz Gilbert and his men would have fled from Lugershall in fear of Patrick and his army. John fitz Gilbert had other ideas; John and his knights ambushed Patrick not far from Winchester and cost Patrick many of his best knights, killed as well as wounded or captured. By this clever ambush, John had acquired horses, armour, and ransoms from Patrick's captured knights (*Hist* 283-354).

This latest event, added to the previous attacks of fitz Gilbert against Patrick's lands, resulted in a bargain being struck between John fitz Gilbert and Patrick. Both had had enough of the destruction of their lands in Wiltshire and sought a compromise. Their compromise entailed John putting aside his wife, Adeliza Pipard, and marrying Patrick's sister Sibyl, and Patrick switching from Stephen's side to the side of the Empress (*Reg Anglo-Norm* iii #339; *Hist* 360-75). Patrick's switching of sides eventually resulted in his being made Earl of Salisbury by the Empress. In fitz Gilbert's actions with regard to Patrick is another clue to the character of the man himself. John fitz Gilbert is offered an opportunity to end the unprofitable fights with Patrick and to form an alliance that will not only protect fitz Gilbert's lands and castles, but will also provide him with a new wife and connections much more powerful than his first marriage. Without a qualm or apparently any regret, John fitz Gilbert divested himself of his first wife and married Sybil of Salisbury. In an article by David Crouch, he provides the identity of the man, Stephen Gay, who married fitz Gilbert's first wife, Adeliza/Aline. According to Crouch, Stephen Gay was a much younger brother of the unnamed woman who was the mother of Robert of Gloucester, natural son of Henry I. Crouch proposes that the arrangements of the marriage of fitz Gilbert to Patrick's sister Sibyl and the marriage

of fitz Gilbert's ex-wife Adeliza/Aline to Stephen Gay was the work of Robert of

Gloucester. Crouch suggests that Robert of Gloucester used this situation to solidify

and strengthen the support for the Empress Matilda in Oxfordshire and Wiltshire

("Robert of Gloucester's Mother" 172-79). A final extant record of John's first wife,

Adeliza, is a charter of April or May 1153 confirmed by Henry II recognizing an

agreement made between fitz Gilbert's and Adeliza's son Gilbert and Stephen Gay,

Adeliza's second husband (*Reg Anglo-Norm* iii #339).

The marriage of fitz Gilbert to Sibyl provides a glimpse not only into the

character of William Marshal's father but also into the importance that marriage

played in the politics of medieval England. John fitz Gilbert had not only neutralized

his most powerful enemy in Wiltshire; he had also greatly increased his social

position by marrying into one of the most important feudal families of England.

John had acquired a powerful ally and brother-in-law, the freedom to plunder the

royalists' lands in Wiltshire, Berkshire, and Hampshire, and the means to build his

own adulterine castle at Newbury in Berkshire.

In 1152, there occurred an incident involving John fitz Gilbert and King

Stephen that was to become an intrinsic part of the life of William Marshal. It was

an incident that William Marshal would recount many times in his later life. Stephen

had laid siege to John's castle of Newbury, and the garrison of the castle asked

Stephen for respite to send word to their lord, John fitz Gilbert. John asked Stephen

for a truce while he sent word to his lord, the Empress Matilda. Stephen granted fitz

Gilbert a truce but on the condition that fitz Gilbert give Stephen one of his sons as surety that John would not break the terms of the truce. Stephen was given William

Marshal, who was not more than five years old, as hostage for his father. Under the

conditions of a truce, if fitz Gilbert used the time to sneak men and provisions into

Newbury, King Stephen had the right to take William's life as forfeit for fitz Gilbert's

betrayal. John, of course not concerned with the niceties of the expected procedure

with regard to a truce called during a siege, used the time to send knights, archers,

foot soldiers, and provisions into Newbury. When Stephen discovered this betrayal,

he sent a messenger to John telling him that William Marshal would be hung because

of his father's actions. John's reply to Stephen's messenger was that he cared little

if William was hanged as he had the "anvils and hammer" to forge even better sons

(*Hist* 460-508).

Stephen actually ordered and accompanied young William to a tree to be

hung. On the way to the tree, the young William saw the knights in their armour

and with their weapons; Earl William of Arundel holding a javelin caught the young

William's attention. The shine of the steel blade in the sun caught William's eye,

and he asked if he could have it. Stephen, witnessing this incident, apparently

could not sustain his anger against an innocent young child, cancelled the order to

hang William, and carried him back to camp (*Hist* 508-38). Stephen held William

as hostage for some months, and it was only William's mother who sent a servant

secretly into Stephen's camp to see how her child fared. Apparently the servant saw

William playing with King Stephen in Stephen's own tent and was so frightened

by William calling out to him that he fled (*Hist* 539-60). Had Stephen been a more

ruthless and brutal man, he could have justly executed William Marshal for his father's betrayal of a truce. There is no record of what William Marshal thought of his father's actions and words, only the recording of the entire incident in the *L'Histoire*. It should be noted, however, that when William later in his own life had to give up two of his sons as hostages to King John, William did not imitate his father in either words or deeds.

John fitz Gilbert was an active and loyal supporter of the Empress and her cause during the civil wars. John's brother, William, became the Empress's chancellor by spring 1141; in a confirmation charter of the Empress to Cowley April/May 1141, William is her chancellor (Lees, Records of Templars 178-79, #4; *Reg Anglo-Norm iii* #88, #274, #377, #382, #369, #647). John and William were witnesses to many extant charters of the Empress and her son Henry during these years, mostly in England (*Reg Anglo-Norm* iii #180, #193, #239f, #299, #316a, #393, #581, #582, #600, #706, # 840, #901). By 1153, both Stephen and Matilda recognized that neither would win this war. Waleran count of Meulan had gone over to the Angevin side in 1141, and his twin brother, Robert earl of Leicester, and Ranulf earl of Chester had switched to the Angevin side by 1153 (*Reg Anglo-Norm* iii #180, #143). With the death of Stephen's eldest son, Eustace, in August 1153, Stephen gave up his ambition to have the crown of England descend within his own family. In December 1153, King Stephen and Henry duke of Anjou signed a treaty to end the civil war. It is of interest to note that three of the witnesses of this treaty were Earl Patrick of Salisbury, Roger de Clare of Hertford, and Richard "Strongbow" de Clare of Pembroke (*Reg Anglo-Norm iii* #272). February 1154 Stephen and Henry of Anjou signed an agreement known as the Treaty of Westminster. By this treaty, Stephen was to rule England unmolested until his death, and Stephen made Henry Plantagenet his heir to the throne of England. The baronial men on both sides were guaranteed their lands and promised immunity from punishment (Bradbury Stephen and Matilda 168). On October 25, 1154, King Stephen died. On December 19, 1154, Henry son of the Empress Matilda and grandson of King Henry I was crowned King Henry II of England by Theobald archbishop of Canterbury.

Henry II gave John fitz Gilbert the manors of Wexcombe and Cherhill in Wiltshire that yielded an annual income of 82 pounds and the custody of Marlborough castle (PR 2 Henry II 5). In the year 1158 Henry II gave Marlborough to Alan de Neville, but John held the rest until his death (PR 4 Henry II 116; PR 10 Henry II 14). John held Tidworth in Wiltshire by sergeanty of his office as marshal and possibly Hampstead in Berkshire (PR 4 Henry II 9). *The Cartae Baronnum* shows John fitz Gilbert also holding Wigan in Oxfordshire and Inkberrow in Worcestershire (Keefe Feudal Assessments 178). John held these lands and the lands he inherited from his father in Wiltshire and seven other scattered knights' fees. He held land of the bishop of Winchester, the bishop of Exeter, the Abbot of Abington, of Richard de Chandos, of Manasser de Arsic, and of Geoffrey de Mandeville (Red Book Exchequer 207, 250, 284, 300, 304, 347).

In 1164 from January 13 to the 28 at the council of Clarendon, the Constitutions of Clarendon were instituted by Henry II who was seeking a clarification of the customs and laws of his predecessors with regard to both cleric and laymen and the rights of the king and of the ecclesiastical court. It was witnessed by John fitz Gilbert and Patrick of Salisbury and was the beginning of the estrangement between Henry II and Thomas Becket archbishop of Canterbury (*Reg Anglo-Norm* plii; Stubbs <u>Select Charters</u> 135). The Constitutions of Clarendon included the provisions that no one might appeal to Rome without royal permission and that once a cleric had confessed or been convicted of a secular crime by the ecclesiastical court, that person was to be turned over to the royal court for punishment Henry was trying to correct a growing problem of injustice which had been created by the fact that men had often claimed a "benefit of the clergy" and gone to church courts for crimes they had committed and had lost only their orders. Many of these claims had been untrue, and therefore the men had escaped justice and punishment for secular crimes committed. Henry believed that men who had committed secular crimes should be tried in secular courts even if they were clerks of the church. This had been the case before Henry's time, but the years of the anarchy had resulted in not only lawless clerics running free, but also a steady encroachment of the church into the area of secular authority. At a great council at Salisbury in January 1164, Henry had presented to those gathered a written text of these customs to be sealed and agreed to by all. Becket had at first argued against this written and sealed codification of these customs but had eventually signed. When Henry tried to obtain Pope Alexander's agreement to the Constitutions of Clarendon and failed, Henry blamed Becket for the failure. The failure of the Pope to agree to the Constitutions of Clarendon brought about Becket's reversal of his own agreement and placed the battle between Becket and Henry II on the level of a power struggle between the universal Church and the rising secular states.

The battle between Henry II and Becket over the rights of the Church and the king spilled over into John fitz Gilbert's suit against Thomas Becket as archbishop of Canterbury. The estate being contested was South Mundham, which was a part of the archbishop's manor of Pagham in Sussex (Cheney "The Litigation John Marshal and Archbishop Thomas Becket" 9). Bosham had been given to fitz Gilbert (or possibly to his father) by King Henry I, and John now claimed South Mundham as his by hereditary right, though he had no charter or record of this. It is possible that he held South Mundham as a fee farm of the former archbishop of Canterbury. Thomas Becket as archbishop of Canterbury had John's men put out of South Mundham, and John was demanding the land back.

The whole issue had come about when Becket became archbishop of Canterbury and started forcibly taking back estates from the barons whom he claimed held the lands only because of prior weak and negligent archbishops. It was a fight to establish the right of nonalienation of ecclesiastical lands and the ancient customs with regard to the procedure of the descent or possession of lands of both lay and ecclesiastical. Among the barons Becket was infuriating were the earl of Clare, whom Becket claimed owed him homage for the castle and honour of Tunbridge; William de Ros, whom Becket claimed owed him seven knights' fees; and Henry II, whom Becket claimed owed him Rochester Castle (Wendover, Giles ii 539). Becket was in effect trying to regain control of the canon law of inalienability of church lands which was in opposition to the feudal custom that allowed a free man to hold a fief or honour of a clerical lord with the expectation that a new lord would allow him to swear fealty to the new lord and keep possession. John sued in the archbishop's court for his land back, but he was losing his case because he had no charter for South Mundham, nor did the archbishop intend to return the land. John left the archbishop's court before the suit was decided claiming that the court had failed to do him justice, and he took his case to the king's court (Giles ii 543-44). John based his action on the "*novella constitutio*" of Henry II that stated:

> If anyone has a case in the court of a higher lord and sees after the first or second day of the plea that the matter is not going well for him and according to his wishes; it shall be lawful for him to fly to the court of a higher lord, provided that he has sworn with two supporters that he has suffered unjust delay and that he or his ancestor had possession of said land at the time of the death of King Henry I. (Cheney "The Litigation John Marshal and Archbishop Thomas Becket" 15)

John brought his case to King Henry II, and Henry summoned Becket to his court on September 14, 1164, to answer this charge as well as other charges. Becket sent messengers to Henry's court saying that he was unable to attend on that day due to illness. Henry then sent a new summons demanding that Becket appear before the king's court October 6, 1164, the first day of the Great Council held at Northampton. Becket was ordered to stand trial before the King's Great Council on a series of alleged offenses committed during Becket's time as Henry II's chancellor as well as answer the charge of fitz Gilbert on the failure of justice.

Henry had summoned bishops, abbots, earls, all the great magnates, and everyone else of any importance to this council at Northampton. Here, Henry II heard three cases regarding the suit between fitz Gilbert and Becket as well as the alleged offenses Becket had committed as chancellor. The first case was one of contumacy against the archbishop for not appearing on the first summons of the king. The second case was the question of justice given or not given to fitz Gilbert in the archbishop's court. The third case was whether fitz Gilbert had complied with the procedure laid down in the king's enactment of the *novella constitutio* that allowed a claimant to withdraw from his lord's court.

In the first case, Becket was found "in mercy" of the king's court for a fine of 500 pounds. In the second and third case, the court found in Becket's favor as fitz Gilbert had not proven his case rather than having been denied justice in the archbishop's court (*Houedene* i 262-63). Henry demanded judgment on Becket for the other charges, but the bishops begged to be excused from this and to be allowed to send a petition to Rome for Becket's disposition. Henry agreed to this, and when asked for permission for Becket to leave Northampton, Henry said that he would decide that question the next day. Becket did not wait for Henry's permission but fled Northampton that night and was in Flanders within three weeks. This began Becket's exile from England and the battle between Henry II and Becket and the church over the division of the authority between church and state.

The records of fitz Gilbert's suit are important in that they provide an insight into some of the steps in medieval history that led to written laws. Becket's actions of putting out all holders of fee farms on the Canterbury estates without hearings or opportunity for the holders to prove their right to the farms, and Becket's claims of lands and homage from some of the most important baronial men in England precipitated the recognition of a serious problem in feudalism. What was the redress of a free man *disseised* [dispossessed] of his lands without a hearing or judgment?

John fitz Gilbert probably just desired possession of the land in question, but one can safely assume that Henry II recognized the issue involved. It is possible that Henry II used John fitz Gilbert as a weapon in Henry's ongoing contention with Becket and with Henry's attempts to clarify and codify the spheres of secular and ecclesiastical authority within England and Normandy. Sometime between 1165 and before 1176, Henry II enacted *novel disseisin* as a procedure that provided the remedies for a man recently *disseised* of his free tenement unjustly and without judgment. This provided a speedy remedy for the man to go to court and prove by what right he held land, and it required the one who *disseised* him to prove or not prove by what right he removed him from the land. Henry II enacted this for the protection of his own position as lord and king, but it also proved to be a remedy for his vassals as fief holders. Knowingly or not, John fitz Gilbert had aided the development of law in medieval England, but he had also provided one more piece to the battle of power between Becket and King Henry II.

As a man, John fitz Gilbert the marshal was a minor baron compared to the great barons in his age, but the extant records of his life prove that he had fulfilled the main purposes of a feudal baron. By his actions during life, he had greatly increased the wealth, status, and possessions of his family; he had not only held onto what he had inherited but had also greatly enlarged it by the time of his death. This was the duty of the head of a feudal household in medieval time. He was known as "a man illustrious as knight," a man of great military skill and of liberality towards his knights (Church Historians of England ii 126). John was also known to be a man of "great cunning" and one who was "fond of stratagems" (*Gesta Regis Henrici* 66,

107). He was a clever and ruthless baron who had more than his share of daring, energy, and ambition. He had put aside his first wife without a qualm in order to better himself. Even in the lines written about him in the *chanson de geste* of his son William Marshal, there seem to be no polished edges to this knight. There was nothing of the later chivalrous knight to be found in fitz Gilbert; he was very much the Norman warrior of William the Conqueror's time.

John fitz Gilbert died in 1165, presumably of natural causes; his son William was in training in Normandy in the household of William de Tancarville at the time and did not come home for his father's funeral (PR 11 Henry II 56). Of the two sons John had by Aline, the eldest, Gilbert, died within a year of his father's death, and the younger, Walter, died before his father (PR 12 Henry II 95). Of the four sons John had by Sibyl, the eldest son, John, inherited his father's lands and the office of marshal. The second son, William, became the Earl of Pembroke, the third son, Henry, became the bishop of Exeter, and the fourth son, Anselm, is little known (*Houedene i* 226-27; *Hist* 381-98, 480-92). Anselm is found in VCH A History of the County of Wiltshire Vol. III where he is noted under the history of Bradenstoke Priory as having given the advowson of the church of Easton to the abbey of Mont St Catherine (281, 281 f 46, f 47). This means that Anselm did reach his majority; otherwise he could not have gifted the advowson of the church of Easton. This reference to Anselm has not been noted in other histories of William Marshal's family. Of John's daughters, Maud married Robert de l'Arche, Margaret married Ralph de Someroy, and an unnamed daughter married William le Gras (Grassus/ Crassus) of Chipping Sodbury, Gloucestershire (Brooks Knights'Fees 72-74; *Hist.*

398; Walker "The Supporters of Richard Marshal" 46).

Sidney Painter states that the most important thing John fitz Gilbert left his sons was the confidence and favor of Henry Plantagenet (Marshal 12). In their world and feudalistic society the most important quality to a lord, be he baron or king, was to have a knight and vassal known to possess great abilities and skills as a warrior and to be loyal to his vow of fealty. John fitz Gilbert's son, William Marshal, would prove to have both of these to a unique and memorable degree as well as a sense of honour that made real the ideal of chivalry.

Since William was sent at an early age to be trained as a knight in the household of William de Tancarville in Normandy, he would not have learned from his father directly, but perhaps he learned from the stories about his father how important it was to be a successful, skilled knight and a generous lord to his vassals in order to insure the fealty of those who served him. William would have learned from his father's example the necessity of skillful strategies in order to not only survive but also to prosper in his feudalistic world of shifting alliances and contending barons and kings. With the advent of the Angevins to the crown of England and dukedom of Normandy, it became essential to survival for a knight or baron to be well informed and sagacious enough to perceive the potential next moves of his overlord. Henry II began the process of strengthening the position of king as feudal overlord, sometimes at the cost of his barons. Richard and John were not slow in learning from the example of their father. This would be William Marshal's world when he came to manhood, and he would prove to be a master at survival in it.

III. Richard "Strongbow" de Clare

Having provided the genesis of William Marshal, we turn to the family that produced the beautiful Isabel de Clare, who would one day be the wife of William Marshal. Isabel's family of de Clare was one of the greatest original Anglo-Norman families of England. The first members of the family in England were the brothers, Richard fitz Gilbert and Baldwin fitz Gilbert. They were kinsmen to William the Conqueror, descended from Gilbert Count of Brionne (d1040) natural grandson of Richard I Duke of Normandy (d996). Richard and Baldwin accompanied the Conqueror to England in 1066. Richard fitz Gilbert was the sixth largest fief holder in the newly conquered England. He held fiefs in Suffolk, Essex, Kent, and Surrey and had scattered estates in Devon, Norfolk, Middlesex, Cambridge, Bedford, and Wiltshire. Richard's chief seat was Clare in Suffolk, but he also held Tunbridge in Kent of the Archbishop of Canterbury and was known in Domesday records as Richard of Tunbridge.

Baldwin fitz Gilbert's lands were centered around Okehampton in Devon, but he also held land in Dorset and Somerset. Baldwin was known as Baldwin the sheriff in Domesday records as he held the office of sheriff of Devon 1070-1086 (Keats-Rohan Domesday People 162). Baldwin fitz Gilbert died in 1095, and his three sons, William [d1096], Robert [c1103], and Richard [d1157] all died with no surviving male heirs. Both Baldwin and his brother Richard were often at court and at the great councils of William I, but Richard was the more active participant in the Conqueror' governing (Reg Anglo-Norm #1, #22, #26, #88, #90, #100, #128,#141,

#162, #209, #212, #220, #260, #276).

Richard I fitz Gilbert married Rohaise [Rohese] daughter and heiress of Walter Giffard earl of Buckingham. Rohaise was a tenant-in-chief in Hertford and Huntingdon, and her marriage to Richard would have a direct bearing on the later gains of land in England and Normandy by William Marshal in right of his wife Isabel.

Richard I and Rohaise had at least seven children; Roger I fitz Richard de Clare was the eldest son and inherited the Norman lands of Bienfaite and Orbec and sided with Robert Curthose, the eldest son of William the Conqueror, in the rebellion of 1077/1078 (*Orderic* ii 382). Roger died 1130/1131 with no surviving children. The second son of Richard I and Rohese, Gilbert fitz Richard, inherited Richard I's English lands and possessions in 1090 and was known as Gilbert of Tunbridge, or Gilbert fitz Richard (*Mon Ang* v 269). Their third son, Walter fitz Richard, was granted the forfeited estates of Roger, son of William fitz Osbern earl of Hereford. This gave Walter the lordship of Netherwent and the castles and lands of Striguil (Chepstow) in south Wales as well as lands in Bedford, Wiltshire, Hertford, and Gloucestershire (PR 31 Henry I 23, 62, 80,104). Walter founded the second Cistercian house in Britain at Tintern, Monmouthshire, in 1130. The fourth son, Richard fitz Richard became a monk at Bec and was made abbot of Ely on the accession of Henry I to the throne in 1100 (*Orderic* iii 340). The fifth son, Robert fitz Richard was granted the estates of Ralph Baynard when Ralph's grandson William rebelled in 1110. Robert's new lands were in Norfolk, Suffolk, Hertford, and Essex with the *caput* at Little Dunmow in Essex. The estates granted to Robert included the great stronghold of Baynard's Castle in London. Robert fitz Richard married Matilda the daughter of Simon de St Liz, earl of Huntingdon, and Robert was the founder of the fitz Walter cadet branch of the de Clares soon after 1110 (Douglas English Historical Documents p154 #186).

Richard I and Rohaise had two daughters; Adelize married Walter Tirel, and Rohese married Eudo, *dapifer* of Henry I (*Mon Ang* iv 609).

Their second son Gilbert of Tunbridge married Adeliza, daughter of Hugh of Clermont. Gilbert was granted the lordship of Ceredigion (Cardigan) by Henry I in 1110 and told he could have whatever he could take and hold (*Ann Camb* 35; *Brut Red* 105, 113). On Gilbert's death c1117, Adeliza married a de Montmorenci and had Hervey de Montmorenci, uncle to Richard Strongbow de Clare (*Mon Ang* ii 602, 603; iii 473).

Gilbert and Adeliza had eight children. Listing the last six of their children first; Baldwin, their third son, married Adeline niece and heiress of William of Rollos, lord of the honour of Bourne in Linconshire. Their fourth son named Hervey was sent on an expedition to Cardigan in 1140 by King Stephen, but nothing else seems to be recorded of him. Their fifth son named Walter went on Crusade in 1142 and apparently died there (*Mon Ang* ii 601). Their daughters were: Margaret who married William de Montfichet, lord of Stansted in Essex; Alice who married Aubrey de Vere, lord of Hedingham in Essex; and Rohese who married Baderon de Monmouth, a Marcher lord. The marriages of these daughters would tie the de Clare family to some of the more important, particularly later in history, barons of England.

Gilbert and Adeliza's eldest son and heir was Richard II fitz Gilbert; he inherited Clare, Tunbridge, and Cardigan on his father's death in 1117. Richard II fitz Gilbert married Adeliz, sister of Ranulf Earl of Chester, and by this marriage acquired lands in Lincoln and Nottingham as his wife's dowry (Farrer Honors and Knights' Fees ii 183, 210-13). Richard was in opposition to Stephen as early as 1136, if not before, although his uncles, Walter fitz Richard and Robert fitz Richard, and his brother Baldwin fitz Gilbert were supporters of Stephen (*Reg Anglo- Norm* iii #387,# 944,#947, #949). This Richard fitz Gilbert was killed in an ambush by the Welsh near Abergavenny either in 1135 or 1136 while Richard was in arms against King Stephen (*Gesta Stephani* 10-11; *Brut Red* 112-13). This Richard fitz Gilbert's eldest son was Gilbert II fitz Richard. Gilbert acquired the lands of his father in Clare and Tunbridge and became earl of Hertford in 1138. This Gilbert II died in 1153 with no wife or heirs; his brother, Roger II fitz Richard de Clare, assumed the titles and lands of his brother in 1153. The de Clare lands and titles descended to the children of Roger II fitz Richard (d1173) and his wife, Maud (d1195) who was the daughter of James de St. Hilary.

It is Gilbert fitz Richard's (d1117) and Adeliza de Clermont's second son, Gilbert fitz Gilbert, that concerns our story; he was the father of Richard Strongbow and the grandfather of Isabel de Clare. Gilbert is described in the *Gesta Stephani* as a poor knight who was raised in honour and wealth by King Stephen (133-34). Gilbert fitz Gilbert de Clare was lord of Orbec and Bienfaite as a result of his uncle's, Roger I fitz Richard, death in 1131. On the death of Gilbert's uncle Walter fitz Richard in 1138, Gilbert was made lord of Striguil (Chepstow) and created earl of Pembroke. Gilbert was the only English earl with a Welsh title. Gilbert fitz Gilbert married Isabel (Elizabeth) de Beaumont, daughter of Robert de Beaumont count of Meulan and earl of Leicester [d1118] and sister to Robert earl of Leicester and Waleran count of Meulan. Isabel had been the youngest mistress of King Henry I, and their liaison had resulted in a daughter, Isabel (Elizabeth), born c1128/1130. It is possible that Isabel became mistress to Henry I as a means of freeing her brother Waleran. Waleran, who had been captured by Henry I at Bourgtheroulde in 1124, was on the wrong side of the rebellion of William Clito, son of Henry's deceased brother, Robert Curthose (*Orderic* vi 350-51). Henry I kept Waleran in close confinement for five years because of his rebellion, and it is assumed that Isabel became mistress to Henry I in order to protect and eventually free her brother Waleran. When Isabel de Beaumont married Gilbert fitz Gilbert de Clare in 1130, she took her natural daughter, Isabel, with her. Richard de Clare was born around the end of 1130; thus he was raised with the natural half-sister of the Empress Matilda and natural aunt to Henry II.

There does not appear to be any extant records or chronicles commenting on this aspect of the marriage of Gilbert fitz Gilbert and Isabel de Beaumont, but it would seem to be unreasonable to think that the Empress Matilda and Henry II were not aware of this connection that bound this branch of the de Clare family to the Angevin family. Richard Strongbow must have been aware that his mother had been a mistress to Henry I and that his half-sister, Isabel, was Henry's natural aunt. There are three charters to the Abbey of St. John Foucarmont for Cistercian monks in the diocese of Rouen that refer to Isabel de Beaumont after the death of her husband Gilbert earl of Pembroke. One charter is Isabel's; one charter is Richard Strongbow's, and one charter is a confirmation charter by Henry II (Cal. Doc. France 63-65). When and where Isabel de Beaumont died and the fate of her daughter by Henry I are not known. All that is known as fact is that the daughter Isabel [Elizabeth] lived with her mother during and after Isabel de Beaumont's marriage to Gilbert fitz Gilbert and that Isabel, the daughter, apparently never married (Given-Wilson Royal Bastards 71).

Strongbow's father, grandfather, uncles, and great-uncles were men favored by both King Henry I and King Stephen. On the death of Roger I fitz Richard de Clare without legal heirs in 1130, King Henry I granted Gilbert de Clare his lands of Orbec and Bienfaite in Normandy. With the death of King Henry I in 1135, Richard's father, Gilbert, supported Stephen as king and was an active military commander for Stephen during the anarchy (*Gesta Stephani* 149, 63, 74, 112, 471, 52: *Orderic* vi 463). When Gilbert's uncle Walter de Clare died in 1138, King Stephen granted Gilbert the lordship of Netherwent, including the castles of Chepstow and Usk. Stephen also granted Gilbert the title and lands of the earldom of Pembroke the same year from lands that had escheated to Henry I when Robert de Belleme, son of Robert de Montgomery earl of Shrewsbury, had rebelled in 1102 and lost all of the Montgomery lands (*Orderic* vi 512, 520; xiii 37). In 1144 Gilbert rebuilt Carmarthen castle and constructed a castle at Dinwileir (*Brut Red* 120-21). It is thought by some historians that Stephen created Gilbert earl of Pembroke as a defense move in west Wales and to compensate for the losses of Richard II fitz Gilbert de Clare lord of Cardigan in 1136. Crouch has suggested that Stephen gave the earldom of Pembroke to Gilbert because of Gilbert's status as brother-in-law to Waleran, count of Meulan (Beaumont Twins 41).

Gilbert and his son Richard supported King Stephen against Matilda until c.1146. In 1146 King Stephen held Gilbert II fitz Richard de Clare, earl of Hertford, as a hostage for the good behavior of his uncle, Ranulf, earl of Chester (*Gesta Stephani* 201). This Gilbert was the son of Richard II fitz Gilbert and Adeliz, sister of Ranulf earl of Chester; he was also the nephew of Gilbert, earl of Pembroke. When Ranulf changed sides and began to support the Empress Matilda, King Stephen forced Earl Gilbert of Hertford to surrender his castles and lands. This action immediately drove Gilbert to support Matilda along with his uncle Ranulf (*Gesta Stephani* 133: *Diceto* i 255-56). Apparently Gilbert de Clare, earl of Pembroke, overreached himself by claiming that his nephew's lands should go to him by hereditary right because of that nephew's rebellion. Stephen refused, Gilbert revolted, and Stephen took the earl of Pembroke's lands and castles into his own hands (Ward "Royal Service and Reward" 276; *Gesta Stephani* 200-03). However, the estrangement between Gilbert, earl of Pembroke, and King Stephen did not last long; by 1148 Gilbert is found witnessing charters of King Stephen, his wife, and his son (Lees Records of Templars 149-50,179,188-89,198-99).

Ward points out that by 1130 five members of the de Clare family were tenants-in-chief of the Crown and that by 1154 the members of the de Clare family that had reached baronial status were the first sons Richard and Baldwin de Clare, Walter and Robert fitz Richard, Gilbert of Tonbridge, and Gilbert of Pembroke ("Royal Service and Reward" 261, 278). The de Clares had proven that they were ambitious, shrewd, and wise; they knew where their interest lay and how to use royal service as a means to achieve their goals.

Earl Gilbert of Pembroke died circa 1148 around the age of forty-eight. Strongbow, at the age of eighteen, inherited all of his father's lands, including Orbec and Bienfaite in Normandy, the lordship of Striguil, and the earldom of Pembroke. Strongbow first appears in official records as "comes de Penbroc" in the Treaty of Westminster, November 1, 1153 (*Reg Anglo-Norm* iii #272). This is the last occasion in any royal document that Richard fitz Gilbert de Clare signs as Earl of Pembroke; from this point in extant records Strongbow signs his name as "comes de Striguil."

The known history of Richard Strongbow de Clare contains almost as many questions as answers. There has been debate about the name *Strongbow* ascribed to both Richard and his father Gilbert. In a charter in "The Chronicle of Melrose" issued by Richard's grandson, Richard Marshal, both Richard and Gilbert de Clare are named as Strongbow (Anderson 82). Both Gilbert and his son Ricard are called Strongbow in the Irish chronicles of Connaught and in the chronicles of Thady Dowling (*Ann Conn* 8, 10; *Ann Hib* 10, 12). The men of Netherwent (Gwent) were known for their skill and use of an unusually long and strong bow (*Ann Camb* 54). Gilbert de Clare's seal shows him holding a long arrow (according to Round an arrow but a lance according to Wagner) in his right hand (Wagner "A Seal of Strongbow" 128-29; Round "The Family of Clare" 227-28). Most historians assume that the ability and skill using this type of longbow or a forgotten incident involving such a weapon earned both Richard and his father Gilbert their nicknames.

The two major sources for Richard's life are the *Expugnatio Hibernica* of Gerald of Wales and the *chanson de geste* called The Song of Dermot and Earl Richard Fitzgilbert. The *chanson de geste* was written by an unidentified Anglo-Norman poet. It is believed that one source for that poet was possibly Maurice Regan who was an interpreter for Dermot MacMurchada, king of Leinster. Both of these sources are primarily accounts of the Anglo-Norman invasion of Ireland in 1169, the principal event of Richard Strongbow de Clare's life. Both sources are more or less contemporary histories of the men and events of this time. Each is colored by the bias of the author; Gerald strongly emphasizes his own family relationship to the fitz Geralds, and The Song emphasizes the family and relationships of the de Clares. Though both sources cover the time period of the Anglo-Norman intrusion into Ireland, they include information from the time before and after the invasion of Ireland

The public records and contemporary chronicles indicate that King Henry II refused to recognize Richard Strongbow's right to the title and lands of Pembroke, though Richard was his father's only son, having one sister, Basilia, and his natural half sister, Isabel. The title of earl and the earldom of Pembroke did not come back into Richard's family until after the marriage of his sole heiress, Isabel de Clare, to William Marshal in 1189. It was King John who *belted* William Marshal in 1199 and created him earl of Pembroke. Henry as Duke of Normandy had also taken Orbec and Bienfaite from Strongbow and had given them to Roger, son of Hugh de Montfort and of Adeline, sister to Strongbow's mother Isabella (Chron. Stephen, i 177-78).

Historians have proposed different answers to the question of why King Henry II refused to recognize Richard's right to the title and lands of Pembroke. Some have believed that Henry II did not trust Richard de Clare and his power in southern Wales, or that Henry II blamed Richard for holding too long to the cause of King Stephen. Some historians have stated that Henry II was determined to not recognize any claim to land based on tenure granted during the anarchy of Stephen's reign. Another possible reason for Henry's denial of Pembroke to Strongbow might have been that the de Clares had no prior claim to these lands by blood and that Strongbow already held a large portion of southeastern Wales with his lordship of Striguil. Looking at a map of Wales; it would seem to be imprudent to give one baron control of both the southeast and southwest sections of Wales. This last reason may be close to the truth as Henry II, on assuming the crown of England, spent the first years of his reign regaining and/or curtailing many lands, castles, and titles granted during Stephen's reign. Henry II had acquired Brian fitz Count's castle of Walingford in 1153, and in that same year with the death of Ranulf, earl of Chester, Henry obtained the castles of Nottingham, Stafford, Newcastle-under-Lyme, Tickhill, Bolsover, and the Peak (Brown "A List of Castles" 250; *Liber Feodorum* i 16). A young man coming as king to an unknown land which had seen more than ten years of war between powerful barons might be well-advised to wait and weigh any decision to grant or confirm power to those same barons.

The answer to this question may never be discovered, but the results of

Henry's actions definitely contributed to Strongbow's reasons for accepting the offer made to him by Dermot, king of Leinster. Though Strongbow had fought for Henry in 1159 against Rhys ap Gruffydd when Rhys attacked the castles of Dyfed and Carmarthen and had accompanied Henry's daughter Matilda to Germany on the occasion of her marriage to the Duke of Saxony in 1168, Strongbow was not a regular member of the king's household (Lloyd Wales ii 511; *Diceto* i 330). King Henry was denying Strongbow the title and lands of Pembroke, and Strongbow was in debt to Robert fitz Harding of Bristol, probably from having been an active fighter during Stephen's reign and from fighting in Wales for Henry II, not from wasting his inheritance as some chronicles have intimated. Dermot's proposal presented Strongbow an opportunity to gain fortune and glory to replace his losses. Dermot offered Strongbow his daughter Eve (Aoife) in marriage as well as the kingdom of Leinster on Dermot's death if Strongbow would help Dermot reclaim his kingdom in Ireland.

Dermot MacMurchada, king of Leinster, had been deposed as a king in Ireland in 1166 by Roderick O'Connor, king of Connaught, Tierman O'Rourke, king of East Meath, and Turkill, king of the Danes of Dublin. The stated reason for this action was that Dermot had in 1152 stolen Dervorgilla, the wife of Tierman. Since no one seems to record for certain whether the wife was a willing abductee and since it was fourteen years between the abduction and the removal of Dermot from Leinster, the supposed excuse for O'Connor's and O'Rourke's actions fails to ring true. Whatever the true cause for the deprivation of Dermot of his title and kingdom, Dermot set sail with a gathering of some of his family and followers, including his wife Mor and his daughter Eve, to find King Henry

II and seek his help in reclaiming what was his by right. Dermot first went to

Bristol and to Robert fitz Harding in August 1166; he stayed with fitz Harding near

St. Augustine's Abbey where he was given directions on where to find Henry II

(*Song* 225-27). Dermot and his company left Bristol, went to Normandy, and then

to Aquitaine seeking Henry II to ask for aid in reclaiming his kingdom in Ireland

(Annals of Ireland i 1161). Dermot found Henry II, and according to Gerald of

Wales, Henry II issued a writ telling the men who held of him in any of his lands

that they were free to aid Dermot in his quest (*Expugnatio* 220-28, 246-48, 299 f

65, f 66). Henry II was shrewd enough to realize that Dermot's plight could not

only remove some of Henry's own disgruntled barons from Wales and keep them

occupied but also should Dermot recapture his kingdom, Henry would have an

ally who would control the Dublin fleet and be of use to him in the event of war in

Wales or Scotland.

From Normandy, Dermot proceeded to Bristol to seek knights to aid in his

forthcoming battle and with fitz Harding's help he found them. Dermot met with

Richard Strongbow de Clare, probably on fitz Harding's recommendation, and

promised him Leinster [Leinster in medieval times was comprised of the present

counties of Wexford, Wicklow, Carlow, Queen's, the greater part of Kildare,

King's, Kilkenny, and the part of Dublin south of the river Liffey] on Dermot's

death and Dermot's daughter, Eve, in marriage (Annals of Ireland 836). Strongbow

promised his aid to Dermot after he had gained permission from his lord, King

Henry II, to do so. After obtaining the agreement of this greater baron, Dermot proceeded to St. David's in Wales to acquire more knights for his endeavor. Here Dermot acquired the aid of Robert fitz Stephen, castellan of Cardigan castle [with the cooperation of Madog who had taken Robert prisoner after taking Cardigan Castle], Maurice fitz Gerald, Maurice de Prendergast, and Hervey de Montmorency.

The Anglo-Normans who participated in the invasion of Ireland were an inter-connected group of men. Many of the men Dermot found to join his expedition were bound to each other by family, land, or fealty. A great proportion of these adventurers were from the lands of Pembroke, Striguil, and Cardigan in Wales; some were tied to the royal princes of Wales and some to the royal blood of the Angevins. They were men skilled in and used to war and trained to take and defend frontier lands. Some of these knights had fought for King Henry in the Welsh wars of 1164/1165 and lost their lands, castles, and/or offices as a result of Rhys ap Gruffydd's successes (*Brut Red* 120-39, 144-49; *Ann Camb* 43-59).

In some ways the conquest of Ireland was similar to the conquest of England. The major figures involved were known to each other and were tied to each other by blood, marriage, and/or vassalage. They were, like those in 1066, seeking lands and wealth by attempting to take another country by force. In order to understand this conquest it is necessary to know the interconnections of these adventurers.

For the largest related group who went to Ireland, it is necessary to begin with the Welsh woman named Nest/Nesta. She was the daughter of Rhys ap Tewdr, king of Deheubarth, sister to Gruffydd ap Rhys and aunt to Rhys ap Gruffydd. Nest was married to Gerald of Windsor, castellan of Pembroke Castle, and by Gerald she had three sons and one daughter. Her legitimate children were: William fitz Gerald of Carew; Maurice fitz Gerald of Llansteffan; David fitz Gerald, Bishop of St. David's in Wales; and Angharad who was married to William de Barri, father to Gerald of Wales. Nest was apparently a woman of high passions and few moral scruples; she bestowed her favors in many places and on many men. Nest had a bastard by King Henry I, Henry fitz Henry who was killed at Angelsy in Wales in 1157; this Henry's son, Meiler fitz Henry, was to play an important role in Anglo-Irish history. Nest also had a bastard by Stephen, constable of Cardiff, and this son, Robert fitz Stephen castellan of Cardigan castle, played a part in the Anglo-Norman invasion of Ireland. Gerald of Wales' brothers, Robert de Barri and Philip de Barri were also part of Anglo-Norman invasion forces. Thus, William fitz Gerald of Carew and his son Raymond le Gros, Maurice fitz Gerald, Robert and Philip de Barri, Miles fitz David (bastard son of David fitz Gerald), Robert fitz Stephen, and Meiler fitz Henry were all related by blood and half-blood, all from Wales, and all took part in the Anglo-Norman conquest of Ireland.

Hervey de Montmorency was Strongbow's uncle; apparently Hervey was a child of Adeliza de Clermont from her second marriage after the death of Gilbert I fitz Richard (d1117). There are no known records that provide the name of Adeliza's second husband; it is only known that he was of the French house of Montmorency.

Miles de Cogan and his brother Richard were apparently knights and vassals from Penarth or Pembroke. Maurice de Prendergast was probably a descendant from a de Prendergast who accompanied William the Conqueror to England, and Maurice may have come from the area of Haverfordwest in Pembroke. Robert de Quenci was connected to the senior branch of the de Clare's who held land in Northhamptonshire. Saher de Quinci had married the widow of Robert fitz Richard de Clare (d1136-1138), founder of the fitz-Walter branch of the de Clare's.

William de Angulo came from the family of that name in Angle on the peninsula in Pembrokeshire. The Bloets were some of the original vassals of Strigoil/Striguil; Ralph Bloet held lands in Helmerton and Lacham in Wiltshire, Silchester in Berkshire, and Daglingworth in Gloucester, and Raglan Castle in Monmouthshire was granted to Walter Bloet by Strongbow (Brooks Knights' Fees 26). Walter de Bloet and at least three other members of this family witnessed Irish Charters of Strongbow, and one brother was granted land in Wexford (Chart St Mary's i 78-79, 83-84, 258; ii 151-54). Walter de Ridelsford belonged to the Lincolnshire family and was probably a vassal of Strongbow's. Gilbert de Boisrohard was from Buckinghampshire and Bedfordshire and also a vassal of Striguil. John de Clahull was a vassal of Strongbow's and would become Strongbow's seneschal of Leinster (Reg. St. Thomas 369-70; Chart St Mary's i 83-84, 258; ii 152-57). Richard de la Roche was descended from Godebert Flandrensis of Ros, near Haverford, and the name de la Roche was probably taken from Roche Castle which was probably held by Robert fitz Godebert of Maurice de Prendergast (Roche "Roches of Wexford" 39-40).

Many of these men had lost their position, castles, and lands during the Welsh wars from 1152 to 1176. In 1157 and 1163 Henry II had led expeditions into Wales trying to curb the Welsh inroads against the Anglo-Norman barons, but these military expeditions were not successful even though they had resulted in

64

treaties. The Welsh merely waited and then began again their attacks on the Anglo-Norman held lands. Henry's expedition of 1165 into Wales was defeated by the weather, and when he left for Normandy in 1166, the Welsh began their attacks on the Norman held lands. Rhys ap Gruffydd retook the lordship of Ceredigion (de Clare's) and demolished Cardigan Castle, attacked the Carew holding of Emlyn, took Cilgerren Castle, and captured Robert fitz Stephen, the castellan (*Brut Red* 146-49; *Brut* 64). All of these factors came together to create a situation that was ripe for the offer by Dermot MacMurchada of lands and wealth in Ireland in return for aid in recapturing his kingdom there. These men from the Anglo-Norman Welsh lordships had lost castles, lands, and/or positions to the Welsh princes, and they were, in essence, ready-made warriors and adventurers for Dermot's purpose. Perhaps Henry II saw Dermot's request as a means of ridding himself of a group of armed and unhappy knights from his own English/Welsh territories and thus reducing his own problems there.

The first contingent of these adventurers arrived in Ireland in May 2, 1169 [August 1169 according to Conlon p 225 f]; they included Robert fitz Stephen, Miles fitz David, Maurice de Prendergast, and Hervey de Montmorency (Orpen Ireland i 451). This first contingent was met at Bannow by Dermot and his army. Combining both forces, they took the city of Wexford after two days. From Wexford, Dermot attacked Ossory and with the help of fitz Stephen and de Prendergast took it. Afterwards Dermot and the Anglo-Normans plundered Offelan and brought under control all of Leinster. Dermot then sent messages to Strongbow and urged him to come to Ireland and honour his promise to aid

Dermot. Meanwhile Strongbow had gone to Henry II in Normandy and received permission to go to Ireland. [There is still debate over whether Henry II actually gave Strongbow permission to aid Dermot or whether Henry gave it in such a way that he could later deny that he had been serious in giving permission.]

May 1170 Strongbow sent Raymond le Gros to Ireland ahead of himself. On landing in Ireland, Raymond and his men were attacked by the citizens of Waterford and the men of Melaghlin O'Phelan, lord of Decies. But Raymond and his men defeated the assault by the men of O'Phelan. Having collected men from Striguil, Gowerland, and Haverfordwest, Strongbow arrived at Waterford on August 23, 1170, with 200 men-at-arms, and about one thousand archers. Once in Ireland, Strongbow and his army were joined by Raymond le Gros and his men, and together they took Waterford on St Bartholomew's Eve. On August 25, 1170, Strongbow and Eve, Dermot's daughter, were married in Waterford Cathedral (*Expugnatio* 255-56; Barnard English History 34-36).

Dermot then turned his attention to Dublin as it was of primary importance in order to secure Leinster. The combined armies immediately moved toward Dublin and arrived September 21, 1170. According to the *Song,* Miles de Cogan led with 700 men including Donnell Kavanagh, natural son of Dermot. He was followed by 800 men led by Raymond le Gros, Dermot with 1000 Irishmen, and Strongbow with 3000 (*Expugnatio* 256-60; *Song* 1159-162). One can assume that the figures are exaggerated, but the actual number of knights and archers would have been significant, with archers outnumbering knights by 10 to 20 to 1. At Dublin, O'Connor, king of Connaught, O'Rourke, king of east Meath, and

Murtogh O'Connoll, prince of Origiall, had gathered to defend Hasculf MacTorkil, lord of Dublin. Because the Irish had blocked all the main southern approaches to Dublin, Strongbow and his men came through Wicklow and the Dublin mountains unscathed. When the Ostmen of Dublin sought terms with Dermot through the efforts of bishop Laurence O'Toole {brother-in-law to Dermot}, O'Connor saw this as a repudiation of his status as high king of Ireland and withdrew his forces from the battle.

On September 21, 1170, on the third day of negotiations, de Cogan and le Gros managed to attack and break through an undefended gate to the city and overcome the Ostmen. Dermot and his allies took the city of Dublin, and many of the Danes fled on their ships. After several days in Dublin, Dermot turned his attention to East Meath, pillaging Clonard and Kells and even invading Briefne, land of O'Rourke. As a result of these actions, O'Rourke killed all of the hostages from Meath, and he persuaded O'Connor to kill Dermot's legitimate son Conchobar as well as a son of Donnell Kavanagh, Dermot's natural son. Dermot returned to his caput at Ferns, and Strongbow left Dublin in the care of Miles de Cogan and returned to Waterford.

After the capture of Dublin, King Henry II, perhaps seeing the threat of another possible Welsh palatine lordship in Ireland, issued a writ. That writ commanded that no ships from any of the lands subject to him could carry men or supplies to Ireland and that all of his men who had gone to Ireland must return by Easter (March 28, 1171) or risk forfeiture of their lands (William of Newburg i 167-68). Strongbow sent Raymond le Gros to find Henry II in Aquitaine and to try and appease and reassure the king that all the lands that the Anglo-Norman knights had captured in Ireland were lands to be held of the king and not held as little kingdoms by the barons. Raymond returned to Ireland in the summer of 1171 after the death of Dermot MacMurchada.

Dermot MacMurchada died at Ferns in May 1171, and Strongbow assumed the kingship of Leinster in right of his wife. (Dermot's right to give the kingship of Leinster to Strongbow is fully discussed in Flanagan's book, Irish Society, Anglo-Norman Settlers, Angevin Kingship chapter four.) At the news of Dermot's death, the Irish kings Roderick O' Connor, Tiarnan O' Rourke, and Murchad O' Connell gathered an army and besieged the city of Dublin for two months. Godred King of the Isle of Man came with thirty ships to help O'Connor. Strongbow, de Cogan, and their men were trapped inside the city. O'Connor encamped with his armies at Castleknock and Finglass (Wright Essays 242). The situation was desperate, and Strongbow devised a plan, with the aid of le Gros, Maurice fitz Gerald, Miles and Richard de Cogan, and Robert Quenci, to send Lawrence O'Toole to O'Connor to propose a compromise. The proposal was that if O'Connor would raise the siege, Strongbow would consent to hold Leinster as a fief of O'Connor (Annals of Ireland 539). O'Connor refused and demanded that all Anglo-Normans leave Ireland forever; naturally Strongbow refused that option. The next morning Strongbow, in a brilliant military move, divided his army and led one of three separate groups of men quietly out of Dublin and attacked the unprepared Irish army at Finglas and Castleknock. The success of this strategy enabled the Anglo-Normans to divert, divide, and defeat the Irish. Godred took his fleet and returned to the Isle of Man.

[According to the Annals of Ireland O'Connor and the men from Brefney were not in the battle because they were busy burning the Anglo-Normans crops (539-40).] While the battle at Dublin was being fought, Robert fitz Stephen was besieged at Carrig, and being told that Dublin had fallen and Strongbow and his men defeated, fitz Stephen surrendered to the Irish. Strongbow left Dublin in the care of Miles de Cogan and went to try to rescue fitz Stephen on his way back to Waterford. Being told by the Irish that fitz Stephen was being held on Beggerin Island and that any attempt to rescue him would result in fitz Stephen's immediate death, Strongbow had to return to Waterford without him (Dolley Anglo-Norman 66).

July 1171 Strongbow sent his uncle Hervey to King Henry in Normandy after Raymond le Gros had failed to reassure King Henry about the aims of the Anglo-Norman knights in Ireland. By September 1171 Hervey returned and urged his nephew to go to Wales and meet King Henry who was preparing to come to Ireland in person to impress the royal authority on all of his subjects. Robert of Torigny says that Hervey settled the problem between Strongbow and King Henry while Hervey was meeting with Henry at Argentan in July 1171, but most sources state that Strongbow and Henry did not settle their differences until they met in Pembrokeshire later (Robert of Torigny 252).

As to Henry II's reactions and reasons for deciding to go to Ireland in person, there were several contributing factors. First, Henry II had supposedly been given a papal bull by Pope Adrian to see that Ireland's ecclesiastical house was brought into line with the current Church's reforms. Second, Henry II was trying to avoid the papal legates who had been sent to inquire into the murder of

Thomas Becket, Archbishop of Canterbury. Third, Ireland seemed to have been already partially conquered without Henry II having to pay or provide anything except men. The inherent danger of the successes achieved by the Anglo-Normans in Ireland was that they might seize on the opportunity to establish Marcher-like palatinates [king-like fiefs where the lord was almost absolute ruler within his fief] as had happened in Wales. Henry II definitely wanted no Anglo-Norman petty kings sitting just off the coast of Wales and controlling the trade between Bristol and Dublin with the potential of invading Wales or Scotland. Henry II ordered the highest-ranking Anglo-Norman baron, Strongbow, to appear before him in Wales, and in the meantime Henry had confiscated Strongbow's lands and castles in Wales and England (Wright Essays 247-48).

Before Strongbow could leave Ireland, he had two problems to solve to provide for stability in Leinster while he was absent. First he used his brother-in-law, Domnhall O'Brien, king of Thomond, to get the assurance of MacGilla Patraic king of Ossory that he would respect the borders of Ui Chennselaig [Hy Kinsellagh] and maintain the peace in Leinster. The second was the problem of Ui Chennselaig [Hy Kinsellagh] itself. Strongbow solved this by recognizing Murchad [Murrough MacMurrough], brother of Dermot, as king of Ui Chennselaig with his son Muirchertach [Murtough, Murtherdath] as his heir and by giving him substantial lands within this territory. Second Strongbow recognized Dermot MacMurchada's natural son Domnall Caemanach [Donnell Kavanagh] as having jurisdiction over Strongbow's Irish vassals there and in other parts of Leinster, entrusting the pleas of these lands to Domnall. Strongbow also gave Domnall vast lands in Ui Chennselaig (Orpen Ireland i 338-39; *Song* 2180-197).

With these problems solved, Strongbow crossed over to Wales and met Henry at Pembroke while the royal muster gathered at Newnham in Gloucestershire. [The *Song* and Robert of Torigny say they met at Pembroke as Henry was preparing to depart for Ireland.] This was a meeting between two men that begs for an eyewitness account, but none seems to be extant. On one side was Strongbow; a knight and vassal from a powerful, influential, and wealthy Anglo-Norman family who had been denied by his lord and king what he believed to be his rightful inheritance. Here was a knight who by his own skills and ingenuity had conquered and claimed by that conquest and by his marriage a large portion of new dominions. Opposite Strongbow was Henry Plantagenet, probably the shrewdest and most gifted medieval lord and king. This was a lord and king who probably understood better than any other medieval king the equation that dictated that no feudal king could rule and control his lands and his vassals without the support and cooperation of the strongest and greatest of those vassals. Yet, Henry was a practical realist who recognized that this cooperation had to be equally balanced by the limitation of the power [the men, castles, and wealth] of those greater vassals. This meeting would have been something like watching a truly great chess match as two minds plotted, feinted, and moved to gain the advantage with each giving-up or yielding only as much as was absolutely necessary. These two men apparently settled most of their differences at this time. According to some records, Henry recognized Strongbow's comital status but not his right to Pembroke, and from this point, Strongbow signed his name as 'comes Richardus' or 'comes de Strigoil.'

King Henry was held at Milford Haven for 19 days due to ill winds and did not sail to Ireland until Oct. 16, 1171. Henry arrived in Waterford on October 17 with 400 ships, 500 knights, 4000 men-at-arms, and around a thousand archers. Henry brought with him his own *familiares* and men of his household, including William fitz Audelin, Hugh de Lacy, Robert fitz Bernard, Philip de Braose, and Bertrum de Verdun (*Gesta Regis Henrici i* 25-29). At Waterford, Strongbow did homage and fealty to Henry II for Leinster and surrendered Waterford into Henry's hands. Henry placed Waterford in the custody of Robert fitz Bernard. At Waterford, the men of Wexford appeared and turned over to Henry their captive, Robert fitz Stephen, as one of those Anglo-Normans who had refused Henry's order to return to England. Needless to say, Henry II did not keep fitz Stephen as a prisoner for long. As Henry proceeded towards Dublin he received the fealty and oaths of the kings of Cork, Limerick, and Ossory on his way (*Expugnatio* 272-73; *Song* 2620-625; <u>Wendover</u>, Giles 20-21).

While en route to Dublin, Henry stopped at Lismore and saw Gilla Crist Ua Connairche, bishop of Lismore and papal legate to Ireland. Gilla agreed to hold a national Church council while Henry was in Ireland. At Cashel, Henry obtained the permission of Archbishop Domnall Ua Hullachain to hold the Church council at Cashel, and Henry put his chaplain Nicholas and Ralph, archdeacon of Llandaff, to work arranging the council for the reformation of the Irish Church.

Henry arrived in Dublin November 11, 1171, and held Christmas there within a quickly provided suitable castle/domicile. Here Henry received the fealty of the Irish chieftains except for Connaught and Ulster. Before he left Dublin, Henry gave

John de Courcy the lands of Ulster on the condition that he would hold what he could conquer, and he gave the lands of Meath to Hugh de Lacy as a fief to be held for fifty knights' fees. Henry also placed the city of Dublin in the custody of Hugh de Lacy. This Hugh de Lacy had married Rose/Rohesia de Monmouth who was very possibly the daughter of Baderon de Monmouth and Rohesia de Clare, sister to Strongbow's father. Henry gave Robert fitz Stephen, Meiler fit Henry, and Miles fitz David to de Lacy to help garrison the city. Henry left Dublin on February 2, 1172, to return to Wexford and from there sail back to England (*Gesta Regis Henrici* i 24-29; *Song* 2665-75).

While Henry II was at Cashel, Strongbow was at Ferns marrying his sister, Basilia, to Robert de Quenci. On this marriage, Strongbow gave de Quenci all of the Duffry as a fief, the constableship of Leinster, and made de Quenci his standard bearer (*Song* 2740-754).

Between March 26 and April 16, 1172, Henry II moved to protect the royal interests in Ireland and limit Strongbow's power. He placed the city and land of Dublin in the custody of Hugh de Lacy and created Hugh lord of Meath. He gave the custody of Waterford and Wexford to Robert fitz Bernard and William fitz Audelin (Cosgrove Medieval Ireland 96-97; *Expugnatio* 287; *Gesta Regis Henrici* i 25-30). Henry separated Strongbow from his most important military commanders by placing fitz Stephen, Maurice fitz Gerald, Milo fitz David, and Meiler fitz Henry in the garrison of Dublin. Henry put fitz Audelin, de Braose, and de Hastings with thirty knights in charge of Wexford, and fitz Bernard, de Bohun, and de Grenville with forty knights in charge of Waterford (Cosgrove Medieval Ireland 95-97;

Houedene ii 34). Though Henry recognized the value and need of his barons, he

wanted no palatine lordships in Ireland as he had inherited in Wales. By separating

his strongest knights into different spheres of power, Henry hoped to have them

counter-balance and check each other. Henry II knew the realities and possibilities

of his world, his vassals/knights, and the seductions and temptations of power.

After Henry II left Ireland late in 1172, Strongbow lost Robert de Quenci in

a battle at Offaly. On de Quenci's death Raymond le Gros demanded de Quenci's

widow, Basilia, his lands and his titles, and custody of de Quenci's sole heir and

child, Maud. When Strongbow refused le Gros' request, Raymond returned to

Wales. Strongbow made his uncle Hervey constable of Leinster.

April 1173 Henry's son, young Henry, began a rebellion in Normandy, and

Henry II called Strongbow to come to Normandy and aid him. Strongbow

left Ireland for Normandy and defended Gisors for the king, which had already

been strengthened in March by Henry (*Diceto* i 375; *Houedene* i 51; Eyton *Itin*

172,176).   Strongbow was at Breteuil, and in August 1173, he was part of the relief

of Verneuil. At Rouen August 10, 1173, Henry II named Strongbow governor of

Ireland (*vice Regis Anglie in Hibernia agens)*, gave him the city of Wexford, the

castle of Wicklow, and made him constable of Waterford and Dublin (*Crede Mihi*

46-47; *Song* 2902-905). Henry II then sent Strongbow back to Ireland before

the end of the war, ordering le Gros to return with him. On reaching Ireland,

Strongbow sent back fitz Bernard, fitz Stephen, and Henry's Irish garrisons to aid

the king in England and Normandy (Eyton *Itin* 176; *Diceto* i 375,377; Cosgrove

Medieval Ireland 100; Brooks "Unpublished Charter Raymond le Gros" 167-69;

74

Lalley "Secular Patronage" 130-32).

On Strongbow's return to Ireland, he had to recall Raymond from Wales where he had gone. Strongbow needed le Gros to take charge of the Anglo-Norman army as Hervey seemed to be ineffectual in commanding military forces. But before the end of 1173, Raymond le Gros had to return to Wales on the death of his father.

During the early part of 1174, Hervey led Strongbow's troops toward Dublin, but at Thurles they were ambushed by the Irish, defeated, and forced to retreat to Waterford. The rebellion of the native Irish led by David of Limerick at the end of 1174 forced Strongbow from Limerick back to Wexford. Strongbow sent for Raymond le Gros in Wales [Gerald of Wales says it was because Strongbow's men would not follow Hervey and demanded the return of Raymond.] Whatever the true reason, le Gros returned to Ireland, and on his return, le Gros was given Basilia, Strongbow's sister, in marriage and custody and wardship of her daughter Maud de Quenci. Raymond was also given the constableship of Leinster, and lands in Fothard, Idrone, and Glasskarrig (Brooks, Knights' Fees 27, 27 f9, 28, 67, 247).

During this same time period, Strongbow gave his natural daughter Alina in marriage to William fitz William, son of William fitz Gerald, and Strongbow's uncle Hervey married Nest, daughter of Maurice fitz Gerald. (There are no known records of the mother of Alina, and as the only marriage Strongbow made was with Eve in 1170, historians can only presume that Alina was Strongbow's natural daughter.) This marrying of Strongbow's family to the Geraldines may have simply been an attempt to lessen the strife between the families and strengthen alliances of the Anglo-Normans in Ireland. Holding and keeping land in Ireland during this time period was difficult enough without the Anglo-Normans fighting among themselves. Most of these men were from Wales. They had personal experience of the necessity of Anglo-Norman barons in a hostile land surviving by ties of marriage, blood, or vassalage; they had seen and lived with such a reality and knew its value.

October 1175 Strongbow was in England, perhaps for the Treaty of Windsor which was signed by Henry II and Roderick O'Connor, king of Connaught (Eyton *Itin* 196; Chart St. Mary's i 79-80). The treaty stated that O'Connor would be king of the Irish and take their homage, he would provide hostages, cattle, and tribute to King Henry II, and he would not interfere with lands held by the king or in the lordships of Dublin, Meath, Wexford, Leinster, and Waterford. It is known that Strongbow was in England at this time because of a re-grant of a charter to Canterbury dated between October 12 and 14, 1175 (Landon *Cartae Antiquae* 93#184). With Strongbow in England, this may have encouraged the Irish princes to revolt in Ireland (Eyton *Itin* 189,196; *Gesta Regis Henrici* i 102-03; *Chart* i 79-80; Sheehy "*Registrum Novum*" 253).

Strongbow returned to Ireland by the beginning of 1176, and in April 1176, Strongbow sent le Gros to relieve Dermot Macarthy, prince of Desmond. After restoring Dermot to Desmond, le Gros headed for Cork. On the way to Cork, le Gros received a letter from his wife Basilia saying: "[. . .] that huge grinder which gave me so much pain has fallen out [. . .]" (*Song* 3208-212; *Diceto* i 407). This was a coded message telling le Gros that Strongbow had died April 5, 1176 (June 1, 1176, according to *Diceto* i 407) of some type of infection in his foot or leg. Only after le Gros arrived in Dublin was Strongbow buried with great ceremony at Holy Trinity Church in Dublin with Lawrence Archbishop of Dublin presiding (*Diceto* i 407). It is written in "The Chronicle of Melrose":

> Ricardus, surnamed Strangboye, died in Ireland, son of Gilbertus
>
> Strongboye and Isabella aunt of kings Malcolmus IV and Willelmus
>
> of Scotland and of earl David. He went with many knights and gentlemen
>
> to Ireland and with the support of a regalus [Diarmait] of that land, whose
>
> daughter he had married, attacked certain cities and the
>
> noblest of them Dublin, and at last took them. (i 41)

There is no mention of Strongbow's wife or children in any of the extant records for this time. It must be assumed that Eve and the children were there in Dublin with Strongbow when he died and was buried in Christ Church.

When Strongbow died, he left a widow Eve, a minor son Gilbert, and a daughter Isabel. According to records, Gilbert died a minor in 1185. At Strongbow's death, Henry II took his lands into royal hands because Strongbow's heir was a minor. William fitz Audelin was the administrator for Strongbow's lands in Ireland (*Houedene i 125)*. Strongbow's widow, Eve, held her own dower rights, and possibly the lordship of Striguil until as late as 1184/1185. Visible proof of the value that Henry II placed on Richard Strongbow de Clare is evidenced in the care and protection Henry II practiced with regard to Strongbow's lands, castles, widow's rights, and with Strongbow's sole heir, Isabel de Clare. Perhaps the best indication of Henry's protection of the lands and rights of Strongbow is seen in the fact that Henry did not re-marry Eve to one of his barons after the death of Strongbow. One of Henry's last acts was to promise Isabel and all of her father's lands in marriage to William Marshal in 1189.

In 1176 on Strongbow's death, Henry II appointed William fitz Audelin as justiciar in his place and placed the custody of all of Strongbow's Irish lands into fitz Audelin's hands. In 1177 Henry II divided the custody, lordships, and lands in Ireland according to Hoveden thus:

> William fitz Audelin had custody of Wexford with all of its appurtenances and Henry enacted that the following should be part of the services due to Wexford; Arklow with its appurtenances; Glasscarrig; Ferns; the lands of Gilbert de Boisrohard to Ferneg Winal; all the lands of Hervey de Monmorency between Wexford and the waters of Waterford; Leinster; the lands of Geoffrey de Constantin [. . .] , and the whole lands of Otweld. To Robert le Poer, Henry's marshal, he gave the city of Waterford and all of its appurtenances including the following which would owe service to Waterford: all the land between Waterford and the water beyond Lismore, and all of the lands of Oiseric were part of this service. To Hugh de Lacy, Henry II gave custody of the city of Dublin and the following which owed service to Dublin: all the lands of Ofellana, Kildare, all the lands of Offalaia, Wicklow, the service of 100 knights from Meath, and the service of four knights due from Robert le Poer from his castle of Dunavet.
> (*Houedene* i 455)

This detail found in Hoveden provides some idea of the division and control of the Irish lands as a result of the Anglo-Norman conquest of Ireland accomplished by Richard Strongbow de Clare, his vassals, and the other knights from Wales in 1170.

There are many years in Strongbow's life for which there are no known records. We do not know of his early years or of his life with his father during the wars of Stephen and Matilda. His time in Ireland is seen only through the eyes of a few contemporary chronicles and the charters and writs Strongbow issued and/or witnessed. We know that Strongbow was generous in ecclesiastical grants, adding to the grants of his father to the Templars at Weston, Baldock, Chesterford, Buckland, and Reed from his English and Irish lands. Gilbert had given the Templars four carucates of land at Weston with the advowson of the churches of Weston and Baldock, about 150 acres of land in the vill of Baldock and the mill at Radwell in Bedfordshire. Strongbow founded the priory of Benedictine nuns at Usk and gifted the church of Iverton in Bedfordshire to St Neots. Strongbow founded the preceptory of Knights Hospitallers at Kilmainham outside of Dublin of which the first Master was Hugh de Clahull, probably the brother of Strongbow's marshal John de Clahull. Strongbow, with fitz Stephen and le Gros, helped Archbishop O'Toole build the choir of the cathedral of Trinity at Dublin with the two chapels of St Edmond and St Mary Alba and St Laud and granted them lands and tithes. He gave charters and lands to St Mary's Abbey in Dublin, including Clonlif, and confirmed his uncle Hervey's foundation of Dunbrody Abbey and added to its lands. Two of Strongbow's Charters 1170-1171 to St. Mary's read:

> To the Church of St. Mary and the white monks who serve God
> there in the present and the future, the land which is called Clonlif,
> with the land which is beside the sea between the abbey of the
> said monks and the water which is called Tulkan, with all its
> appurtenances in land and sea, wood and plain, in meadows and

pastures, its fishponds and fisheries, and all other easements [. . .].
(<u>Chart St. Mary's</u> i 152-54)

To the Church of St. Mary's the land which is called Muninalcon
which was held by Sigerith MacTorkill and the land called Lisloan
which was held by Torphin MacTurkill and the land of Balilugan
near Portmarwock, lands that were vacated by the defeated Norse
chieftains from Dublin

[. . .]. (Gwynn "Origin of St. Mary's" 122; <u>Chart St. Mary's</u> i 78-79;
152-54)

Strongbow thus provided for ecclesiastical foundations in both England and Ireland
from his newly acquired lands in Ireland.

The *chanson de geste* of Richard fitz Gilbert does provide an important
record of the lands and fiefs of the first Anglo-Norman barons in Ireland and are
relevant to those who owed their lands and positions to Strongbow and through his
daughter to William Marshal and their children. It is important to know these men
and fiefs because of their relevance to the descendants of Strongbow and Aoife. To
paraphrase a biblical saying: "How sharper than a serpent's tongue is an ungrateful
vassal."

To Raymond le Gros Strongbow gave his sister Basilia in marriage and
Forth as a fief, as well as Odrone and Glascarrig. Basilia's daughter by Robert de
Quenci, Maud, took her inheritance of the Duffry from her father with her to her
marriage with Philip de Prendergast. Basilia and Raymond had no children, so
Raymond enfeoffed his brother Odo de Carew and Odo's sons from his own lands.
On Raymond's death, Basilia married Geoffrey fitz Robert, seneschal of Leinster,

and after his death she entered the Abbey of St. Thomas in Dublin to which she made many grants of lands in Forth. To his uncle Hervey Strongbow gave Obarthy by the sea, and to Maurice de Prendergast Strongbow gave five knights' fees in Fernegenal and five knights' fees in Schyrmal and Kynaloh (Books Knights' Fees 130-31). To Meiler fitz Henry Strongbow gave Carbury, and to Maurice fitz Gerald he gave Naas in the land of Offelan, and Wicklow. To Walter de Riddlesford Strongbow gave twenty fiefs in O Murethy. To William de Dene Strongbow gave the barony of Keir in Wexford, and to William de Angulo he gave Felmeda Tiro worth forty knights' fees. John de Clahull, marshal of Strongbow, received all the land between Eboy and Leighlin, Obargy, parts of the baronies of Carlow and Idrone West in Carlow, and the manor of Aboy {Obowi, Eboy}. To Adam de Hereford Strongbow gave Aghaboe, in Leixlip the district called Salmon Leap near the river Liffey, Cloncurry, Kill, Oughterard, and Downings (Annals of Ireland 835). Adam divided his lands with his two older brothers, Richard and John, and Adam's third marriage was to Basilia, daughter of William fitz Gerald (brother of Maurice) and Alina (natural daughter of Strongbow). To Miles fitz David Strongbow gave Owerk and Ida in Ossory, to Thomas le Fleming he gave Ardrie, and to Gilbert de Boisrohard Strongbow gave Offelimy on the sea.

It is important to note these men and these lands because some of them and/or their descendants will appear again in the lives of Strongbow's daughter and grandchildren. Recognition and acknowledgement of their debt to the man whose skills and intelligence provided the very foundation of their family and lands in Ireland was due, but not always given. In some instances later in history, the very fealty by which these men owed what they held in Ireland was betrayed.

Gerald of Wales describes Strongbow as a tall man with red hair, freckles, grey eyes and a soft (weak) voice:

> In war Strongbow was more a leader than a soldier [. . .]. When he took-up his position in the midst of battle, he stood firm as an immovable standard around which his men could re-group and take refuge. In war he remained steadfast and reliable in good fortune and bad alike [. . .]. (*Expugnatio* 87-89)

If a man who was Strongbow's contemporary and definitely not an admirer could with faint praise describe him thus, then Strongbow must have been a unique man. Strongbow seems to have shared a trait in common with his future son-in-law; he was a military leader who led from the front rather than the rear. Strongbow had the patience and intelligence to not openly defy King Henry II, despite being denied what he must have seen as his rightful inheritance. He had the military skills and abilities of a commander that enabled him to conquer large lands in Ireland and the sagacity of a diplomat that allowed him to offer those conquests to his king and vassal lord, King Henry II. Strongbow had earned King Henry's respect and affection, and this was evident in the facts that Henry protected and guarded Strongbow's widow, his heiress, and his lands after Strongbow's death. August 1189 Isabel de Clare married William Marshal; she brought her inheritance from her father almost completely intact. Isabel de Clare brought Marshal the lordship of Striguil (Chepstow) in Wales, the lordship of Leinster in Ireland, fiefs in nine shires in England, and claims to the title and earldom of Pembroke and to one-half the barony of Earl Giffard in England and Normandy.

IV. William Marshal: Knight and Tutor

Unlike Richard fitz Gilbert de Clare's life, William Marshal's life is well documented because less than a year after his death in 1219, his eldest son William II commissioned a record of his father's life. *L'Histoire de Guillaume le Marechal* is a metrical history of a man of the knightly class in the late twelfth and early thirteenth centuries. Little is known about the writer of *L'Histoire* except that his first name was Jean, that he personally witnessed some of the events in Marshal's later life, and that he had access to Marshal's squire and knight, John D'Erley, who served William Marshal for most of Marshal's life. The point of view is that of the secular knightly class and not of the ecclesiastical class; the events recorded in *L'Histoire* can be verified in most instances by the official records in the Pipe, Charter, Close, Patent, and Oblatis Rolls and the chronicles of the times.

William Marshal was born c 1147, and as a younger son, becoming a knight was his natural choice of a path to success and survival. Marshal was sent to a cousin of the family, William of Tancarville hereditary Chamberlain of Normandy, to be trained as a knight in c 1159/1160 at about 13 years of age. As was the custom in feudal times, younger sons were sent to relatives or godfathers to be taught all the skills and accomplishments necessary to become knights. They were sent to families that had the position or status that would benefit a younger son in finding his own place in society. Since younger sons did not inherit the lands, castles, and titles of their fathers, it was necessary to try to place them in households that would provide *entre* to the higher avenues open to them. To be trained as a knight in ahousehold that had the reputation of producing skilled and successful warriors and in a household that possessed high political status guaranteed a young knight entry into his society at a significant level. William de Tancarville as hereditary Chamberlain of Normandy held a notable position in his society, and the reputation of the knights of his household was already a known entity. So William Marshal began his training for knighthood from an advantageous position.

The year 1167 saw Henry II at war with Louis VII, king of France. During 1167 Count Philip of Flanders, Count Matthew of Boulogne, and the count of Poitou attacked Eu, and John, count of Eu, was forced to fall back to Drincourt (now called Neufchatel-en-Bray). William of Tancarville and the constable of Normandy met John at Drincourt, and William Marshal was a member of the Tancarville's army (Gervase i 203). It is inferred from *L'Histoire* and other records that this was the point in time that William Marshal was inducted into the order of knighthood by his cousin, de Tancarville (*Hist* 815-22, 1190-191). As John, count of Eu, and the constable of Normandy left Drincourt on their way to Rouen, a messenger overtook them with the news that the French-allied counts were marching on Drincourt. Tancarville turned back with the knights of his household to defend it while the constable and John proceeded on their way. When de Tancarville reached the river of Bethune, he found it held by William de Mandeville, earl of Essex. With their forces combined, they managed to take and cross the bridge and run headlong at full gallop into the attacking force in the middle of the town. The de Tancarville force drove the opposition back across the bridge, through the town, and back over the moat on the road to Eu. There the opposition was re-enforced, reversed, and drove the de Tancarville force back over the bridge over the Bethune.

During one of these rounds, Marshal was caught on the shoulder by an iron hook wielded by a Flemish sergeant; it pulled him from his horse, but Marshal was able to fight his way clear with his sword. Marshal lost his charger and would have a scar on his shoulder for the rest of his life, but his ability with a sword enabled him to return to his cousin. The battle went back and forth at least four times until the citizens of Drincourt joined the battle on the side of de Tancarville and helped rout the opposition. The chamberlain held a great feast to celebrate their victory, and according to the *Histoire*, Marshal learned an important lesson from this battle. At the feast de Mandeville, earl of Essex, asked Marshal to give him a gift from all the spoils Marshal had gained from his victories that day. Marshal replied that he had acquired nothing in the battle (*Hist 827-1162*). The earl was reminding Marshal that battle was a business as well as means of acquiring fame for a knight. The business was to succeed in acquiring horses, equipment, and ransoms in battle by virtue of the skills and successes of knightly valor. The acquisition of spoils of battle or tourney allowed the knight to exhibit the qualities of valor and *largesse*, both essential elements of chivalry and knighthood.

This was a lesson that Marshal learned well; he had lost his warhorse in the battle at Drincourt and was forced to sell the splendid mantle he had worn when he was dubbed a knight in order to buy a baggage horse to carry his armor. This still left him without a *destrier*, essential for any knight. When notice of a great tournament that was to be held near Le Mans between the knights of Anjou, Maine, Poitou, and Brittany and the knights of Normandy, England, and France came to de Tancarville, he decided that Marshal had learned his lesson to always take every opportunity to capture spoils in battle. The Chamberlain provided Marshal with a new, not even broken, warhorse so that he could participate in the tournament (*Hist* 1163-302).

This tournament was a large and splendid occasion for all tourneying knights; the chamberlain took the field with over forty knights from his own household. Unlike some tournaments, this one did not set the price of ransoms before the battle; it was a contest in which those defeated and captured would lose all they possessed, horse, armor, and weapons. Marshal entered the field with cold purpose; he captured Philip de Valognes, a knight of King William of Scotland, and taking Philip's pledge to pay the ransom he owed Marshal, Marshal returned to the battle. Marshal captured at least two more knights and acquired warhorses, arms and armor, palfreys, roncins for his servants, and sumpter horses for his baggage (*Hist* 1302-380). Marshal, in one tournament, had not only repaired but also greatly increased his finances and demonstrated his prowess and skills as a knight.

After de Tancarville had returned to his home with his *mesnie*, word came of another tournament to be held in Maine. The chamberlain did not wish to attend, but he gave permission for Marshal to go. In the first encounter of the tournament, Marshal found himself attacked by five knights from the opposition side. Though Marshal beat them off, he found his helmet had been struck so hard that it had turned completely around on his head. Marshal withdrew from the tournament to a *reset* area and had the blacksmith remove and repair his helmet. While he was in the refuge area Marshal heard a conversation between too well known knights, Bon

Abbe le Rouge and John de Subligni. The Bon Abbe asked John who the knight was who was having his helmet repaired. John replied that it was Marshal who by the device on his shield belonged to the household of de Tancarville. The Bon Abbe replied that any band Marshal led would be one that only gained in reputation for courage and steadfastness (*Hist* 1387-512). Such a compliment from such knights must have provided incentive to Marshal. He returned to the field and fought so well that he was awarded the prize of the tourney, a warhorse from Lombardy, considered one of the best breeds of chargers.

In late 1167, Marshal asked de Tancarville for permission to return to England to see his family; de Tancarville gave him permission to go but reminded Marshal that England was not the place for a knight who wished to gain prizes and fame on the tournament field. William Marshal's father, John fitz Gilbert, had died in 1165. William's older brother John, son of Sibyl, had inherited their father's lands and office (PR 13 Henry II 128). Wiltshire was the family home, but Marshal also went to Salisbury and visited his maternal uncle Patrick, earl of Salisbury (*Hist* 1526-564).

This must have been a brief visit for William. Shortly after arriving, William left again with his uncle Patrick when Patrick was called to the continent to help Henry II with the revolt of barons from Poitou, including the Counts of La Marche and Angouleme as well as the rest of the Lusignan family. Patrick had been called by Henry II to take charge of the castle of Lusignan which Henry II had taken from the Lusignan's and garrisoned with his own men. Apparently Patrick and Marshal were joined or met at the castle of Lusignan by Queen Eleanor, duchess of Aquitaine and countess of Poitou (Robert of Torigny 235-36). The castle of Lusignan belonged to the family of Lusignan who were a constant source of trouble to any who held the crown of England and the dukedom of Normandy. At this time there were five brothers in their family; Hugh who was later count of La Marche, and Ralph who was later count of Eu. The other three were Geoffrey, Guy and Aimery; Guy and Aimery were later expelled from Poitou for their constant rebellions. The latter two would later hold the throne of Jerusalem. None of the family was likely to stay peaceful with another holding their ancestral castle, even if the man holding it was their king and liege lord.

One day near Eastertide 1168, Earl Patrick, Queen Eleanor, and William were riding outside the castle with several accompanying knights; none were dressed for battle as they were not anticipating any danger. They were suddenly faced with an armed company of knights led by Guy and Geoffrey de Lusignan. Though Patrick and his men were unarmed, he refused to flee, and instead sent Eleanor to safety within the castle and prepared to arm himself and his men for battle. Apparently some members of the Lusignan's company had little regard for the customs and rules of chivalry. As Patrick was preparing to mount his charger, a Poitevin knight killed him by a single blade in Patrick's back. William, who had put on his hauberk but not his helmet, mounted his horse and charged the Poitevins eager to avenge the death of his uncle. Marshal killed one man with a single blow from his sword, but before Marshal could charge and attack again, Marshal's horse was killed by the lance of a Poitevin knight. William disentangled himself from his fallen charger, and with his back protected by a hedge, held his own against the Poitevins until one man managed to get behind the hedge and strike William in the thigh with a sword. William was then captured and taken prisoner. There is no record of how long Marshal was a hostage, but there is another story told from this time.

While Marshal's captors were moving from place to place to avoid capture by Henry II, they stopped at a castle of one of the Poitevin supporters. Marshal and his captors engaged in a game of who could lift the heaviest stone; Marshal won but tore open the wound on his leg again. Marshal's captors did not seem too interested in caring for his leg, but an unnamed lady in the unnamed castle on seeing Marshal's wounded leg sent bandages to Marshal hidden in a loaf of bread. Marshal was eventually released when Queen Eleanor gave hostages for his ransom and had Marshal delivered to her. Eleanor provided Marshal with money, horses, armor, and clothes as recompense for his actions in protecting her against the original attack (Robert of Torigny 236: *Hist* 1623-881).

This incident is important to William's life because it produced an undying hatred for the house of Lusignan, and because it marks the beginning of his life-long relationship with the Plantagenets. Eleanor of Aquitaine would not forget the heroic and chivalrous actions of the young Marshal (*Gesta Regis Henrici* i 343).

Eleanor's actions with regard to freeing Marshal from his captors would prove to be one of the most fortuitous and long-reaching acts of her life. Marshal must have had concerns about his fate while he was held by the Lusignan's vassals. He had the memory of his own father's refusal to rescue Marshal when Marshal was held hostage by King Stephen in 1152. Marshal's father was dead by 1168; his powerful uncle Patrick had been killed by the Lusignan family, and Marshal must have wondered who would raise the ransom to free him from his present captivity. To have Eleanor of Aquitaine provide the hostages to Marshal's captors that would guarantee that Marshal's ransom would be paid, and to have the queen personally compensate Marshal for his time in captivity generated a sense of obligation and gratitude in Marshal that would serve not only Eleanor but also her sons throughout their lives.

To understand the hatred this incident created, it is essential to understand the nature of the crime committed in the act of slaying Earl Patrick. It was not only an act of striking and killing an unarmed knight in the back; it was also an act of treason to slay the representative of one's feudal overlord (Strickland War and Chivalry 54). In this incident and in Marshal's reaction to it, one begins to see the values and codes that would rule Marshal for the rest of his life. Of all the crimes a knight could commit, the greatest crime was the act of treacherously betraying one's oath of fealty to one's lord. Marshal would live and die by this inviolate code.

During the years 1168-1169, Marshal was probably once again in service with his cousin William de Tancarville, who succeeded Earl Patrick as the king's lieutenant in Poitou. His status would change in 1170. In the spring of that year Henry II had his son, young Henry, crowned as his heir by Roger archbishop of York (*Gesta Regis Henrici* i 5-6). Young Henry was fifteen at this time, and as his father's heir, he was provided with a suitable household that would see to his care and education. Richard of Ilchester and William de St. John would provide his political education, and King Henry II appointed William Marshal as the young king's tutor in chivalry and head of his *mesnie* household (Eyton *Itin* 151; *Hist* 1929-948). For

90

a young man in his early twenties who was the second son of a minor baron to be appointed to the position of tutor in arms to the heir to the king was an unimaginable achievement. Once again, Marshal would recognize and honour the obligation and responsibility that such a gift from the Plantagenet king placed upon him.

Marshal's job was to teach young Henry how to handle weapons and the knightly virtues and codes, oversee his military household (*mesnie*), and protect his person in battles and tourneys. For a young man in his early twenties, this was a remarkable leap in status. This new position was undoubtedly due partly to his father's services to Henry II, partly due to the influence of Queen Eleanor, and partly to William Marshal's own successes, recognition, and fame as a knight. Marshal was to be tutor, guardian, friend, and companion to the young Henry for most of young Henry's life, until the young Henry's death in June 1183.

The core of young Henry's military entourage was composed of William Marshal, Gerard Talbot, Robert de Tregoz, Simon Marsh, and Adam de Iquebeuf; all of whom witnessed at least three of young Henry's charters (*Gesta Regis Henrici* i 45-47). Some of the men frequently attached to the young king's household were John and Peter des Preaux, Saher de Quinci the younger, and Baldwin de Bethune. The household had two types of knights. One group were ordinary knights, having only themselves and perhaps a servant as their entity, and the other group were bannerets who were knights who had a following of their own of up to a dozen men (*Hist* 4750-776). From 1170 to 1173, Marshal's primary task was to instruct the young king in all the skills and ways of chivalry; he was to prepare the young Henry for his induction into the chivalric order of knighthood since knighthood was required in order for a male to obtain his full majority. This had to be a difficult time for a young man who had the title of heir but not the right to rule or collect the revenues of his future domains. The young king's natural desire to have the power as well as the title of heir to Henry II was aided and abetted by young Henry's father-in-law, King Louis VII of France (*Gesta Regis Henrici* i 34; *Hist* 1959-2000).

The first overt break in the relationship between King Henry II and young Henry occurred in the spring of 1173 at Montferrand. In negotiating with Hubert count of Maurrienne of Savoy for a marriage between Henry II's son John and the count's daughter, Henry II wished to give John the castles of Chinon, Loudon, and Mirabeau. Young Henry refused to agree to this proposal unless his father gave him actual sovereignty in England, Normandy, or Anjou. Needless to say, Henry II refused such a demand, and the disgruntled young Henry was taken with his *mesnie* to Limoges with his father to meet his mother, Richard, and Geoffrey for a family gathering from February 21 to 28 (*Gesta Regis Henrici* i 36-42). On March the fifth Henry II, the young Henry, and his group left Limoges and stopped at the castle of Chinon for the night. As Henry II slept, young Henry and his household fled to Vendome (*Hist* 2020-036). In essence this act of fleeing his father's household and company in the dead of night with no word and going into France was a declaration of war.

However, young Henry had a serious problem. He was not yet a knight and thus was prohibited from taking an active part in war or any knightly sport. Henry could not lead an army against his father unless he was a belted knight, and it was clear that he could not have his father knight him. Young Henry's father-in-law,

King Louis of France, sent his own brother, Peter de Courtenay, Raoul count of Clermont and constable of France, William des Barres, and other barons to solve the problem of knighting his son-in-law (*Hist* 2132-142). It is probable that Louis VII expected his brother, Peter de Courtenay, to knight his son-in-law, but young Henry surprised all by having his tutor in arms, William Marshal, gird him with the sword of knighthood.

The bestowing of knighthood on a young man was a ceremony that inherently carried significant symbolism. The act of girding a young man with his sword of knighthood (*cingulum militiae*) carried with it a bond that tied the giver to the receiver, often with an understood tie of alliance and/or allegiance. It was the investiture of authority, the attainment of a young man's majority, and his entrance into the warrior elite. Perhaps Marshal's reputation for prowess and his successes as knight and warrior overrode the considerations of rank and status, or perhaps young Henry did not wish to be beholden to any noble for this act. Whatever Henry's reasons, he conferred a great honour on Marshal by having him be the one to bestow knighthood on a king presumptive, and Marshal would consider this one of the great events of his life (*Hist* 2079-150).

At Chartres on March 8, the young Henry joined Louis of France, and sometime later young Henry's brothers, Richard and Geoffrey, joined them in Chartres (Eyton *Itin* 171; *Gesta Regis Henrici* i 42). The action of these four caused a general rebellion of the barons of the Angevin domain against Henry II, though all had sworn homage to the young Henry against all but King Henry II. Here it is necessary to clarify a distinction in feudalism custom and law; a knight who held lands and/or titles by gift of the king swore homage and fealty to the king as lord above all others. This was the basis of feudalism, law, and governance for that time period. A knight who held no fief but was a member of a lord's household owed homage and fealty to the lord who provided him with shelter, food, the accoutrements of knighthood, and protection. The latter knight was the *man* of the lord whom he served and who maintained him; the knight would owe his loyalty and service to that lord to whom he had sworn fealty and would follow that lord's allegiance in war. Marshal owed his fealty and loyalty only to the young Henry as his lord, and as a knight who held no fief from King Henry II, he had never sworn fealty to the king as such. Later events show that Henry II did not consider William's support of the young Henry during his rebellion an act of treason against himself as king.

On June 28, 1173, Philip count of Flanders took Aumale, and on July 6, 1173, Philip of Flanders, the young Henry, and the count of Bologne invaded Normandy (*Gesta Regis Henrici* i 49). General rebellion broke out in England. William the Lion of Scotland, David earl of Huntingdon, Robert the younger earl of Leicester, Robert de Ferrers, Hugh Bigod, Hugh earl of Chester, and Roger de Mowbray and his brothers were some of the leading rebels in England (*Gesta Regis Henrici i* 48). In Normandy King Louis of France began a siege of Verneuil that would last for a month. The city was made up of the castle and three burghs which were separated from each other and individually enclosed. Louis laid siege to the burgh known as the Great Burgh, and after a month, the people within asked for a three-day respite while they notified King Henry of their plight. On August the eighth, Henry II was at Breteuil, the castle of Robert earl of Leicester, and after reducing it to ashes, he proceeded to Verneuil (*Gesta Regis Henrici* i 49-50; *Houedene* i 370). On the third day of the respite, Louis failed to keep his word; he did not preserve the peace that he had promised. Instead, Louis took the Great Burgh, looted the property of the burghers, and burned the town (*Houedene* i 371). Henry II ordered the walls of Verneuil rebuilt, proceeded to the castle of Damville and took it, and then entered the city of Rouen. Henry ordered his mercenaries to go into Brittany after Earl Hugh of Chester and Ralph de Fougeres. In September, Hugh and Ralph were taken at the castle of Dol and all of Brittany was brought back under the control of Henry II (*Houedene* i 373).

Meanwhile, Robert of Leicester had crossed from Normandy into England and gone to Hugh Bigod, earl of Norfolk, at Framlingham castle. The first of November, Robert met in battle Hugh de Lucy, justiciar of England, and Humphrey de Bohun, the king's constable. Robert was defeated and captured and sent to Henry II to join Earl Hugh of Chester in prison at the castle of Falaise (*Houedene i* 375). On September 25 Henry II and Louis met at Gisors to talk, but no agreement was reached; a truce between Henry II and Louis and Henry's sons was not arranged until Easter of 1174 (*Gesta Regis Henrici* i 53, 59).

Henry II had one problem that could not be left unfinished. Henry proceeded to Poitiers and took his wife, Eleanor of Aquitaine, prisoner and kept her confined and unheard from until he removed Eleanor to Salisbury Castle in July 1174 (*Houedene* i 381). Henry apparently blamed Eleanor for their sons' rebellion and as the cause of all his current problems (*Wendover* ii 20, 23). The contemporary chronicles agree that it was Eleanor who had encouraged and supported the sons' rebellion against their father. She had been in Aquitaine and Poitiers since 1169, and the three oldest sons had been with her at least some of that time. Eleanor had drawn away from Henry II and established her own household and life in Poitiers with her daughter Marie de Champagne and with her older sons occasionally staying with her. Whatever Eleanor's reasons, it is safe to assume that she had played an active part in the 1173-1174 rebellion of her sons Henry, Richard, and Geoffrey.

After Easter 1174, William king of the Scots invaded Northumberland and ravaged it; Earl Robert of Ferrers took and burned Nottingham, and Hugh Bigod took and burned Norwich (*Houedene* i 377-78). William then laid siege to Carlisle castle but could not take it, so he moved on to Prudhoe castle with the same results. William next moved on to the castle of Alnwick and laid siege to it (*Houedene i* 380). In Normandy, the young Henry and Philip of Flanders had proceeded to Gravelines to try to cross to England, but the winds were not favorable. Henry II had better luck and set sail from Barfleet and arrived in England in July. On the day after Henry's arrival, Henry made a pilgrimage to the tomb of Thomas Becket, and on that very day William king of the Scots was defeated and captured at Alnwick castle. When Louis heard of the defeat of William, he ordered the young Henry and Philip of Flanders to leave Gravelines and meet him at Rouen where he was laying siege to the town (*Houedene i* 382; *Wendover* ii 29).

In England, Henry II took Huntingdon back and proceeded to Framlingham castle where Hugh Bigod surrendered his castles, Framlingham, Walton, Thetford, and Bungay, and himself to the king (Brown "List of Castles" 252). From here

Henry went to Northampton where Hugh bishop of Durham surrendered his castles of Durham, Norham, and Northallerton to the king. At Northhampton, Roger of Mowbray surrendered his castles of Thirsk, Kirby-Malzeard, and Kinardferry, and Robert de Ferrers surrendered his castles of Tutbury and Duffield. The constables of the earl of Leicester surrendered the earl's castles of Leicester, Mountsorrel, Brackley, and Groby to Henry II. Henry had all of these castles demolished with the exception of Mountsorrel, Durham, and Norham which he kept in his own hands (Brown 252). So in a matter of a month's time, Henry II had completely crushed the rebellion of his barons in England (*Houedene* i 382-83). Henry II set sail for Normandy the end of August and marched to the relief of the city of Rouen. This ended the rebellion of his sons and the war with King Louis of France (*Wendover* ii 31).

Henry II agreed to terms of peace with King Louis and his three sons at Mt. Louis between Tours and Amboise on September 30, 1174 (*Gesta Regis Henrici* i 77). The Treaty was confirmed at a great council at Falaise on October 11, 1174 (*Foedera* I 1, 30). There are two points of hypothesis to ponder about this rebellion for which there are no known extant records to verify. One is the probability that it was at this point, while at the French court with the young Henry, that William Marshal established the mutual respect and friendship of such important French nobles as William des Barres and Phillip Augustus, heir to Louis VII. This friendship and respect of the higher nobility of the French court would exist for the rest of Marshal's life. The other point to consider is the possibility that William Marshal met Richard Strongbow de Clare during this time period. Henry II had called Strongbow from Ireland to aid in stopping this rebellion, and Strongbow had been active and successful in fighting on Henry II's behalf (*Gesta Regis Henrici* i 51). It is not beyond the realm of possibilities that two such known knights, though on opposite sides, would have made the acquaintance of each other at some point during this time period. It teases the imagination to contemplate what Strongbow thought of the young knight leading the young Henry's *mesnie,* considering that this young man would one day marry Strongbow's only legitimate daughter and sole heiress. Neither point can be proved from existing records, but they are both worthy of consideration in regard to William Marshal's life.

The Treaty of Falaise gave the young Henry two castles in Normandy and the yearly revenue of fifteen thousand pounds Angevin. Henry II and the young Henry both forgave each other's men and allies and promised to bear no malice to them. Marshal was at the council and was one of the witnesses to the treaty of peace (*Gesta Regis Henrici* i 77-78). In May 1175, Marshal accompanied the young Henry and Henry II to England; Henry II had decided that it was time for his son and heir to act his age and learn the duties and responsibilities of being a king (*Recueil des Actes de Henry II* intro., 258).

The year 1176 saw the betrothal of Henry II's son, John, to Isabella daughter of William earl of Gloucester. With this betrothal, Isabellla was granted most of her father's lands while her older sister Mabel was married to Aumauri of Everaux and her other sister Amicia was married to Gilbert de Clare. This same year also saw the death of Richard Strongbow de Clare in Ireland and the appointment of William fitz Audelin who was given custody of Strongbow's lands as agent for King

Henry II. Young Henry had apparently had enough of the close supervision of his father in England, and perhaps he was also missing the opportunity of having great tournaments to participate in and attend. In May 1176, young Henry and his *mesnie* returned to Normandy with the stated objective of a pilgrimage to St. James of Compostella (*Gesta Regis Henrici* i 114).

V. Marshal as Tourneyer Knight

Leaving England in May 1176, the young Henry and his household went to Henry's cousin, Philip of Flanders. Philip was considered the epitome of a chivalric knight, and the arrival of the young Henry gave him the opportunity to exhibit that admired quality of *largesse.* A tournament was announced that was to be held between Gournay and Ressons in the county of Clermont. For some reason not explained, the young Henry and his *mesnie* were without their knightly equipment, and Philip provided the warhorses and armour needed for the upcoming tournament *(Hist* 2443-496). Thus, the young Henry and his military household were launched into the chivalric world of tournaments with great panoply and fanfare.

From May 1176 until the fall of 1180, William's life was one of tutoring the young king and leading and protecting him in an active round of tournaments on the continent. We know that Marshal led young Henry and his *mesnie* to many victories on the tournament fields of Normandy. It is during the years from 1170 to 1183 that William Marshal established his status as an undefeated knight in tournaments and his friendships with the powerful and influential men of his day. His reputation and his character were built through his own actions and abilities.

The greatest patrons and/or participants of the tournaments of this time period were the young Henry, Count Philip of Flanders, Theobald of Blois, Robert of Dreux, the duke of Burgundy, Raoul count of Clermont, and William des Barres (Painter Marshal 57). The *Histoire* records some twelve tournaments; of these twelve, two were held in the county of Clermont, two in the county of Deux, three in the lands of Henry count of Champagne, and four in the lands of Count Theobald of Blois.

Tournaments were the best means of teaching and refining the skills and abilities necessary for medieval warfare within a more confined and controlled circumstance than actual warfare. The tournaments of the late 1100s were far different than the usual vision of two knights jousting against each other over a dividing barrier before a gathering of distinguished lords and ladies that was the norm in the late thirteenth century. The tournaments of William Marshal's time were more of a "free-for-all" melee. Two weeks prior to the date of the expected event, the time and place of each tournament would be announced by messengers to the households and lords who were known to be interested, sometimes providing the composition of the two parties involved. Those notified would then gather a group of knights who might come from their own households or be men who would be interested in participating in the tournament with that lord. All participants would arrive at the set place either the day of the tournament or perhaps the day before if the group participating came from a greater distance. Some great tournaments could last several days, and on the eve preceding the actual tournament, the young knights might show their skill with weapons and horse without having to compete against the more experienced knights.

The site of the tournament would encompass several square miles of territory between the two towns or sites specified. They could, and did, include farmland, small villages or towns, fields, and even vineyards. The property and welfare of the bystanders were not necessarily a major concern, and often these people were swept up in the tournament and its mayhem to the detriment of their lands and dwellings. It was not until 1194 that rules were set that protected the bystanders and their property, and that was only in England by order of King Richard. Richard decided that tournaments would be held in England in order to train his English knights to the level of skill of the knights on the continent, but he also decided to control those tournaments and make them a means of collecting revenue while protecting the peace and welfare of his realm.

Richard's writ to Hubert Walter, *justiciar* of England, set five sites as places of tournaments. Richard's designated sites were: between Salisbury and Wilton in Wiltshire; between Warwick and Kenilworth in Warwickshire; between Stamford and Warinford in Suffolk; between Brackley and Mixbury in Northhamptonshire; and between Blyth and Tickhill in Nottinghamshire. These sites straddled major roads to London and were in areas controlled by the three men that Richard appointed as guarantors of the charter. All tourneyers were required to take an oath before they set out to participate in a tournament. They had to swear to pay their fees in full on pain of arrest, to not endanger the peace of the kingdom, to pay reasonable market price for food and other necessities, to take nothing by force or unfairly, and to not breach the royal forests or impinge on the royal rights of vert and venison (*Foedera* i 65; *Diceto* ii lxxx, lxxxi). The license for holding a tournament was ten marks. The fee a participant paid to enter was based upon his standing; an earl paid twenty marks, a baron paid ten marks, a landed knight paid four marks, and a landless knight paid two marks. All fees required for each individual tournament were paid to and collected by Theobald Walter, brother of the *justiciar* (*Houedene* iii 268). Richard appointed three earls as guarantors for the tournament charters; they were William

fitz Patrick earl of Salisbury and cousin to William Marshal, Gilbert de Clare earl of

Hertford and Clare, and Hamelin de Warenne earl of Surrey and Warenne (*Houedene*

iii 268). Richard allowed tournaments in England under these concise rules for the

purpose of providing the Crown revenue, maintaining order, and training his English

knights so they would no longer be accused by the French knights of lacking skill

(*Foedera* i 650). It was only in England in this time period that tournaments were

closely regulated; this was not the case on the continent.

The tournaments on the continent usually began in the morning and

lasted until dusk. There were few restrictions on who could or could not enter a

tournament until the thirteenth century, and no prohibition that prevented a knight

from entering a tournament that had already begun. There were few prohibited

strikes and no rules that prevented a group of knights or foot soldiers from banding

together to attack a single knight. The count of Flanders used *serjeants* as well as

knights in one tournament, and in another tournament he used over 300 infantry to

cover a retreat (*Hist* 3247, 2829-830).

Mounted knights fought with lance, sword, and mace, and foot soldiers used

arrows and lances. There were specified areas, *recets*, where a knight that had been

unhorsed or captured could go to make arrangements for the payment of his ransom,

or could re-arm, or simply rest. In this area no one was allowed to harm any other

(Barker Tournament in England 141). After a knight had made his arrangements for

the payment of his ransom to the knight who had defeated him, he could return to the

fight if he wished and it was not prohibited (Barker 144).

Tournaments were fought either *a l' plaisance* meaning that they were fought with blunted weapons, or they were fought *a l' outrance* meaning that they were fought with unsheathed weapons. It was only in tournaments fought with bare weapons that ransoms and booty were taken. Depending upon where the tournament was to be held, the participants would arrive a day or several days before the actual event. Those men who were barons, counts, or princes would appear in their finery leading their company of knights. If a castle or large manor was near, the greater nobles would reside there and the lesser knights in tents on the grounds or in the barracks of the castle. The day of the tournament the knights would don their equipment. Beginning with pants--possibly leather as cloth would catch on the mail leggings--they would add a *gambeson* or *aketon* which was a quilted and padded garment with long sleeves for the torso. Then the knight would put on mail chausses which would cover the foot and the entire leg. These were tied to the gambeson or to a leather belt to hold them up and were sometimes gartered with leather strips at the knee. The weight of the mail chausses could be as much as thirty pounds. Next the knight would put on his hauberk which was a shirt of mail that included the coif and covered the knight from head to hands. The hauberk extended to knee length and was split in the front and back to enable the knight to sit his warhorse. The hands were covered on the top with a mitten-like mail (called mufflers) that tied at the wrist; these left the palm of the hand bare to allow the knight to grip his sword. The weight of the hauberk, including the coif, ranged from thirty to forty pounds. By the late twelfth century, the wealthier knights wore a great helm, or helmet, that totally encased the head and the face. Either under or over the mail coif, a knight would put on an arming cap. This was a heavily quilted skull cap that might have an additional roll of padding at the brow to ease the weight of the helmet off the top of the knight's head and provide greater padding to his skull. The helmet would have one single slit or two equal slits for the eyes and breathing holes at the level of the knight's nose.

The weapons carried by a knight were first a shield made of wood strengthened with steel and usually kite-shaped to protect the knight's entire left side when he was mounted. The shield would often carry the coat of arms of the knight and help identify not only who that particular knight was but also to what lord or group that knight was attached. Secondly the knight carried a sword which was his most prized possession. The sword was a broad double-edged weapon used primarily for cutting and slashing; it was usually 36 inches long with a blade of 28 inches and a width of blade about one and a half inches. It had a slightly rounded point, a simple cross-guard of about seven and a half inches wide, a hilt of about eight inches long, and a rounded, flat, or brazil-nut shaped pommel. The sword weighed from three and a half to four and a half pounds. It was carried in a scabbard that hung from the belt on the left hip (if the knight was right-handed). Considering the weight of the sword and the chain mail and the fact that a tournament could last all day, it is easier to recognize the amount of strength of the arms and shoulders required of a medieval knight. The lance carried by a knight was on the average ten feet long, made of ash, and had a head of steel or iron, sometimes barbed. The lance was carried under the right arm of a charging knight and primarily used in the first maneuver or action of the tournament. Some knights carried a mace which was made of metal with a slim, straight shaft and a metal trilobate head (*Hist* 2510, 2966,

3797, 5003). Bows were used by the foot soldiers, and with their reach and their barbed, iron arrowheads could be deadly in battle; they could pierce chain mail with their force. Crossbows were used but not in tournaments because of their ability to pierce the shield and hauberk and therefore kill a knight. In war, crossbowmen were often killed because of their effectiveness against a knight and his armour. The Church banned the use of crossbows against Christians because of their deadly abilities, although this did not prevent their use in war.

The war horse of a knight was of value equal to that of his armour and sword; it was the charger that provided the speed and force of a mounted knight. The war horse was also trained to bite and kick in defense of his rider. The saddle was made with a high bow in front and an equally high cantle behind, and the stirrups were long leathers which provided a deep straight-legged seat. In effect, the knight rode almost standing in the saddle which gave him the ability to use the saddle as a fighting platform, providing a secure seat from which he could deliver and receive blows of lance, sword, or mace.

The actual tournament began with the military maneuver of an ordered charge of mounted knights with couched lances. This was one of the most important skills required of a medieval knight and one that the tournament fields proved to be the best at training. The charge of the mounted knights with couched lances was the opening move of a tournament and the most important in determining which side would be victorious. It required that the knights in each army work together as an ordered and disciplined unit. Maintaining their serried ranks and moving as a group in a full charge made that army almost impossible to defend against (*Hist* 1417-422,

2477-500). The ability to time the charge exactly right and maintain a concentrated force provided the maximum effect. The sheer force of such a charge usually resulted in the opposing army scattering and thus making individual captures more likely. In actual war the archers were to use their weapons to create an opening for the cavalry charge, and the foot soldiers' job was to resist the enemies charge with their lances and arrows. Any knight who was over-confident or over-eager could destroy the entire purpose of the charge of the whole company. The great benefit of the tournaments was to provide an arena for this military training for knights while reducing the possibility of permanent injury or death to the knight. The organized and highly skilled abilities required of a medieval knight had to be constantly re-enforced and refined, and the tournament field provided the arena for that training.

The reckoning and collection of the ransoms was done at the end of the day when the tourneyers would call at the tents or abodes of the great lords. The winner of the tournament would be either the army that held the field at the end of the day, or the one who had collected the most booty or ransoms, or in the event of no clear winner, the army selected by all those participating. Any knight who believed that he had been mistreated or cheated of his ransoms or booty during the tournament could present his case to the lord of the offending knight and ask for justice. There were unwritten customs and rules governing the action of the knights at this time, and some things were not permitted. A knight could not take advantage of a disadvantaged knight such as striking an unprepared opponent or taking a horse or booty from a knight who was not in a position to defend his captured booty. Such actions violated the codes of chivalric behavior and were not tolerated. If you were a knight in a tournament, the object was to unhorse your opponent, to take his helmet, or to clearly defeat him in hand-to-hand combat. This made the opponent your captive and as such he would have to ransom his freedom. It was expected of all knights participating to avoid at all costs actually killing or seriously maiming an opponent.

It was on the tournament field that the medieval knight developed a sense of professional solidarity, identity, and a universal code of acceptable conduct and custom that would also permeate the conduct of medieval warfare. This arena also provided a way for knights to meet and know knights from other regions and countries and thus provided a social as well as a military environment. The knight could meet men from France, Flanders, Normandy, Scotland, and England; he could even find such a variety within his own lord's household. The fact that many of the opposing teams in tournaments were formed on political divisions and alliances meant that in actual warfare many of the opponents were well known to each other. The tournaments were in many ways the entrance point for the young knight into his world of the military order of chivalric knighthood. It was the arena where he could, by his own abilities and skills as a knight, make the contacts and friendships that would aid and guide his future possibilities in his society. This was the arena in which William Marshal developed his reputation, his status, and his sense of honour that would influence and govern the rest of his life.

The highest accolade that could be bestowed on a medieval knight was that he was a *prudhomme*. This meant that the knight displayed loyalty to his lord and kin, that he was known for wise and sagacious counsel in both war and diplomacy, that he practiced *largesse* (generosity) to his vassals and companions-in-arms, that he showed *franchise* (piety) to the Church and its institutions, and that he possessed *courtoisie* (the ability to conduct oneself properly in courtly circles and with the ladies). Above all of these, the knight must be known for his *prouesse* (prowess), his ability to prove in combat and in feats of arms that he was a superbly able and skilled fighting knight. It was not only a knight's pride in himself and his estimation of his own worth, but the acknowledgement of society of his right to that pride that made a *prudhomme*.

According to Kaeuper, Marshal was a knight who used his prowess in causes that were honourable to his king and country as well as causes that advanced himself and his family (Chivalry and Violence 281-82). Marshal earned his rewards by his sword, his counsel, and with his careful and prudent loyalty. His *largesse* was openly displayed with style and flair with regard to his own men and family as well as to his opponents. Marshal's piety was practical and realistic; he founded priories and abbeys and gave to those that were in his lands, went on crusade to Cologne, and fought as a Knight Templar in the Holy Land. Marshal possessed and lived by a strong sense of loyalty and honour that perfectly balanced and complemented his prowess as a medieval knight (Kaeuper 297). This was the world of the tourneying knight and the world in which Marshal would live for the next seven years.

In the first tournament Marshal attended back on the continent with young Henry and Philip of Flanders in May 1176, Marshal noted that Count Philip of Flanders employed a very practical approach to tournaments. The count tended to hold back in the tournament until the other combatants were disorganized and somewhat exhausted; then the count would charge into the fray and capture many knights and much booty. Based on this critical observation of the count's approach to the tournament, Marshal advised the young Henry to use this tactic in future tournaments when it was not specifically prohibited (*Hist* 2715-772).

After this tournament, the young Henry and his household returned home and were soon engaged in another tournament. This tournament was held between Anet and Sorel-Moussel in the valley of the Eure. Henry's company was so successful that they managed to drive the French company completely from the field in their first charge. While pursuing the French through the streets of Anet, Marshal and the young Henry found themselves surrounded by French foot soldiers led by the baron Simon de Neauphle. Completely undaunted by the men on foot, Marshal simply charged into their midst with Henry close behind him. Marshal grabbed the reins of Simon's charger and pulled Simon and horse with him until they were clear of the Frenchmen. While Marshal raced through the town with Simon in tow, a low-hanging drainpipe knocked Simon off his horse. Henry, who was following close behind Marshal on his own charger, said not a word as he and Marshal returned to their camp. When Marshal ordered his squire to take charge of the horse and knight that he had captured, Marshal discovered that he had taken the charger as booty but had lost the knight (*Hist* 2773-874). Marshal laughed at himself as loudly as the knights who witnessed this event proving that he was a fighter of even temperament and humour and not one of excessive pride.

Another tournament was held in 1177 at Pleurs in the valley of the Marne. Young Henry decided not to go, but he gave permission for Marshal to attend. At this tournament were some of the greatest knights of that time. Count Philip of Flanders, Theobald of Blois, James d'Avesnes, and Guy de Chatillian were there; these men would soon take the Crusader's vow and go the Holy Land. Raoul count of Clermont, Hugh duke of Burgundy, the count of Beaumont, and William des Barres were also participating in this tournament. This was a gathering of what was considered some of the best knights of that time and apparently filled with glorious combat. At the end of the tournament a lady, who was not named, presented a great pike to the duke of Burgundy as a reward for an outstanding display of prowess. The duke, wishing to increase the value of the reward, gave it to Count Philip of Flanders. The count in another gesture of *largesse* gave it to Theobald. At this point, it became obvious that they needed to call a halt to the somewhat overdone gestures. Philip suggested that the pike be given to the knight that they thought had truly fought the best during the tournament and suggested William Marshal. The great nobles agreed to this, and they sent a squire holding the pike before him and accompanied by two knights to find Marshal. Having searched everywhere for Marshal, they finally discovered him with his head in his helmet on the anvil of the blacksmith. Marshal had received so many blows on his helmet during the tournament that it had to be hammered back into shape before it could be removed. Once free of his helmet, Marshal received the pike as the accolade for the best warrior on the field that day with the required amount of humility and probably a great deal of humour (*Hist* 2875-3164).

At another tournament in 1177 at Eu, a Flemish knight, Matthew de Walincourt, had his horse taken by Marshal in combat. Matthew went to young

Henry and asked that his horse be returned to him as a gesture of *largesse*; Henry ordered Marshal to return the horse, and Marshal did. Later in the same tournament, Marshal again took Matthew's horse, but he kept it this time. Marshal personally took ten knights and twelve horses in ransom and booty in one day, and quickly increased his wealth and reputation on the tournament field (*Hist* 3372-376). Even young Henry could not attend all of the tournaments being held on the continent, so Marshal and another knight from Henry's *mesnie*, Roger de Gaugi, formed a partnership. Marshal and Roger would attend tournaments as partners and split the booty and ransoms they gained when fighting as partners. Henry agreed to this business relationship of these two men from his household, and his clerk, Wigain, recorded that Marshal and Roger took one hundred and three knights in ransoms and booty during a ten-month period (*Hist* 3381-424).

At a tournament at Joigny in the Seine valley is recorded one of only two instances where ladies are mentioned in relationship to tournaments in the entire *Histoire*. Marshal and Roger had armed themselves at the castle of Joigny with the company they had joined for that day. These men all arrived at the tournament field before their opponents. While waiting for the tournament to begin, the countess of Joigni and her ladies joined the men, and the knights and ladies entertained themselves by dancing to a song that was sung by Marshal. This must have been a rare sight; to see knights already dressed in their hauberks dancing with ladies in their finery! After Marshal's song, a young minstrel sang a song of his own composition that included the refrain, "Marshal, give me a good horse." When a mounted knight of the opposition rode onto the field, Marshal mounted his charger,

112

unhorsed the knight, and gave the charger to the minstrel (*Hist* 3426-562). At this tournament, or another held later at this same place (the *Histoire* does not often date the tournaments recorded), Marshal gave all his earnings to be divided between those knights that had to be ransomed and those who had taken the Crusader's vow. Marshal was practicing the knightly virtue of *largesse,* and by doing so Marshal increased his own reputation as a successful and generous knight. A knight was expected to share and to give of the rewards he acquired in the tournaments; this added to the knight's status as a *prudhomme.*

During the year of 1179 three great tournaments were held in the region of Dreux and Chartres. By this time, Marshal and de Guagi had dissolved their partnership and returned to young Henry's household. At one tournament held in the valley of the Eure, Marshal led the young king's men while Henry remained at home. Marshal and his company arrived after the tournament had started and the French were winning, but Marshal and his company helped turn the tide of the event. During this tournament, Marshal discovered a group of Frenchmen who had taken refuge on an old motte; they had left their chargers outside of the enclosure. Marshal saw a perfect opportunity to acquire booty. He dismounted, crossed the old moat, took two of the French horses, and brought them back across the moat. As Marshal was coming back, two French knights that Marshal recognized relieved Marshal of his prizes. Since Marshal was on foot, he could not defend his booty at that time, so he made note of the men. Marshal remounted his charger and continued across the combat field. Marshal came across another group of fifteen French knights who were being besieged in a farm building by a group of English knights. They called out to Marshal and told him that they would surrender to him. This annoyed the besieging party who were technically Marshal's companions in this tournament, but none wished to challenge Marshal for the French knights. Marshal took the Frenchmen's surrender, escorted them to a safe area on the field, and refused to accept ransoms for the capture. Once again Marshal had practiced that prized virtue of *largesse* in regard to his opponents.

After the tournament, Marshal went in search of the lords of the two French knights who had taken Marshal's first prizes. He went first to William des Barres whose nephew had been one of the two knights who had taken Marshal's captured warhorses. William des Barres ordered his nephew to return the horse or leave his household. It was suggested that Marshal give the nephew one half of the charger as a gesture of *largesse* and that they throw dice for the other half of the horse. Marshal agreed; the nephew threw a nine and Marshal an eleven. One horse regained and one more to go! Marshal went to the household of the other French knight, and it was suggested that Marshal give half of the horse to the knight and the whole horse would belong to whoever could pay for the other half. The French knight, thinking that Marshal did not have any coins on him, set the price of the horse at fourteen pounds. Marshal tossed seven pounds on the table and walked away with his second horse having paid only one-fifth of the value of the horse (*Hist* 3884-4284). These two tales are clear examples of the concepts of what was considered right and proper behavior and customs of a chivalric knight and of the forms and customs of *largesse*. It was wrong for any knight to take advantage of an unarmed knight in tourney or combat, and it was expected of a knight to openly display generosity and sportsmanship. In these tales of Marshal's tournament career there are clear images of Marshal's values, of what he considered honourable and right in a knight, and of the humor and character that made him a valued man among his contemporaries.

There is a record of a grand tournament held at Lagni in the *Histoire,* but the date is not given. It might possibly be the tournament given by Henry count of Champagne on the coronation of his nephew, Philip, son of Louis VII of France. Philip was crowned on November 1, 1179, at the cathedral of Rheims by his uncle Archbishop William. Henry count of Champagne held a tournament at Lagni-sur-Marne to celebrate the occasion. Henry was one of the richest and most powerful barons of France; he was married to Marie, daughter of Louis VII and Eleanor of Aquitaine, and his sister Adela was married to Louis VII king of France. On the day of the tournament a truly magnificent gathering of nobles and knights appeared. The duke of Burgundy and his household, Robert count of Dreux, David earl of Huntingdon and brother to the king of Scotland, the counts of Eu and Soissons, Henry count of Champagne, Count Philip of Flanders, Theobald of Blois, the young Henry, some thirteen other nobles, and close to a thousand ordinary knights appeared in all of their glory. The young Henry's household, alone, arrived with two hundred knights of whom some sixteen were *bannerets* with *mesnie* of their own (*Hist* 4457-796). During this tournament Marshal had to rescue young Henry from capture twice, and Henry's brother, Geoffrey, is noted and described as a skillful tourneyer (*Gesta Regis Henrici* i 242; *Diceto* i 438; Robert of Torigny 287). Lances were broken, shields were lost or destroyed, many mighty blows struck, and vast acres of vineyards and fields were destroyed under the hooves of the warhorses charging over the ground (*Hist* 4820-970). This must have been one of the most outstanding and splendid tournaments of the 1100s. It also illustrates one of the most difficult realities of medieval knighthood for today's world to grasp and comprehend.

Most of these men would find themselves either fighting with or against each other within less than three years. They knew one another well and formed friendships and bonds that would transcend their positions as opponents. The tournaments not only provided the training ground for all the skills necessary to a medieval knight in warfare, but they also engendered a sense of common values, customs, and practices these men would display and employ on both fields of combat, tournament and war. In their society where honour and reputation were as important as wealth and status and shame and reproach were abhorred and feared, these warrior-knights were bound by the same significant ties and strictures of chivalry whether they were companions or opponents. Perhaps the greatest irony is that the melee tournaments of the 1100s produced the ethic of chivalry that placed some of the restrictions on the barbarity that could rule medieval warfare. They were the training ground for the warrior, and yet they also instilled and imposed customs and rules that set parameters for what was acceptable in actual warfare. One of the most difficult realities of medieval life for today's world to understand and comprehend is that not only a man's own value and opinion of himself but also the value and opinion of his own contemporaries were standards against which he measured and ruled himself. The highest and most difficult measures a knight had to meet were those of honour and knightly prowess; his physical abilities and skills had to be met equally with his sense and practice of what was honourable behavior for a medieval knight.

These incidents of his early life provide insight into the mind and character of the man William Marshal. They show that Marshal had taken and made his own some of the higher values of chivalry. He was developing his own standards of right and wrong based upon the customs and attributes of medieval chivalry and feudalism as he knew it. He swore fealty to the young king Henry and served him faithfully and well even when the young king fought against his own father and king. In his actions as a tourneying knight, Marshal overtly conveyed his sense of right and wrong, just and unjust as regarded the behavior of a chivalric knight and warrior. He practiced the qualities of *largesse*, giving generously to his own men and displaying courtesy to his opponents. He proved his prowess again and again in his successful capture of opponents, warhorses, and armour, and he maintained his undefeated status as a knight through many tournaments. Marshal learned and practiced many military strategies that he would later put to use in actual battles during war. It was during this time that Marshal acquired the respect and trust of men, both royal and noble, ally and opponent. This trust and respect would last Marshal's entire life.

One other incident from the earlier part of Marshal's life gives insight into the man and his sense of honour. In 1180/1181, Marshal was accused by some envious men of young Henry's *mesnie* of being the lover of Margaret of France. Margaret was the daughter of King Louis VII of France and Constance of Castile and the wife of the young Henry. Marshal denied this accusation and was defended by others in young Henry's mesnie, including Baldwin de Bethune and Peter des Preaux. Apparently the tale was carried to the young king's father, Henry II, who had several reasons to be interested in the tale (*Hist* 5095-668). William's relative, William de Tancarville, was out of favor with Henry II at this time, and King Henry II was far from happy with the lavish spending of his eldest son and heir (Walter Map 232). Did Henry II believe this tale? In all probabililty he did not. No matter how idealistic and romantic the idea of being the gallant and lover of a married noble lady may sound, it was a serious breach of feudal custom and law. The minstrels might sing of such love, but woe to any knight who touched more than the silk favors of a married lady. One thing clear from the history and life of William Marshal is that he believed, practiced, and upheld the ideals and beliefs that were considered most dear to a chivalric knight. Marshal would have considered any type of liaison with any married lady, let alone the wife of his feudal lord, an act of betrayal of his vows of fealty and a completely dishonourable act.

As a knight and vassal accused of a crime that he swore he did not commit, Marshal was entitled to face his accuser and challenge him to trial by combat to prove who was telling the truth. He was not given this opportunity until Christmas of 1182. That Christmas, Henry II celebrated in Caen with his sons Henry, Richard, and Geoffrey. Apparently there was a great gathering of nobles, barons, and prelates for Christmas that year (*Hist* 5693-714; *Gesta Regis Henrici* i 291). On Christmas day just before the great feast began, William de Tancarville charged into the hall, seized the vessels of water used for the cleaning of the hands of the king and his sons, and performed the task himself and then left. The next day, de Tancarville defended his actions by reminding the king and his guests that as hereditary chamberlain of Normandy, he alone had the right to pour water on the duke of Normandy's hands for all state occasions, and he alone had custody of the vessels used on such occasions (Walter Map 232-34). William Marshal, having accompanied his uncle to the Christmas court, presented himself before young Henry and denied the accusations made against him with regard to the young king's wife (*Gesta Regis Henrici* i 291; Walter Map 232; *Hist 5693-714)*. Marshal demanded his right to prove his innocence in battle by offering to fight three of the strongest of his accusers over three days. When that was refused him, Marshal offered to fight the strongest after one finger on his own right hand was cut off. When the young Henry refused Marshal his right to trial by battle, Marshal asked King Henry II for a safe conduct to the frontier of the Angevin lands and was granted his request (*Hist 5715-848; Gesta Regis Henrici* i 290-91). Under feudal law and custom, if the lord refuses a hearing or justice in his court to his vassal, that vassal can freely sever all ties between himself and his lord.

Marshal left the court with his own *mesnie* and went into the county of Chartres. He seemed to be enjoying his freedom and wandered from the lands of his friend, Count Theobald, into the lands of the count of Champagne. In January he participated in a tournament in the county of Clermont, fighting for the count of St. Paul. As always, Marshal did well and even saved the count from capture at least twice. After the tournament, the barons sent for Marshal. Philip count of Flanders and the duke of Burgundy each offered Marshal an annual income of five hundred pounds if he would serve in their *mesnie*. The advocate of Bethune offered Marshal five hundred pounds a year and his daughter in marriage (*Hist 5923-6170, 6260-277). Marshal refused these three offers, but he may have at this time accepted a grant of land from the count of Flanders (*Chart* 46a). Marshal did not give up his freedom as an independent knight, however, but instead went on a pilgrimage to Cologne.

The separation between Marshal and the young Henry did not last long. In February 1183, young Henry and his brother Geoffrey invaded Poitou in support of their brother Richard's rebelling vassals. Richard called on his father for help, and Henry II entered Limoges in March and laid siege to the castle where young Henry and Geoffrey had withdrawn. Geoffrey advised young Henry to send for Marshal because they needed his skills as a knight. The young king sent his chamberlain to find Marshal and bring him to his court (*Hist* 6408-512, 6525-552). The chamberlain found Marshal returning from Cologne and delivered the message from young Henry.

Marshal sent word back to the young Henry that he would join him after Marshal received safe conduct from King Henry II. Marshal obtained letters of recommendation from Philip count of Flanders, William archbishop of Rheims, Count Robert of Dreux, and Count Theobald of Blois and sent them to King Henry asking for safe conduct so that Marshal could return to the young Henry. Henry II replied with letters authorizing Marshal's return to the household of the young king (*Hist* 6553-656). Sidney Painter's view of this supposed reversal of Henry II was that Henry II knew Marshal's loyalty to his son, and Henry probably hoped that Marshal would control the young Henry's recent penchant for ravaging and plundering the countryside and the abbeys and shrines (<u>Marshal</u> 51). Marshal met his friends Baldwin de Bethune and Hugh de Hamelincourt just twenty miles from

Paris, and they all rejoined the young Henry near the river Dordogne (*Gesta Regis Henrici* i 296-99).

On May 5, 1183, while still rebelling against his father, the young Henry fell sick with a fever at the castle of Martel on the river Dorodogne. On the seventh, Henry confessed to his chaplain, Gerald, received the sacrament, and renounced his rebellion against his father. May 11, 1183, knowing that he was dying, the young Henry asked Marshal to take his cross and make the journey to the Holy Sepulchre in Jerusalem and fulfill young Henry's crusader vow. Marshal agreed, and young Henry died (*Gesta Regis Henrici* i 300-02; *Houedene* ii 278-79; *Hist* 6891-911). The young king's body was sprinkled with salt and wrapped in bulls' hides and lead to make the journey to Rouen. According to Hoveden, when the party stopped at Le Mans the bishop of the city and clergy of the Church of Saint Julian the Confessor and Pope buried the young Henry's body within their church. The people of Rouen were enraged, and King Henry II had to force the people of Le Mans to give the body of his son to the Church of St. Mary in Rouen to be buried (*Gesta Regis Henrici i* 303-04). Marshal met King Henry II at Limoges, and Henry ordered William to escort the bier to the cathedral at Rouen where the young king had wished to be buried. On July 22, 1183, the young Henry was interred in the cathedral at Rouen (*Hist* 7003-184).

One incident that happened near Saint-Pierre-sur-Dive in Normandy after the burial of the young Henry illustrates the humour and resourcefulness of Marshal. Marshal, Baldwin de Bethune, and Hugh de Hamelincourt arrived for a tournament. They stopped at a tavern for food and discovered that the tournament had already begun when the opposition and their own men poured into the town. Suddenly one

of the opposing knights was thrown from his horse right in front of the tavern and

was in danger of being trampled. Marshal rushed out, grabbed the fully armoured

knight in his arms, and deposited him on the table where his friends were eating.

Marshal said, "Take this knight's ransom and pay for the meal" (*Hist* 7204-232).

Marshal had cheerfully proven that necessity stimulates ingenuity.

     After this, Marshal obtained permission from Henry II to take the young

Henry's cross to Jerusalem and fulfill his crusader vow. Henry II took two of

Marshal's warhorses as a pledge that Marshal would not stay in Jerusalem but return

to join the king's *mesnie*. Marshal was given one hundred pounds Angevin to cover

the expenses of the pilgrimage and permission for a quick trip to England to see his

family before he left for Jerusalem. Marshal saw his brother John, who had inherited

the title of marshal of England from their father, his sister who had married Robert

de Port de l'Arche, and his cousin William earl of Salisbury who was the son of

Patrick (*Hist* 7239-274).   Marshal then left on his pilgrimage, spending two years

in the Holy Land fighting for the Knights Templar. The *Histoire* states that Marshal

accomplished more in two years than any other man could in seven (*Hist* 7275-295).

There are no known extant records of his time in the east, but it was during this time

that William Marshal became a member of the Knights Templar.

     In order to understand the importance of being a member of the Knights

Templar it is necessary to provide the facts and dispell the half-truths and mis-

information currently prevalent. The Knights Templar was one of the two military

orders of knights that in essence belonged to the Church, the Pope. The Knights

Templar were an order of knights created by Hugh de Paynes and Godfrey de St. Omer in 1118 as an order of knights whose purpose was to protect the pilgrims who came to the Holy Land (Wendover, Giles 469). Bernard of Clairvaux took upon himself the sponsorship of the order and drew up the provisions for the order at the Council of Troyes in 1128 (Williamson The History of the Temple 12). Pope Honorius II confirmed the rule of the Templars and gave them the characteristic white habit as their coat. There were five classes of brethren of this order: knights (*milites*) who were all men of noble birth; sergeants (clients) who were all freemen but were serving brothers, not knights; priests/chaplains (*capellani*) who provided spiritual services; squires (*armigeri*) who were freemen who carried light arms; and associates (*affilies*) who were temporary members. The associates could be married brothers, brothers who joined the Templars and fought for only a certain time, or brothers who joined the Templars when they were near the point of dying (Lees Records of the Templars lxi, n 9).

The Order was divided into provinces for administrative purposes; three were in the East. These were the Kingdom of Jerusalem, the Principality of Antioch, and the Principality of Tripoli. There were nine provinces in Europe: France with the Netherlands and Holland; England with Scotland and Ireland; Portugal; Castille with Leon; Aragon; Germany with Hungary; Central Italy; Sicily with Apulia; and Greece (Williamson History of the Temple 16, n 1). The supreme head of the Templar Order was the Master of the Order of Jerusalem, known as the Grand Master, and the head of the given province was called Preceptor, or Grand Preceptor. In England the Preceptor became known as the Master of the Temple for the center of the Templars built in London and dedicated in 1185 (Williamson 16). This military Order was not only important as an Order that answered only to the Pope with the purpose of defending Christianity, but it also became an organization that served the royal courts as counselors, financial agents (banks), envoys, and negotiators for both Church and state (Williamson 16-17). To be a member of this Order was to achieve a unique status as a knight in medieval times, and to have been an actual fighting Crusader in the Templars was the highest honour and recognition a knight could achieve.

VI. William Marshal and King Henry II

Marshal returned to England in the spring of 1187 and met King Henry II at Lyons-la-Foret (*Hist* 7302). Henry II granted Marshal his first fief, Cartmel in Lancashire, in 1187 (<u>PR 34 Henry II</u> 50). Henry also gave Marshal the custody of the person and lands of Helwis, daughter and heiress of William de Lancaster. Marshal could marry Helwis and obtain permanent possession of her lands, or he could just hold custody of her and her lands until she came of age to marry. As custodian of a minor heir, Marshal was entitled to receive the revenues from her lands as long as there was no destruction or diminishment of the value of Helwis' lands and property (*Hist* 7304-318). With this fief Marshal became a vassal of King Henry II and swore fealty to him as his lord and his king. Until Henry II's death in 1189, William Marshal served as his knight, his counselor, and his ambassador. Marshal became a *familiaris Regis*; this status meant that Marshal served as a counselor/advisor, military captain/knight, and ambassador for King Henry II (*Gesta Regis Henrici* ii 46).

The time period of 1187 to 1189 was a chaotic one with raids, sieges, battles, conferences, and truces between Henry II and Philip Augustus of France, son and heir of King Louis of France. The barons of Henry II on the continent could, and some did, sway from Henry's side to Philip's side at any given moment. To make matters even more difficult for King Henry, his son and heir count Richard Plantagenet of Poitou flirted with both camps frequently. Henry's son, young Henry, died in 1183, and his third born son, Geoffrey, died in 1185 in a tournament in Paris.

Queen Eleanor of Aquitaine had been comfortably imprisoned in England by King Henry II since 1173/1174 for her part in her sons' rebellion. Historians agree that Richard was definitely his mother's son, and this did not endear him to his father. King Henry was left with only his son John whom he made lord of Ireland c 1177 (*Houedene* i 455). For reasons that ranged from disliking Richard because he was his mother's son to disliking to release any of his own powers, Henry II chose the worst possible time to try to push John to the forefront. Henry decided that he wanted John to have the duchy of Aquitaine, the domain of Eleanor and the land that had been Richard's since the 1170s. Henry could not have chosen a worse path had he wanted to maintain some semblance of peace with his oldest son. Richard reacted to every move Henry II made during this time; if Henry seemed to be supporting Richard's position, Richard stayed with his father. If Henry's actions seem to presage a danger to Richard's inheritance, Richard was fighting for Philip.

During January 1188, Henry and Philip agreed to a truce in order to combine their military strength and rescue Jerusalem from Saladin (*Gesta Regis Henrici* ii 29-30). Henry left the continent and went to England to make preparations for this crusade, and Marshal went with Henry to put his own affairs in order (*Gesta Regis Henrici* ii 32-33). It was at this time that Marshal took possession of Cartmel and hired a new squire, John d' Erley, who would serve Marshal the rest of Marshal's life and be a source for the *Histoire* (PR 34 Henry II 50).

The stay of Henry II and Marshal in England did not last many months because Richard managed to entangle himself in a war with Philip of France by engaging in a military quarrel with Count Raymond of Toulouse. Henry had to raise a force of Welsh mercenaries and return to Normandy in July. To avoid an actual

war with his suzerain and fellow crusader, Henry sent the archbishop of Rouen,

the bishop of Evreux, and William Marshal to Philip to demand that Philip present

reparation for his raids into Maine and the Norman marches. Philip apparently

refused and informed Henry's representatives that he intended to take Berry and the

Norman Vexin. This resulted in Henry's ambassadors giving Philip formal notice of

their lord's defiance, and official war between the two kings on the continent began

again (*Gesta Regis Henrici* ii 34-36).

Henry II and his men assembled at Gisors and Philip and his army at

Chaumont-en-Vexin (*Diceto* ii 55; *Gesta Regis Henrici* ii 47). Philip, apparently

in jest, offered to settle the differences between Henry II and himself by a contest

between four champions for each side. Philip offered the counts of Flanders,

Clermont, Dreux, and Dreux de Mello against William fitz Ralph, seneschal of

Normandy, William de la Mare, Richard de Willequier, and Richard d'Argences

for Henry II. Since the seneschal was too old to fight and the other three were not

skilled knights, no one could take Philip's offer seriously. William Marshal saw this

jest as an opportunity for Henry II and advised Henry to turn the jest into reality and

suggest that the contest take place in a neutral court. This would allow Henry II to

choose his own champions, and Marshal recommended that Henry select Marshal,

William de Mandeville, John de Fresnai, and Osbert de Rouvrai. King Henry

immediately sent Marshal and de Mandeville to confer with Philip's representatives

and counteroffer this new contest. Philip, being caught in his own jest, immediately

refused the counter suggestion (*Hist* 7429-781). After a minor skirmish at the river

Epte between Henry's forces and Philip's, Philip returned to his own lands and disbanded part of his army (*Guillaume le Breton* 69-72).

Marshal, perceiving another opportunity in Philip's actions, advised Henry to disband his own army but give secret orders to have it re-assemble in several days at Paci-sur-Epte. Henry followed Marshal's counsel, and on August 30, 1188, Henry, Marshal, and his army swept over the border and raided Philip's lands as far as the outskirts of Mantes. The results of this raid were large amounts of plunder gathered from the destruction of more than fifteen villages (*Guillaume le Breton* 76-77; *Hist* 7782-852; *Gesta Regis Henrici* ii 46). Ravaging the lands of an opponent was an accepted and often practiced form of combat in medieval time; it greatly reduced the resources of one's opponent and garnered the attacker vast supplies and booty.

A conference between Philip, Richard, and King Henry was held at Bonmoulins near Mortain on November 18, 1188. Philip and Richard demanded that Henry II deliver Alix, Philip's sister and affianced bride of Richard, and formally recognize Richard as his heir. When Henry II refused, Richard swore fealty and homage to Philip of France for all the Angevin lands on the continent, saving the fealty and homage he owed to Henry II. All three men agreed to a truce until January 1189, and then each returned to their own bases (*Gesta Regis Henrici* ii 50).

Henry II and his court spent the winter and spring of 1189 in Anjou and Maine, and it was during this time that Henry II suffered the first attack of the illness that would eventually cause his death (*Giraldus* viii 29). During spring, Henry II promised to give William Marshal in marriage the lady Isabel de Clare, daughter and heiress to Richard Strongbow de Clare (*Hist* 8303-305). Unlike Helwis of Lancaster,

Isabel de Clare's lands were held as a tenant-in-chief of the king. Isabel as sole heiress of her father held fiefs in England which owed more than 65 and a half knights' fees, the lordship of Striguil in eastern Wales which owed over 65 knights' fees, the lordship of Leinster in Ireland which owed 100 knights' fees, and claim to the earldom of Pembroke in south west Wales (Red Book of the Exchequer 288, 444, 568).

Henry was too ill to meet with Richard and Philip in January 1189, and in March Philip and Richard raided Henry's lands (*Gesta Regis Henrici* ii 61). Henry sent William Marshal and Ralph, archdeacon of Hereford, to try to separate Philip from Richard, but Richard's agent at Philip's court, William de Longchamp, sabotaged Henry's ambassadors' efforts (*Hist* 8311-334). Spring of 1189 was spent in rounds of pointless and unfulfilled conferences between the three men on the frontier of Maine and in half-hearted small battles and sorties. (*Diceto* ii 67; *Hist* 8362-380; *Gesta Regis Henrici* ii 67)

Henry's forces were at Le Mans in June when Philip and Richard appeared with their armies on the south bank of the Huisne. Henry had ordered the destruction of the bridge over the river to impede the French army from taking the city, and he proposed that if the French army managed to ford the river, his men would set fire to the suburbs south of the city to halt the advance (*Hist* 8479-752). Unfortunately, once the fire was started in the suburbs, it could not be controlled and soon the city of Le Mans was burning. Henry decided that he had to withdraw his men and head for Fresnai, and as he did, the French were in hot pursuit. It is here that the often-told tale of the confrontation between William Marshal and Richard the Lionheart occurred. William Marshal and William des Roches turned to act as rear-guard for Henry II against the approaching men of the French forces. Marshal confronted Richard, who was wearing nothing in the way of armour but his helmet. Richard seeing Marshal ride toward him with his lance at the ready cried, "By the legs of God, Marshal, do not kill me for that would not be right for I am unarmed." Marshal replied, "No, let the devil kill you for I shall not" (*Hist* 8773-862). Marshal ran his lance through Richard's horse killing it, and then turned to follow and protect King Henry.

Henry II rested at Fresnai, sent Marshal to take command of the barons at Alencon, and Henry then moved into Anjou and stopped at the castle of Chinon. When Henry learned of the taking of Tours by Richard and Philip, he sent a letter to Marshal at Alencon and ordered him to leave the army at Alencon and to come to Chinon with only the knights of his own *mesnie* (*Hist* 8877-920). Not long after Marshal arrived at Chinon, Philip proposed a conference between Tours and Azay-le-Rideau in July. Henry was so ill by this time that he had to rest at the commandery of the Templars at Ballan, but on July 4, 1189, Henry met with Philip and Richard (*Hist* 8995-9028). The terms of peace were humiliating: Henry had to surrender his continental lands to Philip who then would re-grant them in return for Henry's homage; he had to pay Philip 20,000 marks; Richard was to marry Alix and receive the homage of all barons of England and the continental lands of the Angevins as heir to his father; and Henry's barons were to swear to support Richard and Philip if Henry violated this treaty. As an added surety for Henry's support of this treaty, the allies were to hold certain castles until all the terms of the treaty had been fulfilled (*Gesta Regis Henrici* ii 70). Henry accepted these terrible terms, returned to

Chinon, and there he died on July 6, 1189 (*Gesta Regis Henrici* ii 70-71). Geoffrey,

bastard of Henry II, Marshal, Gilbert Pipard, Gilbert fitz Renfrew, and a few other

knights who were loyal to the king were with Henry II until his death (*Giraldus* iv

70, viii 304; *Hist* 9135-143). They escorted the body of Henry II to the Abbey of

Fontrevault, and there the abbess and the nuns stood watch over the man who had

been King of England for thirty-five years.

One wonders what Marshal thought of his dead king for there are no personal

opinions expressed in the *Histoire* of Marshal regarding any of those who were

important or critical to his life. Marshal had known Henry for at least nineteen years

and had known him personally and well. That Marshal had learned a great deal

about royalty, nobility, government, politics, and war from his association with King

Henry II cannot be denied. Did Marshal mourn the loss of both the realized and

the unfulfilled greatness of Henry II? Perhaps he did, but all that is known is that

Marshal seemed to be unafraid of what the future would bring to him when Richard

assumed the throne.

According to the *Histoire,* while the barons loyal to King Henry II awaited

the arrival of Richard at Fontrevault, they feared for Marshal's safety and offered

Marshal their aid should Richard confiscate Marshal's property (9253-276).

Marshal's reply was:

> Lords, it is true that I slew his horse, and I do not regret it. I thank you for
> your offers, but I would be ashamed to take your gifts if I were not sure of
> being able to return them. Ever since I was made a knight, God by his
> great mercy, has cared for me so well that I trust him for the future. His

wishes will prevail. (9276-290)

Apparently, Marshal did not fear that Richard would exact some type of revenge against himself for his loyal and faithful service to Richard's father. Marshal had known and fought with and against Richard for many years, and by this time, Marshal's own reputation as a knight and a loyal and trustworthy vassal was recognized by most of the important men of both the Angevin and French lands. Honour and loyalty were not simply words in this time period; they were the essence of the character and value of a man of the knightly class and were the most valued commodity a man might possess. William Marshal not only had these qualities to a high degree but was also known and recognized as such by the men who were his contemporaries whether ally or opponent. Who and what Marshal had become as a man could not be taken away from him for he had earned it himself without debt to any other. He had no cause to fear any other man because his honour was his and could be diminished or destroyed only by himself.

VII. William Marshal and Richard Lionheart

The conversation between Richard and Marshal at Fontrevault has often been quoted. Richard said to Marshal, "Marshal, the other day you wished to kill me, and you would have done it had I not turned aside your lance with my arm." Marshal replied, "Sire, I had no intention of killing you nor have I ever tried to do so. I am still strong enough to direct my lance. If I had wished, I could have struck your body as I did your horse. If I had slain you, I would not consider it a crime, and I do not regret having slain your horse." Richard replied, "Marshal, I pardon you, and I will bear you no rancor" (*Hist* 9291-341). Under the customs and regulations of feudalism, Marshal had been fighting in defense of his feudal lord and king, Henry II, and Richard had been in rebellion against his feudal lord and king, Henry II. In chivalric and feudal terms, Richard had been engaged in an act of treason by virtue of his war against his vassalic lord, King Henry II. He was fighting against his lord who happened to be his king and his father. But more importantly, he was rebelling against the lord who had given him his fiefs; Richard was making war against the lord to whom he had sworn fealty and homage for the lands that lord had given him.

While still on the grounds of the Abbey of Fontrevault, Richard ordered Marshal and Gilbert Pipard to England to free Richard's mother, Eleanor, and attend to Richard's business until Richard arrived (*Hist* 9341-354). It was Geoffrey, chancellor to Henry II and Henry's bastard son, who told Richard of Henry's promise to William Marshal of the heiress Isabel de Clare. Richard's reply was that his father merely promised Isabel to Marshal, but that he, Richard, would give her to Marshal as well as all of her lands (*Hist* 9367-371; <u>Chron. Reign Richard I</u> ii73).

Here once again is a Plantagenet gifting Marshal with the second wealthiest heiress in their kingdom. Not in his greatest imaginings could Marshal as second son of a minor baron have ever anticipated that he would be given such a prize. Richard I was no man's fool when it came to judging a vassal's worth. What he saw in and knew of William Marshal assured him that by placing Isabel de Clare and all of her lands into Marshal's hands Richard would guarantee that this part of his kingdom would be safe and loyal to the Plantagenet crown. Richard knew that Marshal's own sense of duty and responsibility would insure this.

After Henry II's funeral at Fontrevault, Marshal and Pipard headed for the coast to board a ship at Dieppe for England. William went first to Winchester to see that Eleanor was freed and to give her Richard's letters, and then he dealt with his own personal affairs (*Hist* 9439-512). Probably while still at Winchester, Marshal had a writ of Ranulf de Glanville by order of Queen Eleanor to send sixteen knights and twenty-five sergeants from the sheriffs of Devonshire and Gloucestershire with thirty pounds for expenses to defend Pembrokeshire from Rees ap Griffith (*Giraldus* vi 80; <u>PR I Richard</u> 130, 163). The lands and castles of Pembrokeshire were lands that Isabel de Clare could claim as part of her inheritance from her father and grandfather. Though Henry II had withheld the earldom of Pembroke from Strongbow, Marshal as Isabel de Clare's husband could put forth a claim for its return to Isabel de Clare as the sole heir of her grandfather, Gilbert fiz Richard earl of Pembroke c.1137.

Marshal then headed for London to take possession of his bride Isabel, who was in the Tower of London and in the custody of the justiciar Ranulf de Glanville

(*Hist* 9515-516). This union of William Marshal and Isabel de Clare would begin

in a room in the Tower of London in late July/early August 1189. There a knight in

his forties and a lady in her late teens met for the first time. They would be married

before the end of August and become a union that would impact the course of

medieval English history. By a twist of fate or destiny's plan, Marshal and Isabel

would be main characters in English, Norman, Welsh, and Irish history during their

own lifetimes and permanently in medieval history's timeline.

This is where the *Histoire* and other contemporary sources fail the reader.

There is no record or description of the first meeting between Isabel de Clare and

William Marshal. Isabel was a young girl who had been kept in the Tower of

London for at least two years as a precaution against some unruly English baron

trying to kidnap and force her into marriage for her vast lands.

Isabel's mother, Eve de Clare is found in Sweetman's <u>Calendar of Documents</u>

<u>Relating to Ireland</u> in 1184-1185 in two cases; one under Northumberland where

Adam de Cardhill is to render his account to Ranulf de Glanville of 40 pounds of

which 20 pounds is to be loaned to the Countess of Ireland for her support in the

March of Wales. The other case is found under Cambridge and Huntingdon where

Ralph Bardulf renders 40 marks to be paid on loan to the Countess of Ireland by

writ of Ranulf de Glanville (p 11, #69, #70). It is known from the records that

Eve de Clare was alive in 1186-1187 as she is found on the <u>Pipe Roll 33 Henry II</u>

under the military scutage for the honour of Striguil (142). Eve is identified as the

countess of Striguil here rather than the countess of Ireland and remitted ten pounds of the sum owed by Striguil out of 65 and a half knights' fees in scutage answered for by Ralf Bloet who held custody of the Chepstow castle (PR 33 Henry II xxvi, 16). Eve is also found in *Crede mihi* where she issued a charter that confirmed to John Cumin, archbishop of Dublin, the prior grants donated to Trinity Cathedral with the confirmation of count John (50). The date of this charter could be any time between 1185 and 1189; it might be in the year 1189 before Marshal assumed control of Leinster (Flanagan Irish Society 133-34). It is not known what year Henry II confined Isabel to the Tower of London; it could have been in the spring of 1188 after Henry II had taken the vow as crusader, returned to England to prepare for a crusade, and had once again put Eleanor in close confinement at Winchester or Salisbury. Since Henry returned to Normandy in the winter of 1188 and died there in 1189, he might have thought it safer to hold such a wealthy unmarried heiress in the Tower and thus in royal hands.

It is not known what year Eve de Clare died, but what is known is that she was buried in the north part of Tintern Abbey not far from the chapter house where her father-in-law, Gilbert fitz Richard de Clare, first earl of Pembroke, was buried (Visitations, Siddons p 38 #9). This means that Eve MacMurchada de Clare, princess of Leinster and widow of Strongbow, died in England or Wales in 1188/1189. Otherwise as princess of Leinster and Strongbow's widow, Eve would have been buried in Trinity Cathedral in Dublin, Ireland, with her husband and her people. The *Histoire* makes no mention of Eve, so it is not known if she lived to see her daughter and heiress married to William Marshal.

Meanwhile, Eve and Strongbow's daughter and heir, Isabel de Clare, waited in the Tower of London. It is possible that Glanville's clerk, Hubert Walter, may have told Isabel that she was to be married to William Marshal (*Hist* 8303-310). One wonders if she had any knowledge of the man who was about to claim her as wife. It is assumed from the scant sources that Isabel had no family with her in the Tower. What must have been her emotions as she awaited the arrival of a man, unknown to her, coming to claim her body and her lands as her husband on order of the king? Marshal was between forty and forty-two years old, and Isabel was between eighteen and twenty years old [it is not known the year of birth of either]. Marshal is described as well-shaped physically, tall, with dark brown hair, darkly tanned skin from his years in the Holy Land, a face like a Roman, and a physique equal to a Greek sculpture (*Hist* 717-36). Isabel is described as beautiful, good, fair, and wise. Physically, Isabel was probably slender like her father and either blonde or strawberry blonde since her father was red-haired and her Irish mother was probably fair haired and skinned. There are no extant records of Isabel's actual physical description, but it is safe to assume that the young lady was definitely not an antidote. Something of Marshal's character and personality is known from the *Histoire*, but there is no description of Isabel's.

Isabel had been raised by her mother, a princess of Ireland, daughter of King Dermot MacMurchada of Leinster. Flanagan has shown that Irish women were not like their counterparts in England. They could and did hold and rule lands that they held in their own right, and by the end of the twelfth century children of the upper classes in the medieval world of western Europe were being educated as a rule rather than an exception. Isabel was not simply a daughter; she was the sole heiress of immense lands and vassals with a mother that was Irish. It is known that the extant

records of Eve show that Henry II must have had confidence in her to allow her

charge over Chepstow at least up to the Welsh rebellion in 1185. It is not beyond the

realm of possibilities that Eve would have taught her daughter of the responsibilities

and duties of a woman who would hold such vast lands one day. Mothers have

always taught daughters by their example and by specific instruction. Eve would

have fulfilled both her role as mother and father in teaching Isabel not only of the

lands and vassals she would inherit, but also of the obligations and responsibilities

that were inherent to her position as lady of Leinster and Chepstow and possible

lady of Pembroke. The de Clares were always known as a family who knew what

belonged to them in lands and castles and what might belong to them because of

past history. Eleanor of Aquitiaine had proved that given certain circumstances,

a woman in medieval time was quite capable of being the equal of a man in

understanding how to be and rule as a feudal lord. Because of the lack of primary

sources providing information on Eve and Isabel de Clare for the years 1176 to 1189,

it is not possible to know what kind of person Isabel was by the time of her marriage

to William Marshal. The only clear indication of who and what Isabel actually was

as a woman is the fact that she is seen often as a counselor to her husband, as privy

to Marshal's discussions within the group of his *familiares*. Isabel was never a

decoration, a trophy, nor a cipher as William Marshal's wife.

William had intended to take Isabel to her lands, probably Chepstow, for

the marriage ceremony as William lacked sufficient funds of his own to wed her in

London in the style her status demanded. Richard fitz Renier, a sheriff of London, informed William that the couple must be married before they could leave London. Since Marshal lacked funds for the marriage, fitz Renier provided the necessary monies to see them married in style and with the proper ceremony due on such an occasion (*Hist* 9519-536). There are no records regarding the marriage of William and Isabel. It is not known what church they were married in, who married them, or who attended the wedding ceremony (Landon <u>Itin.</u> <u>Richard I</u> 3). All that is known is that Engerrand d'Abernon provided his home at Stokes d'Abernon in Surrey for the honeymoon of William and Isabel (*Hist* 9537-550). Again, there are no details of either the wedding or the honeymoon. There is a lacuna in medieval history with regard to the knowledge of how two almost virtual strangers managed to accept and adapt to the reality of being married to each other. In the case of William and Isabel they truly were complete strangers to each other, and yet they had to be physically and religiously married to each other within days of their first meeting. One can conjecture that the honeymoon must have been a lively and interesting start to a marriage that would survive for thirty years and produce ten living children.

What William Marshal acquired as a result of his marriage to the second greatest heiress in England was staggering to a man who held only two or three small fiefs of his own. Isabel was the granddaughter of a king of Ireland, Dermot king of Leinster, and she was the sole heir of her father Richard Strongbow de Clare. In her own right as the heiress of Strongbow, Isabel held the lordship of Chepstow/ Striguil in southeast Wales, claim to the earldom of Pembroke in southwest Wales, the lordship of Leinster in Ireland, and a claim to one-half the honour of Giffard as a descendant of Richard fitz Gilbert de Clare (d.1090). The honour of Striguil alone consisted of some 60 or more knight's fees through nine shires and included the demesne manors of Weston in Hertfordshire, Chesterford in Essex, and Badgworth in Gloucestershire (*Rotuli de Dominibus* 66, 76; PR 33 Henry II 142). The lordship of Striguil, which had its caput at the great castle of Chepstow, was more than one hundred square miles of lands, and it was a Marcher lordship which meant that the king's writ did not run inside its territory except for ecclesiastical cases. The lord of these lands owed the king homage, fealty, and military service. As a Marcher lordship this was a type of palatine lordship that had its own *juria regalia;* the lord had his own civil and criminal courts, own court of the chancery, and the right of wreck, fines, reliefs, aids, escheats, wardships, and other feudal incidents (Evans Monmouthshire 69). The lordship of Leinster was held under much of the same terms, and it comprised the counties of Kildare, Carlow, Kilkenny, Wexford, Queens, and a portion of Kings (Orpen Ireland i 258-59, 326). The earldom and lands of Pembroke included the great castle of Pembroke as well as claim to Usk, Emlyn, and Cilgerran castles and lands (Taylor "Usk Castle" 252; PR 36 Henry II 203; PR 38 Henry II 2; *Ann Camb* 63; *Chart* 47). By virtue of Marshal's marriage to Isabel de Clare, he claimed "in right of his wife" the opportunity to acquire one-half the honor of Giffard. Marshal paid Richard I two thousand marks in relief for the demesne manors of Crendon in Buckinghamshire and Caversham in Oxfordshire including the homage and service of forty-three knights *(Liber Feodorum* 637-1138; PR 2 Richard I 145, 58). Marshal's share of the Normandy lands of the Giffard honor included one-half the barony of Longueville, the castles of Longueville and Meullers near Dieppe, and Orbec near Lisieux as well as lands owing more than sixty knights' service (<u>Red Book of Exchequer</u> 633). Marshal's share of the Giffard lands in right

of his wife went from the eastern Pays de Caux west to Cany and Montivilliers and

south to the river Seine. The honor of Giffard was split between Marshal, holding

in right of his wife, and Earl Richard de Clare of Hertford; de Clare held the lands

in England as lord, and Marshal held the lands in Normandy as lord. With this

marriage, William Marshal became in right of his wife one of the greatest lords and

magnates in the Plantagenet kingdom, and he held most of these lands as tenant-in-

chief, meaning he held them directly of the king with no intermediary lord with the

exception of the Irish lands which Marshal held in right of his wife from count John

as lord of Ireland.

Marshal considered the lands that he held to be one unit, not separate units

of English, Irish, Welsh, and Norman lands. They were a compact whole to be

preserved and improved for the inheritance of his children. Marshal used what he

had learned while fighting in Normandy and the Holy Land to improve his fiefs

and castles. The great Tower, the Horseshoe Gatehouse, and the fighting gallery in

the outer curtain wall at Pembroke were built under his guidance (Brown <u>English</u>

<u>Medieval Castles</u> 61; Somerset-Fry <u>British Medieval Castles</u> 136-37). The tower

keep at Pembroke was seventy-five feet high, fifty-three feet in diameter, and had

walls fifteen feet thick. When Marshal re-built Pembroke in stone, he created a

defense system that would encompass the castle and the town. This design pre-

dated the great castles in Wales of Edward I by almost a century (Walker "Henry II's

Charter" 133). At Chepstow he was responsible for the gate in the middle bailey,

the rebuilding of the upper level of the keep, the wall dividing the present middle and lower bailey, the drum tower, the west barbicon, and the upper bailey (Brown Castles From the Air 83-84). Marshal was also responsible for the building of the castle at Kilkenny, the new castle at Emlyn, and for taking and improving Cilgerran. From a list of castles by R. A. Brown for the period from 1153 to 1214, Marshal held Chepstow, Cilgerran, Emlyn, Goodrich, Haverford, Inkberrow, Pembroke, Tenby and Usk in England and Wales ("A List of Castles 1154-1216" 249-80). Just these castles would have produced more than two hundred knights' fees owed by Marshal to the Crown. Without including his lands in Normandy and Ireland, as feudal lord Marshal controlled a vast amount of land, wealth, knights, and vassals in the Angevin kingdom.

By his own actions, Marshal had gained the favor of Queen Eleanor, and this interest and his skills and reputation as a knight had resulted in Marshal's appointment as the head of the young king Henry's *mesnie*. That stage of his life gave him the opportunity to know and acquire the friendship and respect of some of the most important men of his time. Marshal then added to his reputation and status as an honourable, courageous, and loyal knight with his two years as a crusader. Marshal's service as knight and vassal to King Henry II increased his own knowledge and skills both as a warrior knight and as a political entity at the level of kings and kingdoms. The man who married Isabel de Clare and became one of the most powerful and respected magnates of the realm was a man whose character and values were already formed. Had William Marshal been less of a man, his promotion to the highest level of power and status by his marriage to Isabel de Clare might have corrupted or destroyed him.

While Marshal married and became acquainted with his wife and the lands and vassals he had acquired with her, Queen Eleanor, through acts of Ranulf de Glanville, had curbed the abuses of the forest officials, removed the royal horses that had been stabled in religious communities by Henry II, ordered the liberation of all prisoners, and allowed those who had been exiled to legally return to England (Chron. Reign Richard I 18, 26, 76, 87-88). Diceto says that Richard had given Eleanor the power to demand whatever she wished in England for the good of the realm (ii 67; Gillingham Richard I 128). Eleanor ordered clergy and laity to establish and maintain peace and to take the oaths of all freemen of allegiance to Richard as king and lord (Chron. Reign Richard I ii 74-75; *Houedene* ii 4).

On August 13, 1189, Richard arrived in England with his brother John; Marshal had several pressing problems that he needed to resolve with the latter. John had been given the honor of Lancaster, and Marshal had to swear fealty and homage for his fief of Cartmel to John because it was part of that honor (Chron. Reign Richard I ii 75, 78). Marshal's other problem was that John, as lord of Ireland, had treated Marshal's wife's lands in Leinster as if they were John's own lands. John had made many grants of the Leinster lands to his own men, which he had no right to do as the lands were not his but were merely in his custody until Isabel de Clare was married. Marshal had to ask Richard to force John to give up the lordship and to return the lands he had granted to his own followers. With the exception of the fief of Theobald Walter, John's butler, all the lands were returned to Marshal. Walter would now hold his fief as Marshal's vassal, and Marshal swore featly and homage to John as lord of Ireland for Marshal's lordship of Leinster (*Hist* 9582-616, 10312-

0340). Marshal obtained permission from John to establish a priory of regular canons at Cartmel in an act of gratitude and piety for all that he had just acquired. Marshal took a group of canons from the priory of Bradenstoke in Wiltshire, a favored priory by Marshal's maternal uncle, and created a house at Cartmel (VCH History of County Lancashire Vol II 143).

When Richard arrived in England on August 13, 1189, he was not crowned immediately; instead, Richard and his mother Queen Eleanor made a leisurely progress to London. On their way to London, they stopped at Marlborough to witness the marriage of Prince John to Isabel of Gloucester, who was the wealthiest heiress in the land. King Henry II had arranged that Isabel would inherit the title and most of the lands of her father, William earl of Gloucester who was the son of Robert earl of Gloucester and natural cousin to Henry II. This arrangement had to all intents and purposes disinherited Isabel's sisters, Amicia married to Gilbert de Clare, and Mabel married to Amaury de Montfort.

On Sunday, September 3, 1189, Richard was crowned at Westminster Abbey in a coronation ceremony that was, at least partly, devised by his mother Eleanor (Diceto ii 68-69). The coronation of Richard I was an elaborate ceremony performed in Westminster Abbey. Entering through the nave of Westminster, Richard was preceded by abbots and the bishops. In the midst of the bishops walked four barons carrying four candlesticks of gold. Behind these barons was Geoffrey de Lucy bearing the king's cap and with him John Marshal, marshal of England, carrying two great spurs of gold. Next came William Marshal, lord of Striguil, bearing the royal scepter of gold with a cross of gold on top, and William fitz Patrick, earl of

Salisbury, carrying a rod of gold with a golden dove on top. After these two came, David, earl of Huntingdon and brother to the king of Scotland, John earl of Mortain and brother to Richard, and Robert earl of Leicester. Each of these men carried a golden sword with scabbards worked in gold. Behind them came six earls and six barons carrying a *chequer* with the royal arms and robes for Richard's coronation placed on top. Behind the earls and barons came William de Mandeville, earl of Albemarle, carrying a massive gold crown with precious jewels on each side. Then Richard came walking between the bishop of Durham on his right and the bishop of Bath on his left; these three men walked under a silken canopy carried on four spears by four more barons (*Houedene* ii 117).

As Richard kneeled at the altar he swore to observe peace, honor and reverence to God, the Holy Church, and its ordinances; to exercise true justice and equity to the people whom he ruled; and to enact good laws with no evil intent or fraud and abrogate bad laws and customs if any existed in his kingdom. After his vows, Richard was anointed with holy oil by Baldwin, Archbishop of Canterbury, clothed in the royal robes, given the sword of rule, shod with the spurs, and swore again at the altar that he would observe the vows and oaths with the help of God. Richard I was then crowned, observed a mass, gave a mark of pure gold as offertory, and was led from the church to his chamber (*Houedene* ii 118-19). Thus was born the coronation ceremony for the kings and queens of England that in many ways is still being used in the coronation ceremony of England today.

Richard was a crusader, and therefore he had to prepare for the joint crusade with Philip of France for which they had both taken the cross in 1188. November

1189 Richard sent Marshal to France as his proxy to swear to Philip that Richard would meet Philip at Vezelay on April 1190 to begin their crusade. The date was later postponed until June 24, 1190 (*Houedene* iii 19-20). In the meantime, Richard had to raise the money for his crusade, and his solution to this problem was to put everything up for sale including castles, towns, manors, lordships, offices, charters, and privileges. Every sheriff had to buy back his office or lose it to some other man who paid the price for it.

Marshal used his new position to acquire the shrievalty of Gloucester and custody of Gloucester castle as well as the forest of Dean and the castle of St. Briavells (PR 2 Richard I 58; PR 6 Richard I 239). Marshal's standing with Richard also allowed him to obtain the deanship of York for his brother Henry on September 16, 1189 (*Diceto* ii 85-86). William's brother John, who was head of the Marshal family, was appointed sheriff of Yorkshire and given the manors of Wexcombe and Bedwin in Wiltshire and Bosham in Sussex (PR 2 Richard I 58). William's bastard nephew John Marshal was appointed escheator in Anglia (*Houedene* ii 376; Chron. Reign Richard I ii 91).

William de Longchamp, Bishop of Ely, was justiciar of England and papal legate in England, but Richard appointed four barons to serve as associate justiciars with Longchamp. These men were Marshal, Geoffrey fitz Peter, William Brewer, and Hugh Bardolf *(Diceto* ii 83, 91; *Houedene* iii 1, 28; Chron. Reign Richard I ii 101-06). These four itinerant justices covered the shires of England hearing cases, sat in the *Curia Regis* at Westminster and elsewhere, and acted as barons of the exchequer. Longchamp was expected to seek their advice and counsel on important issues of policy and the government of the realm while Richard was gone on Crusade (Chron. Reign Richard I ii 213-14).

Richard and Marshal left for Tours on June 27, 1190, on their way to Vezelay. Apparently Isabel accompanied Marshal on this trip as their first son, William, was born in Normandy during this year. At Vezelay Richard received the scrip and staff of a pilgrim, and on July 5, 1190, Richard and Philip set off on their crusade to the Holy Land (*Layettes du Tresor* #369).

In England, Richard had given John almost regalian rights in the counties of Nottingham, Derby, Cornwall, Devon, Dorset, and Somerset. This meant that John appointed the sheriffs, collected the revenue, and exercised all powers of government in these counties (*Houedene* ii 115). John was lord of the marcher fief of Glamorgan in right of his wife Isabel of Gloucester, and Richard had also given him the honours of Lancaster, Wallingford, Tickhill, and Peverel (Chron. Reign Richard I ii 78, 99). Richard as an unmarried king had no heir, but there was the son of his brother Geoffrey, Arthur, and Richard's brother John. According to Norman law, John would be the preferred heir if Richard should die on his crusade (History of English Law 281-84). Richard had apparently named Arthur as his heir in a treaty with Tancred of Sicily and had definitely informed Longchamp of his decision during the winter of 1190-1191 (*Foedera* i 1, 52; William of Newburg 335).

A power struggle was pre-ordained by the disposition by Richard of lands and castles between his brother John and Longchamp. Marshal was brought into this power struggle while Marshal was still in Normandy. Longchamp removed Marshal's brother, John, from the shrievalty of Yorkshire in the spring of 1190 on the grounds that he could not control the anti-Semite riots in York (Chron. Reign Richard I ii 108; *Houedene* iii 34-35). Longchamp replaced John Marshal with his own brother, Osbert. Longchamp then had the audacity to besiege Marshal's castle of Gloucester in August 1190, but withdrew when Geoffrey de Lucy, bishop of Winchester, returned from the continent and advised Longchamp to desist if he wanted to maintain peace (*Diceto* ii 83; Richard of Devizes ii 391). Longchamp had thus in two strokes managed to insure the hostility of Marshal to any of his future attempts to seize control of England in Richard's absence.

These and other complaints against the heavy-handed rule of Longchamp reached Richard in Sicily at the end of 1190 (Chron. Reign Richard I ii 157-58). Richard decided that he had to send Walter de Coutances, archbishop of Rouen, to England to assist and even supersede if necessary Longchamp in England. Richard gave a series of letters patent to Walter; one was addressed to Longchamp and his four associates, Marshal, fitz Peter, Bardolf, and Brewer. This one stated that Richard was sending de Coutances to England to serve as advisor and counselor in all matters to the five men addressed. There was also a letter addressed to each of the four associates advising them to act only with the counsel of de Countances, and if the chancellor should refuse to follow the advice of the archbishop of Rouen and the associate justiciars, they were to rule without him (*Diceto* ii 90-91; *Houedene* ii 123).

Walter arrived in England and found that Longchamp had instigated another war by removing John's appointee of sheriff of Lincolnshire, Gerard de Camville, and had actually laid siege to Lincoln castle. This was doubly illegal as Gerard was hereditary custodian of Lincoln castle and under John's control and right (Chron. Reign Richard I ii 207; William of Newburg 338). John had taken the castles of Tickhill and Nottingham, which were in the chancellor's custody, and mustered an army to relieve the siege of Lincoln castle. Walter de Coutances arranged a treaty at Winchester on July 28, 1191, that provided that Tickhill and Nottingham be returned to Longchamp, de Camville reinstated as sheriff of Lincolnshire, and Longchamp recognize John as Richard's heir should Richard die on crusade (Round Commune of London 207-18).

No sooner was this problem solved, than Longchamp managed to commit an even graver crime. Geoffrey, bastard brother to Richard and John, was consecrated archbishop of York by Bartholomew, archbishop of Tours, on August 19, 1191. At Flanders, Geoffrey received a letter from Longchamp forbidding him to come to England; Geoffrey ignored the letter and landed at Dover on September 14, 1191 (Wendover, Giles 103). As soon as Geoffrey landed at Dover, he went to the priory of St. Martin to prevent Longchamp's constable of Dover from arresting him. Unfortunately, the agents of the constable went into the priory, seized Geoffrey, and removed him to Dover castle. This act of the violation of sanctuary roused the anger of all barons and prelates of England, and the bishop of London persuaded Longchamp to release Geoffrey and allow him to come to London on October 2, 1191 (*Diceto* ii 96-97).

Longchamp's actions had given his opponents the opportunity to remove him from office. John called a meeting of the associate justiciars, the prelates, and barons at Reading to discuss the chancellor's actions (*Diceto* ii 98). Longchamp declined to attend and retired to the safety of the Tower of London while John and the barons took control of the city. On October 8, 1191, Geoffrey, archbishop of York, and Hugh, bishop of Durham, presented their grievances against Longchamp to Walter de Coutances and a council of barons and prelates at St. Paul's in London. The associate justiciars and de Coutances pointed out the chancellor's failure to consult and abide by their counsel. Marshal read Richard's letter authorizing the associate justiciars and de Coutances to take any measure necessary to insure the good of the kingdom in the event that the chancellor refused to follow their advice (Chron. Reign Richard I ii 213-14; *Houedene* iii 31, 38, 43, 50). Longchamp was removed from the justiciarship and de Coutances put in his place; the entire assembly swore fealty to Richard while Richard lived and to John as his heir if Richard died.

Longchamp tried to regain his place by going to Pope Celestine; Celestine ordered the English prelates to excommunicate anyone who injured his legate. Longchamp wrote his fellow bishops to excommunicate Walter de Coutances, the bishops of Coventry and Winchester, all the associate justiciars except Hugh Bardulf, as well as fifteen barons (*Houedene* iii 150-54). The bishops did not obey these orders, and de Coutances sent agents to Rome to persuade the pope to remove the excommunication order. Celestine did remove the order, but he refused to remove Longchamp as papal legate (*Houedene* iii 155, 188-92). Longchamp also sent his agents to Richard in Syria telling him that John planned to steal his throne and that the barons of England were willing to permit it. Richard demanded to know the men who had gone over to John, and Longchamp's messenger accused Marshal. Richard replied, "The Marshal! By the legs of God, I deemed him the most loyal knight who was ever born in my lands. I am trusting in your loyalty." This responsibility was too much for the messenger; he then told Richard that he had been ordered to accuse Marshal. Richard answered, "I believe that the Marshal would never be evil or false." (*Hist* 9828-858; *Houedene* iii 155)

Longchamp was probably doomed to failure from the beginning as he was Norman, of servile stock, short and lame, tactless, arrogant, avid for power, and totally unknown to and unfamiliar with England. He probably distrusted Marshal and Richard's brothers from the beginning and foolishly did everything he could to diminish and undermine their power and influence. Just as John did later in his reign as king, Longchamp failed to grasp the reality that no king or king's agent ruling under a feudalistic system of law and custom could rule and maintain power without the help and cooperation of the greater barons of that kingdom. The system could only work and survive if both king and at least some of the most powerful barons cooperated in the endeavor. This fact, plus Longchamp's abuse of power, caused Longchamp to fail so abysmally in his efforts to govern England in Richard's absence.

December 1191 Philip returned to France, and on January 20, 1192, Philip met William fitz Ralph, seneschal of Normandy, near Gisors and showed him a document purported to be a treaty between Richard and Philip. The document said that Philip's sister Alix was to be delivered to him as well as the castle of Gisors and the counties of Eu and Aumale (Chron. Reign Richard I ii 23; *Foedera* i 54). Needless to say, William fitz Ralph refused to turn anything over to Philip without direct written orders from King Richard. Philip apparently then wrote to John in England offering him Alix as wife and France's aid taking all of his brother's domains. This action was stopped by Queen Eleanor immediately crossing to England, and with the help of de Coutances, forbidding John to cross to the continent to join Philip on penalty of losing all of his English lands (Richard of Devizes 60-61; Chron. Reign Richard I i 236-37; Gillingham Richard I 219-20).

With one problem solved, another immediately arose. In the summer of 1192 Rees ap Griffith, prince of south Wales, invaded south Wales and laid siege to Swansea castle on the Gower Peninsula (*Ann Camb* 58). Walter de Coutances and his associates ordered the feudal levy to muster at Gloucester for an expedition against Rees (PR 5 Richard I 158). Marshal, Geoffrey fitz Peter, and count John took command of the operations. Ships were brought together at Bristol and sent to Swansea with supplies, weapons, and re-inforcements for the garrison (PR 5 Richard I 113-14, 148). The army proceeded from Gloucester overland and engaged the enemy under the walls of Swansea and forced them to withdraw (PR 5 Richard I 93). Marshal as sheriff of Gloucester furnished money from the revenues of that county to pay for the ships sent to Swansea and other supplies (PR 5 Richard I 113-14). Out of his own pocket Marshal loaned money to William de London to maintain and strengthen the castles of Kidwelly and Swansea, loaned count John one hundred marks to sustain himself during the expedition, and gave twenty pounds for the ships sent to Swansea (PR 5 Richard I 148). Marshal was not only occupied with his feudal military obligations during this time, but he was also an itinerant justice, and with the bishops of Hereford and Coventry, Richard of the Peak, and Robert of Shrewsbury, Marshal visited the counties of Gloucestershire, Worcestershire,

Herefordshire, Warwickshire, Shropshire, and Staffordshire fulfilling his duties as a justice itinerant (PR 5 Richard I xxiv-xxv).

On December 28, 1192, Henry of Hohenstauffen, Holy Roman Emperor, sent a letter to Philip informing him that Richard had been captured by Leopold, duke of Austria, while Richard was on his way back to England. Walter de Coutances somehow obtained a copy of this letter and thus was instantly aware of the danger this presented to England and Normandy (*Houedene* iii 195-96). Philip had another card to play in this game; he sent a letter to count John again offering Alix in marriage, acceptance of John's homage for Richard's continental fiefs, and aid in taking England (*Houedene iii* 203). Thus the proverbial fat was in the fire, and Walter summoned the associate justiciars, prelates, and barons of England to a meeting at Oxford to determine the defense of the realm (PR 5 Richard I 158; *Houedene* iii 196-97).

Queen Eleanor had returned to England on February 11, 1192 (Chron. Reign Richard I ii 161, 235; *Houedene* iii 160, 179). Gervase of Canterbury says that Eleanor assumed direct authority for the conduct of all English affairs on the news of Richard's capture (i 515). Eleanor gave orders to fortify the castles of the kingdom, especially those that were on the channel coast; they were all strengthened, provisioned, and garrisoned (Gervase i 514-15; PR 5 Richard I xvii). Marshal immediately gathered forces in the castles of Gloucester and Bristol; at Bristol he garrisoned ten knights and five hundred sergeants, and at Gloucester twenty knights, four hundred and fifty sergeants, and forty archers (PR 5 Richard I 148). Marshal now had at hand an army that could become mobile in case of civil war or an invasion by the French.

John left for Normandy in January 1193, and when the seneschal and the barons of Normandy refused to do John homage for their lands, John left Normandy and went to King Philip and the French court. Here John made a formal alliance with the French king and did homage for all the continental lands of the Plantagenet house (*Houedene* iii 204). In the spring of 1193 John returned to England with an army of mercenaries, and when the justiciars refused his demand to recognize him as king, John retired to his lands to prepare for war (*Houedene* iii 204-5).

John at this time held the castles of Nottingham, Tickhill, Wallingford, and Windsor. Walter de Coutances decided that Windsor was the greater danger as it commanded the Thames valley. Marshal came from the west at the head of five hundred sergeants who were probably Welsh mercenaries. Marshal was joined at Windsor by Geoffrey fitz Peter and William de Braose, sheriff of Herefordshire, with additional Welsh forces (*Hist* 9893-904; PR 5 Richard I 148, 87, 99). While Marshal, fitz Peter, de Braose, de Coutances, and Queen Eleanor laid siege to Windsor, Hugh bishop of Durham laid siege to Tickhill (*Houedene* iii 208). Marshal's ability to find the money to pay for the troops during this time proved a valuable experience. In February 1193 he received four hundred pounds from the royal treasury (PR 5 Richard I 148). As sheriff of Gloucestershire Marshal collected as many debts owed to the crown as possible and used these to pay his men (PR 5 Richard I 119-20). On expectations of the payments to the exchequer at Michaelmas, Marshal borrowed from the abbot of St. Augustine of Bristol and from several Jews to cover the costs of the men needed to subdue John (PR 5 Richard I

118-20, 148). Marshal also used about one hundred and twenty pounds of his own revenues which was later reduced from the fine he owed for the honour of Giffard. Painter says that these lessons in the means of meeting financial emergencies would serve Marshal well a decade later (Marshal 98). Timely fate played a hand in this potential disaster when messengers arrived at the beseigers camp with the news that Richard would be released for a ransom of one hundred thousand marks (*Houedene* iii 205). With Richard alive and the possibility of his return, John became a negligible factor which needed to be resolved quickly in order to devote time to raising the ransom for Richard.

In November 1193 a truce was concluded with the aid of Queen Eleanor. Eleanor would be given the castles of Windsor, Wallingford, and the Peak to hold until the expiration of the truce. Nottingham and Tickhill were to be left to count John, much to the dismay of Hugh of Durham who had almost totally reduced the castle of Tickhill (*Houedene* iii 207-08; PR 5 Richard I xxi). The justiciar, Walter, had to set about collecting the one hundred thousand marks ransom demanded for the release of Richard. According to Devizes, Eleanor was responsible for seeing that the ransom for Richard was raised and that his kingdom was defended (Richard of Devizes intro. xvi, 58-63; *Houedene* iii 210, 212). One pound from each knights' fee was levied as the customary aid due from all of Richard's vassals; a quarter of everyman's yearly income was levied by the government; and monastic establishments were ordered to give a year's crop of wool as well as the gold and silver in church treasuries (*Houedene* iii 210-11; Gervase i 519). William Marshal contributed so generously to the aid for Richard's ransom that Richard, on his return to England, gave the see of Exeter to Marshal's brother Henry (*Hist* 10000-0008).

As Walter de Coutances and Queen Eleanor set out for Cologne to meet Richard, Hubert Walter, archbishop of Canterbury, was made justiciar of England (*Houedene* iii 203, 210, 212, 226). John was in France, but in February, Hubert's agents intercepted a message from John indicating that he was planning to resist Richard's return. Hubert summoned a council in England and ordered the confiscation of all of John's lands and castles. Hubert laid siege to Marlborough, Hugh of Durham returned to attack Tickhill, and the earls of Huntingdon, Chester, and Derby invested Nottingham (*Houedene* iii 236-37). Marshal seized the town of Bristol and some of John's property in Dorsetshire and Somersetshire (PR 6 Richard I 194, 241). Meanwhile, Eleanor was at Cologne by January 6, 1194, Mainz on February 2 and by March 13, 1194, Richard and Queen Eleanor finally returned to England (Chron. Reign Richard I ii 82, 86, 89, 91).

When Richard landed in England on March 13, 1194, Marshal was at his castle of Striguil. Marshal learned of Richard's safe arrival at the same time he learned of the death of his own brother John Marshal (*Hist* 10018-0048). John was sheriff of Sussex when he died and held the hereditary office of marshal of England (PR 4 Richard I 204; Red Book of Exchequer 812, 759; Round Commune of London 82-90). With John Marshal's death, William became the head of the Marshal family and his brother's heir (*Chart* 47; *CRR* i 50). The manors of Wexcombe and Bedwin in Wiltshire were held in fee farm by John and his heirs granted by Richard I in 1189, and these went to William Marshal because John Marshal had no male heir. The manor of Spleen in Berkshire had been given to John Marshal on his marriage from his father-in-law Adam de Port (PR 2 Richard I 121). In Worcestershire, John held the manor of Inkberrow as fief of the bishop of Hereford who in turn held it of the bishop of Worcester; this fief dated back to John fitz Gilbert (Cal. Pat. Rolls 1354-1358 197; Cal. Chart. Rolls 1327-1341 337). Upleden in Herefordshire belonged to John. Tidworth in Wiltshire was held by sergeanty of the office of marshal by John fitz Gilbert and William, and the manor of Hampstead in Berkshire may have been held by the same office (Red Book of Exchequer 487; *Liber Feodorum* 100, 298). Bosham manor in Sussex belonged to the office of marshal and had been held by John Marshal; it was confirmed to William Marshal as part of his inherited office as marshal of England by John in 1200 (Salter, Newington Longueville 15, 14 f 1). The manor of Mildenhall in Wiltshire originally was held by Patrick earl of Salisbury of the abbey of Glastonbury and later was held by Marshal as simply a fief, but not of Glastonbury Abbey (*Liber Feodorum* 748).

On notice of John's death, Marshal sent knights from his own household to escort John's body to the abbey at Cirencester where Marshal met them for the funeral ceremony. After the ceremony, Marshal left three of his knights to accompany his brother's body to Bradenstoke Priory where it was buried, and Marshal himself hurried to meet Richard at Huntingdon. Richard was on his way to reduce John's last castle at Nottingham (*Hist* 10049-0112).

On March 28, 1194, Nottingham castle fell to Richard, and two days later Richard called a council of the ecclesiastic and baronial leaders of England. Eleanor was with Richard at the council and may have helped prevent John from being tried for treason (*Houedene* iii 232, 236-38, 241). Once again Richard was in desperate need of money to pay off the remaining fifty thousand marks for his ransom and to help finance his coming campaign against Philip in France (*Houedene iii* 240). Unfortunately, Longchamp had returned with Richard, and this new process of selling offices to gain money caught some of Longchamp's enemies in its grip. Geoffrey fitz Peter lost the shrievalties of Essex, Hertfordshire, and Northamptonshire; William Brewer lost the shrievalty of Oxfordshire, and Marshal lost the shrievalty of Gloucestershire (PR 6 Richard I 28, 68, 88, 231). Marshal did receive the promise of the shrievalty of Sussex as his brother's heir (PR 6 Richard I 226).

According to the *Histoire*, Longchamp tried once again to reduce Marshal's status by convincing Richard that he should try to get the Irish barons to do homage to Richard for the lands they held in Ireland of count John as lord of Ireland. Walter de Lacy, lord of Meath, did swear homage to Richard for his lordship of Meath, but Marshal refused. Marshal replied to Longchamp:

> I shall never be a sycophant. I tell you that if any man should wish to take Ireland, I would support to the best of my ability my liege lord whose man I am. I have loyally served our lord the king for the land I hold from him, and I fear nothing (*Hist* 10289-0340).

Marshal knew that he held his lands in Ireland as tenant-in-chief of John as lord of Ireland and not of Richard. These lands had been granted to Isabel de Clare's father as a lordship held directly of King Henry II. When Henry II gave Ireland to John in 1177, all who held land in Ireland before and after 1177 held their lands as vassals of John as lord of Ireland. Ireland did not belong to Richard; it was not part of his inheritance, not granted to Richard by his father, King Henry II, and therefore not part of the English crown.

Ireland had not been a part of Henry II's inherited or "in right of his wife" domains; Ireland had become Henry II's by the sword of Richard Strongbow de Clare and other Anglo-Norman barons who had invaded Ireland in 1169/1170 at Dermot's request. As an acquired land instead of a patrimony, Ireland was free to be granted to whomever Henry II chose, and he chose John "lackland." Richard held Aquitaine as his mother's designated choice and heir. John had no claim to Aquitaine as long as Eleanor was alive and until and unless she chose to grant it to him or until both Eleanor and Richard were dead. From the point of a vassal and the homage due to his lord, the lands Marshal held in right of his wife were divided. The lordship of Leinster and the English fief of Cartmel were held of Prince John who was lord of Ireland and the holder of the honour of Lancastershire. For these, Marshal's homage and fealty were due to John in all things "save rebellion against the king"; the difference between the two was that Ireland was held totally and completely of John and not part of the Crown's lands. Cartmel was part of England and therefore part of the English Crown's lands, Marshal would support John there only as long as John was not in rebellion against Richard and the Crown of England.

Marshal viewed all the lands he held, both his and those in right of his wife, as one single group of lands which were to be protected, preserved, increased, and passed down to the children of Marshal and Isabel. This was the primary goal and purpose of any medieval baron and lord; his duty was to insure that the patrimony, titles, lands, vassals, castles, power, and status were there to be handed to the next generation. Marshal's generation was composed of sons and daughters whose fathers had paid in blood and with the sword for what they held and passed to their children, and Marshal and his own children would still be doing the same in some instances. Children were married to increase and secure holdings that their parents already held, but they were also married to provide the power of vassals and swords to protect both what they held and what they might acquire. This was a world primarily still based on the power, skill, and acumen of a military elite; it protected and defended the individual and his own lands as well as the kingdom as a whole.

From May 1194 to Richard's death in 1199, the story of Marshal's life is more a series of incidents and events than a continuous tale. Richard returned to Normandy in May 1194, but it is not known for certain when Marshal arrived there. John came to Richard and Queen Eleanor in Normandy in May 1194 and made his peace with Richard (Chron. Reign Richard I ii 93-94). It is known from Marshal's Sussex accounts that two ships were provided to take Marshal and his men to Normandy; this proves Marshal was in Normandy with Richard by July (PR 6 Richard I 226). In early July, Richard was at Vendome while Philip was at Freteval. When Philip did not advance upon Richard and his troops as he had told Richard he would, Richard advanced toward Philip. Discovering that Philip was withdrawing his army, Richard decided to pursue him, but he commanded Marshal to hold together his men where they were in case the French should turn and fight (*Houedene* iii 253-55). While Richard and his men took great plunder from Philip's treasury and equipment, Marshal remained with his men until Richard and all of his men had returned from their pursuit of the French (*Houedene* iii 256; *Hist* 10632-0662). Even at the age of forty-seven, Marshal as a warrior would have found it hard to stay back and take no part in a pursuit and the chance for gain of spoils of war, but stay he did and kept his men there ready and able to provide a reserve force of men should the occasion arise. According to Painter, this is visible and factual proof that Marshal was not only an extraordinary knight but also a leader who held the respect and trust of the men who served under his command (Marshal 110). Marshal was not simply a warrior; he was a loyal and skilled commander of warriors.

The next recorded event of note in Marshal's life occurred at Milli castle near Beauvais. Richard had led a force from Gournay in May 1197 to attack the castle. Richard's men had used ladders to reach the top of the castle walls and overcome the defenders; however, the defenders had pushed the ladders away from the walls, throwing Richard's knights to the ground. Unfortunately, a Flemish knight, Guy de la Bruyere, was caught by his neck with a fork and held dangling from the top of the castle's wall. Marshal, seeing the predicament of the knight, left his position as director of the attack, leaped the moat, climbed the bank, and mounted a ladder with sword in his hand. Apparently Marshal attacked the defenders holding Bruyere so ferociously that he found himself in sole possession of that section of the castle wall. Richard's men seeing Marshal on the wall renewed the attack and charged once more up the walls. Meanwhile, Marshal was seen and attacked by the constable of Milli castle, but Marshal with one blow of his sword cut through the constable's helmet all the way to his scalp. The constable fell to the parapet apparently unconscious. Justifiably feeling he had done his own part in the attack, Marshal sat down on top of the constable and waited for the rest of Richard's men to finish taking the castle. When Marshal presented the constable to Richard as his due as king, Richard reproved Marshal for forgetting his rank and his already established prowess. Richard informed Marshal that even if the constable had been worth a hundred times more in ransom, he would have still been given to Marshal rather than kept by Richard (*Hist* 11205-1264). Marshal exhibits the adage followed by the most gifted of military leaders, "a true commander of a fighting force leads from the front, not the rear." Here was an almost fifty-year-old knight, fully armoured with helmet, hauberk, shield, and sword, climbing a ladder tall enough to reach the top of a castle wall, and then proceeding to fight and defeat the younger fresher knights on that section of the wall! What a feat that must have been to have witnessed!

In January 1199 Pope Innocent III sent his legate Peter of Capua to arrange a truce between Philip and Richard. Peter met Richard near Vernon, and Richard agreed to a truce for five years with Philip holding the castles that were currently in his possession, but giving up all lands that had formed a part of the Angevin domains (Wendover, Giles ii 176*)*. Richard was furious at losing any of his castles to Philip, but Marshal persuaded Richard that the truce was to his advantage since any castles that Philip held in Angevin lands would have to be supplied from France with great cost to Philip (*Hist* 11655-1688).

During these five years serving with Richard in Normandy, Marshal made several trips to England. At Michaelmas 1194, Marshal was there to answer for his county of Sussex and close his accounts as sheriff of Gloucester (PR 6 Richard I 226, 231). However, Marshal retained the custody of the forest of Dean (PR 6 Richard I 239). Marshal was in England on at least two other occasions, once in the spring of 1196 and once in the autumn of 1198 (PR 6 Richard I 110; Feet of Fines 176).

By two charters, one issued in 1196 by Henry of Longueville and witnessed by Marshal, and one issued by Marshal himself at Meullers near Dieppe in 1198, it is possible to identify some of Marshal's *mesnie* (Salter <u>Newington-Longueville Charters</u> 54; *Recueil des actes de Henry II* intro., 493-94). John Marshal was a bastard son of one of William Marshal's brothers. Nicholas Avenel held land in Striguil and was William's deputy sheriff of Gloucester. Hugh de Sanford was a vassal of the honor of Giffard; and John d'Erleigh (Erley) had been Marshal's squire since 1188 and was now a knight of Marshal's household. A charter issued in 1199/1200 for the priory of Longueville was issued with the consent and the seal of Marshal's wife Isabel, proving that Marshal had taken Isabel with him to Normandy (<u>Cal. Doc. France</u> 79 #239).

In March 1199 Richard, Count John, Robert earl of Leicester, Marshal, William de Braose, and other knights were in the valley of the Loire. A messenger arrived for Richard telling him of a treasure found by one of the vassals of Aimar, viscount of Limoges. Aimar was sending Richard a gilded shield decorated with several golden figures as his share of the treasure found on the land of the lord of Chalus (*Houedene* iv 82). Richard decided that he wanted the whole treasure and took some of his knights and his mercenaries to besiege the castle of Chalus. While Richard was before the walls of the castle, he was hit by a bolt from a crossbow of one of the defenders of the castle. Marshal was at Vaudreuil on April the seventh with Hubert Walter, Archbishop of Canterbury, and others when a courier arrived bearing the news that Richard had been seriously wounded at Chalus. Marshal was ordered to take command of the Tower of Rouen where the state treasury of

Normandy was lodged (*Hist* 11791-1805). Marshal and Hubert left for Rouen where Marshal occupied the Tower, and Hubert went to the priory of Notre Dame de Pre across the river Seine (*Hist* 11844-1845). Queen Eleanor had been at Fontevrault when news reached her of Richard's injury, and she left immedediately for Chalus. By the time she arrived, there was no hope for Richard Lionheart, and he died on April 6, 1199.

The *Histoire* records a conversation between Marshal and Hubert Walter about the successor to Richard on the evening of April 10, 1199, when Marshal received the news that Richard had died (*Hist* 11804-1805, 11855-1908). The claimants to Richard's throne were Arthur, the son of Richard's next brother Geoffrey count of Brittany, born after Geoffrey's death, and John, the youngest and last living brother of Richard. There were two major questions confronting Marshal and Hubert. Who was the rightful heir to the Angevin domains? Who would make the least satisfactory king? Hubert thought that Arthur was the rightful heir as the son of the oldest younger brother of Richard. Marshal believed that John was the closer and more rightful heir as the son of Henry II, and not Arthur who was Henry's grandson. The choice of the next king was between the lesser of two evils, the devil or the deep blue sea. John had proved that he had neither honour nor loyalty; he had deserted his father Henry II at the last hour, and he had tried at least three times to usurp Richard's throne while Richard was on crusade and being held for ransom. John was a known entity to the barons and knights of the Angevin Empire, and he was a grown man of thirty-two. Arthur was a child of twelve, raised by his mother, Constance of Brittany, whom contemporary chroniclers describe as a woman who

164

hated the Plantagenets and all things English. Arthur had been raised from 1196 with Louis, son of Philip of France. Given such a choice, John looked to be less unsatisfactory than Arthur, but Hubert warned Marshal that one day he would rue his support of John. Eleanor supported John not because he was her son, but because she chose the welfare of the Angevin lands against a possible destruction of all that she and Henry II had built at the hands of Philip of France.

VIII. William Marshal and King John

John was in Brittany on April 10, 1199, visiting his nephew Arthur, and Marshal decided that word must be sent to the justiciar, Geoffrey fitz Peter, in England. Marshal sent John d'Erley to notify Geoffrey fitz Peter that Richard was dead and that he had chosen John as his heir (*Hist* 11909-1916). William and Archbishop Hubert Walter stayed in Rouen waiting for John to tell them what he wished for them to do (*Hist* 11917-1918). John ordered them to England while he himself proceeded to Chinon to secure the Angevin treasury (*Houedene* iv 86-87).

When Marshal and Walter reached England, they joined with the justiciar to notify all the magnates that they must swear allegiance to John as Richard's heir. Because there was a group of barons who saw this as an opportunity to force John to "buy" their allegiance, Marshal, archbishop Walter, and Geoffrey fitz Peter met with them at Northhampton. Some of the most important of these men were David, earl of Huntingdon and brother to William king of Scotland, Richard de Clare earl of Hertford, Ranulf earl of Chester, William de Ferrers earl of Derby, Waleran earl of Warwick, and Roger de Lacy, constable of Chester castle. Each of these men had claims or issues of lands, castles, and/or titles that dated back to King Henry II, and they saw this as a chance to resolve them by bargaining with John on the basis of their support or nonsupport of John's claim to the Crown. Apparently they were satisfied by the assurance of John's representatives at Northhampton that John would see that each man received whatever privileges or rights that he was entitled to receive (*Houedene* iv 86-88). They swore the oath of allegiance to John on the understanding that John would consider their demands once he arrived in England (*Houedene iv* 89).

Meanwhile on the continent, Arthur and his mother Constance had taken Angers, and the barons of Anjou, Maine, and Touraine had accepted Arthur as their sovereign. On the Monday after Easter, Philip and Arthur took Le Mans, and Arthur swore homage to Philip for Anjou, Maine, and Touraine. The opposition now had the capitals of Anjou and Maine in their hands. John was proclaimed duke of Normandy on April 25 in Rouen, but it was Eleanor who took the first physical steps to ensure John's inheritance. Eleanor, from her position at Fontevrault, called Richard's mercenary captain, Mercadier, and his army of *routiers* from Chalus to her. Despite her age of over seventy, Eleanor led this army and retook Angers; Arthur and Constance and their men fled back to Le Mans. John gathered his own army and marched on Le Mans, but Arthur and his mother had fled before John arrived (*Houedene* iv 88; Strickland War and Chivalry 266-67, 285-87). Once Le Mans was secure, John returned to Normandy and was met by Marshal at Dieppe on May 21, 1199. Leaving Eleanor and Mercadier in charge of Anjou and Maine, John and Marshal returned to England (Cal. Doc. France #112).

John was crowned king of England on May 27, 1199, at Westminster in a ceremony much less grand than Richard's, possibly because his mother, Eleanor, was still in Normandy trying to secure his inheritance (Meade Eleanor of Aquitaine 334-35). At John's coronation, he granted Marshal comital status by girding him with the comptal sword and making Marshal Earl of Pembroke (*Houedene* iv 90). In essence the title merely increased Marshal's social status, making him an official member of the upper ruling class; in reality Marshal had had the power and the status since he married Isabel de Clare and become a *familiaris Regis* of Richard I. John also appointed Marshal sheriff of Gloucestershire, gave him custody of the castles of Gloucester and Bristol, and confirmed Marshal's shrievalty of Sussex, custody of Chichester castle, and custody of the forest of Dean (PR 1 John 124-25; *Claus* i 54, 68; *Liberate 27*).

Eleanor once again proved that, like Elizabeth I, she might have the body of a woman but she possessed the heart and intelligence of a king. Knowing that John could likely lose Anjou, Touraine, and Maine, she determined that he would not lose her patrimony of Aquitaine. Beginning the end of April she started a tour of her lands from the border of Anjou to the edge of Spain. On April 29 she was at Loudon, by May 4 at Poitiers, then on to Niort and La Rochelle, and by July 1 and 4 she had been in Bordeaux and Soulac. Eleanor, being a shrewd politician, visited her lands as duchess of Aquitaine and realized that the only means of securing the support of her people for John lay in judicious grants. By using castles, tithes, and privileges from her own ducal inheritance, she managed to obtain the support of barons, abbots, and castellans. Eleanor was aware of the new importance of towns, cities, and their burghers and artisans, and her grants during this time reflect that acute understanding. These charters issued by Queen Eleanor are not issued under a delegated power, nor do they require the confirmation by any other (Richardson "The Letters and Charters of Eleanor of Aquitaine" 206). These charters were issued between April and August 1199 and contain the charters which granted Poitiers its charter of freedom and release from local lords and confirmed or granted franchises and/or corporation status to La Rochelle (Cal. Doc. France #1248, #1307, #1304, #1096; *Foedera* i 52). With Eleanor releasing the men of the towns from their feudal obligations to local lords and giving them charters of independence and corporation, Eleanor gave the towns the means and the responsibility for defending and preserving themselves and their rights. Eleanor's tour through her lands and her charters and grants of this time not only removed some of the potential problems for John but also greatly helped to stabilize a large portion of the Angevin continental lands.

In July 1199 Eleanor met King Philip at Tours and personally did homage for Aquitaine which Eleanor held herself by hereditary right. This event is not recorded in any English chronicles, but it was an act that inherently contained great political and legal ramifications. By this act Eleanor countered any claims that Arthur might hope to make for her lands as Richard's heir and thwarted any action that Philip might hope to take in order to obtain them (Powicke Loss of Normandy 195-97; Martingdale "Eleanor of Aquitaine" 156-57). There was a second part to this strategic move and because this was a subtle and deft action, it is most likely that it was Eleanor's plan. Two months after Eleanor gave homage to Philip, she and John came to a written agreement. Eleanor asserted that John was her rightful heir to all her hereditary lands; she accepted John's homage and transferred the fealty, homage, and service due her from her lands to John as king and liege. John's agreement stated that he had done homage to Eleanor, but that she was "the lady to us and all our lands and possessions" and that "except for the salvation of our souls, neither party would give away anything without the consent of the other" (*Chart* 30,

31; *Foedera* i 113). These actions were a masterful use of law and custom in an effort to forestall Philip from any legal attempt to take the Angevin continental lands. It presupposes that Eleanor was the rightful and legal holder of Aquitaine and that she had the right to designate her own successor. As lady of King John's lands and possessions Eleanor had done homage to Philip for her lands; therefore, Philip could demand of Eleanor service, but not from John. This was a brillant legal maneuver worthy of de Glanville, but it would prove to be only a temporary deterrent to Philip, who had no regard for legality when it stood in the way of what he desired.

In August 1199 John was reminded of Richard's talk of a family alliance between the Plantagenet and Capet house. In January 1200 John and Philip concluded the Treaty of Le Goulet which set up a five year truce. John was recognized by Philip as Richard's heir for the Plantagent lands on the continent; John did homage to Philip as John's overlord for those lands and paid Philip twenty thousand marks of silver for *seisin*. Philip relinquished his own claims to Maine and Anjou in Arthur's name, and agreed that Arthur should do homage to John for his land of Brittany (Painter Marshal 126). Philip acquired the Norman Vexin, except the area around Les Andelys, the city of Evreux, and half the land. Eleanor left for Spain to see her daughter Eleanor II, wife of Alphonse VIII of Castile, and to obtain her granddaughter to marry the son and heir of Philip Augustus. Eleanor and the third daughter of Eleanor II and Alphonse VIII, Blanche, arrived in Bordeaux by Easter 1200. On May 23, 1200, at Portmort in Normandy, Blanche the granddaughter of Queen Eleanor of Aquitaine and King Henry II married Louis Capet, son of Philip Augustus King of France and Isabella of Hainault. Eleanor retired to Fontevrault thinking that she had managed to obtain a period of peace between the Capet and Plantagenet kings.

John, who had become a bachelor again with the annulment of his marriage to Isabelle of Gloucester, decided to take a tour of Aquitaine in the summer of this year. It was in Poitou in July 1200 that John took the first step in losing the continental possessions that his mother and father had fought so hard to defend and preserve. Poitou had always been a turbulent land with constant war between the counts of Angouleme and the lords of Lusignan. Richard had controlled them by force and subjugation, but John managed to undo all that by his ill-advised actions. Isabella, daughter and heiress of Aymer of Angouleme, was betrothed to the son of Hugh de Lusignan count of Le Marche. John proceeded to fall in lust with the young Isabella. While John, Aymer, and Isabella were at Lusignan, John made an offer for Aymer's daughter to be his wife. Aymer immediately removed Isabella from the Lusignan household and returned with her to Angouleme. This violated feudal law and custom; John had actually stolen a betrothed young girl from John's own vassal. John and Isabella were married August 24, 1200, at Angouleme and then left for Chinon. In October 1200 John returned to England with his new bride and stayed there until June 1201. John came back to Normandy in June, met Philip at Gaillard, and then John and Isabella made a state visit to Paris. Philip and John reached a compromise on the Lusignan question with Philip agreeing to not press the Lusignan appeal for redress against John if John would agree to give them a chance to submit their just grievances at a formal trial (Powicke Loss of Normandy chapt. iv).

In March 1202 Pope Innocent III legalized Philip's daughter and son by

Agnes of Meran as heirs to the house of Capet. With this church issue resolved, Philip ordered John, as duke of Aquitaine, to appear before Philip's feudal court on April 28, 1202. John had seized the lands of the Lusignans in the spring of 1201 and had refused to give them a proper hearing in John's court as duke of Normandy. The Lusignans had appealed to Philip as John's feudal lord for John's continental possessions. John refused to appear, and Philip declared John contumacious, deprived him of the lands he held of the French crown, and began the war to conquer Normandy from John.

The part of Normandy that lay north of the river Seine was protected in the northeast by a line of castles some twenty miles within the Norman border. These castles were Arques, Drincourt, and Gournay; the land that lay between Gournay castle and the Seine River was protected by the castle of Lyons (the French held the great castle of Gisors), and the valley of the Seine was protected by Richard's great castle of Gaillard. In April 1202 John tried to take the lands of Eu from Ralph of Exoudon, a Lusignan brother who held Eu in right of his wife. Ralph with the help of the count of Boulogne overran the land between the Bresle and Bethune rivers and recovered his castles of Eu and Drincourt (*Pat* 8b, 9b). John ordered Marshal to take the Norman possessions of the count of Boulogne and the castle of Lillibonne (*Pat* 9b). At John's directions, Marshal divided these lands among the Norman barons who had lost lands to the French (*Rotuli Normanniae* 45). Marshal himself kept Lillibonne castle until June; then he gave it to Earl William de Warenne who had lost his Norman lands to the count of Boulogne (*Pat* 47).

Marshal held the Pays de Caux area including Lyons and the castle of Arques that protected the access to Dieppe (*Rotuli Normanniae* 23, 35). This was the main line of defense of Normandy, and command of this region was a great responsibility. In April 1202 Marshal received letters patent dated April 25, 1202, at Les Andelys that orderd the inhabitants of Arques and Caus to obey Marshal as the king's representative (*Pat* 9b). On April 26 Marshal received money from the Exchequer to provision the castle of Arques and strengthen its garrison, and a month later Marshal was given one hundred marks to further strengthen the knights and sergeants at Arques ("Misc. Rec. Norman Exchequer." 67). At the end of May, Marshal received one hundred fifty marks to pay the troops there ("Misc. Rec. Norman Exchequer" 67). Between June 3 and 28, 1202, Marshal received and distributed over one thousand six hundred pounds Angevin for improving the fortifications and paying the garrison of Arques. The castle itself was commanded by William de Mortimer and William Martel as Marshal's constables while Marshal himself was the commander of the entire area ("Misc. Rec. Norman Exchequer" 67; *Hist* 12052-2054).

In July 1202 Philip had taken Gournay and marched against Arques. John ordered the barons of the Cinque Ports to prevent Philip from getting supplies from the sea and sent Marshal another four hundred pounds for the garrison of Arques (*Pat* 15; "Misc. Rec. Norman Exchequer" 67). While William de Mortimer defended Arques, Marshal, William Longespee, earl of Salisbury, and William de Warenne harassed the French besiegers (*Hist* 12119-2132).

While Marshal was defending the Arques area from Philip, John had gone to Le Mans to watch Arthur. Here John learned that Arthur had taken his army and was besieging Queen Eleanor at Mirabeau. John, in one of his rare bursts of speed, swept from Le Mans to Mirabeau and captured and/or destroyed Arthur's entire army. In one sweep, John had captured Arthur and two of the de Lusignan brothers as well as a good portion of the rebelling nobility. Philip, learning of the defeat of Arthur, raised the siege of Arques and left. Marshal, William Longspee, and William de Warenne decided to watch the French army leave with some of their cavalry. Not intending to fight they had ridden out without their helmets and hauberks and were seen by Philip. Philip knew that they were too few to offer him battle and decided that the three earls would make good bargaining chips to trade with John for the prisoners taken at Mirabeau. Philip sent William des Barres and three hundred knights to capture the earls and their party, but William and his lightly armed group outran the French and headed to Rouen with their troops (*Hist* 12132-2398).

Here another event in Marshal's life is recorded in the *Histoire* that illustrates the customs and laws of feudal time. As Marshal, Longespee, and de Warenne approached the city of Rouen, the citizens were alarmed by the arrival of the three earls and feared that the French were not far behind. Marshal, knowing that the privileges of the city prevented Marshal from demanding the city entertain his men, told the burghers that since he knew the French were near, he and his men had come to see the city safe. The grateful city then provided Marshal and his men the best of food and wine. The earls and their men were "given wines clear and sparkling, sweet and dry, and spiced wines; they were given pears, apples and nuts for dessert" (*Hist* 12398-2400).

Meanwhile, John was once again making every conceivable mistake that a feudal king and lord could make with regard to the men he had captured at Mirabeau.

John had taken Mirabeau on August 1, 1202, with the aid of William des Roches, seneschal of Anjou. William had made an agreement with John that none of the rebels would be put to death, that the captured would not be removed from the county until a truce was established, and that des Roches would be the final judge of the disposition of Arthur. John in a letter to his English barons told them that he had captured Arthur, Geoffrey de Lusignan, Hugh de Lusignan, Andrew de Chauvigni, the viscount of Chatellerault, Raymond of Thours, Savary de Mauleon, Hugh Bauge, and other knights numbering up to two hundred (Wendover, Giles ii 204-05; *Pat* x). John then had the prisoners put in chains and taken by carts to various castles. Hugh de Lusignan, the former fiance of Isabella of Angouleme, was taken to a tower in Caen; others were shipped to the castle of Corfe in England, and Arthur was put in a dungeon at Falaise (Wendover, Giles ii 204-05; *Coggeshall* 137-39; *Histoire des ducs* 94-96). Eleanor, sister to Arthur, was also taken at Mirabeau and put in Corfe Castle, and later Bristol Castle, where she spent the rest of her life (*Claus* xxxv, 144, 150, 157, 168, 466). From the Pipe Roll for the fourth year of John, we know that some prisoners were sent to London, York, Newcastle-on-Tyne, Lancaster, Corfe, Wallingford, Sherburn, the Peak, Nottingham, and Ipswich (xv, xvi, 79, 284, 68, 48, 85, 187, 144, 104). One of John's greater mistakes was his betrayal of William des Roches who had helped John take Mirabeau and had helped maintain John's control of Anjou and Touraine. William believed that Arthur was the rightful heir to Anjou and Touraine. John had made des Roches seneschal of Anjou and had promised to heed des Roches' advice with regard to those regions and to the disposition of Arthur. By his handling of the prisoners of Mirabeau, especially Arthur, John lost des Roches who went to Philip's side and proved a formidable foe to John.

John's treatment of the prisoners from the battle at Mirabeau was so insulting and so brutal that it was perceived by all as such (Strickland War and Chivalry 197). The *Histoire* states that the treatment of men held at Chinon was so horrible that it brought shame on the men who assisted John in this (12507-2512). The *Annals of Margam* states that twenty-two prisoners held at Corfe were starved to death (i 26; *Pat* 24, 33b). The capture of Arthur by John was to prove to be one of the greatest disasters of John's reign. Had John been his father or his brother Richard, he would have known that a free Arthur as count of Brittany could have been controlled and contained. As a prisoner, unseen and unheard, Arthur became the rallying point and focus of war and rebellion for not only King Philip of France, but also the nobles and knights of Touraine and Anjou.

John spent Christmas 1202 at Caen, and in January he went to Falaise to see Arthur. Wendover says that John tried to make peace with his nephew by offering him many honours if Arthur would separate himself from Philip of France and give fealty and homage to John as heir to Richard and king. Arthur apparently answered John by demanding that John give up England and all the Angevin possessions on the continent to him as Arthur was the rightful heir to Richard, and that as long as Arthur lived he would fight John (Wendover, Giles ii 205). According to Coggeshall, John ordered that Arthur be castrated and blinded, but Hubert de Burgh countermanded that order and put out word that Arthur had died. This news raised an outcry and war threats from Arthur's supporters, and de Burgh immediately swore that Arthur was still alive and healthy which was not believed by those same supporters (*Coggeshall* 140-41). In February or March 1203 John ordered Arthur removed to a new tower at Rouen and kept in close confinement (<u>Wendover</u>, Giles ii 205). John lacked honour, finesse, and political acumen; when he should have acted with honour with regard to the knights taken at Mirabeau, he treated them with disdain and cruelty, and when he failed to honour his oath to William des Roches who had gained Poitou, Maine, Anjou, and Mirabeau for him, John himself lost his strongest and best ally and best chance to save his continental lands. Both des Roches and Amaury of Thouars turned from John and gave their allegiance to Philip of France.

The fate of Arthur once he disappeared into the tower at Rouen was to plague John the rest of his life and prove to be a constant incentive to all those barons who saw him as an untrustworthy lord and king. Not without justification did rumors and tales circulate as to Arthur's fate. One source that deals with the fate of Arthur is the *Annals of Margam*. Margam Abbey was a Cistercian abbey supported by the de Braose family, and William de Braose had custody of the castle of Rouen where Arthur had been sent. Margam Abbey was supported by de Braose, and it is assumed that the story of Arthur's fate came to the chronicles of Margam Abbey via William de Braose while in exile in France in 1211. The Margam chronicle states that on the Thursday before Easter, April 3, 1203, John got drunk, killed Arthur, and threw his body into the Seine with a stone tied to it. The body was found in a fisherman's net; they recognized Arthur, and the monks of Saint Mary of the Meadow buried the body (*Ann Mon i* 27).

John was at Moulineaux on April the first and second, from the third to the seventh he was at Rouen, back at Moulineaux on the seventh and the eighth, and back in Rouen on the night of the eighth. William de Braose was with John the entire time; the justiciar, Geoffrey fitz Peter, joined them on the second at Moulineaux. Arthur disappeared on April 3, 1203 (*Rotuli Normanniae* 85-87).

Though some historians have implied that Marshal might have known of Arthur's fate, of all things that Marshal might have condoned or excused in time of war, the killing of a young man who was grandson of King Henry II, nephew to King John, and a helpless prisoner at that time would not be one. The laws and customs of knighthood and feudalism defined the act of murder of a noble prisoner as unthinkable and heinous. Marshal would have had no part in this insane act of John. All that Marshal was as a man and a knight would have been repulsed by the act of killing a young, defenseless man and been horrified by an act of killing one who was a grandchild of King Henry II. Marshal had been in the young Henry's household in 1170/1171 and in Normandy, and he had seen the reaction of the nobility on the continent to the murder of Thomas Becket. Marshal would have had no illusions about how the nobles would react to an act of murder committed against Arthur of Brittany. Even the *Histoire* makes no effort to hide the contempt and dislike Marshal had for King John; Marshal had spent enough time with and around Eleanor of Aquitaine to know the realities of power with regard to the continental domains of the Angevins. Marshal was never seen by his contemporaries as one of John's men, and if he had ever been anyone's man besides his own, he would have been Queen Eleanor's. More to the point, had there been any rumor or taint of suspicion of Marshal having been involved with the murder of Arthur of Brittany, it would have been known then and would have definitely prohibited Marshal from ever being trusted as negotiator later during the time of the baronial rebellion and still later being elected as regent for John's son.

While John seemed to be merely spending time at Rouen with his new bride; the Angevin lands and barons were falling to Philip of France. Hugh of Gournay and Peter of Meulan had gone over to Philip in April/May of 1203 (Robert of Torigny 342; *Rotuli Normanniae* 89, 92, 93). Philip took Domfort, Le Mans, Falaise, Bayeux, Lisieux, Caen, and Avranches (Wendover, Giles *ii 206-07)*. In June Philip had set his sights on the castle of Vaudreuil which would have left only Pont de l'Arche and Roche Orival between Philip and John who was at Rouen. The garrison was commanded by Robert fitz Walter and Saher de Quinci and had been provisioned and paid in February. John had moved his army to Roche Orival and sent messages to speed up the supplies to the castle (Robert of Torigny 342; *Rotuli Normanniae* 69, 74, 80-82; Pat 30a, 31b). Then suddenly with no warning and not a single arrow shot or a single stone catapulted, the garrison surrendered to Philip. By August Philip had laid siege to the town of Andeli at the foot of Chateau-Gaillard which was commanded by Roger de Lacy, constable of Chester. John mustered enough energy to try to relieve Gaillard with a night convoy up the river and by land, but they miscalculated the tides in the Seine and arrived at different times and were beaten back (William le Breton *Gesta Phillippi Augusti* 213-16). There was little left that John held on the continent but Rouen, Aruqes, Gaillard, and the Norman shores of the Channel. On December 5, 1203, John left for England with Marshal, the earl of Arundel, Robert of Vieuxpont, William de Braose, Baldwin of Bethune, Thomas

Basset, Warin Fitzgerald, the bishop of Norwich, and others (Cal. Doc. France #545, p 304; *Historie des ducs* 97; *Pat.* 36b). Queen Eleanor remained on the continent and was in all probablility at Poitiers. Thus all the players were positioned at the beginning of 1204.

There are no records of Eleanor for the last few months of her life, and it is not even certain whether she died at Fontrevault or Poitiers. What is known is that Eleanor of Aquitaine, who had been ill for several months, died on April 1, 1204, and was buried at Fontrevault Abbey where she had often gone for respite and had been a generous benefactor. One wonders what she thought of the events of the past three years. This intelligent, beautiful, and feisty woman had lived, fought, and survived for more than eighty years, had married two kings, and had given birth to three kings. Eleanor had brought to Henry II huge fiefs with lands, castles, and vassals greater than the king of France held. Eleanor had loved, fought with and against Henry II, and in the end, she had used all her power, intelligence, and political acumen to preserve that which she and Henry had inherited and acquired. Eleanor had to have known her son John; she had to have recognized all the inherent faults and traits that John carried. With no records to guide the modern day reader, one cannot know if Eleanor foresaw the eventual destruction of the Angevin empire. But, one can assume that seeing John lose so much of the Norman lands that had been held by Henry II, Richard I, and Eleanor herself must have grieved Eleanor of Aquitaine beyond repair. While Eleanor might have made errors in judgment with regard to her husbands, she had proved while Richard was on crusade and in captivity that she could wield power and rule a kingdom as well as any man.

History can view with a cautious eye the aspersions cast upon Eleanor by the clerical chronicles and honestly acknowledge the phenomenal accomplishments of an extraordinary and rare woman and evaluate her by her own time and place.

After his return to England, John held a council at Oxford in January 1204; John taxed his barons two and a half marks for every knight that they owed for service, and he fined every tenant-in-chief four to seven marks if he wished to be exempt from service. While John was in England, Chateau Gaillard fell to Phillip on March 6, 1204. In April, John sent Hubert Walter, archbishop of Canterbury, the bishops of Norwich and Ely, Robert of Leicester, and William Marshal to Bec to meet with King Philip of France. Their mission was to try to come to some sort of compromise with Philip. Philip was not in a mood to compromise; he demanded that John give him either Arthur or Arthur's sister Eleanor and that Arthur or Eleanor would hold all of the continental lands of the house of Anjou. Philip stated that if John had killed Arthur, he would dedicate his life to forcing John from the English throne (*Coggeshall* 144-45). Philip also announced that any baron holding lands in Normandy that wished to keep those lands would have to do liege homage to Philip or lose them.

Robert of Leicester and Marshal both held extensive lands in Normandy, but they could not do homage to Philip without the consent of John who was their king and lord for the lands they held in England. In May 1204 Robert and Marshal came to a compromise with Philip who gave them one year respite to come to their decision with regard to the Norman lands. Each earl agreed to pay Philip five hundred marks for this year of grace. Marshal immediately gave Philip the castle of Orbec which Philip garrisoned with his own men, and turned over the castles of Longueville and Meullers (according to Le Verdier this was the castle of Moulineaux not Mouliers *Guillaume le Marechl, comte de Striguil* 167 f15) to Osbert de Rouvrai, a French knight, who would hold them until June 24 at which time they would also be garrisoned with French knights (Cal. Doc. France #1315, p 475-76). Osbert de Rouvrai held lands in the Pays de Bray and the Norman Vexin and had been a friend and companion of Marshal well before Marshal's marriage to Isabel de Clare. Osbert was a perfect tool for both Marshal and Philip of France in that his brother John de Rouvay was a vassal and knight of King Philip. If by May 1205 Marshal came to Philip and did homage for these Norman lands, they would be returned to him in the same state as when he gave them to Philip, but if Marshal did not do homage by May 1205 and/or did not pay the five hundred marks, Philip would keep the castles and the lands to do with as he willed.

After this meeting, Philip proceeded to take the rest of Normandy, taking Argentan, Falaise, and Caen by May 1204. In July, Rouen under Peter de Preaux finally fell to Philip who now held most of Normandy, and thus John lost most of the lands and vassals that his father and mother had inherited and fought so hard to control and hold.

In the spring of 1205 Marshal persuaded John to allow Marshal and Hugh, archdeacon of Wells, to go to Philip and try to negotiate a peace. Before leaving, Marshal brought the question of his Norman fiefs to John's attention. Marshal said, "Sire, I am not certain that I can make peace, and the respite for my Norman lands is almost over. If I do not do homage to Philip, I shall suffer great loss." John replied, "I know you to be so loyal that no consideration would draw your affection from me. I wish you to do the homage to save yourself from loss, for I know that the more land you hold, the better you will serve me" (*Hist* 12948-2966; Gervase ii 96). John gave letters to Marshal for Philip authorizing Marshal to do the required homage (*Layettes du Tresor* #1397). Hubert Walter, archbishop of Canterbury, did not trust any effort to make peace with Philip and saw it as the destruction of any chance John might have of regaining Normandy (Powicke <u>Loss of Normandy</u> 291). Hubert, therefore, sent Ralph d'Arden to Philip with a private message that stated that Marshal and Hugh had no authorizaton to make peace between John and Philip (*Claus* i 28). When Marshal and Hugh appeared before Philip at Anet, Philip refused to negotiate and accused them of deceiving him about their power to conduct such a meeting on John's behalf (*Hist* 12995-13020). Despite the failure to negotiate a peace, Marshal did present Philip with John's letters authorizing Marshal to do "liege homage on this side of the sea" (*Layettes du Tresor* i #1397). This phrase *hominagium ligium citra mare* meaning liege homage on the continental side of the British channel had not been used anywhere else and may have provided a unique interpretation of what homage meant with specific regard to Marshal and his Norman lands.

This act of Marshal's doing homage to Philip for his Norman land is one of the several puzzling facts in Marshal's life. It presents a podium for legalistic and perhaps ethical debates. Painter resolved the issue by pointing out that Bracton had stated that Marshal and several other Anglo-Normans could plead in both England and France because they owed fealty to both kings. In case of war between the two kings, Marshal would physically fight for the king to whom he had sworn allegiance, John, and send feudal knight service owed for Norman lands to Philip. Painter also pointed to Glanville who made a distinction between allegiance and homage and fidelity of a vassal who owed to several lords (Marshal 139, 139 n 44, 140, 140 n 45). Marshal, however, seems to have drawn an even sharper line of distinction between what he owed to John and what he owed to Philip as evidenced by the next events in his life.

When Marshal returned to England, Hubert's agent Ralph d'Arden had told John of Marshal's oath to Philip. John asked Marshal why he had done homage to Philip to John's disadvantage (*Hist* 13062-3064). Marshal replied that he had done nothing against John, and the homage he had given to Philip was with John's permission (*Hist* 13068-3090). John denied that he had given Marshal permission to do homage to Philip, but John had sent letters to Philip stating that he had authorized Marshal to do homage to Philip for his Norman lands.

This action of William Marshal with regard to the Norman lands of his wife Isabel has provided much debate for historians, but the one factor never before considered in the debate is the fact that Marshal's position and role in his society had changed. Marshal had been given in marriage one of the greatest heiresses in the Angevin kingdom. With this marriage and his fathering of children, particularly sons, Marshal had changed his position and his obligations within his society. Now Marshal was a greater magnate, a man who held vast lands and the service of hundreds of vassals from Normandy to Ireland. Though he was still an excellent military fighter and commander, advisor, and ambassador for the Angevins,

Marshal's first duty and obligation was to his family and the vassals of the lands he held in right of his wife. Marshal had paid Richard 2,000 marks for his wife's right to one-half of the Giffard barony. By 1204 Marshal held the castles of Longueville and Meulers near Dieppe and the castle of Orbec near Lisieux. The Norman lands of the Giffard barony included fiefs that ranged from the west in Cany and Montivilliers to as far north as the Seine river and included a port at Leure which is now part of Le Harvre (*Chartes du prieure de Longueville* #xxiv, lxix-lxxiii). The monks of Longueville had been granted freedom of toll at Shoreham and the lastage from Langeston in Havant to Pevensey was added to the manors of Bosham and Shoreham and other towns in Sussex by Marshal (Salter "Newington Longueville Charters" 14-15). Marshal had also acquired the fief of Abenon near Orbec, Chambois from King John, and the port of Le Pollet from the monks of Longueville Abbey (*Chart* 65, 75; *Rotuli Normanniae* 39; *Chartes du prieure de Longueville* 103-04 #xcii).

Since Marshal had begun his life as a household knight of limited means, he knew the importance and necessity of a lord to provide for those who served him. From the lessons of his father and from his own experiences, Marshal recognized the duties and obligations expected of a greater lord by his family and by those who were tied to him through vassalic bonds. To think that Marshal would blindly and easily throw away his wife's vast Norman lands with their knights, vassals, merchants, towns, and the potentialities of each without doing all in his power to retain them is to negate an important dimension of the man himself. Marshal was still a superb knight and military commander for the Angevin king, but he was more than this. Marshal had become one of the greater barons who understood and did all that was expected of one in such a position.

This question of Marshal's homage to King Philip came up again in June 1205 at Portsmouth when John demanded that William go to Poitou with John and help John regain his inheritance. Marshal refused saying that for him to do so would be a felony against Philip. John, by now enraged, called the assembled knights and barons to witness that Marshal had committed a felony against his lord, John. Marshal denied this and offered to prove his innocence in combat with any man in the realm, but John wanted the barons to condemn Marshal. Marshal spoke to the barons: "Lords, look at me. Today I am an example and mirror for all of you. Attend closely to the king, for what he plans to do to me, he will do to you all and worse yet if he can." John replied, "By the teeth of God! I see that none of my barons are on my side. I know whom I can trust. I shall converse in private with my bachelors about this treason" (*Hist* 13098-3106). These bachelors who were in the king's pay as semi-permanent members of his own household and led by John de Bassingbourne agreed that a man who refused to follow his lord in battle could not hold land from that lord. In other words, these paid hirelings of John were saying that John had the right to take all the lands, titles, and castles that Marshal held in England and Ireland. Baldwin de Bethune, count of Aumale and faithful vassal of the Angevins, replied to these bachelors, "Be silent, it is not fitting for you or me to judge in court a knight of the Marshal's eminence. On all this field there is no man strong enough to prove in combat that he had failed his lord" (*Hist* 13107-13256). John had to let the matter drop because no one would challenge Marshal, and also because none of the bachelors had the right to judge Marshal as they were not his peers and certainly not his equals.

As far as an expedition to Normandy in 1205 was concerned, Marshal and Hubert Walter, archbishop of Canterbury, advised John against trying to take a large army of English knights into Normandy to retake his lost lands. It was well known at this time that the count of Boulogne, Renaud of Dammartin who had married the heiress of Boulogne, was planning to invade England and regain the English lands that belonged to his wife (*Coggeshall* 152-54; Powicke Loss of Normandy 390-91). If John and a large army were on the continent, this would leave the way clear for such an invasion. Marshal, having recently been in Normandy, would have seen and gauged the size and strength of Philip's army as well as the amount of support that Philip had from the Norman barons. John could not fight the reasoning and objections to a 1205 war in Normandy, but this did not mean that he would forget Marshal's homage to Philip.

John, as usual, was infuriated at being denied what he wanted when he wanted it. John could at best be talked out of rash and ill-considered actions on occasion, but John at worst trusted no one, even those whom he had bought and paid for by his gifts and grants. Marshal owed nothing of his status, prestige, and power among his fellow Anglo-Norman barons to John; Marshal was a man of honour, loyalty, and integrity. John having none of these qualities could neither understand Marshal nor forgive him for who and what he was. John had proved that he could not and would not protect the Norman lands of his vassals. Marshal as a typical medieval feudal baron knew that his first duty above all else was to protect and hold what was his wife's inheiritance and what would be their heir's. John's greatest fault was in not recognizing what every other Plantagenet had known about William Marshal; Marshal was not capable of treason, and he would never ruin his own sense of honour by betraying his vows of fealty.

This incident was the first in a series of incidents that would cause the complete estrangement between Marshal and John. John sealed this one by demanding and getting Marshal's oldest son, William II who was no more than 8 years old, as a hostage for Marshal's behavior (*Hist* 13272). Once John decided that Marshal was not his man, John looked at what power Marshal had. Marshal was earl of Pembroke and controlled the castles, knights, vassals, and income from this large earldom; he was lord of Cheptsow and controlled and could call on the same from this large lordship. John had given him the shrievalty of Gloucestershire and the castles of Gloucester and Bristol (*Claus* 54, 68; <u>PR 4 John</u> 172, 290). Marshal had custody of the forest of Dean and the castle of St Briavell's (*Pat* 65b). Marshal held custody of the castle of Cardigan and an annual allowance of four hundred marks for its maintenance since 1202 (*Liberate* 27, 71, *Claus* 54b, 68b). In the summer of 1204 Marshal had taken the castle of Cilgerran from Maelgwyn ap Rhys, lord of south Wales (*Chart* 44; *Brut* 261; *Ann Camb* 63). In 1204 John had given him custody of the castle of Goodrich *(Chart* 124). Marshal was second only to Ranulf earl of Chester in his power and control in Wales. Equally if not more important, Marshal was lord of Leinster in Ireland, and one of the strongest and most important barons there as an almost palatine lord. The true rulers of Ireland were Marshal as lord of Leinster, Hugh de Lacy, earl of Ulster, Walter de Lacy, lord of Meath, and William de Braose, lord of Limerick.

IX. Marshal, King John, and Ireland

Even though John was titular lord of Ireland, he held in his own hands or
the hands of royal servants neither the lands, knights, or castles to enable him to
authoritatively rule. In 1200 John appointed Meiler fitz Henry as justiciar in Ireland;
Meiler was the son of a bastard of Henry I. Meiler's father was Henry fitz Roy,
bastard son of Henry I and the busy Nest, the occasional wife of Gilbert castellan
of Pembroke for Henry I. Meiler was a vassal of Marshal's for lands that he held
in Leinster and a minor baron, but he had ambition for his own interests and the
royal duty to carry out John's orders. By the end of 1206 Meiler had managed to
antagonize and alienate most of the lords in Ireland including Walter de Lacy, son-
in-law to William de Braose, and Marshal. He had taken Marshal's castle of Offaly,
with or without John's written consent (*Pat* 72). With Marshal and de Braose not in
Ireland, Meiler felt that he had a more or less free hand in what he did. This was not
to last. The Irish lands Marshal held were potentially the richest that his wife Isabel
had inherited from her father, and he was not about to allow some lackey of John's to
pillage at will these lands.

In 1207 Marshal recognized that he needed to be in Ireland to deal with
the problems that Meiler was causing. Marshal asked John for permission to go
to Ireland and see about these lands, but John knew that if Marshal was there,
Meiler's free-wheeling days would be numbered (*Hist* 13318-3320). John gave
Marshal permission in February 1207 to go to Ireland and issued letters patent for
the protection of Marshal's vassals Henry Hose's and John d' Earley's possessions in

England (*Pat* 69). Apparently several days later, John received letters from Meiler in Ireland asking John to keep Marshal in England as he was a serious threat to Meiler's activities (*Claus* 78b). On receiving these letters, John immediately sent Thomas de Sanford to Striguil to stop Marshal from going to Ireland and demand Marshal's second son, Richard, as hostage for Marshal's behavior. Thomas was brother to Hugh de Stanford who was a knight and vassal of Marshal's. After feeding Thomas and consulting his own men and his wife, Marshal took Thomas aside and asked, "Sir, you know well that if the king wished, I would send him all of my children, but tell me, for God's love, what has he against me?" Thomas told him that John was most anxious to prevent Marshal from going to Ireland. Marshal replied that he would give his son Richard as hostage but that he was going to Ireland whether the king liked it or not (*Hist* 13355-3419). Marshal sailed for Ireland with his wife and men of his *mesnie,* leaving his two oldest sons, William II and Richard, in England as hostages for his behavior.

John, naturally seeing traitors behind every bush and door, took this opportunity to strip Marshal of as much power as possible in England. John gave the custody of Cardigan to William de London and gave the shrievalty and castle of Gloucester to Richard de Mucegros, a mercenary of John's (*Pat* 70b, 71, 74b; *Claus* i 81, 95). The castle and forest of St. Briavells were granted to Hugh de Neville as part of the forest administration (*Pat* 71). William had lost the shreivalty of Sussex in 1205, and now John took back custody of the castle of Chichester (*Pat* 79). According to the *Histoire*, John also took Marshal's castles in England and Wales, though there is no extant official record for this seizure or a contemporary source that states that John had actual control of Marshal's castles and lands (14334-4335; *Pat* 98b).

There are few contemporary records of this time period regarding Marshal's and John's relationship. There are enough records and chronicles to recognize that John's greatest failure as king was his inability to gain and hold the support and trust of some of his most important Anglo-Norman magnates. Trusting only mercenaries of his pay and men that John himself had created by bribes, gifts, and grants of lands, castles, and/or titles would not suffice. These men had neither the power nor the respect of the other, more established barons, nor did they have the knowledge and experience of the Anglo-Normans in England and in English custom and law. Because John had already proved how untrustworthy he himself was and how capable he was of obligating his barons by exorbitant fines and/or destroying them, the men John most needed were as wary and distrustful of John as he was of them. Somehow John had failed to learn from his father, the expert, how to rule and govern not with fear but with a judicial use of power and force and equal measure of *largesse* and reward. Whether John actually thought Marshal was a disloyal vassal or, more likely, saw Marshal as a powerful check on John's own ambitions to rule like a god on earth answering to no man is a question that cannot be completely answered. Marshal did have the power, wealth, and respected status to thwart John in England and definitely in Ireland with regard to any unilateral and arbitrary rule. This may be the closest to the truth about the real nature of John's mistrust of William Marshal. Whatever the reason for John's actions, the result of them was to be of great benefit to Ireland and the lordship of Leinster.

Marshal had sent to Leinster in 1192 a ranking member of his own household, Geoffrey fitz Robert, to act as Marshal's representative. Geoffrey had married first Basilia, sister to Strongbow and widow of Raymond le Gros, and after Basilia died sometime in 1200, Geoffey married Eva de Bermingham, widow of Gerald fitz Maurice who died c.1203 (Empey "A Case Study" 33). Geoffrey held the lordship of Kells, and he probably governed the whole area of Kilkenny. In addition, Geoffrey held Grean County in Limerick and Dysart County in Kilkenny (Orpen Ireland ii 34, 34 f 8-9; 211,225). Geoffrey's lands would have incorporated over 40,000 acres which provides some idea of the scope and size of the Anglo-Norman barons' fiefs in Ireland. It is likely that he at least built the first foundation of Kilkenny castle and either established the burghs of Kilkenny and Carlow or fixed the burgage rates for them and the town of Wexford (*Chartae, Privilegia et Immunitates* 33, 34, 37, 47). Geoffrey was appointed seneschal of Leinster by 1204, but because he was instrumental in setting the burgage tenures in Leinster at 12d a year, he was probably seneschal as early as the 1190s (Reg. St. Thomas #125-26, #154-56, #398; *Liber Primus Kilkenniensis* 73). Geoffrey also established the town of New Ross on the river Barrow as Marshal's seneschal (*Chartae, Privilegia, et Immunitates* 80). This town with its port served the river traffic on the Nore and Barrow and also the burghs of Kells and Kilkenny. New Ross became the principal port of south Leinster and took a great deal of traffic from the royal port at Waterford (Orpen Ireland ii 230). Geoffrey also provided for the religious as well as the secular welfare of Marshal's lands. He founded the Priory of Kells on his own lands and founded Tintern Minor on Marshal's orders (Cal. Ormond I #30, p 14-16; *Mon Ang vii 1136*).

In the spring of 1204 Marshal had sent his nephew, John, to take the position of seneschal of Leinster. John carried letters patent from Marshal that directed Meiler, justiciar of Ireland, to receive John as seneschal of Leinster, and they forbade Meiler to infringe on the palatine privileges guaranteed by Marshal's charter for Leinster (*Pat.* 40b, 42). John Marshal, however, proved to be less than loyal to his lord and uncle, William Marshal. John Marshal accepted from King John the office of marshal of Ireland and a substantial fief in Ireland as part of that office (*Chart* 173b). This action on the part of John Marshal may have contributed to William Marshal's decision to go to Ireland and protect his lands and his rights.

In the spring of 1207 Marshal and his men landed in Ireland. This may not have been Marhsal's first visit to Ireland. The Chartularies of St. Mary's Dublin states that Marshal came in the fall of 1200. As a result of having survived a bad storm in the Irish Sea coming over, Marshal founded Tintern Minor in fulfillment of a vow Marshal made during that voyage (ii 307-08). The first act that Marshal took on arriving in Ireland in 1207 was to summon Meiler to appear before Marshal's court to answer for taking the castle of Offaly, which belonged to Marshal and had been held by Adam de Hereford as Marshal's vassal. Since Meiler was a vassal of Marshal's and the land in dispute belonged to Marshal's lordship of Leinster, this was a correct and proper procedure. Meiler, however, declined to appear on the basis that he had taken Offaly on command of King John in Meiler's capacity as justiciar of Ireland. Meiler's action immediately produced a reaction among the great Anglo-Norman barons of Ireland. If Meiler was taking one baron's castle and land on the pretext that it was at King John's command, then all Anglo-Norman barons in Ireland were vulnerable. They held their lands originally by conquest and sword and not by gift of King Henry II, who had only come to Ireland after the first Anglo-Normans had taken it with their own blood and the blood of their own vassals. King John's reputation was as well known in Ireland as in Normandy and England. This was a threat to their lands, wealth, power, and vassals, and they were not going to tamely accept any attempt at royal usurpation. If John would try to displace Marshal on his own lordship, then all lesser lords were in jeopardy.

The major barons of Ireland sent a letter of protest to King John with regard to Meiler's contumacy and actions, and John's reply to their letter is found in Sweetman's <u>Calendar of Documents Relating to Ireland</u>:

> The King to Walter, Hugh, and Robert de Lacy, William Petit, Richard de Tut, Adam de Hereford, Philip de Prendergast, William baron of Naas, John de Clahull, Maurice de London, Thomas de Hereford, and other barons of Leinster and Meath. He marvels at what they tell him in their letters from which it appears that they are about to create a new assize in the King's land without the King. It is unheard of that a new assize should be established in the land of another without the consent of the Prince of that land. Unjust, indeed, and unusual is what they ask, namely that the King's justiciar of Ireland should restore, without the King's order, what had been taken into the King's hand by his order. The King, therefore, commands them to desist from their demand to the justiciar touching Offaly. For the King wills not that the justiciar answer to anyone without his order concerning tenements taken into the King's hand by his order. As to what they write, that they will not be wanting in seeking the right of their Lord, the King notifies that by the help of God he will seek his right according to time and place. (49 #329; *Pat* 72)

John's letter was received with the amount of distrust and disdain that one would expect from magnates who had learned well the nature of the man and the king who ruled them. Their reaction was justifiable since John followed this letter with a summons to Marshal, John Marshal, Meiler, and other barons of Leinster to return to England to discuss the matter (Pat 8 John.72; *Chart* 171b-173)

Marshal recognized the danger of this summons because once he left Ireland, Marshal knew that Meiler's men would begin attacking Marshal's lands trying for more illegal gains. Marshal also had the added worry of the safety of his wife, Isabel, who would have to remain in Ireland as she was pregnant at the time and could not endanger herself and child by a rough sea crossing. Trying to provide for Isabel's safety and the safety of their lands, Marshal left John d' Erley and Jordan de Sackville who were charged with the defense of Leinster, and Stephen d'Evreux, Ralph fitz Pagan, Mallard, Marshal's standard bearer, and six more knights of Marshal's household charged with guarding the Countess. Geoffrey fitz Robert, seneschal of Leinster, Walter Porcel and Thomas fitz Anthony who were all powerful and trustworthy barons of Leinster were to counsel and advise Marshal's knights on how best to defend and govern Leinster in Marshal's absence. Marshal called all of his vassals to Kilkenny castle before he left for England and addressed them. In this speech recorded in the *Histoire* one perceives a glimpse of William Marshal's feelings regarding Isabel de Clare and the truth regarding men who were their vassals in Ireland:

> Lords, you see before you the countess whom I lead by the hand. She is your natural lady, daughter of the earl who invested you with your fiefs when the land was first conquered. She remains among you, with child, until such time

as God restores me. I beg you all to care for her kindly and by nature since she is your liege lady, and I have no right in this land except through her. (13464-3550)

Marshal does not treat Isabel as a nonentity nor as merely a possession. Marshal never forgot that it was through Isabel that he had acquired the fiefs and vassals that lifted him to the status of a greater magnate. Isabel has accompanied, and will continue to accompany Marshal, wherever he is, and many of the charters that Marshal issued will contain the phrase "with the assent of my wife" and often carry Isabel's seal as well as Marshal's own (Cal. Doc. France 75-79). Isabel was not a cipher, nor simply a breeder of heirs. Mullally points out that Isabel was an active member of Marshal's councilors, and Marshal often sought Isabel's opinion and council ("The Portrayal of Women" 359).

The truth contained in this speech regarding the vassals in Ireland is the fact that most of them were fief-holders and barons only because Isabel's father, Richard Strongbow de Clare, had conquered Leinster and large portions of southeast Ireland and had enfeoffed these barons with their lands. It is important to acknowledge and remember these facts and men because later some of them and/or their descendants will be found guilty of that greatest of feudal crimes, *felonie*, against Strongbow's descendants.

William Marshal arrived in Wales on Michaelmas day and went directly to John. According to the *Histoire*, John was less than gracious in receiving Marshal (13552-3584). When Meiler arrived in England in early November, John began to plot. It is in John's actions regarding Marshal at this particular moment that a clear and concise picture of John's character and the extent to which he would go to gain his own ends is vividly revealed. Whether John merely wanted to take all of Marshal's lands in Ireland or whether he wanted to completely destroy Marshal is not known, but John's actions are capable of being interpreted to fulfill either purpose. Either at Meiler's suggestion or by his own, John wrote letters demanding that John d'Erley, Jordan de Sackville, and Stephen d'Evreux return to England (*Hist* 13616-3652). Next, John proceeded to bribe and detach Marshal's own vassals from Marshal. John offered John Marshal, William's bastard nephew and his supposed loyal vassal, the office of marshal of Ireland and granted him a substantial fief in Ireland (*Chart* 173b). John granted John Marshal the "marshalry of all Ireland and the cantred in which the vill of Kylmie is situated to hold of the king for five knights' fees" (Sweetman Doc. Ireland 53 #353). Next, John gave impressive grants of lands to David de la Roche and Philip de Prendergast (*Chart* 173b, 171b). Philip de Prendergast had married Maud de Quenci daughter of Strongbow's sister, Basilia and Robert de Quenci, Strongbow's constable of Leinster and holder of the Duffry. Strongbow had given to Maurice de Prendergast ten fiefs, five of which were in Fernegenal (*Song* 177, 198, 197). To de Prendergast, John granted "fifteen knights' fees in between the ports of Cork and Insovenach and twenty-five knights' fees elsewhere to hold of the king saving the ports and the king's demesne lands" (Sweetman Doc. Ireland 52 #348). David de la Roche was the eldest son of Robert fitz Godebert and the grandson of Godebert of Flandrensis; he held land in Fernegenal and land in the barony of Shelmalier East, county Wexford (Brooks Knights' Fees 146-47, 316-19). All three men owed Marshal their fealty and homage for the lands and positions they held for he was their lord. But all three men obeyed John's orders, through Meiler, and attacked their feudal lord Marshal's lands and vassals. All three men knew that in accepting the grants from King John and binding themselves to Meiler in Ireland they would eventually be involved in attacking Marshal's lands and vassals there. They are perfect examples of the double-edged sword which was inherent in the vassalic bond of fealty. When a vassal swore fealty to both a baron and a king for his fiefs, which lord did he follow in case of conflict between his two lords? This dilemma was intensified when what the king sought to achieve was contrary to the laws and customs of the land; this was often the case when it came to King John's actions with regard to his vassals.

While Meiler had been in England, he had orderd his men to attack Leinster since Marshal was in England, and they attacked it in early October and killed twenty of Marshal's knights. However, Marshal's custodians, d'Erley and Sackville, had managed to capture these raiders and throw them into prison (*Hist* 13557-3574). When Meiler returned to Ireland in early winter 1208, he brought with him the king's messenger carrying the letters demanding that d'Erley, de Sackville, and d'Evreux come to England. John d'Erley, de Sackville, and d'Evreux, trusting neither Meiler nor the king, did not return to England but mobilized the men of Leinster and prepared to defend their lord's lands as best they could. Jordan de Sackville sent word to his lord, Hugh de Lacy earl of Ulster, of their need for help. Hugh came to their assistance with sixty-five knights, two hundred mounted serjeants, and a thousand infantry. Meiler's lands were devastated, and he was captured and forced to give his son as hostage for his own freedom. Philip de Prendergast and the other disloyal vassals were also captured and forced to give hostages for their own good behavior (*Hist* 13692-3786, 13873-3888). Thus the greedy and ambitious were given a salutary lesson in the perfidy of disloyalty.

Due to the winter weather and the inability of ships to cross the Irish Sea at this time of year, Marshal was in the uneasy position of being forced to accompany John and his court to and fro across England with no word of what was happening in Ireland to his wife and vassals. John, with a sadistic and vicious turn of mind, sought to torment Marshal. In late January as they were leaving Guilford, John asked Marshal if he had heard from Ireland. When Marshal replied that he had not, John proceeded to give him an imaginary account of events there. John said that d'Erley had sortied from Kilkenny castle with all the men but two serjeants left to guard Isabel, and that Meiler had laid siege to the castle. When d'Erley had returned to attack the besiegers, he had been mortally wounded, and Stephen d'Evreux and Ralph fitz Pagan had been killed. Knowing neither he nor John could have received word from Ireland because of the weather, Marshal replied, "Certainly Sire, it is a great pity about the knights. They were your men which makes the affair still more regrettable" (*Hist* 13787-3866). As John and Marshal rode up and down England together waiting for news from Ireland, John consoled himself and his frustration by taking the English lands of John d'Erley and Jordan de Sackville into his hands (*Chart* 103, 106b). Both men were tenants-in-chief to the king and therefore primarily the king's men in England. To take their lands for their disobedience of his summons seems unjust as no ships could navigate the Irish Sea at this time of year. Finally word arrived to both King John and Marshal of the events in Ireland in late February, and John was forced to accept the true account of Meiler's failure in Ireland, however galling it was (*Hist* 13904-3930).

On March 7, 1208, John sent a letter to Meiler informing him that Marshal had appeared before him at Bristol on March 5 and submitted, "showing himself sufficiently submissive to the king's will" (Sweetman Doc. Ireland 56 #375). He informed Meiler that there was to be a council at Winchester on the affair in Ireland on the Wednesday before Lent. Meiler was to keep the peace in Ireland and make what amends he could for any raids that he had carried out in Leinster. John also informed Meiler that Marshal was sending similar orders to his vassals in Ireland (*Claus.* 105; Sweetman Doc. Ireland 56 #375, #376). The terms of the compromise reached by John and Marshal were formulated by March the twentieth. Marshal agreed to accept a new charter for Leinster and to pay three hundred marks for the return of his castle of Offaly (*Chart* 176; *Oblatis* 434; *Pat* 80b). John sent William Petit, Roland Bloet, Philip of Worcester, and Robert of Cirencester to Meiler to inform him of this agreement and to order him to see that is was put into effect (*Claus* 106b, 107; Sweetman Doc. Ireland 56 #377, #379). John also at this time turned over the custody of d'Erley's and de Sackville's lands in England to Marshal to be returned to them (*Claus* 106b).

The crux of this matter was the new charter issued to Marshal for the lordship of Leinster, and it is important to note the changes in this charter from the original charter granted by Henry II to Hugh de Lacy, lord of Meath [the charter of Henry II to Strongbow did not survive, but the charter for Meath was issued at the same time and with the same powers as were granted to Strongbow for Leinster]. The

200

original charters for Meath and Leinster had been for palatine lordships. The lord exercised total countrol over the courts for criminal and civil cases, and the revenues proceeding from these courts were solely the lord's. They constituted their own judges, seneschals, sheriffs, coroners, and escheators, and they could build their own castles without license of the king. The king's writ did not run in their lordships except for church lands and for cross-lands, where the sheriff was appointed by the king's representative. The charter of Henry II of Meath to Hugh de Lacy gave:

> the land of Meath with all its appurtenances for the service of fifty knights [. . .] to hold all liberties and free customs which I have or can have there on the service aforesaid of me and my heirs [. . .] in wood and plain, in meadow and pasture, in waters and mills, in fishponds and pools, and fisheries, and hunting grounds, in ways and by-ways, and seaports and in all other places and things pertaining thereto, with all the liberties which I have there or am able to give by this my charter. (Barnard English History 62-63)

By the new charter of King John, Marshal held Leinster for the service of 100 knights, but John reserved for the king's court the pleas of the crown for treasure-trove, rape, arson, and ambush as well as all appeals for felonious breach of the peace. In the case of default of justice in the lord's court or in the case of complaints against the lord himself, the question could be taken on appeal to the king's royal court. The regalian right over the sees of Leinster was also taken into the king's hands. If a tenant-in-chief of the king who held lands in Leinster died leaving a minor heir, the lord would have custody of the fees held of him, but the king would have the right to arrange the marriage of the heir or heiress (Sweetman Doc. Ireland 57 #381; Chart 176). A month later, King John issued the same type of charter to

Walter de Lacy for the lordship of Meath and his fiefs in Fingal for 57 knights' fees (Doc. Ireland 57 #382; *Chart* 178). John had managed to clip some of the sources of revenue of the two strongest magnates in Ireland by these charters, but by no means had he clipped the power they held in vassals and castles.

Marshal requested leave to go to Ireland in April 1208, and John freely gave that permission. When Marshal arrived at Glasscarrick near Wexford, he was met by d'Erley and de Sackville. Since they were wearing hauberks, Marshal questioned this saying that he thought that peace had been proclaimed. His two knights told Marshal of those who had been disloyal in Ireland, and the first two men who met Marshal were de Prendergast and de la Roche proclaiming their loyalty. Marshal informed them that all men in the towns and countryside knew the two for traitors, and both begged Marshal's pardon for their actions. Marshal acted more generously than most lords would have done and pardoned them. The next day the Countess Isabel met Marshal, and they traveled to Kilkenny together. Isabel was not in a forgiving mood since she had suffered the betrayal of Marshal's vassals directly being in Ireland when they attacked her and her lands while Marshal was in England. These Irish lands were hers by right of her mother and father, and these rebellious vassals by and large owed their very existence to the generously given fiefs of her father. She wanted them all to be treated as the traitors they were and to forfeit the lands they held and any position of favor with their lord. This is one of the two times in the entire *Histoire* where her opinions and her disagreement with her husband are recorded (Mullally "The Portrayal of Women" 359). Marshal forgave the men and returned their hostages, with the exception of Meiler, realizing that they had acted according to the king's will and command. Meiler was forced to give Marshal his castle of Dunamase immediately and promise to make Marshal his heir to all of his lands when he died (*Hist* 13941-14136). For the moment, there was peace in Leinster, and Marshal could turn his attention to the development and care of his Irish lands.

Before proceeding to the next crisis in the relationship between William Marshal and King John, it is important to take note of Marshal's activities regarding his Irish lands. He was not a medieval lord who neglected his far-flung fiefs and lordships; these lands that he had acquired "in right of his wife" were fiefs that not only required care and defense, but also required settlement and development. Marshal was not lax in this obligation and once again proved that his position as a greater magnate and lord was as important a part of his life as knight and *familiaris regis*. Marshal had a keen business sense and knew from his experience with his English estates that grain was in great demand by the commercial areas of the low countries of Europe. He recognized the potential of agricultural products in his Irish lands and introduced the European process of winter and spring sowing and three-crop rotation. Marshal brought men and sheep from his Welsh and English lands to cultivate the land and provide meat, wool, leather, and cereal crops (Cosgrove Medieval Ireland 151-52). Marshal and Isabel were instrumental in founding New Ross, a deep water port that was close to one of Marshal's manors. New Ross lay on an estuary of the Barrow River and was capable of accepting ships that crossed the Irish Sea from Bristol and Wales. Marshal had a bridge built over the Barrow to the town by 1210 (Cosgrove 117). Marshal granted the town the rights of free trade and a degree of self-government under the Law of Breteuil, and he eventually

obtained the right of free passage for ships bound for New Ross past the royal town

of Waterford as well as favors in trade for the merchants of Leinster (Sweetman Doc.

Ireland #674, #725, #862). Marshal actively established boroughs and towns in his

Irish lands including Kildare, Kilkenny, New Ross, and Carlow. Marshal founded

and/or endowed Tintern Minor, Duiske Abbey, St. John's priory, Graiguenamanagh,

and the Augustinian abbey of St. Columba and St. Mary at Inistioge (Phelan

"William Marshal" 501-02; Cal. Ormond I #52, p 25-26). He built, or had built,

castles to provide protections and caputs; Marshal was responsible for Kilkenny,

Ferns, Dunamase, Carlow, and Carbury castles (Sweetman, Medieval Castles Ireland

34, 36, 40-43). Marshal's policy was directed towards establishing English law and

custom in both civil and ecclesiastical affairs, and he gave charters to the principal

towns of his lands in the Anglo-Norman fashion providing them with a degree of

self-government ("The Charters of Cistercian Abbey Duiske" 12). He continued the

sub-infeudation by granting fiefs to men such as John d'Erley, Geoffrey fitz Robert,

Thomas fitz Anthony, William de St. Leger, and Mallard, Marshal's standard bearer,

in the underdeveloped county of Kilkenny. Erleystown {Earlstown}, Mallardstown,

and Eve's Castle were founded by these men, and they were responsible for the

initial development of this part of Kells (Orpen Ireland ii 225-26; "The Charters

of Cistercian Abbey Duiske"14, 15; Walsh "Castle Eve" 42-43). Marshal built, or

rebuilt, Strongbow's original castle of Kilkenny and made it his principal seat in

Ireland, and Marshal granted the Priory of St. John's the tithes and provisions of the

castle. The priors were appointed the chaplains of the castle and granted the oblating there whenever the Marshal and his heirs were elsewhere (Clohosey "Kilkenny Castle" 50). Marshal was equally diligent in providing for the welfare of the soul by founding the monastery of Tintern Minor {St. Mary de Voto} and the abbey of Duiske {St. Salvator}, and confirming and adding to the grants of Strongbow to St. Mary's Abbey, and Trinity in Dublin ("The Charters of Cistercian Abbey Duiske" 17-19; Chart St. Mary's Abbey ii 158-59; Reg. St. Thomas 137, 356). Marshal thus provided for the success of the lands in Ireland by combining settlement with agriculture, urbanization, and trade, and he remembered to provide for the welfare of the soul as well as the body by founding and/or endowing abbeys, priories, and cathedrals.

X. King John, William de Braose, and the Pope

Peace and tranquility was not to last long for Marshal, however, as John was soon to drag him into another crisis. This one involved one of Marshal's peers, William III de Braose, lord of Bramber and a great magnate in Wales. William was a descendant of the de Braose who had accompanied William the Conqueror to England. The family came from Briouze in Orne in the south of Normandy, and William I de Braose was given the Rape of Bramber in Sussex as his Domesday fief and center of the family's holdings. William III's grandmother was a daughter of Judhael de Totnes, and thus he had acquired Totnes and Barnstaple in England c. 1196. His mother was Bertha, daughter and co-heir of Miles of Gloucester, and through her William III had acquired the lordships of Abergavenny and Brecon in Wales. Through his father, William III had the centers of Builth and Radnor in Wales. William III had served Richard I and was one of the barons who swore that Richard had named John as his heir before his death (*Ann Mon.* i 24). Walter de Lacy, lord of Meath, was married to William III's daughter. Giles, one of William III's sons, was bishop of Hereford, and William IV, William III's son and heir, was married to Matilda de Clare, daughter ot Richard de Clare earl of Hertford and Clare.

King John's battle with William III de Braose was another of John's great mistakes. This was not only a great magnate whose family in England dated back to William the Conqueror, but also a baron who fought for and with both Richard I and John. John himself had helped to create the power and status that de Braose had by 1208. In 1200, John had given de Braose the right to add any Welsh lands that he took to his lordship of Radnor (*Chart* 66). In 1201 John granted de Braose the right of holding the county of Hereford at farm and gave him the lordship of Limerick, with the exception of the city of Limerick (*Rotuli Cancelleri* 106; *Chart* 94). In 1202, John gave him custody of the castles of Glamorgan and Gwywllwg, and in 1203 John gave de Braose the lordship of Gower and the city of Limerick at farm (Cal. Pat. Rolls i 91; *Chart* 107). In 1205 John gave de Braose custody of the castles of Skenfirth, Grosmont, and Llantilio (*Chart* 160). King John's charter to de Braose for Limerick was given for a fine of 5,000 marks with the stipulation that de Braose would pay this fine at the rate of five hundred marks a year. This was a ridiculously high fine, and one that John knew would be almost impossible for any baron to pay. This was a common practice used by John to make barons so indebted to him that they had to obey him or lose their lands and chattels in default. William III had made the mistake of paying John very little since 1201 on this debt; from the records still extant, it seems that de Braose had paid only 700 marks for the lordship of Limerick by 1207.

In the spring of 1208 John sent men to demand de Braose's sons as hostages, but de Braose's wife, Maud de St. Valery, answered this demand by saying, "I will not deliver my sons to your lord, King John, because he basely murdered his nephew Arthur, whom he ought to have taken care of honourably" (Wendover, Giles ii 248-49). When the men returned to John and reported Maud's reply, John went into an absolute rage. Despite the fact that the rumor of John having killed Arthur had existed and been known to all since 1204, it was not known to be true from any reliable source. Of all people, de Braose was the only one of standing that could know unequivocally how Arthur had died, and therefore de Braose and his wife were

a tremendous threat to John. In November 1207 de Braose gave John his castles

of Hay, Radnor, and Brecon along with seven hostages as guarantees for de Braose

paying what he owed John, and John put the castles in the custody of Gerard de

Atheis (Rees "The Medieval Lordship of Brecon" 181). Because of the Interdict

placed upon England in March 1208, William III's son Giles bishop of Hereford

had already left England for France. William III's wife Maud, his son William IV,

daughter-in-law Matilda de Clare, and his grandson John fled to Ireland in the winter

of 1208/09 (Rees "The Medieval Lorship of Brecon"181).

Before continuing with the politics and relationships of John and his barons,

it is necessary to record the battle that John was waging with the pope and the

church as it is another seed which added to the crop of baronial rebellion. On July

12, 1205, Hubert Walter, archbishop of Canterbury died; Hubert had served Richard

as archbishop of Canterbury and justiciar and John as archbishop and chancellor.

Hubert had been an older, wiser, and restraining hand on King John, and John was

determined to not allow a second such man to fill the post of archbishop. The

Angevin kings seemed to have difficulties with their Pope and the Church when it

came to the archbishops of Canterbury. The kings wanted secular, supporting men

in such a position of power in England, and the Church wanted more ecclesiastical

and church-minded men. Ever since William the Conqueror, the king had and

maintained the right to assent, have a voice, in the man elected to the archbishopric

of Canterbury. For over 130 years the man who held the role of Archbishop of

Canterbury had been a man who could and did wield great power in the governing of

England, often as regent or justiciar in the king's absence.

King John had the misfortune to be confronted by Pope Innocent III who was very conscious of his and the Church's power and rights and wanted to see them enforced and strengthened. On Hubert Walter's death, John went immediately to Canterbury, took possession of the late archbishop's effects and got a promise from the chapter that they would not elect a new archbishop until November 1205. Some of the monks at Canterbury, not wanting another such secular man as Hubert had been, elected one of their own, sub-prior Reginald, without the king's assent and without the suffragan bishops' vote. The bishops appealed to Rome because the election had been made without them, and the monks appealed to Rome against the bishops. John, discovering this election of the sub-prior, forced the monks left at Canterbury to elect John de Gray, bishop of Norwich and John's own very secular man. On November 11, 1205, the monks elected John de Gray as archbishop in John's presence. John swiftly gave de Gray the temporalities of Canterbury and sent some of the monks to Rome ordering that they vote for no one but John de Gray as archbishop and that they obtain the pope's confirmation and the pall of office. Innocent, confronted with some monks who had Reginald as their elect archbishop and other monks from King John with de Gray as their elect, quashed both elections. Then Innocent III had the Canterbury monks gatherered before him vote and elect the pope's choice, Cardinal Stephen Langton as archbishop of Canterbury. John refused altogether to accept Langton as archbishop saying that Langton was a man unknown to him; Langton had been teaching in Paris, and therefore he had to be an ally of Philip of France.

Since John refused to allow Stephen Langton even to enter England, let alone be consecrated as archbishop of Canterbury in England, Innocent personally consecrated Stephen as archbishop of Canterbury on June 17, 1207, in Rome. John acted immediately by sending armed mercenaries to turn the rightful monks out of Canterbury, seizing their property, and placing Canterbury in the care of the monks of St. Augustine's. On August 27, 1207, Innocent wrote the bishops of London, Ely, and Worcester requesting that they try to persuade John to accept Langton, and if John still refused, they were to place England under Interdict. In February 1208 John met with Stephen Langton's brother, Simon, but since Simon could neither make nor agree to terms with John in the pope's name, the talks failed. Bishop Mauger of Worcester, bishop Eustace of Ely, and bishop William Sainte Mere Eglise of London tried to convince John to accept Langton and avoid an interdict. John in typical ill-conceived fashion and totally lacking in diplomatic skill, vowed that if they issued the interdict, he would send all prelates, clerks, and monks in England to the pope and seize all their goods, lands, and churches. The three bishops published the interdict on March 23/24, 1208, and left England with two other bishops. The interdict suspended all church services and all sacraments except for baptism and confession for the dying, and no one could be buried in consecrated ground as long as the interdict lasted.

John being enraged about the Interdict sent his sheriffs and men to all districts telling all priests to leave his kingdom immediately and ordered all ecclesiastical revenues put into John's hands. The corn was locked up and distrained for the benefit of the king's revenue, and the mistresses of the priests and clerks were taken by the king's servants and forced to ransom themselves at great expense (Wendover, Giles ii 246-47). It was during this time that John, fearing that the pope would excommunicate him and release all his barons from their oath of fealty, sent his men to demand hostages of all the barons of rank in his kingdom. This is the time when Matilda de Braose refused to give her children as hostages.

In January 1209 Innocent sent King John a letter telling him that if he did not yield within the next three months in the matter of Langton and the exiled bishops, the pope would excommunicate John. John demanded security of William the king of the Scots, and when he did not appear, John gathered an army and went to Northumberland. At the castle of Norham, August 4, 1209, William the Lion of Scotland agreed to give John his two daughters, Margaret and Isabella, pay John thirteen thousands marks of silver, and give hostages from other Scot lords. John left Norham and returned to England where he ordered all fences to be removed from the forests of England and that all free tenants over the age of eleven swear fealty to King John. King John also forced the Welsh to meet him at Woodstock and give hostages and swear fealty to him (Wendover, Giles ii 248-49). In September 1209 John turned out all the Cistercians, except those at Beaulieu and Margam Abbey, from their houses and made them ransom themselves for twenty-seven thousand marks.

William de Braose and his family fled England and arrived at Wicklow in Ireland in the winter of 1208/1209. The de Braoses were met at the town of Wicklow by William Marshal, and Marshal took them to stay with him for twenty days, probably at Kilkenny (*Hist* 14193-4198). When John de Gray, justiciar of

Ireland for King John, learned that de Braose was in Leinster, de Gray ordered Marshal to deliver the fugitives to him. Marshal declared that he knew nothing of a quarrel between de Braose and King John and that it would be treason on the part of Marshal to turn his lord and guest over to de Gray. Either in Wales or Ireland, Marshal must have held a fief from de Braose which would have made de Braose one of the lords of whom Marshal was a vassal. Marshal instead conducted William III and his family to the border of Meath and gave them into the care of William's son-in-law, Walter de Lacy (*Hist* 14199-4232). William de Braose and his family spent the year 1209 in Ireland in relative safety because John was preoccupied with his problems with the Church in England and trying to secure his hold over his barons as well as the local lords in Scotland and Wales.

Finally John turned his attention to the problem of de Braose. On May 31, 1210, King John arrived at Haverford and by June 3 he was at Pembroke and remained there until June 16 (*Liberate* 172-78). John had already summoned William Marshal to join him at Pembroke, and Marshal did (*Hist* 14240-4246). William III de Braose came to John at Pembroke and attempted to resolve his difficulties with John. John's solution to settling the differences between himself and de Braose was a fine of 40,000 marks, which he knew could not be paid by a king let alone a baron (Sweetman Doc. Ireland #408). John invited de Braose to go with him to Ireland, convinced that no promise de Broase made was worth anything without the agreement of de Braose's wife Matilda. William de Braose, however, stayed in Wales while John and his army proceeded to Ireland in June 1210. For John to gather an army and to launch an attack (for that was exactly what it was) into Ireland merely for the purpose of punishing Matilda de Braose, the de Lacys, and other barons who had supported de Braose fails to be believable. According to a letter patent from the fourteenth year of John's reign, John states the various reasons he had for persecuting the de Braose family:

> We therefore, being no longer able to bear with excesses so enormous, assembled an army to march into Ireland [. . .]. When in the meantime we had arrived with our army as far as Pembroke, on the Irish Sea, William earl Ferrers, his nephew came to us offering a fine of 40,000 marks for peace with William de Braose; and we informed de Braose that we were about to sail for Ireland and that he might come with us under our convoy thither, to confer with his wife and friends, but he chose rather to remain in Wales and after we crossed over into Ireland he did us all the injury he could do. When we were at Carrickfergus our friend and cousin Duncan de Karye informed us that the wife and daughter of de Breouse, etc, were captured. After this we left Carrickfergus, on our return to England we took under our custody the wife, son, daughter, etc. And after our return to England, whilst the same Matilda and her friends were under guard at Bristol, she prayed of us to permit her husband to come and converse with her privately, and we allowed it: and thereupon William himself came to us and consented to the fine his wife had made with us before, but de Breouse fled our country etc [. . .]. (*Pat* xxxiii)

As an excuse and a justification for John's actions regarding William III de Braose and his family, this is a mockery. There was some darker more virulent reason for John's brutal persecution of de Braose's family.

Obviously John wanted to revenge himself on the Anglo-Irish barons who had thwarted John in his attempt to break their power and control in Ireland, but John's final solution to the de Braose problem goes much farther than mere subjugation. John arrived in Ireland on June 20, 1210, and proceeded to Kilkenny by way of New Ross the next day (*Liberate* 178, 179). John and his entire army spent two days at Kilkenny being housed, entertained, and fed at the expense of Marshal. Perhaps yet another example of John's petty revenge on those who crossed him, John's long stay in Pembroke and his arrival and travel through Leinster as the first stop in Ireland were all at the expense of Marshal as lord of these lands (*Hist* 14258-4266). From Kilkenny, John proceeded to Naas, held by Marshal's vassal William fitz William, and on June 28 arrived in the royal city of Dublin (*Liberate* 181). Refusing to accept the submission of Walter de Lacy's barons in de Lacy's name, John proceeded to take all the lands, castles, and the lordship of de Lacy in Meath. Walter's brother, Hugh de Lacy earl of Ulster, tried to defend his lands but finally fled from his castle of Carrickfergus with Matilda de Braose, William IV, Matilda de Clare, and the latter's two children to Scotland (Orpen Ireland ii 246-60). Matilda, William IV, Matilda de Clare, and the two children were captured by Duncan of Carrick and were turned over to John at Carrickfergus (*Chron Maj* ii 530). John took the castle of Carrickfergus and was back in Dublin by August 18, 1210. John had managed to seize all the lands and castles of the de Lacys and to gain possession of Matilda de Braose, her son, daughter-in-law, and grandchildren. John had also gained more control over Ireland on this expedition. He received the homage and fealty of some of the petty kings of Ireland, appointed sheriffs and administrators to see that English law was adopted and practiced in Anglo-Ireland, and ordered the creation and adoption of official coinage in Ireland (Wendover, Giles ii 254-55; Duffy "King John" 8-10).

Before he left Ireland, John made one more attempt to reduce the power of Marshal. John demanded that Marshal give him the castle of Dunamase, which Marshal had taken from Meiler as security for Meiler's behavior. John also demanded that Marshal give him John d'Erley, Hugh de Sanford, Geoffrey fitz Robert, Jordan de Sackville, and Walter Purcel as hostages (*Hist* 14319-4372). Apparently at this time John demanded other hostages to hold until all of the above five men were in his custody, but one, David de la Roche, refused to serve as a pledge for Marshal's conduct. According to the *Histoire*, because of David de la Roche's refusal to serve as hostage for his lord, he was thereafter scorned by other barons (14402-4446). Marshal's hostages were sent to England; Jordan was held at Gloucester, Hugh at Winchester, John at Nottingham, Geoffrey at Hereford, and Purcel at Gloucester with Peter fitz Herbert, the sheriff of Gloucestershire (*Hist* 14447-4468).

William III de Braose was not the man Marshal was; though he had gained power and wealth from his own family and from service to both Richard and John, he was apparently seen by many of the other barons as John's man. William de Braose had been in control of his Welsh lands since 1175 and must have been well into his fifties by 1210 (*Diceto* i 401). But de Braose did not have the standing nor the power with other Anglo-Norman magnates that Marshal possessed; other barons might do their best to protect de Braose and his family but not at the risk of their own castles and lands. John brought Matilda de Braose, William IV, and Matilda de Clare back to England; Matilda de Braose and William IV were starved to death by John in the castle of Windsor according to Welsh records (*Brut Red* 187; *Ann Mon ii* 265). Even by the standards of that time, this was an excessively brutal act and another one of King John's many mistakes.

The act itself of starving to death the wife and the son and heir of an Anglo-Norman magnate by a king indicates some powerful, irrational motivation on the part of that king. This had nothing to do with the matter of failure to pay a fine for seisin of Limerick. John could have simply confiscated de Braose's lands as distraint for de Braose's non-payment. Some speculate that this was the result of John's vitriolic hatred of Matilda de Braose for shouting out to the world the truth of John having killed his nephew Arthur. Most historians believe that the only near contemporary account of the fate of Arthur of Brittany is found in the Margam Abbey Chronicles and the account of William le Breton and that both of these had as their source William III de Braose who fled to France in September 1210 and died there in 1211(*Ann Mon i* 34-40; Legge "William Marshal" 19-20). Rowlands, however, says that according to both versions of the *Brut*, John's vengeance and brutality was aimed at William IV, elder son and heir of William III, whom John apparently hated. "That year King John out of hatred and envy expelled William de Breos and William the younger and their wives and grandsons to Ireland with disgrace and the loss of their possessions" (*Brut Red* 187; Rowlands "William de Braose" 127). "John having seized the wife of William de Breos and William the younger and his wife and children, John returned to England and there he put William the younger and his mother to an unmerciful death in the castle of Windsor" (*Brut* 189).

There is another reason that John might have taken the younger William prisoner; apparently William de Braose the father had demised part or all of his lands in England and Wales to his son William IV by 1203 (Holden "King John and the Braoses" 11-12). But there is also an interesting not often noted fact regarding the members of de Braose's family involved in this incident. When John took Matilda de Braose and William IV prisoner, he also took William IV's wife, Matilda/Maud de Clare. Matilda and William IV had been married before 1197, but it is not known what her age was at the time of the marriage. John eventually released Matilda de Clare to her father, Richard fitz Roger de Clare (d1217), but it is a curious fact that John took her back into custody as a hostage for her father in 1213 (*Pat* 101b; *Chart* 192, 197). As a point of further clarification, the de Clare women were noted to be beautiful women. Rohese de Clare, daughter of Richard fitz Gilbert de Clare (d1090), was considered as a possible second wife for King Henry I. King Henry II apparently had less than platonic thoughts about one of the daughters of Richard fitz Gilbert de Clare earl of Hertford (d1136). "Nearly all the nobles of England were related to the Earl of Clare, whose sister, the most beautiful woman in England, had long been desired by King Henry II" (Round "The Family of Clare" 223). The unnamed daughter of Richard fitz Gilbert de Clare is said to have married Cadwaladr, brother of Owain Gwynedd. Owain Gwynedd was son and successor of Gruffydd ap Cynan, and in 1157 Henry II pressed Owain to reinstate Cadwaladr in Maelienydd (Roderick "Marriage and Politics in Wales" 14). Taking this point one step further, King John was known and recorded by contemporaries as being a lecherous man who ignored all rules of honour, respect, and propriety when it came to the wives, sisters, and daughters of his barons. Could John have also desired and attempted to lay more than eyes on the wife of William de Braose the younger?

King John's hatred of the de Braose family could easily entail more than one level or motivating factor, especially as his revenge was such a vicious and brutal one. Once William III de Braose and his family had been forced to flee to Ireland and John had possession of all of his Welsh and English lands and castles, John had nothing to fear from either him or his family. John's actions betray a hatred of at least some members of the family and a will quite simply determined to destroy them. William Marshal, John disliked and feared because he had the power and standing to effectively challenge John as king and lord, but John's actions toward the de Braose family evince much darker and stronger emotions. Whatever King John's reasons for the destruction of the de Braose family, the results would make a lasting impression on the barons and lords who lived and served John in both Ireland and England. King John once again sowed seeds that would eventually be reaped in the whirlwind of rebellion.

XI. The Road to Rebellion

From June until the end of August 1210, John was pre-occupied with his pursuit and destruction of the house of de Braose in Ireland. John landed back in England on August 29, 1210, and hurried to London where he demanded that all prelates of England assemble. Here Templars, Hospitallers, abbesses, and abotts, men of all rank and order assembled. John demanded that they pay an enormous ransom to hold their lands and rights totaling up to one hundred thousand pounds sterling, with the Cistercians paying forty thousand pounds alone (Wendover, Giles ii 255).

In July 1211 John assembled an army at Whitchurch to march into Wales where John subdued the Welsh, including his son-in-law, Llywelyn ap Iorworth, and forced the Welsh to give him twenty-eight young men of the nobility of Wales as hostages. In August 1211, Pandulph, a cardinal of the apostolic see, and Durand, a Templar, came to John at a council at Northampton to try to restore peace beteen the pope and John. John agreed to allow Langton and the exiled bishops to return to England in peace, but he refused to make good the losses that the ecclesiastical houses had suffered as a result of John's confiscation of their lands and property. The messengers returned to France without a peace being established between John and Innocent, but before they left Pandulph announced to the prelates and barons assembled at the council at Northampton that King John was exccommunicated. This papal bull of exccommunication released all men in King John's lands from their vows of fealty and allegiance to John and ordered them to avoid association with

John at table, in council, or in converse (<u>Wendover,</u> Giles ii 256). Thus the year 1211 ended.

1212 was, to quote Queen Elizabeth II, an *annis horibulus* for King John with regard to Pope Innocent III and his bull of excommunication. The release of the feudal barons of England, Wales, Scotland, and Ireland from their oaths of fealty and homage to King John was fuel to the fire of discontent already rampant within John's lands. In the summer of 1212, the Welsh rose in rebellion and proceeded to attack John's castles and men in Wales and destroy towns and acquire great spoils from these raids. John was forced to put all of his plans of re-taking Normandy on hold and restore order at home. John ordered Marshal and de Gray, justiciar of Ireland, to muster at Chester with two hundred knights and as many serjeants as they could spare from the defense of the Anglo-Norman lands in Ireland (*Claus* i 131b). John postponed the muster and moved it to Nottingham in mid-September. At Nottingham John proceeded to hang the twenty-eight Welsh hostages that he held there, including the seven-year-old son of Maelgwn (Davies <u>Wales</u> 137). While there, John received word from the king of Scotland that there was treachery planned against John. Following this message, John received a letter from his bastard daughter Joan, wife of Llywelyn of Wales, telling him of a plot to kill John by some of John's barons (<u>Wendover,</u> Giles ii 257-58). Two of John's leading barons in the north, Eustace de Vesci and Robert fitz Walter, fled England at this time, and that action with the two messages were enough to verify the threats to John's life and cause him to cancel the muster of the army (*Pat* 99).

Whether Marshal and de Gray had actually made it to Chester in the summer of 1212 is doubtful; they had to contend with an Irish rebellion at that time (Orpen Ireland ii 281-89). However, Marshal was definitely aware of the dangers that John faced with the threat of baronial rebellion, the reality of excommunication, and the possibility that Philip Augustus would accept the role of papal representative and try to remove John from his throne. Marshal was a knight and wholly secular in his reasoning and purpose; he saw the threats as dangers to the Angevin throne and the English lands, and Marshal's defense was a defense of these, not of King John as a person. Marshal wrote to King John urging him to make peace with Innocent III and included the renewal of the oaths of allegiance of the barons of Ireland to John and an offer to go to England and serve as negotiator for John with regard to the pope (*Claus i* 132b). John's response to Marshal's letter is found in letters close. He was grateful that Marshal had overlooked their quarrel and come to John's aid and appreciated Marshal's offer to come to England, but Marshal was needed in Ireland to protect the king's interest there. John thanked Marshal and the barons of Ireland for their service and oaths of allegiance and asked if the barons in Ireland would issue letters patent similar to the ones John enclosed to Marshal that had been issued by the barons of England supporting King John. On a personal note, John added that Marshal's son Richard needed a horse and clothing which John would provide and that he, John, would place Richard in the custody of John d'Erley or any other knight of Marshal's at the king's court (*Claus i* 132b). Apparently, Marshal was now restored to the king's favor; John did provide clothes and horses for both of Marshal's sons, William II and Richard, and placed William II in John d'Erley's custody and Richard in Thomas de Sanford's custody (*Hist* 14533-4578).

Marshal persuaded twenty-six barons in Ireland to join him in issuing letters patent in support of King John in the form that John had sent to Marshal. The content of the letters patent are obviously John's own version and words. The barons stated that they were grieved and astonished to hear that the pope was absolving the king's subjects of their oaths of fealty because of the king's refusal to accept Stephen Langton who had been elected without the assent of the king. These letters patent stated the right of the king's assent had been established and practiced since William the Conqueror, and that the king had acted thus to protect the rights which the English Crown had always enjoyed. They also stated that the king had been faithful to his vassals and never offended against their rights and that the barons were prepared to live or die faithful to the king (Sweetman <u>Doc. Ireland</u> #448). These words and statements must be accredited to John as his creation as they could not have been truly or accurately the words of any of his barons at this time. That Marshal succeeded in getting twenty-six barons to sign and send such letters patent is a tribute to his own powers of persuasion and argument. This was not an honest tribute to John as king, but an attempt to mitigate a serious threat to what those barons held and protected as fiefs of the Angevin crown. If the barons were released from their oaths of fealty and allegiance and the pope was encouraging Philip Augustus of France to conquer England and depose John, then how and by what right would any baron in any Anglo-Norman lands hold those lands and fiefs he now held? Self-preservation was the root and rule of those letters patent issued in John's behalf.

In April 1213 Pandulph had arrived in France with the papal letters deposing

John and ordering Philip of France to conquer England for himself and his heirs as the papal representative. Philip had summoned his vassals to meet at Rouen on April 21, 1213, to form the expedition to England. In late March, John had summoned Marshal and de Gray to England. Marshal and de Gray arrived at Barham Down with a force of five hundred knights (Sweetman Doc. Ireland #455). Both sides were now prepared and ready for the anticipated struggle for the English Crown. Into this charged situation arrived Pandulph on May 13, 1213, at Dover; Pandulph was there to make one last attempt to reconcile King John and Pope Innocent III. Pandulph and John met at a house of the Knights Templar near Dover with the nobles of the realm present. On May 15, 1213, King John agreed to accept Stephen Langton as archbishop of Canterbury, to receive in peace all the bishops and monks that had fled England, to make restitution to all the prelates and their houses, and he resigned his crown and the kingdoms of England and Ireland into the hands of the pope and agreed to hold them as fiefs of the pope (*Foedera* i 111; Wendover, Giles ii 268-69).

William the Conqueror must have been rolling in his grave. John had just done what William the Conqueror refused to do; he had given the Anglo-Norman Plantagenet lands to the pope. John also agreed to pay the pope one thousand marks sterling annually, five hundred at Michaelmas and five hundred at Easter. This charter was witnessed by Henry archbishop of Dublin, John de Gray, Geoffrey fitz Peter, William earl of Salisbury, William Marshal, Reginald count of Boulogne, William earl of Warenne, William earl of Arundel, William earl of Ferrers, William Briuere, Peter fitz Hubert, and Warin fitzGerald at the house of the Knights Templar near Dover on May 15, 1213 (Wendover, Giles *ii* 268-70). On May 24,

1213, Marshal and eleven other barons sent letters patent to the exiled bishops guaranteeing the fulfillment of John's charter to the pope (*Foedera* i 115; *Pat* 98b, 114b). Pandulph returned to France with eight thousand pounds to begin restitution to the archbishop, bishops, and monks in exile, and he urged the prelates to return to England. Pandulph also hurried to Philip of France and ordered him to cease and desist in his invasion of England (<u>Wendover,</u> Giles ii 271).

Philip was furious; he had spent sixty thousand pounds equipping his ships for the invasion and providing food and arms. According to Wendover, the only reason that Philip yielded was trouble with his vassal, Philip count of Flanders. The count of Flanders had refused to accompany King Philip to England because the count had made a treaty with John, because King Philip had no claim to the English throne, and because the king of France had illegally seized the count's lands and castles. Philip, therefore, turned his attention to dealing with the count of Flanders and with the fact that an English naval expedition led by William earl of Salisbury had destroyed Philip's invasion fleet anchored off the coast of Damme in Flanders the end of May (*Ann Mon* iii 35-36).

John, having been absolved by the pope, summoned his feudal levy to Portsmouth in July 1213. However, a number of the northern barons refused to cross to Poitou saying that they had no obligation to serve in Anjou or Aquitaine. John saw their refusal as rebellion and proposed to gather his mercenaries and take military action against these barons. Langton, having arrived in England, insisted that John proceed against these northern barons only in accordance with the judgment of his court, and that if John persisted in his actions, Langton would excommunicate John's soldiers (Wendover, Giles ii 275-76). The majority of the barons refusing to serve merely gave the excuse that they were exhausted by the number of summons they had answered within England in the past year. According to Vincent, the barons had been called to serve in Poitou, in Wales in the summer 1212, to the army of defense at Barham, and then to Poitou before August 1213 (Vincent "A Roll of Knights" 90). This effectively brought an end to John's attempts to mount an expedition to Poitou in the year of 1213.

In August 1213 a council was summoned to assess the damages suffered by the prelates attended by bishops and magnates. Marshal was one of the commissioners appointed to estimate the damage done to the see of London (*Claus* i 164b). There were representatives from the townships in the king's demesne, and the purpose was not only to estimate damage done to church lands but to also discuss the state of the realm and the laws of Henry I that John had promised to observe. On October 2, 1213, Geoffrey fitz Peter justiciar of England died. John is reported to have said that he and the justiciar would meet in hell and that "by God's feet" he, John, was for the first time truly lord and king of England. John appointed Peter des Roches, bishop of Winchester and a Poitevin, justiciar of England (*Pat* 110). This move of appointing a foreigner to the position of justiciar did not sit well with John's barons. On November 3, 1213, John met the bishops and barons at Wallingford and promised to make restitution to the prelates and was reconciled with the northern barons (*Ann Mon* iii 40).

In October 1213 John gave Marshal the castle and fief of Haverford for a fine of one thousand marks (*Pat* 105; *Oblatis* 499). John also gave to Marshal custody of the castles of Cardigan, Carmarthen, and Gower as well as money to maintain them (*Oblatis* 522; *Pat* 109b). John was preparing once again an expedition to Poitou, and he needed a loyal and powerful man to ensure the safety of southern Wales. Marshal was respected as knight and warrior, and he was capable of mustering knights and Welshmen to the defense of the realm. John also created Marshal's nephew John custodian of the marches of Shropshire and Staffordshire, gave him the manor of Hengham as a fief, and the office of sheriff of Lincolnshire (*Pat* 109; 109, 109b)

John had planned carefully for his next attempt to regain his lands; he had made an ally of Philip count of Flanders, Otto of Brunswick, the counts of Boulogne and Holland, and the dukes of Brabant and Louvain. John's plan was to get to Poitou in northern Aquitaine and attack Philip through Poitou while the German and Flemish allies attacked France from the northeast. John already had a large force under William earl of Salisbury and Raymond VI count of Toulouse in Flanders.

John called for the muster to meet for the expedition to Poitou in February 1214. There were fifteen earls in England in 1214; Ranulf earl of Chester, William de Ferrers earl of Derby, Aubrey de Vere earl of Oxford, Harry earl of Warwick, and William earl of Salisbury all accompanied John to Poitou. Roger Bigod earl of Norfolk and Saher de Quenci earl of Winchester sent their sons with John (*Claus* i 206). William earl of Arundel, William de Bethune earl of Devon, and William Marshal earl of Pembroke sent their contingents to the host. Richard de Clare earl of Hertford and Clare, William de Warenne earl of Surrey, David earl of Huntingdon, and Geoffrey de Mandeville earl of Essex neither went nor sent contingents to John (*Claus* i 212). One-third of the English earls took part in the campaign; one-third

226

sent their contingents, and one-third abstained altogether from John's expedition. According to the *Histoire* John also took Marshal's second son, Richard, with him as a hostage, and Richard almost died while there (*Hist* 14712-4727).

John arrived in Rochelle, which he still held, on February 15, 1214. In March John went to Limousin and ravaged the county of Le Marche of Hugh de Lusignan, and in April he marched into Gascony to La Reole. John then took Geoffrey de Lusignan's castle of Mervant in May and besieged his castle of Voucant where Geoffrey and his two sons were located at that time. They surrendered to King John, and at Parthenay the count of Le Marche, Eu, and Geoffrey de Lusignan did homage and swore fealty to John. John sealed this with the marriage of his daugher Joan to Hugh de Lusignan's son (*Chart* i 197). In June John took Ancennis and Nantes, taking King Philip's cousin, Peter of Dreux, prisoner. Later in June, the city of Angers surrendered to John; John's complete control of Anjou was blocked by William des Roches, Philip's seneschal. William had built a castle at Roche-au-Moine, and when John approached to attack it, the Poitevin barons hearing that Louis, King Philip's son, was leading an army to defend it, refused to fight for John against their own lord (Warren <u>King John</u> 221-23). John had no choice but to fall back to La Rochelle (*Coggeshall* 167-70). While John stewed at the betrayal of the Poitevin barons, the English and Flemish mercenary forces under William earl of Salisbury met King Philip's army at Bouvines in Flanders on July 27, 1214. At the end of the battle, Count Ferrand, Count Renaud of Boulogne, and William Earl of Salisbury were captured by the French; only Otto of Brunswick escaped (*Foedera* i 124-25; Warren <u>King John</u> 223-24)). A truce between Philip and John was arranged by Cardinal Robert Curzon to last until Easter 1220, and John sailed for England in October 1214. This last of John's attempts to regain the continental lands that had belonged to his family ended in defeat.

John returned to an England that was rife with unrest; John's failure to succeed in his expedition to regain his Norman lands greatly weakened his position as king and encouraged the dis-satisfied barons of his realm to actively seek acknowledgement of their demands. In November the barons met at St. Edmunds and formed a confederation to force John to give them their liberties guaranteed by a document based on the coronation charter of Henry I. What the barons wanted was a new charter that abolished the old, unjust practices and established new customs that were guaranteed in a written document signed by the king. For once John governed himself and used negotiations to play for time. When the barons came to London at Christmas 1214 with their demands, John persuaded them to wait until the Sunday after Easter, and he would meet them at Northampton and give them his answer. Stephen Langton, the bishop of Ely, and William Marshal gave the barons their oath that John would give the barons satisfaction (Wendover, Giles ii 305).

Meanwhile John, in his usual double-dealing fashion, had sent envoys to Rome to tell Pope Innocent of his problems with his rebelling vassals. But the rebelling barons were not two steps behind John and sent envoys of their own to Rome to plead the justice of their cause. John also called for Poitevin mercenaries to come to England. When the barons discovered this, they protested and demanded an explanation of John. John sent the barons letters patent of safe conduct to go to Oxford and meet with John's representatives, including Langton and William

Marshal (*Pat* 129). On March 4, 1215, King John took the crusader's vow; this proved to be a masterstroke of guile and strategy. A crusader's vow put his person and his property under the protection of the Church and gave him a crusader's respite of three years in meeting his secular obligations.

While John still had Poitevin mercenaries in England, Stephen Langton refused to act as a negotiator for John; so on March 13, 1215, John thanked his Poitevin vassals for their loyalty to him and sent the ones in England back and told the others to stay at home (*Pat* 130). John did not hear from the pope until after April 29, 1215, so the date was postponed for his meeting with the rebels. When John did get a letter from Innocent III, it ordered the barons to abandon their conspiracies and give up any thought of using force. The rebel barons were now determined to force John to meet their demands, and they called a meeting to be held at Brackley. On April 27, 1215, John sent Langton and Marshal to Brackley to obtain a list of the rebels' demands. When John read their demands, he categorically refused to accede to them. Marshal and Langton were unable to get John to yield on anything, and they had to return and tell the rebel barons that John refused all of their demands. The enraged barons set off and laid siege to Northampton castle that was held for the king by Geoffrey de Montigny. John also prepared for war by sending the earls of Pembroke, Salisbury, and Warenne out to gather the king's allies and to put the royal castles in a state of defense (*Pat* 135, 134b).

May 3, 1215, the rebelling barons formally renounced their homage and fealty to King John and in feudal terms defied the king as their feudal lord. The barons made Robert fitz Walter their leader at this time (Warren <u>King John</u> 234).

On May 9-10, 1215, John issued letters offering to put old grievances before papal arbitration saying that, "Know that we shall not take them or their men, nor disseize them. Nor go upon them by force or by arms, except by the law of our realm or by the judgment of their peers in our court" (*Chart* i 209). John was prepared to settle outstanding grievances but not bind himself under any terms for the future. Feeling less than secure, John sent Marshal and the earls of Salisbury and Warenne to put the royal castles in order (*Pat* 135). Marshal then left to join the muster of the other marcher lords at Gloucestershire (*Pat* 134b). John also called the mercenaries with Savary in Ireland to Winchester and ordered the earl of Salisbury and the Flemish mercenaries to move to London (Warren <u>King John</u> 232). But William, earl of Salisbury, was too late; the rebel barons finding that Northampton was too difficult to take had gone to Bedford where William de Beauchamp welcomed them. On May 17, 1215, the rebel barons were allowed to take London and welcomed by London citizens.

In June, John sent Marshal to London to inform the barons that John would grant them the liberties that they demanded in order to preserve the peace and welfare of the realm. The rebels and the king met at Runnymede in June 1215. John set his seal to the preliminary draft of the document on June 15, and on June 19, 1215, it was issued as a charter freely granted by King John.

The barons were rebelling, not revolting; they did not want to overthrow the king or the Crown. The rebellion of the barons was an action taken because of the argument and contention between King John and his vassals over the definition of the rights of lords and vassals. Other Angevin kings had abused the customs of feudalism, but John's character and the types and brutality of his abuses had forced the rebellion of his barons. John could not distinguish between loyalty and subservience; he used the conventional ties of loyalty as instruments of discipline and used homage and fealty as bargaining chips in his attempts to control his vassals. John used the customs of inheritance, wardship, and marriage as rights to be held up to the highest bidder. No matter how careful and wise a baron might be, he would inevitably find himself at John's bargaining table. A vassal had to pay relief for the inheritance of his father's lands, had to provide military service to the king or pay scutage if he did not serve personally, and had to secure the marriage of his heir and his other children. John had set arbitrary amounts for the fines demanded from his vassals for exemption from jury service, for rightful *seisin* by a son of his father's lands, for the marriage of an heir or heiress, for a widow's right to her dower and her right to remarry or not, for wardships, and for scutages and aids other than the three customary aids.

Some examples of John's abuses with regard to the customs of feudalism provide an idea of just how far John had gone in his idea of his power as lord and king. In 1211 John had charged John de Lacy seven thousand marks for livery of his inheritance though de Lacy was the sole heir (*Oblatis* 494-95). Robert de Vere was charged one thousand marks for livery of his brother's, Aubrey de Vere, lands (*Claus* i 173). Nicholas de Stutville had to pay ten thousand marks for *seisin* of his brother's, William, lands (*Claus* i 173). As far as widows were concerned, Amabile, widow of Hugh Bardulf, had to pay two thousand marks and five palfreys to remain a widow and not be forced to remarry (*Oblatis* xxxii). Hawaise, countess of Aumale, had to pay John five thousand marks to regain her dower and to not be forced to remarry, even though she had already been married three times at the king's pleasure (*Oblatis xxxii*). Geoffrey de Mandeville, earl of Essex, was charged 20,000 marks to marry King John's ex-wife Isabella, countess of Gloucester (*Oblatis* 520-21). For wardships and guardians, John had charged Simon de Montfort ten thousand marks to have custody of the lands and heir of Gilbert de Umfraville (*Oblatis xxx*). Thomas de Eardinton paid five thousand marks for the custody of the fitz Alan barony though the barony provided less than five hundred marks a year in revenue (*Oblatis* 531).

The Magna Carta was an attempt to create a general statement of legal principles that would help establish a regime of accepted law for the land of England. The content of the Magna Carta shows the haste and the bargaining of many voices in its text. There is no single author of the Magna Carta; it is the result of the many voices of men who were trying to rectify an abuse of what was perceived as the usual practiced custom of a given aspect of feudalism. The crafting of this document was virgin territory in which the men involved had few precedents to guide them. Given the time and the context of this document, it was a remarkable achievement. The clauses of the Charter are the pragmatic and practical solutions the barons and King agreed upon in 1215. It was the attempt of medieval man in England to create a formal, written code of law that would be recognized, obeyed, and enforced to provide for efficient and just governance of the land, people, and king. Though the clauses prove that there were many voices and views addressed in this charter, it is unique in that it is primarily national in its scope. The rebellious barons did not seek to exclude royal government; they sought to make that government respect the customary rights of all free Englishmen. Implied in the clauses is the overall concept that there was a body of law that circumscribed the power of the king, and this concept was what the barons tried to embody within the Magna Carta.

The Charter grants to God and the English Church all of its rights and liberties, including the right to select its own officials without royal interference. It is addressed to all free men of the kingdom. Clauses two and three provide that relief paid by an heir to a barony is to be one hundred pounds, for a knight's fee it is to be five pounds, and for a fief which is inherited by a minor it is to have no relief charged. Clauses four and five state that guardians/wardships shall be answerable for any abuse of the lands, men, or property of a minor and that all shall be returned to the heir when he comes of age. Clauses seven and eight state that a widow shall have her marriage portion and inheritance at once and shall not have to pay anything for it, and that she shall not be compelled to remarry. Clauses nine, ten, and eleven address John's practice of freely seizing his vassals' estates and lands, whether the vassal was in default of debts to John or to others. Clauses twelve, thirteen, fourteen, and fifteen state that any aids or scutages that are not one of three customary ones cannot be levied without the common counsel of the kingdom. Clauses twenty and twenty-one deal with fines/amercements and limit the amount to the seriousness of the offense and the ability to pay of the offender and any such against earls or barons can be obtained only through a fair hearing by their peers. Clauses thirty-eight, thirty-nine, and forty are concerned with justice and are the root of common law. They state that no man will be put on trial on the basis of an official's unsupported statement, that "no free man shall be seized or imprisoned, or stripped of his rights or possessions, or outlawed or exiled, or deprived of his standing in any other way, nor will we (the king) proceed with force against him, or send others to do so, except by the lawful judgment of his equals or by law of the land." Forty states that the king will neither sell nor deny nor delay justice to any man. Clauses fifty and fifty-one deal with the foreign mercenaries that John had brought into England and placed into positions that the barons felt should not have gone to foreigners. They demand that John dismiss them and remove them from England. The Charter also provides that twenty-five barons be elected to keep and enforce the clauses of the Charter by all, including the king.

Painter originally proposed the possibility that William Marshal had been an active participant with Stephen Langton in formulating the clauses of the Magna Carta, but he later reasoned that Marshal had probably not been actively involved with the actual writing of the Magna Carta (Marshal 181-82). Marshal saw and understood the inherent faults of feudalism and of a king who ruled by his own whim or decree. Marshal knew his world as well as any man alive and knew that in order to preserve the Angevin/English throne and lands some of the most obvious injustices of feudalism and of a feudal king and lord unchecked had to be remedied before the entire country fell in rebellion and to an invasion by Louis of France. Marshal had his eldest son and heir in the party of the rebelling barons; he had to know what the major issues of the rebels were and what could and could not be granted without losing the whole of England in the process. Marshal was the only baron and earl of great enough stature and respect who could be trusted to deal with both the rebels and the royal partisans with honour. It was this one man whose word and whose honour were such that he could talk with and for both king and rebel. If Marshal gave his word to either side, it was trusted as no one else's. Stephen Langton was the genius and political thinker who created the legally crafted clauses of the Magna Carta; he was the gift that destiny granted to medieval England in the time of her need (Powicke <u>Stephen Langton</u> 102-28). Langton was aided in his purpose by having in Marshal a man of experience, wisdom, and power who listened and understood the political realities that Langton presented and did his utmost to preserve England from the horror and devastation of civil war. Marshal hated the war that John's actions after Runnymede brought down upon England, and according to the *Histoire*, he believed that the war should never have been allowed to happen.

Whether Marshal actually helped in the formation of the text of the Magna Carta is so far an unprovable theory, but the undeniable fact of this time period is that had Marshal not been there, no one else had the statue and power to bring John to Runnymede, to the realization that the survival of the realm depended upon the concessions demanded in the Magna Carta. It is in the fact that Marshal, of all the magnates of England, was the man whose word was trusted by both sides during this time that refutes any later historical attempts to ascribe to Marshal any part in the murder of Arthur of Brittany. Had Marshal carried any taint of such a heinous act, he would have never been trusted by those barons rebelling against the excesses of King John. William Marshal remained true to his honour and his belief that the preservation of the realm, the preservation of the Angevin crown, despite the man who held it, was the heart and soul of his oath as earl, vassal, knight, and man of honour.

XII. The Baronial Revolt: John's Last Years

John sealed the Magna Carta on June 15, 1215, at Runnymede, but it is certain that John had no intention of keeping any of the concessions he had made to the barons. John's immediate reaction was to send letters to the pope asking that the pope annul the Charter as it had been given under duress. At the end of September when the pope's reply reached England ordering the annulment of the Charter, there was already war within England.

After the gathering at Runnymede, a meeting had been arranged for July 16 between the barons and John to discuss certain questions that had not been addressed in the Charter. On the fifteenth of July, John sent Marshal and other envoys to the barons with the message that John could not make a council on the sixteenth of July (*Pat* 149). This was the last time that Marshal served as a negotiator between the king and the barons.

In late July, Marshal went west to supervise the defense of the marches against the Welsh who had allied themselves with the rebel barons. Giles de Braose, bishop of Hereford, and his brother, Reginald, and Geoffrey de Mandeville, earl of Essex and Gloucestershire, were three who sided with the Welsh. In June and July, de Braose had invaded Brecon and raided Pembroke and Gower capturing castles and ravaging the countryside (*Brut* 282-87). John had given Marshal custody of the royal castles of Cardigan and Carmarthen and possession of Swansea, and possibly other castles in Gower (*Pat* 109b, 157b). Marshal had as his allies in the Welsh Marches, Walter de Lacy, John de Monmouth, and Hugh de

Mortimer.

In June and July the de Braose brothers invaded Brecon and were welcomed by their father's vassals. Maelgwyn ap Rees and his nephew young Rees raided Pembroke and Gower and captured castles and ravaged the countryside (*Brut* 282-85). But on October 21, 1215, Giles de Braose made peace with King John and received custody of the castle of Swansea and the lands of his family in Wales (*Brut* 286-89; *Pat* 157). Unfortunately, Giles died in November 1215, and his brother Reginald was still allied and fighting with Llywelyn of Wales. John had ordered that all of Giles de Braose's lands and castles be placed into Marshal's custody, but undoubtedly some were held and kept by Reginald (*Pat* 159; *Ann Mon* iii *47)*.

The pipe rolls, both Closed and Patent, show Marshal in Wales the summer of 1215 and the winter 1215/1216 acting as John's chief representative to the region and holding vice-regal powers. All the king's writs for delivery of castles and lands in the region were addressed to Marshal (*Claus* i 239b, 240, 240b; *Pat* 166b, 169b). Marshal assigned manors on his own authority and made treaties with repentant rebels during this time and acted as commander-in-chief in South Wales (*Claus* i 262, 270). John showed his appreciation of Marshal's efforts at this time by granting several favors to Marshal's Irish lands. Thomas fitz Anthony, who had succeeded Geoffrey fitz Robert as Marshal's seneschal of Leinster, was given the custody of all of the county of Waterford, except for the city itself, and custody of the county of Desmond and the city of Cork (Sweetman Doc. Ireland #526). On August 20, 1215, John issued two writs in Marshal's favor; one gave permission for all ships to go to Marshal's port of New Ross, instead of the royal port of Waterford, and John ordered Geoffrey Luterel to return the castle of Dunamase to Marshal (*Pat* 153b, 161b, 184).

While the rebel barons held London, John systematically ravaged their lands and reduced their castles. The rebels' major action from London was to send word to France offering the throne of England to Louis, son of King Philip of France. Louis based his right to the throne on the fact that he had been elected to the throne by the rebelling barons and that he could claim it in right of his wife, Blanche, Henry II's granddaughter. Louis promised the rebels that he would come, and in the meantime he sent two forces to their aid, one of 140 men and one of 120 (*Histoire des ducs* 160-64).

To forestall Louis from coming to England, King John sent Marshal and Peter des Roches, bishop of Winchester, to Philip in France to try to persuade Philip to stop his son from landing in England. Marshal's mission to France failed to convince Philip to stop Louis, and Louis left Calais for England on May 20, 1216 (*Coggeshall* 180-81).

After Marshal returned to England, John issued letters of safe conduct to Marshal's son, William II, to meet with his father under the aegis of Aimery de St Maur, master of the Templars in England, on April 10, 1216 (*Pat* 175b). The purpose of this meeting was to allow William senior to try to persuade his son to return to the side of the king. William senior's attitude to the rebellion was that it was completely unnecessary and wrong. Marshal was the king's liege man; though he had suffered a great deal of injustice from King John, William had never crossed the line into open rebellion against his lord. Marshal's own sense of honour and feudal propriety forbade him from such an action, and he was wise and knowledgeable enough to know that the future of England did not lie with a French king. Painter suggests that Marshal may have been also wise enough to "hedge his bets" when it came to preserving and protecting his family's future (Marshal 186). By having his son on the side of the rebels, no matter the outcome of the war and possible French invasion, either outcome of the war was covered for the family. Whatever the true purpose of the meeting between father and son, the son refused to join the king's side and left the meeting still supporting the rebels.

On May 21, 1216, Louis landed in England, and John proposed to meet him in battle on his landing. On second consideration, heeding Marshal's advice that a pitched battle could cost John everything and recognizing that most of his mercenary troops had been born vassals of Philip of France and were greatly in arrears in their pay, John withdrew from the field (*Ann Mon* iii 46; *Hist* 15088-5094).

Louis took Canterbury and the castle of Rochester after a siege of a week, and entered London on June the second. William Marshal, Jr. was one of the first barons to do homage to Louis (*Claus* i 260b; *Histoire des ducs* 171). On June 6 Louis began a siege of Winchester castle, despite the fact that the legate Gualo had excommunicated Louis and all of his partisans. While at Winchester, Louis received the homage of the earls of Arundel, Warenne, and Salisbury, and they brought with them the feudal power of Surrey, Sussex, and Wiltshire (*Histoire des ducs* 169-74). Louis had more or less free rein in the eastern counties, taking control of England from the English Channel to the Scottish border. By the end of July only a few castles, Dover, Windsor, and Lincoln, still held out against Louis.

William senior was busy in the south Marches watching and checking the actions of Reginald de Braose and Llywelyn (*Claus* i 276, 280b, 283, 288b; *Brut* 288-91). In July 1216 the younger William managed to overstep the allowed boundaries of his father, William senior. William II took Worcester castle which was under the custody of his father. William strongly advised his son to leave Worcester castle immediately, which the son did. After the young William left Worcester castle, William senior, Ranulf earl of Chester, and Faulkes de Breaute retook it (*Ann Mon* iv 406; iii 48; *Claus* i 282b).

From this time until the time of King John's death, William Marshal's specific actions are not recorded; it is known that Marshal was responsible for protecting and defending the Marches of Wales from actions of the Welsh and the rebel barons. Painter states that Marshal's very character prevented him from being strongly identified with John and John's policies against the rebel barons. Unlike Peter des Roches, Hubert de Burgh, and Faulkes de Breaute, Marshal held the core of royal support in the marches together and fought or made treaties with rebels there without participating in the harsh treatment meted out in the east and north of England by these active supporters of John's retribution against those who opposed him (Painter Marshal 191). Had Marshal joined the rebels or identified himself with John's policies towards his own barons, Marshal would have likely never been elected regent on John's death.

John had spent July and August of 1216 in the west between Corfe on the channel coast and Shrewsbury resupplying castles and seeking allies within and without the kingdom. In August, Alexander king of Scotland moved south to join Louis, and by September he reached Dover and did homage to Louis. In September, John moved with his mercenary army down the Thames towards the besieged royalists at Windsor castle. John retook Cambridge and several Essex castles and relieved the siege of Winsdor by drawing the besiegers after himself. John then made a lightning raid on Lincoln, which was under attack and remained in that area until October. Next, John made a raid into Norfolk, but by October he returned to Lincolnshire. John was apparently seriously ill by this time and stopped at the bishop of Lincoln's castle, Newark. He died there on October 19, 1216, but he managed to die with some dignity. Before he died he received the Church's consolation, made a will to try to safeguard his Crown and his son, and requested burial in the church of his patron St. Wulfstan at Worcester. When John died only a few loyal servants were with him; Peter des Roches, John de Monmouth, Walter and Roger Clifford, and John Marshal were there.

According to two records John's words were:

> Lords, I must die. I cannot resist this disease. For the love of God beg the Marshal to forgive me the wrongs I have done him, for I repent them fully. He has always served me loyally and he has never acted against me no matter what I did or said to him. For God's sake, lords, pray him to pardon me. As I am more sure of his loyalty than that of any other man, I ask you to entrust to him the care of my son who will never succeed in holding his land unless by his aid. (*Hist* 15153-5190; *Histoire des ducs* 180).

Thus, John Lackland died, but he had not died a defeated king. John had control of the west of England and the midlands; the royal castles of Windsor, Dover, and Devizes in the southeast; he had his loyal foreign military captains installed in strongholds throughout the country; and he had the support of Marshal, earl of Pembroke, and Ranulf, earl of Chester, who controlled the Welsh marches. John had the loyalty and support of the citizens of most of the southeastern ports, of the papacy, Archbishop Langton, and many abbots of the religious houses of England. There was a stalemate of sorts in England on the death of King John, but not a triumph of the rebels and the French prince.

XIII. William Marshal Regent of England

Marshal learned of John's death while he was at Gloucester, and Marshal hastened to meet his nephew and the other barons who were escorting John's body to be interred in the church of St. Wulstan. They met at Worcester, and the legate Gualo also joined the party here. After John was buried in the church of St. Wulstan, Marshal and Gualo summoned the chief men of the royalist party to a council at Gloucester. Thomas de Sanford was sent to bring the young Henry Plantagenet from the stronghold of Devizes to Gloucester (*Hist* 15206-5286). The royalists were facing a critical decision with the death of King John; they had no king to support because there was no king between the death of one king and the coronation of another king. Therefore the council decided to knight and consecrate the young Henry immediately to solve their dilemma. Marshal was awarded the honour of knighting the young king, as he had done once before for the son of Henry II. Henry was dubbed a knight, took the customary oaths, performed homage to the legate Guala as he was the representative of the king's lord, the pope, and was then crowned king of England by the bishop of Winchester (Wendover, Giles ii 379; *Hist* 15287-5332).

England now had a king, but a nine-year-old young boy cannot rule. The barons had to devise a way to govern England until Henry III came of age. They needed a force that could remove the invaders from their shore and restore order to the kingdom. There were several men who could have been selected to rule England for Henry III; Peter des Roches, bishop of Winchester, Hubert de Burgh, justiciar, William Marshal, earl of Pembroke, Ranulf earl of Chester, William de Ferrers, earl of Derby, or Guala, papal legate for England. Peter des Roches was a foreigner and definitely disliked by most of the barons, and Hubert de Burgh was not of the nobility. Both of these men were too closely allied to all of John's policies that had created the rebellion in 1215. Guala was an ecclesiastic and a foreigner and had no knowledge or any experience in ruling a secular entity; plus he was the representative of the pope which would not endear him to any of the barons. William de Ferrers was a minor baron with no great standing or wealth among the English barons. Marshal and Ranulf of Chester were the only great magnates who had the power, wealth, and standing among their peers to hold the position of regent. Both had the reputation of loyalty to the Angevin household, both were experienced soldiers, and both were men of great wealth and power. Ranulf was the younger, only in his mid-forties, but he lacked the administrative experience and the respect that Marshal possessed on all levels. According to David Carpenter, Marshal had abundant material resources to use in defense of the king and the kingdom; he had years of unswerving loyalty to the Angevin crown; he had the earned reputation as one of the greatest and most successful knights of the time; and he had the understanding and experience of the use of patronage in contemporary politics (Minority of Henry III 14-16). Marshal understood the need and the methods of the use of patronage to bind those loyal to the young king more tightly and how to use a carrot to bring those rebelling barons to the young king's side. The fact that Marshal did not grab or easily accept the role of regent after Henry III's coronation is another proof of Marshal's political acumen. Marshal knew that the only way any regent could rule in the current chaotic land was with the consent and support of those gathered at the council. Ranulf of Chester arrived at Gloucester the day after the king's coronation and urged Marshal to accept the position of guardian to Henry III, and Guala added his endorsement with the addition of a spiritual reward of the remission and pardon of all of Marshal's sins if Marshal accepted the position. Marshal accepted the role of guardian of the king and of the kingdom on the "common counsel" of all those gathered there (Walt Cov 233). Because Marshal could not personally look after the king while he commanded the armies in defense of the kingdom, he placed the king in the custody of Peter des Roches (*Hist* 15580-5610).

Having accepted charge of the king and the kingdom, Marshal faced a daunting situation on October 29, 1216. According to Sidney Painter's figures, Marshal faced ninety-seven baronies in revolt with only thirty-six on the side of the new king (King John 297). Louis of France controlled London and the entire eastern half of England, and he had an alliance with Alexander of Scotland and Llywelyn of Wales. Louis lacked any ecclesiastical support because the pope had excommunicated Louis and all of his supporters. However, all was not lost in the east to the royalists; there were castles in that region held by Henry's supporters. Peter de Maulay held Corfe; Hubert de Burgh held Dover, and Engelard de Cigogne held Windsor. Falkes de Breaute and his men held Northampton, Oxford, Buckingham, Hertford, Bedford, and Cambridge. Robert de Gaugi held Newark; Hugh de Balliol held Newcastle upon Tyne, and Philip Marc held Nottingham. Brian de Lisle held Knaresborough; Philip of Oldcoats held Bamburgh, and Nicola de Hay held Lincoln (Holt The Northerners 228; *Histoire des ducs* 181). Many

of the men holding these castles were foreigners of non-noble birth who had been

brought to England by John and therefore were totally dependant upon the survival

of the Angevin crown. They were as ruthless as any man and could and did survive

by their own means including extracting money from ransoms and extortion from

the local populace (PR 1215 45; PR 1216-1225 95; *Coggeshall* 204; Walt Cov

232). This was Marshal's reality when he assumed control of the kingdom for

Henry III.

Early in November 1216 Marshal summoned a great council to be held at

Bristol. The first matter to be resolved was the title that Marshal was to hold in his

new position. Marshal had been calling himself *justiciar* since the justiciar under

the Angevins had controlled the kingdom in the absence of the king (*Claus 293;*

Recueil des actes de Henri II xix 625). The problem with this title was that King

John's justiciar, Hubert de Burgh, was still in that office, and as he attended the

council at Bristol, he protested being removed from his office. Marshal was given

a new title for his position; he was called by the king *rector noster et regni nostri*

[our ruler and the ruler of our kingdom] (Chaplais Diplomatic Documents 32-33

#25; Shirley Royal Letters I 6-8).

The next problem Marshal faced was the position of the rebelling barons.

Since the reason for their rebellion had been the actions of King John, the

succession of the young Henry removed the crimes of his father from the Crown.

Henry III declared in a royal letter, "We hear that a quarrel arose between our father

and certain nobles of our kingdom, whether with justification or not we do not know. We wish to remove it for ever since it has nothing to do with us" (*Foedera* 145). In accordance with this letter, in November and December eighteen letters of safe conduct were sent to rebels giving them the right to come and speak with the king or with Marshal with regard to their grievances (Cal. Pat. Rolls 2-16).

On November 12, 1216, a revised version of the Magna Carta was issued by Henry III on the advice of Gualo, Marshal, eleven bishops, Ranulf earl of Chester, William de Ferrers earl of Derby, the count of Aumale, Hubert de Burgh, William Brewer, and eighteen other ministers and magnates. The version of the Magna Carta issued in 1216 was sealed by the legate and by William Marshal under his new title (Stubbs Select Charters 336-39). In several ways this was an amazing document. The pope had condemned the original Magna Carta, and Guala had had no time to consult with the pope about a reversal of policy towards the document. Henry III was a minor and under law could not make permanent gifts that would reduce his patrimony. Yet this document granted fundamental liberties to Henry's subjects for himself and for all his heirs in perpetuity, and it was to shape the future of the monarchy of England. Those responsible for the Charter of 1216 did leave out some of the clauses that most closely infringed on the rights and revenues of the crown (Holt Magna Carta 271-72). Clause 25 that forbade the exaction of revenue above the old farm of the counties was removed, as well as Clause 50 that ordered the king to remove alien sheriffs. The council also put into abeyance a group of clauses that they classified as *gravia et dubitalia* (Stubbs Select Charters 339). These latter clauses were to be used as subjects of negotiation because they were ambiguous and because the king wished to deal with them after further discussion so that they could be made useful to the common good of the people, the king, and the kingdom. This charter was meant to provide a balance between the state of the king and the common utility of all the freemen.

Louis took the castle of Hertford between November 3 and December 5, and then proceeded to take Berkhampstead between December 13 and 20 as his price for a Christmas truce (*Wendover* iii 2-8; *Ann Mon* ii 287). On January 13, 1217, Marshal agreed to another truce that would last until April 23, 1217, and this truce cost the royalists the castles of Hedingham, Orford, Norwich, and Colchester (Walt Cov 235). Marshal could not take the offensive yet because he lacked the resources to pay the army; what resources the regency had were the remains of John's treasury in Corfe and Devizes castles, mostly silks and jewels (*Claus* 602b-603b). The only influx of money was primarily from ransoms and extortions. Marshal was also faced with in-fighting among the royalists. Brian de Lisle would not give the castle of the Peak to de Ferrers, earl of Derby (PR 1216-1225 7-8). Ranulf earl of Chester was threatening to go on crusade because he could not get all the lands, castles, and baronies that he wanted (*Claus* 335b). In general, this time was like the period of King Stephen's anarchy; many opportunists were seeking everything they could obtain from the regency government as their price to support the young Henry III.

A reprieve came for the royalists when Louis left for France on February 28, 1217, and did not return to England until April 23, 1217 (*Historie des ducs* 182-87). The first good news that Marshal received was on March 5, 1217. On that date as Marshal left Shoreham-by-Sea, he was met by his son, William the younger, and William Longespee, earl of Salisbury (*Hist* 15873-5888; PR 1216-1225 35). These two former supporters of Louis of France had decided to return to the faith of the young king Henry III. A series of letters cover their absolution from excommunication and the terms under which they rejoined the royalist party (*Claus* 299, 299b; PR 1216-1225 109). Their defection from Louis's party was followed by nearly one hundred more men, men who were mostly from Wiltshire, Somerset, Dorset, and Berkshire (Walt Cov 235; *Ann Mon* iii 47; *Coggeshall* 185). During March and April, the royalists took the castles of Rochester, Southampton, Porchester, Farnham, Marlborough, and Winchester (*Historie des ducs* 187-8; *Hist* 15889-16033). One very important action for the royalists' party was an act of Pope Honorius on January 17, 1217. The pope granted Guala the power to suspend the crusading vows of those men who were supporting Henry III. Guala not only suspended existing vows, but he also granted them remission of their sins and signed them with the cross (Walt Cov 235-36; Shirley Royal Letters I 527-29). In effect Guala made the royalists crusaders fighting against the pagans, those supporting Louis of France. This may have added incentive to those choosing to leave Louis' side for Henry III.

Louis landed at Sandwich on April 22 or 23, 1217, just as the truce was about to expire. He still held the support of Robert fitz Walter, Saher de Quenci, earl of Winchester, the earl of Hereford, Gilbert de Gant, Nicholas de Stuteville, William Maudit, and many of the Northerners (Walt Cov 236; Holt The Northerners 141, 141 f 1). On Louis' return, he sent de Quinci and the count of Perche to relieve the siege at Mountsorrel. After this the two men were to proceed to the castle of Lincoln and try to take it from Nicola de Hay who held it for the king. Louis himself once again lay siege to Dover Castle on May 12 and tried to take it from Hubert de Burgh (*Historie des ducs* 191-92; *Chron Maj* 15-18).

On May 13, 1217, Marshal learned that Louis had split his forces and decided to attack the half of Louis' army currently laying siege to Lincoln castle. This was a great gamble for Marshal because set-piece battles were not common practice in this time period. A man ran the risk of losing all on one set battle or on losing so many of his army that he could no longer continue a war. A set, pitched battle involved great strategic, political, and physical risks; Bovines in 1214 had cost King John most of the Angevin possessions in Normandy. On one battle and one throw of the dice, John had lost it all, and no commander willingly or easily took such a risk (Strickland War and Chivalry 43).

The royal forces gathered at Newark on May 17/18, 1217. One recorded incident of this gathering gives an idea of just how difficult commanding an army at this time could be for a leader. The Normans who made up part of the army went to the young William Marshal, because he had been born in Normandy, and asked that he put forth their ancient right to strike the first blow in the coming battle. This was a recognized custom and right of those who were native born to Normandy in the Angevins' domain. Ranulf, earl of Chester, immediately protested that he had the right to strike the first blow, and if it was not allowed to him, he would withdraw from the entire coming battle. The regent had to yield to the earl of Chester on this in order to keep his military force intact (Carpenter Minority of Henry III 36). The royalist army faced another big problem in that the city of

Lincoln sat on a ridge, two hundred feet high. In front of the walls of the city was a hill that sloped down one hundred seventy-five feet. The city, castle, and cathedral were all within one encompassing wall. This physical lay-out of the city and castle made it suicidial to try to enter the city from the wall on the south, fighting one's way up that one hundred seventy-five foot hill to the castle (Strickland War and Chivalry 37). The only sensible approach to the battle was to get the army to the top of the ridge, away from the city walls, and then attack the castle and the city wall from the northwestern side. On May 20, 1217, the royalist army was before the northern wall of the city of Lincoln at the northwestern side of the castle.

When the royal army appeared, Louis' army was within the city walls laying siege to the castle itself. At first, Louis' army led by the count of Perche went out of the city walls to meet the royal army, but they immediately turned and hastened back inside the city walls. The count of Perche and the Marshal of France concluded that their force was greatly outnumbered and that they should stay within the city walls and fight the royalist army until they were joined by the rest of Louis' army (Walt Cov 237).

Marshal's problem was to get inside the city walls and then attack Louis's forces. The Earl of Chester was to attack the north gate of the city wall and Falkes de Breaute was to attack the west gate of the castle which merged with the city wall (*Ann Mon* iii 49). Peter des Roches, bishop of Winchester, had entered the castle by a postern gate and reconnoitered the area from inside the castle itself. He had found a solution for Marshal in a western gateway to the city that had previously been blocked, but not in a manner that prevented it from being reopened by the royalist's army (*Hist* 16500-6520). As Falkes took the castle walls, he used his crossbowmen to attack Louis'men who were laying siege to the eastern side of the castle. As soon as Louis' men withdrew from the castle walls back into the town, Falkes and his men poured out of the castle in hot pursuit. This foray gave the regent the opportunity to get through the opened western gateway into the city. Marshal was in such haste to enter the battle that he almost charged without his helmet. Marshal was saved from this possibly costly error by his squire who halted the regent's horse and handed Marshal his helm before he charged. The young Marshal and the earl of Salisbury galloped through the gateway and immediately wheeled to the right to meet Louis' forces who were still attacking the east gate of the castle. The regent charged forward with such force that he managed to plunge through three rows of lancers in his initial charge. Fast behind Marshal was Peter des Roches calling in a high voice "*Ca! Dieu aide du Marechal.*" In the words of *Histoire* Marshal is described:

> Quicker than a falcon, he spurred his horse and all those who were with him grew reckless at the sight. A squire had to point out to him that he had not got his helm. He said to the young Marshal, Wait for me while I get my helm! With his helm on he looked the finest of them all and as light as a bird. He spurred his horse. A hungry lion is not quicker to fall upon its prey than was the Marshal when rushed upon his enemies. He carved his way three lances deep into the throng, scattering his adversaries and forcing them to turn tail. The bishop following him crying, Now! God help the Marshal! (16577-6768)

With these words one can begin to see what R. Allen Brown imparted to his students of Anglo-Norman history of the power, strength, and skill required of a medieval knight in a couched, cavalry charge.

The battle of Lincoln was fought in a series of fierce fighting contests from the walls of the castle and city, down and through the streets of the town. In front of the cathedral the count of Perche had taken a stand, and though mortally wounded, he was fighting on valiantly. When the regent saw him, he charged forth and grabbed the count's bridle. The count took his sword in both of his hands and delivered three blows to Marshal's helm, leaving three deep dents, and then the count fell from his horse dead (*Hist* 16577-6768). Those of Louis' army who had been driven from the castle wall and down the hill gathered reinforcements and tried to fight their way back up the hill. They were met on the right by the earl of Chester and his men and attacked from the rear by Thomas and Alan Basset and their forces (*Chron Maj* 21; Walt Cov 237).

When the battle was over the recorded dead were the count of Perche, an unknown serjeant, and the English knight Reginald Croc (Wendover, Giles 215-19). Those of the infantry killed were not recorded, and those of the French and rebel barons who had escaped through the southern gateway of the city were not listed except for William de Mandeville, earl of Essex, and John de Lacy, constable of Chester. Forty-six rebel barons and three hundred knights were captured at the end of the battle. Saher de Quenci, earl of Winchester, the earl of Hereford, Gilbert de Clare, heir to the earldom of Hertford and Gloucester, Gilbert de Ghent, Robert fitz Walter, Richard de Muntfichet, William de Mowbray, William de Beauchamp, and William son of Robert de Ros were among the barons captured (Wendover, Giles ii 215-17, 219; Gervase 111)

The victory at Lincoln was the deciding factor in this war for control of England; because of this victory of the regent and the royalists' forces, England would be ruled by the house of the Angevins and not by the house of the Capetians. After the battle the royalists were granted some long sought prizes. Brian de Lisle was granted Knaresborough castle to hold until Henry III reached his fifteenth birthday, and William Longespee, earl of Salisbury and bastard brother of King John, was granted the custody of the city and county of Lincoln (PR 1216-1225 64, 65). Neither grant was a permanent alienation, but only granted until King Henry III reached his majority. The earl of Chester was granted the third penny of the county of Lincoln and thus the earldom of Lincoln and the castle of Mountsorrel, which he razed to the ground (PR 1216-1225 64, 65; *Claus* 308b; *Ann Mon* i 224; iii 50).

At the close of the battle for Lincoln, Marshal allowed all to depart with their prisoners so that they could make arrangements with the said prisoners for their ransoms to be paid. The regent commanded the men to re-assemble early in June at Chertsey to continue the fight to rid England of the French forces. Louis learned of the loss of Lincoln on May 25, 1217, while laying siege to Dover castle. Louis withdrew from Dover and returned to London with his forces (*Histoire des ducs* 195-96). From London, Louis sent the count of Brittany and Nevers to Chertsey to open negotiations with the regent for peace (PR 1216-1225 68).

On June 12, 1217, four members of Louis' council and four members of king Henry's met between Brentford and Hounslow. The delegates reached an agreement on June 13 (Smith "Treaty of Lambeth" 566-67). Louis agreed to release his supporters from their oaths of homage and fealty and to restore the lands that he had taken. All of his supporters, both lay and clerical, were to be absolved of the sentence of excommunication and to recover the lands and possessions that they had held at the beginning of the war. All prisoners taken after Louis' first arrival in England and all who had been his supporters before Louis reached England were to be released. Their ransoms were to be paid up to the installments due at the time peace was declared. Louis' supporters were to enjoy all liberties and customs of England including any improvements made to those liberties (Stubbs Select Charters 339). These negotiations broke down because the legate Guala insisted that the ecclesiastical supporters of Louis, especially Simon Langton, Gervase of Heybridge, Elias of Dereham, and Robert de St Germain, be excluded from the settlement. Louis refused to make peace without all his supporters being included in the treaty (Smith "Treaty of Lambeth" 566-67).

Louis remained safe in London, but with the breakdown in negotiations, some of his English allies used the time to return to the royalists' side. Between June 15 and the middle of August, some one hundred fifty Englishmen returned to the allegiance of Henry III (*Claus* 310b-318b). Reginald de Braose returned to Henry's side by June 23, the earl of Arundel by July 14, and John de Lacy, constable of Chester, by August 9 (*Claus* 310b, 311b, 312, 314, 318; PR 1216-1225 72-73).

Reginald de Braose's return to King Henry's side infuriated his father-in-law, Llywelyn ap Iowerth, prince of north Wales. Llywelyn immediately took Swansea castle and the lordship of Gower and placed Rhys Gryg, son of Lord Rhys of Deheubarth (d1197), in charge. Llywelyn then proceeded to attack the regent's castle at Haverford and took hostages from the lordship of Pembroke (*Brut* 95-96). The regent hurriedly left for his castles of Goodrich and Chepstow to survey the situation, but he could spare neither the time nor the resources to launch an attack against Llywelyn at this time (*Claus* 319; PR 1216-1225 71, 81, 85, 86). The regent had to return to England to hold assemblies at Oxford, held between July 21-25 and August 7-13, in order to attend to the reconciliation of the former rebel barons to King Henry III.

On August 24, 1217, Marshal was at Sandwich to meet another major crisis. Blanche of Castile, who was Louis' wife and the granddaughter of Henry II and Eleanor of Aquitaine, had raised a large French fleet which was coming to Louis' aid. This French fleet was led by the pirate Eustace the Monk and was off the coast of England. The regent was at Sandwich to lead the knights and serjeants who would fight the French fleet once the Cinque Ports' ships had brought them alongside of the French. The regent was persuaded that it was too dangerous for him to be in this battle because of the risk to England of losing him, so Hubert de Burgh was given command of the English troops and ships (*Hist* 17197-7210, 17253-7261; *Chron Maj* iii 28-29). By luck and skill, the English were victorious in this battle at sea, losing only fifteen ships of the French fleet and taking at least thirty-two men of rank for ransom (*Historie des ducs* 200-02; *Hist* 17573-7574).

Peace negotiations began August 28, 1217, and continued until September eleventh by which time the regent had blocked the Thames with the barons of the Cinque Ports (PR 1216-1225 89). On Tuesday, August 12, 1217, Louis met with the regent, Guala, King Henry III and his mother, and Hubert de Burgh on an island in the Thames near Kingston (*Histoire des ducs* 204-05; *Hist* 17704-7706). On September 20, 1217, at Lambeth the treaty was ratified by a formal assembly gathered on the island.

The new treaty stated that only the laymen of Louis' supporters were to have their lands and seisins as at the beginning of the war. The ecclesiastical supporters could recover their lay fees but not their ecclesiastical offices and properties; thus Simon Langton and his men were forced to leave England and go directly to the pope to obtain absolution (*Histoire des ducs* 201). Louis released his supporters from their oaths of allegiance to him. The rebel barons, once they gave security in the form of oaths and charters to King Henry III for their future behavior, were given their lands as they held them before the war and guaranteed all the liberties that they had held. All prisoners on both sides since Louis' first landing in England were to be freed. All ransoms already paid were to be kept, and if a prisoner had arranged to pay his ransom in installments, all arrears were to be paid but all future payments were cancelled. All debts owed to Louis were to be paid, and he could retain the hostages taken in connection with them. Not in the text of the treaty but an understood part of the treaty was a payment of 10,000 marks to Louis as "compensation for the damage he had suffered in England" (PR 1216-1225 284, 114-15, 168; Chaplais Diplomatic Documents #25, #26). This was in reality an incentive to speed Louis on his departure from England. The regent placed his own lands in Normandy as surety for this payment when Florence the Rich, a merchant of St. Omer, advanced two-thirds of this sum (PR 1216-1225

114-15, 168; <u>Patent Roll 1218</u> xvii-xviii). Also not written in the text of the treaty but understood was a vague promise by Louis to try to get his father to return the Angevin Norman lands or to do so himself once he became king (*Ann Mon* iii 81).

Later in English history the regent was blamed for missing an opportunity at this moment and for agreeing to pay Louis 10,000 marks and for not capturing Louis and holding him for ransom, the ransom being the return of the Angevin Norman lands (*Historie des ducs* 204). Hindsight is always ready to re-write history, or as Mark Twain once quipped, "The very ink with which history is written is merely fluid prejudice." As evidence of this in 1241 King Henry III told Marshal's son Walter that it was known that his father had acted as a traitor in neglecting to capture Louis (*Chron Maj* iii 25-26; iv 157; *Historie des ducs* 204). Louis had a strong force of the best knights of France still in London, and the citizens of London were more loyal to Louis than the royalists. Marshal would have had to besiege London, and the cost in men, time, and money would have been more than the government could bear. This is always supposing that Marshal could have kept the army together and that those who had abandoned Louis would have not returned to his side. King Philip would not have tolerated this treatment of his son; he would have raised an army--which he could afford--and taken the rest of the Angevin lands in Normandy, and invaded England. Neither the legate nor the pope would have approved holding a prince of the realm for this type of ransom. If a prince, why not a king or even a pope? No one would have seen this as a reasonable or acceptable method to peace in a time when the paramount objective was to secure the crown and restore peace and order to the kingdom and get the French knights out of England. That Louis considered his promise to try to return the Angevin lands as part of this agreement is found when Louis ascended to the throne in 1223; Louis said that he had not returned the lands because the English had failed to observe the treaty of 1217.

The terms of the peace treaty were narrowly defined; they did not apply to those men taken at Rochester in 1215, as they had not been supporters of Louis. They applied to only those who were still prisoners at the end of the war (Smith "Treaty of Lambeth" 576; *Claus* 358b). The latter did not have to make any payments due later than September 12, 1217 (Smith "Treaty of Lambeth" 576). The earl of Norfolk had paid 800 marks toward the ransom of his son Ralph by 1218/19 (*Claus* 392b). Many men had to give up some of their lands in order to pay their ransoms. John fitz Hugh had to give John Marshal land in Cowley and Oxford in order to pay his own ransom, and Simon of Kyme paid his by leasing five manors to the earl of Chester (Gervase 111-12; Holt The Northerners 248). The rebels were lucky that John had not still been alive as he would have taken their lands or made the fines so high that the men would have lost them as escheats for debt, and he would have certainly abolished the Charter of 1216.

Marshal knew that the Charter was a benefit to all the magnates regardless of their allegiance in the war, and he and the legate wanted no disinheritance. The legate wanted the rebels to receive penance and absolution so that they could depart for the crusade in the Holy Land. One important factor in the minimal amount of bloodshed among the nobles during the war was family ties. Marshal's daughter Maud was married to the rebel Hugh Bigod, heir to the earldom of Norfolk. Ranulf earl of Chester's sister was married to the brother of Saher de Quenci, earl of Winchester. None of this stopped the collection of ransoms, and even Marshal took advantage of this by marrying his daughter Isabel to Gilbert de Clare, Marshal's own captive (*Ann Mon* i 61; PR 1216-1225 79).

Marshal now had the monumental task of returning men to seisin of their lands that they held before the war, deciding about the amendments to the Charter, recovering the authority of the king, and rebuilding the structure of his government. The government needed to conciliate former rebels and begin dispensing justice. The king's local agents had to rebuild their castles and get control of their local sheriffdom's administration. Some of the sheriffs had custody of royal castles and through that custody had control of the counties. They would not easily give up such power and source of revenue. Philip of Oldcoates held the sheriffdom of Northumberland, Philip Marc held Nottingham-Derbyshire, the earl of Salisbury had Wiltshire, the earl of Chester had Lancashire, Shropshire, and Staffordshire, and Falkes de Breaute had Oxfordshire, Northamptonshire, Bedforshire, Buckinghamshire, and Cambridgeshire-Huntingdonshire. Most of these men held their offices primarily through appointment by King John, and these men and their control of the sheriffdoms had been a major contributor to the success of the royalists' army. They felt that since they had been appointed by King John, no one but a king could remove them from office; Henry III was eleven years away from being of age to rule in his own right as king.

Until a seal could be made for Henry III in November 1218, Marshal as regent authenticated royal letters with his own seal and attested to the majority of letters issued during his time as regent. Marshal was not a figurehead; in the first memoranda roll of the exchequer from Michaelmas 1217 to Trinity 1218, writs ordered the sheriffs to account "by the Marshal" or by "writ of the Marshal" (*Claus* 343, 371; West <u>Justiciarship</u> 234). Guala as papal legate was closely associated with Marshal in the governing of England, and his presence insured that there was cooperation between the Church and the state. He encouraged the clerical community to take government offices and made certain that those appointed were loyal to the king. Ecclesiastics were thus in office as barons of the exchequer and justices in the eyre (<u>PR 1216-1225</u> 206-08).

The Magna Carta had engendered the belief on the part of the barons and greater magnates that their obedience to the king was conditional on the reasonableness of the king's orders. The barons believed that with their king being a minor the only true orders of the king had to be those that were sanctioned by the council of the magnates of England. In other words, only those orders that had been agreed upon by the greater council of the barons and magnates of England would be recognized as binding. This meant that the regent and the legate often had to consult with both small groups of fellow ministers and with greater gatherings of barons. Carpenter says that the regent's authority, and that of those who followed him, depended in actual practice on securing the common counsel from meetings with those barons (<u>Minority of Henry III</u> 55).

Marshal had to balance the rights and liberties granted by the Magna Carta with the rights of the king. He had to implement the terms of the peace treaty and at the same time restore the structure of the king's administration. He was faced with a government that had little or no income because of the war, and yet the magnates who had defended England for the young king were demanding rewards for their service. The only way to reward these men was to use the king's resources of his escheats, wardships, demesne manors, and sheriffdoms. This would mean diminishing the king's power and authority by allocating some of the sources of both to the barons. There was no other way for Marshal at this time, but it would result in a problem that would plague the entire minority of Henry III.

A great council was held at Westminster from October 21 to November 8, 1217. There was a gathering of the rebels to swear fealty and do homage to Henry III, to give charters of their faithful service to the king, and to obtain seisin of their land from the chancery. Among those attending were Robert fitz Walter, Saher de Quenci earl of Winchester, Gilbert de Clare, Gilbert de Gant, Roger Bertram, Walter de Dunstanville, and John fitz Alan (Walt Cov 240). On November 6, 1217, a new version of the great Charter was issued as well as a Charter for the Forest.

In the new Charter clause 39 forbade any free man from alienating land if it meant that he was no longer able to provide the service he owed to his lord for his fief. Clause 43 tried to prevent a vassal from evading the customs and services he owed his lord by granting lands to a religious house and then receiving those lands back as the house's tenant. A stipulation was included ordering that everyone, particularly the magnates, were to observe the liberties granted by the Charter towards their own vassals. Clause 42 gave new regulations with regard to the customs of the counties holding county and hundred courts. The scutage and aids clause of 1215 was altered to vaguely define the right of the king to take scutage and aid as in the reign of Henry II.

The Forest Charter was issued under the seal of the regent and Guala on November 8, 1217. For the first time it subjected the forest to laws other than the king's will. It pardoned all past offenses and purprestures and assarts made in private woods within the forest since the time of Henry II. It regulated the entire forest administration including the holding of its courts, the actions of its officials, and the level of punishments allowed. Henceforth no man was to lose life or limb for any offense against the protected beasts of the forest. It granted privileges to those who had private woods within the royal forest. Most importantly it attempted to reduce the bounds of the royal forest itself. The afforestations of King Richard and King John were to be deforested immediately. The afforestations of Henry II were to be established by surveys of "law-worthy" men, and then the amount of deforestation would be determined.

These Charters were to the benefit of all men, magnates, knights, burghers, and common populace. New clauses protected great magnates from being judged by anyone less than their peers. The new clauses regarding county and hundred courts protected the knight, gentry, and local society. The relief for a barony was set at one hundred pounds no matter the size of the barony. Clauses 14 and 15 restored the judicial bench which was to hear all assizes of *darrien presentment* and all cases too difficult to determine by the petty assizes judges in the counties. As of 1218 the justices were to be paid a salary, and the regular sessions of the bench at Westminster were held from the Hilary term of 1218 (*Claus* 344). Beginning November 1217 the Exchequer office was open with Eustace de Faukenburg as treasurer and William

Brewer returned as clerk (PR 1215 20). Beginning Michaelmas 1218 the sheriffs were to account only for the last half year of peace, Michaelmas 1214 to Easter 1215. The Exchequer gave-up any effort to try to secure accounts for the time period of the war (*Claus* 340b, 343, 343b; PR 1214 xi-xii, 12; PR1215 56). The new Magna Carta did not include the clause that gave the twenty-five barons the right to force the king to uphold the laws of the Charter.

Marshal still had the problem of Scotland and Wales. The Treaty of Lambeth had stated that if King Alexander of Scotland and Llywelyn prince of north Wales wished to be included in the peace they should return the castles, lands, and prisoners which they had taken during the war. Alexander met the king, regent, and Guala at Northampton the week before Christmas. Alexander had already surrendered Carlisle castle, and now he was absolved from excommunication and did homage to Henry III for the earldom of Huntingdon and other lands which his predecessors had held from the king of England.

Marshal left the king at Northampton and was at his castle of Usk by December 28. From here Marshal surveyed Caerleon, which his bailiffs had taken from Morgan of Caerleon sometime after Michaelmas 1217. After his visit, Marshal returned to Westminster via Marlborough, and his manors of Hampstead Marshal and Caversham (*Brut* 96; *Hist* 17748-7786; *Claus* 349b). From February 21 through 28, 1218, Marshal, Guala, and a large body of magnates met at Sturminster. The council agreed to give William Marshal the younger the proceeds of the royal exchange in order to provide him with 1000 marks a year to sustain him in the king's service (PR 1216-1225 138-39). On February 22, 1218, the sheriffs were ordered to distrain all tenants-in-chief who had not paid the scutage of February the second, and to have the monies paid into the Exchequer by March 25, 1218. The sheriffs were also ordered to read their copies of the new Charter and the Charter of the Forest in their county courts where all knights, barons, and free tenants could hear, and to take oaths from the same of fealty to the king and oaths to uphold the laws of both charters (*Claus* 377b). Thus was allegiance to the king tied to allegiance to the Charters.

In March 1218 the Treaty of Worcester was made with Llywelyn prince of north Wales. Llywelyn agreed to not receive any enemies of the king in Wales and to insure that all magnates in Wales did their customary homage and fealty to the king. Llywelyn then did fealty and homage to Henry III and became the king's baliff for Wales. Llywelyn surrendered Montgomery and the other lands of Gwenwynwyn, Cardigan, and Carmarthen, but he got them back to hold until the king came of age (*Foedera* 150-51). Llywelyn also kept Marshal's castles of Emlyn and Cilgerran, fitz Martin's castle of Cemais, the de Lisle's castle of Laugharne, the Camville's castle of Llansteffan, the Londres's castle of Kidwelly, and the de Braose's castle of St Clears and their Gower lordship (*Brut* 92, 95, 98; Walker "Hubert de Burgh and Wales" 469-70). According to the *Brut*, sometime in 1218/1219 Rhys Gryg married Matilda de Clare, widow of William IV de Braose (k1210). John de Braose, son of Matilda de Clare and William IV de Braose, married Margaret, the daughter of Llywelyn prince of north Wales (*Brut* 219).

The reason for the regent's inaction with regard to the castles and lands held by men who had been ordered, or could be ordered, to return them to their rightful lords was the poverty of the government at the time and the lack of a king's military household that could be used to extract these men from their possession of said castles and lands. Marshal did get de Gaugi out of Newark castle and returned it the bishop of Lincoln, but for the rest, they remained in the hands of those that had held them during the war (*Claus* 365, 380; PR 1216-1225 164; Ann *Mon* iii 54). Philip of Oldcoates kept Roger de Bertam's castle of Mitford, Falkes kept William de Beauchamp's castle of Bedford, Henry fitz Count kept Totnes, Henry de Tracy kept Barnstaple from Reginald de Braose, and the count of Aumale kept de Colevill's castle of Bytham and Hugh de Neville's forest of Rockingham (*Claus* 379b). Many of the castles' custodies could really only be settled in court where the right to them would have to be proven.

However, in July 1218 at Leicester, Marshal decided that he not only could but he would get control of the deforestation process before the shires removed all the forests from royal hands. He ordered the men of Huntingdon to pay a fine of 40 marks for their deforestation and to make a new survey (perambulation) of the forest to determine what was Richard's and John's afforestation and what was Henry II's. The regent then ordered twelve knights for each country to attend to the survey of their individual forests; the results were to be sent to the king who would decide what was to be deforested and what was not (PR 1216-1225 162, 197).

The rest of the summer Marshal spent at his manors of Hampstead Marshal and Long Crendon, the castle of Marlborough, and his manor at Caversham. During this summer Ranulf earl of Chester, William de Ferrers earl of Derby, and John de Lacy constable of Chester castle left on a Crusade to the Holy Land (Walt Cov 240-

41; *Ann Mon* ii 289; iii 54). This may have alleviated some of the pressure on the regency government because as crusaders, no change in the lands they held could be executed until they returned.

Now to attend to the acquisitions Marshal made to his family and *familiares* and himself during his regency. Marshal's bastard nephew, John Marshal, was made chief justice of the forest, given the custody of all the royal manors pertaining to the forests and the custody of fees in Dorset and Somerset; Marshal's knight Henry fitz Gerold was granted markets on three of his manors (PR 1216-1225 123-24). Marshal's knight John d'Erley was given the custody of an heir with his lands (*Claus* i 344, 368, 369b, 370). Jordan de Sackville, who had lost his lands in Ulster under King John, got them back and was appointed a justice itinerant in the fall of 1218 (Sweetman Doc. Ireland #775; PR 1216-1225 208). William Marshal the younger was given the custody of the lands of eight rebels during the war, including the lands of the earls of Winchester and Huntingdon, and of Gilbert de Gant (*Claus* i 299b, 305b, 309b, 310, 31; PR 1216-1225 45). At the time of the peace, thirty fees of de Gant were still held by the young Marshal. The younger William had the custody of more than forty-six fees in Buckinghampshire and Bedfordshire. In Febraury 1218 the younger Marshal had been granted the proceeds from the money exchanges (royal monopolies) in the cities of London, Winchester, Durham, York, and Canterbury (PR 1216-1225 138). As regent Marshal can be shown to have used his position to grant favors to his family and *familiares,* but with the exception of his own son, not excessive favors.

The grants made to William Marshal are divided into two groups; those he was given as earl of Pembroke and lord of Leinster, and those that Marshal was given as regent of England. When Llywelyn appealed to the king against Marshal for Marshal's taking of Caerleon, it was the earl of Pembroke's bailiff who answered for Marshal's side in the case. It was as the earl of Pembroke that Marshal received 100 marks from the bishop of Lincoln for helping him retake his castle of Newark and therefore not answerable to the exchequer (*Claus* i 602). Some time before the death of King John, Marshal had apparently taken some of the bishop of Ferns' lands in Ireland. Albin O'Molloy was the bishop of Ferns and a friend of King John's and he appealed to Rome. Felix, bishop of Tuam, and Henry, bishop of Dublin, informed Marshal that his lands in Ireland were under interdict because he was unlawfully detaining property of the see of Ferns. Marshal was warned to make restoration or the bishops of England would excommunicate him. Pope Innocent III did not confirm the excommunication of Marshal, and the case disappeared from the records (Way "Letter from the archbishops of Tuam and Dublin"138). Early in 1218 the bishop of Ferns brought the case before an ecclesiastical court and the archbishops of Tuam and Dublin and demanded the manors of Temple Shanbo and Ferns be returned to him. On April 18, 1218, the king wrote a letter prohibiting them from bringing a case against the regent. The letter stated that the ecclesiastical court was prohibited from hearing a plea against a lay fee which Marshal claimed to hold of the king (PR 1216-1225 148-49). Since the king, as a minor, could not warrant Marshal in this case, the prelates were forbidden to hold the plea until the king came of age. Letters were also sent to the justiciar to see that the judges did not hear this case, and they were attested by Peter des Roches, not by Marshal as regent. Other letters were sent to Geoffrey Marsh ordering him to take security from the bishops that they would appear before the king to answer their offense if they heard the case, and from the bishop of Ferns if he prosecuted the case (PR 1216-1225 173-74). These letters bore the attestation of Marshal himself as regent. Marshal also wrote to Rome on this matter, and on June 29, 1218, the pope ordered the judges to compromise on the case and requested the bishop of Ferns and Marshal to come to an agreement. According to Painter, Marshal, acting as regent in the king's name, prohibited the holding of a plea against the earl of Pembroke according to the law of England (Marshal 269, 269 n186).

In another case in Ireland, Meiler fitz Henry in 1210 had rebelled against his lord Marshal as lord of Leinster. John had given to Marshal Meiler's castle of Dunamase, but he had kept the homage, service, and fees of Meiler in Leinster to himself. Two royal letters under the seals of Peter des Roches and the legate on December 2, 1216, ordered the justiciar to return to William Marshal, lord of Leinster, the service of Meiler, and to allow ships to go freely to Marshal's port of New Ross (PR 1216-1225 9). The other letter to Meiler ordered him to answer to William Marshal for the fief that he held of him and render him the service due for, "William was always faithful and devoted to our father while he lived and now he adheres steadfastly to us, and we have greatly commended his humility before all the magnates of our realm; he has proved himself in this time of need to be like gold tested in a furnace" (PR 1216-1225 10). Marshal could have asked the legate to order the justiciar to return Meiler's fee to him, but he could hardly have dictated the words used to Meiler. Marshal thus was completely reinstated in all of his possessions in Ireland.

As regent, Marshal made certain that ships were not prevented from going to his port at New Ross in Ireland, and he saw that his English lands were well supplied with markets and fairs. On March 3, 1218, he granted himself an annual fair at his manor of Sturminster in Dorset to be held on Tuesday, Wednesday, and Thursday of Pentecost week (*Claus.* i 353). Marshal established a weekly market at his manor of Speen in Berkshire (*Claus i* 354). On June 3, 1218, Marshal ordered the sheriff to allow him to hold a market every Thursday on his manor of Crendon (*Claus i* 363b). In August Marshal granted himself a fair every year and a market every Thursday on his manor of Toddington in Bedforshire, and in September he established a weekly market at Bosham in Sussex (*Claus i* 368, 370). These measures were taken by Marshal to encourage and support trade and commerce within his lands and to greatly increase his own revenue resulting from those fairs and markets.

As for castles, Marshal had taken custody of Marlborough in 1217 and received thirty-two pounds a year from the revenues of Wiltshire for its maintenance (*Claus* i 521). To repair the castle at the end of the war, Marshal had appropriated the hidage of the manor of Wantage, and also took possession of a mill near the gates of the town of Marlborough (*Claus i* 574b, 466). In February 1219 Marshal had granted himself custody of the castle of Gloucester with a manor to provide for its maintenance (*Claus i* 388, 399). Thus Marshal had used his power as regent to gain custody of two royal castles, but in all fairness to Marshal, he could possibly plead a case of inheritance for Marlborough dating back to John fitz Gilbert, and who better than the regent to have custody of the royal castle of Gloucester? Marshal took custody of a few fiefs that were in the hands of the crown, but they were somewhat small and unimportant (PR 1216-1225 117; *Claus* i 361, 367b, 368b).

The one questionable act of Marshal with regard to his acquisition of lands involves the royal escheat of the lands of the count of Perche. When the count of Perche was slain at the battle of Lincoln in May 1217 his uncle, the bishop of Chalons, became his heir. Since the bishop was a Frenchman, the honour of Peche remained in the hands of the king until such time as peace was declared. The regent placed the honour in the hands of William earl of Salisbury (*Claus* i 311b). The manors involved were Aldbourne and Wanborough in Wiltshire, Newbury in Berkshire, and Toddington in Buckinghampshire (PR 1216-1225 7, 9b, 66b; *Claus* 3b, 311b, 333). On December 2, 1217, the regent issued letters of safe conduct to the bishop to come to England. The bishop apparently sold his rights to the honour of Peche to Marshal and the earl of Salisbury (*Liber Feodorum* 154; PR 1216-1225 129). Marshal got the demesne manors of Newbury and Toddington, except for land worth one hundred shillings a year, and half the manor of Shrivenham. The earl of Salisbury got the manors of Aldbourne and Wanborough and the other half of Shrivenham (*Feodorum* 748, 864, 866). These lands apparently rounded out the lands that Salisbury and the regent held in Berkshire and Wiltshire. In 1229 the king conceded these lands in hereditary right to Salisbury and the regent's heirs (Cal. Charter Rolls 102). It is worth noting that William Marshal was the nephew of the grandfather of Ela, heiress to the earldom of Salisbury and wife to William Longespee. However, the regent had no right to buy these lands from the bishop without the king's consent, and there is no record of a contemporary granting of this right by Henry III. With the exception of this one instance, no other case is known where Marshal allowed his personal interest to interfere with the proper governing of the realm.

In September 1218 Marshal paid his last visit to his lordship of Striguil (*Claus* i 370). On October 2, 1218, Marshal stopped at his manor of Crendon, the caput of the honour of Giffard, and was at Westminster on October 9 (PR 1216-1225 169; *Claus* i 370). It may have been in this time away from London that Marshal arranged for the marriage of his daughter Eve with Reginald de Braose's son William.

Between the end of October and first of November 1218 a great council met at Westminster. The Legate Guala was there, though within a month he would leave for Rome having resigned his position as papal legate to England. Stephen Langton was back from Rome and again active as the archbishop of Canterbury. Fourteen bishops, nine abbots, eight earls, and fifteen greater barons are known to have been at this council with Marshal, the legate, two archbishops, and the justiciar (PR 1216-1225 177). Henry III was to be given his own seal which was entrusted to the keeping of the chancery clerk, Ralph de Neville (*Chron Maj* iii 74, 364; iv 367). The first royal letter issued under the king's seal announced the use of this seal. There would be no charter, nor letter patent that conferred any grant in perpetuity issued under the king's seal until the king came of age. If any charter should be issued contrary to this decree, it would be considered invalid. William Marshal could issue writs in the king's name, but from this point so could de Burgh as justiciar and des Roches, and the seal would follow the king. Marshal was preparing for his retirement, his exiting of the stage. After the introduction of the king's seal, des Roches attested to almost as many letters/writs as Marshal. Painter says it is a tribute to Marshal's remarkable abilities that because of Marshal's careful planning the government of the realm would proceed without confusion on Marshal's death (Marshal 262).

Marshal's last important administrative act was the inauguration of the first general eyre. On November 4, 1218, the whole of England, except the west midlands, was divided into eight groups of judges. They were to start on November 25, 1218, and hear all pleas, criminal and civil. These groups were usually headed by a bishop or abbot and included a justice of the bench. They were to summon all archbishops, bishops, abbots, earls, barons, knights, and free tenants in the county, four legal men from each vill, the mayor and twelve legal burghers from each borough, and anyone else who would come by common practice before the justices. All pleas of the crown which had accumulated since the last eyre, all assizes and pleas which had been set for hearing at the first visit of the judges, and all pleas and assizes which had been before the bench at Westminster but not terminated were to be brought before the justices itinerant. The sheriffs who held that office now were to appear before these judges with the judicial writ that had given them their office. The sheriffs were sent letters patent ordering this and providing the names of the judges who were commissioned for their counties (*Claus* i 403b; PR 1216-1225 206-08). The letters patent and the instructions to the justices and the form of oath they were to obtain from the assembled counties were given to one justice of each circuit. The supervision of the eyre required the vigilant participation of the regent;

he had to aid and facilitate their work and answer their complaints and questions. Any amercement of an earl or baron must be sent to his peers of the council, not addressed by the eyre, and any great lord, ecclesiastic or lay, who claimed special privileges was to be ordered to appear before the great council at Westminster fifteen days after St Hilary's. The same disposition was to be made in any case that proved too difficult for the justices of the eyre to handle (*Claus* i 383b). One example of Marshal's job and duties with regard to this eyre is that he was forced to remind the justices in Lincolnshire that they had no authority to amerce earls or barons, that the Charter had reserved that right for the council (*Claus i* 387b). One other important function of the eyre was the administration of an oath to all knights and free tenants of the counties. They were to swear "to observe firmly and faithfully the peaces of the Holy Church, the king, and the realm and to maintain and defend in good faith, all who deserved it" (*Ann Mon* iii 53). The justices also had other duties that might arise in their circuit; the justices in Lincolnshire were to see that a castle burned during John's reign and still standing was completely destroyed (PR 1216-1225 182). The justices were used for any work that the government might want done in the counties they visited. Marshal died before the justices completed their eyre, but he set them on their way and provided careful and defined guidance for their purpose.

XIV. Death of an Earl

Marshal returned to Westminster from Marlborough in mid-January 1219.
Apparently he fell ill near February 2, 1219. Marshal's illness would last over
three and a half months before he died. He was subject to sharp internal pains,
and according to the *Histoire,* the last fifteen days of his life he could eat only
mushrooms and sodden bread (*Hist* 17880-18456).

By March 1219 Marshal decided that he did not want to die in the Tower of
London, and on March sixteenth he left the Tower in one boat, with the countess
following him in another, for his manor of Caversham arriving on March 20 (PR
1216-1225 189; *Hist* 17897-7936). With his resignation in view, the regent called
the prelates and barons to Caversham; on April eighth and ninth the regent requested
the king, legate, now Pandulf the papal chamberlain who had replaced Guala, Hubert
de Burgh, Peter des Roches, and the earls to attend him at Caversham (*Claus* i 390).
Addressing the young king, Marshal said:

> Good sweet lord, I wish to speak to you before these barons. When death
> came upon your father, the legate Guala and the men of rank who were loyal
> to you met at Gloucester, and there, by God's will, you were crowned. They
> entrusted you to me. Defending your land at a time when the task was most
> difficult, I have served you faithfully, and I would continue to do so if it
> pleased God to give me strength. But He wills that I remain no longer in this
> world. Therefore your barons must choose someone to care for you and your
> realm to the satisfaction of God and man. May He give you a guardian who
> will do you honor. (*Hist* 17949-7992)

This speech angered the bishop of Winchester, who had cooperated with the regent and the legate, but who had no desire to see the office of regent transferred to another man unless it was transferred to him. The bishop's protest revealed to Marshal how difficult it would be to name another regent who would not arouse the jealousy of others and produce in-fighting that the realm could simply not withstand at this time. Marshal asked the legate to take the king back to Reading and allow Marshal time to think the problem through (*Hist* 18019-8030).

Before the king, legate, and barons returned the next morning, Marshal called his wife, son, and *familiares* to him and told them that he had decided to place the king and his realm in the hands of the legate as the representative of the pope. When the council appeared, Marshal addressed the legate:

> Sire, I have thought at length over what we talked of yesterday. I
> wish to entrust my lord the king to God, to the pope, and to you
> his representative.

Marshal then addressed the king:

> Sire, I pray God that if ever I have done anything pleasing to Him, He will
> give you the grace to be a good man. If it should happen that you follow the
> example of some evil ancestor, I pray Him not to grant you a long life. (*Hist*
> 18063-8087).

Marshal's resignation had taken place before a small group of barons because of the lack of space about his bed; Marshal then ordered his son to take the king back to Reading, and, as the regent's representative, turn the king over to the legate before the council of the whole realm. The younger William did this before the great barons in spite of an attempt by des Roches to prevent the younger William from doing as his father ordered.

276

Remember Marshal's words to Henry III for they will come back later in this tale to demand justice of the king. Marshal had effectively prevented the election of a new regent, knowing that he had no legal right to name a successor to his position, but also knowing that there was no baron of equal stature to take the position and command and get the cooperation of the greater magnates of the realm. The only possible choice was Ranulf earl of Chester who was still on crusade in the Holy Land and might or might not make it back to England. Marshal did the best he could for the protection and governing of the realm once he had gone.

Now that the office of regent had been resigned, Marshal thought to provide for the welfare of his family. This was the next ritual and obligation of a dying baron. His wife, the countess Isabel, had been with him since he first became sick and was with him now (*Hist* 17896). His eldest son William was there, his nephew John Marshal, and his five daughters. Marshal's second son Richard was at the court of Philip king of France (*Hist* 19120-9121). John d' Erley, his most faithful knight, was there; his knights Henry fitz Gerold and Thomas Basset were there also (*Hist* 18149, 18172-8174, 18204, 18308-8310). His clerk Philip and his almoner Geoffrey were with him; Geoffrey was a brother of the Knights Templar (*Hist* 18318-8320, 18685). There is no doubt that the dying earl was attended by a suitably impressive number of knights, squires, and servants.

William told them that it was time to complete his will; he had made one at least by 1200 and probably added to it each succeeding year or so, but it was time to make certain that all was taken care in regard to his family and his lordship (*Mon Ang* vii 1136). Therefore, William reviewed in his mind and out loud to those gathered the provisions of his will. The countess would hold for her lifetime all of the vast lands of her own inheritance of Striguil, Pembroke, Leinster, and her half of the honour of Giffard (*Claus* i 392 b; PR 1216-1225 195; *Layettes du Tresor* i #1354). William the younger would inherit immediately the office of marshal of England, the Marshal lands and those lands that his father had acquired, and on his mother's death would inherit all of her lands. Marshal's second son Richard received Longueville and at least part of the Giffard lands in Buckinghamshire, both groups of lands from his mother's inheritance (*Layettes du Tresor* i #13971; *Claus* ii 98b; Cal. Charter Rolls 1226-1257 142). The third son Gilbert received lands, but it is not known which lands he received at this time. Gilbert was being trained for the clerical order and in 1225 received two benefices in the gift of the crown (PR 1216-1225 531-40). The fourth son Walter was given Sturminster which William had acquired from the count of Meulan (Bracton's Note Book #71). The fifth son Anselm was given lands worth one hundred forty pounds a year (*Hist* 18149-8157). Four of Marshal's daughters were married; Maud/Matilda was married to Hugh Bigod, heir to the earldom of Norfolk. Isabel was married to Gilbert de Clare earl of Gloucester and Hertford. Sibyl was married to William de Ferrers, heir to the earldom of Derby. Eve was married to William de Braose, heir to Reginald de Braose lord of Bramber and Abergavenny. Joan/Jeanne was not married, and so William left her land worth thirty pounds a year and two hundred marks in cash to care for her until she was married (*Hist* 18158-8168). Now that his family was taken care of in his disposition of his earthly goods Marshal had to turn to the caring for his eternal soul.

Marshal had provided a legacy of thirty carucates of land for the Cistercian monks at Tintern Minor as well as 3600 acres of land he had granted to them in 1200 by a charter issued at Hampstead Marshal; Marshal had established this abbey in Ireland early in the 1200s (*Mon Ang* vii 1136). He had bequeathed the manor of Upleden in Herefordhsire to the Templars. Marshal now left fifty marks to the abbey of Nutley and a similar sum to each abbey in his lands beyond the sea. To each chapter in the same lands he left ten marks (*Hist* 18653-8665). Marshal had founded the Cistercian Duiske Abbey in Kilkenny, the Abbey of St Mary in New Ross, a sister priory of the priory of St John the Evangelist which he also founded and had given the tithes of provisions of his castle of Kilkenny. Marshal had also supported and made grants and/or confirmations of charters to Dunbrody Abbey, St Mary's Abbey in Dublin, the Abbey of St Thomas in Dublin, Abbey of Ferns, St Mary and St Columba at Inistioge, and St Canice and the priory of Kells in Kilkenny. Thus the Marshal put his worldly and spiritual house in order as befitted a great noble because in his time the care of the soul was of great importance. Brother Geoffrey drew up Marshal's testament in its final form, and Marshal's seal, Isabel's seal, and the younger William's seal were affixed to the document (*Hist* 18319-8332). The will was then sent to the legate, the primate, and the bishops of Winchester and Salisbury for them to confirm it with their own seals and be honorary executors (the abbot of St Augustine Bristol, Henry fitz Gerold, and John d'Erley were the actual executors of Marshal's will).

Marshal then turned to the matter of his lands. Having heard that Llywelyn was raising forces for an attack on the Marcher lands in south Wales, Marshal ordered John d' Erley to go to Chepstow and make certain that Marshal's men and

d'Erley's son were prepared for the possibility and did nothing rash in the meantime.

John was also ordered to get two silken cloths that Marshal had left with his man

Stephen d'Evreux and bring them back to Marshal (*Hist* 18171-8188). According to

the *Annales Cambriae* Llywelyn turned back from his attack on south Wales when he

heard that Marshal was still alive (74).

When John returned to Caversham, Marshal showed the silken cloths to

Henry fitz Gerold and asked if they were still in good condition. Then Marshal

called his son and other knights in for a judgment on the cloths. He told the men

that he had brought the cloths from the Holy Land thirty years before to be used to

cover his body when he was carried to his place of burial. When his son said that

they did know where Marshal wanted to be buried, Marshal replied that when he was

a crusader he had promised that his body would be buried in the Temple Church in

London (*Hist* 18203-8242)

Then William gave his specific instructions for his burial. John was to

see that the silken cloths were to cover him when he died, and if the weather was

inclement, to make a protective covering for the cloths when he was borne to his

grave. After he was buried, the cloths were to be given to the Templars to do with as

they wished. On the day of Marshal's funeral, his son was to provide food, drink,

clothes, and shoes for one hundred poor as such generousity was expected on the

burial of any great lord (*Hist* 18243-8260, 18605-8608).

Marshal had sent for the master of the Temple in England, Aimery de

St Maur, on the day he signed his testament. When Aimery arrived, Marshal summoned his wife and his men and told them that he wished now to join the order

of the Templars (*Hist* 18351-8358). Marshal sent Geoffrey for his templar's mantle

with the red cross on it, and then said to his wife Isabel to come and kiss him for the

last time. According to the *Histoire* as they embraced, they both wept. Then the

countess called her daughters to her, and they left the room as the Templar's mantle

was spread over William (*Hist* 18359-8397). Once a man had entered the militant

Order of the Templars he was supposed to eschew the company of all women.

After the women had left the room, Aimery de St Maur addressed Marshal

and his knights:

> Marshal attend! It pleases me that you give yourself to God. He has
> granted you a great favor that you will never be separated from Him. He
> has shown you this in your life and He will do the same after your death.
> In the world you have had more honour than any other knight for
> prowess, wisdom, and loyalty. When God granted you His grace to this
> extent you may be sure that He wished to have you at the end. You depart
> from the age with honour. You have been a '*prudhomme,*' and you die
> one. I am going to London to see to our affairs. (*Hist* 18389-8406)

This epitomizes the ideal of a chivalric knight. It is an accolade to the man who had

the true strength, skills, abilities, and qualitites that an Anglo-Norman knight had

to possess and to master in order to survive in his world. This speech by Aimery

in the *Histoire* gives the clearest example of what was the pinnacle of success in

the mind of a medieval knight. In the blending of the virtues of knighthood of

prowess, *largesse,* wisdom, and loyalty with the virtues of piety, devotion, and

support pleasing to the Church and God, the ambitions of a true chivalric knight were realized. If God gives man the power to be a perfect knight and grants him entrance into Heaven on his death, then a knight's greatest ambition is to achieve that perfection that grants him that greatest of rewards.

But a knight's world was one of brutal reality, and in the following speech by Marshal to Henry fitz Gerold, one perceives that the medieval knight did not confuse the ideal of the spiritual with the reality of the corporal. When Henry asked Marshal how he could hope to be saved if the clergy taught that a man could not be unless he returned everything that he had taken from anyone during his life. Marshal answered Henry by pointing out that if the clerics thought that he should return the ransoms he had acquired during his life of more than five hundred knights in order to obtain the kingdom of God they asked the impossible. Unless the clergy desired his damnation, they could ask no more of him than he repent his sins and give himself to God (*Hist* 18480-8502). Marshal's piety was realistic and pragmatic. The Church and the soul were not casual and intangible things in his medieval world; they were important in real ways. Thus, Marshal had founded and/or supported abbeys and churches during his life in preparation for the salvation of his soul and in recognition of the very practical necessities required of a baronial lord in his time. Like most medieval warrior knights, Marshal had balanced the spiritual expectations of the Church against the temporal realities of a military lord.

Several days after this incident, the abbot of Nutley came to see his patron Marshal. The abbey of Nutley had been founded by the earls of Giffard, and Marshal's wife, Isabel, had inherited the manor of Crendon, where the abbey had been established, as part of her share of the Giffard barony. King John had given

Marshal the *regalia* of the abbey in 1200 (*Chart* 74b). The abbot told Marshal that he had just returned from the chapter general of his order of Arrouaise (*Claus* i 378b). He had informed John II, abbot of the order of Arrouaise, of Marshal's illness and asked the abbot to admit the regent to the benefits of their order and to command that prayers be said for Marshal in their chapters. John II said that he would grant Marshal a share in the good works of their order and command that prayers for his soul be said in every house under the rule of Arrouaise. As Painter pointed out, if prayers and pious works of monks were pleasing to God, then Marshal's salvation was certain (Marshal 287). With Marshal's gifts and grants to the abbeys and chapters of his lands, there would be prayers for Marshal's soul issuing from all of the houses of the Arrouaise order, from the Cluniac priory of Longueville, from the black canons at Bradenstoke and Cartmel, from the Cistercian abbey of Tintern Minor in Ireland along with the other many monasteries there, and from that great and beautiful Cistercian abbey of Tintern in Wales (*Mon Ang vi* 337-40, 1135-136; v 267-69). Marshal had completed the duties and obligations of a dying noble by providing for his family and for his soul.

Marshal's last obligation as a feudal lord was performed on the day before he died; for the final time, he distributed robes to all the knights of his household. When this was accomplished, Marshal ordered his son William to take leave of his knights and vassals who were not with Marshal at Caversham and to thank them for their loyalty to Marshal as their lord (*Hist* 18679-8735). Marshal had thus performed his last act as a feudal baron and lord. All that was left for him to do was to die well; however, one last great boon was granted to the earl.

On the last day of his life, Marshal called to d' Earley, "John, hasten to open the doors and windows. Summon the countess and the knights, for I am dying. I can wait no longer, and I wish to take leave of them." As Marshal's household gathered in the room around his bed, the abbot of Reading came to give Marshal an urgent message:

> Sire, the legate salutes you. He sends you word by me that last night
> at Cirencester he had a vision about you. God has given to St. Peter and his
> successors, the popes, the power to bind and unbind all sinners. By the
> virtue of this power, delegated to him by the pope, the legate absolves
> you from all the sins you have committed since your birth which you
> have duly confessed. (*Hist* 18788-8976)

Thus Marshal was given the supreme gift of the church militant; he had been given the plenary indulgence of the Apostolic Vicar (Painter <u>Marshal</u> 289). Marshal's last confession was heard and forgiven by the abbots of Nutley and Reading, and the great earl died with dignity and grace, surrounded by his family, the two abbots, and his knights. A more fitting end could not have been found for a knight who served his kings and his lands for more than fifty years. Marshal had fulfilled his duties and obligations, and now others must see that the rest of the form and ritual of the death of a great noble was completed.

Marshal's body was taken to the abbey of Reading and placed in the chapel that he had founded. After a mass was said for his soul, his casket was taken to Staines. It was here that the funeral cortege was joined by a group of the greater magnates of England, who would provide suitable escort of Marshal's bier to London. William de Warenne, earl of Surrey, William de Mandeville, earl of Essex,

Robert de Vere, earl of Oxford, Gilbert de Clare, earl of Gloucester and Hertford, and many other barons and prelates joined the procession that would see Marshal's body to its final resting place. Marshal was taken first to Westminster abbey where another mass was celebrated, and there his body rested overnight. The next day, Marshal was buried in the Temple church beside his friend Aimery de St Maur, who had predeceased Marshal by several days (William of Newburg 526; *Hist* 18989-19046). Stephen Langton, archbishop of Canterbury, and William St Mere Eglise, bishop of London, officiated at Marshal's burial. Langton gave the eulogy:

> Lords, you see what the life of the world is worth. When one is dead, one is no longer more than a bit of earth. Behold all that remains of the best knight who ever lived. You will all come to this. Each man dies on his day. We have here our mirror, you and I. Let each man say his paternoster that God my receive this Christian into His Glory and place him among His faithful vassals, as he so well deserves. (*Hist* 19047-9084)

The last act of the life of the man Marshal had been played, and as much of his living life, it had been played center stage to his world.

This was not the end of the tale of Marshal's life as he had left a legacy of ten living children, and they would add to his complete story. But the vital elements of Marshal's life had been those that he had added in the living of that life. Marshal had spent more than fifty years of his life protecting, defending, and preserving the crown and realm of his land. He had lived and exemplified the virutes and characteristics of a medieval knight to the best of his ability as mortal man. Marshal had preserved the Angevin crown and the young king Henry III and had done his best to restore order, peace, and justice to an England that had been ripped apart by conflict and revolt. Marshal had earned his place in medieval history, and his act of re-issuing the Magna Carta twice during his regency insured that written law would become fact and reality in western civilization. With a bow to the crown and to his wife, Marshal exits this tale for now.

After William Marshal's death and burial, Isabel de Clare Marshal did not fail in her role as widow and heiress in her own right. She remembered well what had happened to her lands in Ireland under Prince John, and she immediately took measures to insure that all she held in her own right and all that William Marshal had held was secured for their children. In Sweetman's <u>Calendar of Documents Relating to Ireland</u>, part II, there is a letter from Isabel countess of Pembroke to Hubert de Burgh dated April/May 1219. Isabel requests writs to the sheriffs of England and to Geoffrey de Marisco, justiciar of Ireland, ordering that she be given seisin of all of the lands, castles, and vills of her inheritance as she has done homage to the king (#871, #880). Isabel quickly went to France and did homage for her Norman lands to King Philip and obtained a promise that her sons William and Richard might do the same on her death (*Layettes du Tresor* i #1354). The office of marshal of England passed to Isabel's and William's oldest son, William junior, and William junior was belted and given the title of earl and the earldom of Pembroke by Henry III on the death of his father. But the lands, castles, manors, towns, and vills that were solely Isabel de Clare's by right of her inheritance from her father Strongbow remained Isabel's until her death. It is another glimpse into the character and person of Isabel herself to note that she was not slow in reasserting her right to the lands that were hers by virtue of being the sole heir of her father Strongbow. Like Eleanor of

Aquitaine, Isabel de Clare Marshal took every action necessary to insure that all she and William Marshal held and acquired as medieval lords was preserved for their children.

XV. William Marshal's Daughters

William Marshal and Isabel de Clare were married in August 1189. They had ten children; five sons and five daughters, and all of the children lived. The birth dates of these children are not known, but it is known that William and Richard were the first two born. They are both mentioned in a marriage contract dated November 6, 1203. This was a contract to marry William the younger to Baldwin de Bethune's daughter Alice, and if William should not live to fulfill the contract, then Richard would be married to her. It is known that William the younger was born in Normandy, but this is the only known fact of the birth of any of these children.

Taking into consideration the ages of Marshal and Isabel, the frequency of Marshal's being out of England accompanying the king and his army, and the survival of all ten of the children, it is possible to frame the births in terms of roughly twenty or twenty-four month intervals between 1190 and 1207. In 1207 Isabel would have been thirty-five years old, and Marshal would have been in his sixties; this would be the possible age limit for both to have children during their time period. By using this conjectured time frame one can speculate as to the ages of the children when they married.

This part of the story will begin with the five daughters of Marshal who were all married, some more than once, and all had children. The daughters will be presented in an abbreviated form giving whom they married, when they married if known, and the names of the children they had by each marriage.

Maud/Matilda married Hugh Bigod, third earl of Norfolk, in 1206. Maud would have had to be born by 1193 in order to be at least thirteen when she married Bigod. Hugh and his father Roger, earl of Norfolk, had been among the leading rebel barons in the war against King John, and both were listed as members of the twenty-five barons in the Magna Carta who served as guarantors that the Charter would be kept by free men and by the king. Roger had regained possession of his lands and castles in 1217; on Roger's death in 1221, Hugh succeeded to the earldom and all the lands of his father. By Hugh, Maud had three sons: Roger (dsp1270) came of age in 1233 and married Isabel sister of Alexander of Scotland; Hugh (d1266) married first Joane, daughter of Robert Burnet, and second married Joan, daughter of Nicholas de Stuteville; and Ralph married Berta, daughter of the baron of Furnival. Hugh and Maud's daughter Isabella married first Gilbert de Lacy and second married John fitz Geoffrey. Hugh Bigod third earl of Norfolk died in 1225, and Maud married William of Warenne, earl of Surrey and son of Hamelin Plantagenet, bastard of Geoffrey of Anjou. By William, Maud had two children; John de Warenne (d1304) who married Alice of Lusignan, and Isabella who married Hugh de Albini, earl of Sussex. William de Warenne died in 1240 and was buried at Lewes priory. With the death of Maud's brother Anselm in December 1245, Maud received royal recognition of her right to succeed to the marshalcy of England (Close Rolls 1242-1247 443). Maud died March 29, 1248, and was buried at Tintern Abbey with her mother and two of her brothers (*Mon Ang* v 266). Before her death, Maud passed the office of marshal of England as well as the castle of Striguil and all of its appurtenances to her son and heir Roger Bigod (Morris The Bigod Earls 26, 216; Edwards Cal. Wales 29 iv 65).

Isabel married Gilbert de Clare, seventh earl of Clare and fifth earl of Hertford, on October 9, 1217. This was less than five months after her father had captured Gilbert at the battle of Lincoln in May 1217. Gilbert and his father Richard had been active rebels against King John, and both were restored to their allegiance to Henry III in the Treaty of Lambeth. Richard died in November 1217, and Gilbert succeeded to his earldoms and lands, including the earldom of Gloucester. Gilbert was at least thirty-seven years old at the time of his marriage to Isabel, but Isabel's age in not known. Between 1217 and 1230, when Gilbert died, they had six children. These children were: Richard (b1222 d1262) came of age in 1243, married (1232) Margaret, daughter of Hubert de Burgh, and married second (1237) Maud, daughter of John de Lacy; William (b1228 dsp 1258); Gilbert (b1229 dsp?); Amicia (b1220 d1283) who married (1226) Baldwin de Redvers and married second (1247) Robert de Guines; Agnes (dsp 1226); and Isabel (b1226 d1254) who married (May 1240) Robert V de Brus of Annandale. Isabel would be the mother of Robert VI and grandmother of Robert I, King of the Scots (Blakely The Brus 82). Gilbert de Clare died October 25, 1230, at Penros in Brittany. Gilbert's body was brought back to England and buried at Tewkesbury Abbey.

In April 1231, William Marshal the younger married his sister Isabel to Richard, earl of Cornwall and brother to King Henry III. By Richard of Cornwall, Isabel had four children: John (b1232 d1232); Isabel (b1233 d1234); Henry (b1235) who was killed by his cousin Guy de Montfort in Viturbo, Italy, in 1271; and Nicholas (b1240) who died with his mother. There is evidence of Isabel Marshal's true feelings with regard to her marriage to Richard of Cornwall not noted by other historians. On July 7, 1235, there is a mandate from Pope Gregory IX to Richard of Cornwall and one to Isabel countess of Gloucester. This mandate stated that they were to lay aside any doubt about the legality of their marriage and to remain married despite the fact that Richard of Cornwall was connected to Isabel's first husband, Gilbert de Clare, in the fourth degree (Cal Papal 147). By canonical law, marriage to anyone who was related to either party in the fourth degree was prohibited; this included relationship to a previous husband or wife. It is safe to assume that Richard of Cornwall did not institute this inquiry to the pope voluntarily as it would have meant that he would lose a great deal in wealth and property with the dissolution of his marriage to Isabel Marshal de Clare. This new fact plus the fact that Cornwall had been bought by his brother Henry III and supported Henry against Richard Marshal gives new understanding to the act of Isabel asking that she be buried next to her first husband, Gilbert de Clare, in Tewkesbury Abbey.

Richard de Clare, son of Gilbert and Isabel and Gilbert's heir, was given into the custody of Hubert de Burgh until 1232 when he was placed in the custody of Peter des Roches. After the murder of his uncle Richard Marshal and the removal of des Roches from King Henry III's inner circle, Richard was in the custody of his uncle Gilbert Marshal. Richard de Clare came of age in 1243 and died in 1262, but Richard of Cornwall held onto his mother's lands until Cornwall's own death in 1272 at which time Richard de Clare's son Gilbert fitz Richard inherited his grandmother's lands. Isabel Marshal died in 1240; her grandson Gilbert "The Red" inherited her lands in 1272, having already inherited the de Clare lands on the death of his father, Richard, in 1262. Matthew Paris records Isabel's death:

About the same time the noble lady Isabella, countess of Gloucester and

Cornwall, was taken dangerously ill of the yellow jaundice and was

brought to the point of death, and when her time for lying-in arrived

(for she was pregnant and very near child-birth) she became senseless,

and after having had the ample tresses of her flaxen hair cut off and made

a full confession of her sins, she departed to the Lord, together with a boy

to which she had given birth, and which not being likely to live, had been

baptized and received the name of Nicholas [. . .]. Richard returned and had

her body buried with honour at Beaulieu, a house which King John had

founded and built and appropriated to the Cistercian order. (*Matt Paris iii*

255)

Isabel wished to be buried at Tewkesbury next to her first husband, Gilbert de Clare,

but the earl of Cornwall refused her last request. According to Thomas Dingley and

the Annals of Tewkesbury, the monks of Tewkesbury did obtain Isabel's heart:

Before the altar place in the choir, the heart of Lady Isabella, wife of

Richard king of the Romans, daughter of William Marshal earl of Pembroke,

sister and co-heir of Anselm, widow of Gilbert de Clare earl of Gloucester.

Her body was buried at Beaulieu but her heart was brought in a silver cup to

the Abbot of Tewkesbury to be buried with her husband. (Dingley cccxliii;

Mon Ang ii 54-55)

Though Richard of Cornwall denied Isabel's wish to have her body buried next to

Gilbert de Clare, her first husband, Isabel achieved her ultimate wish in having her

heart next to him. Thus in the end, Isabel declared the truth of her life; it was Gilbert

de Clare that held her heart and her love.

Sibyl (d after 1238) married, before 1219, William de Ferrers, earl of Derby,

another former rebel in the war with King John. They had seven daughters and

292

no sons. Their daughters were: Agnes (d1290) who married William de Vesci of Alnwick; Isabel (d1260) who married Gilbert Basset of Wycombe; Maud (d1299) who married Simon de Kyme of Sotby; Sybil (d1273/4) who married Franco de Bohun of Midhurst (d1273); Joan (d1268) who married John de Mohun of Dunster (d1253/54) and married second Robert Aguillon; Agatha (d1306) who married Hugh de Mortimer of Chelmarsh (dc1275); and Eleanor (d1274) who married first William de Vaux, second Roger earl of Winchester, and third Roger de Leyburne of Tutbury. Sibilla died sometime after 1238, and William de Ferrers died in 1254.

Eve (d1246) married before 1219 William de Braose (Briouze), son and heir of Reginald de Braose lord of Bramber. Eve and William had four daughters. William de Braose was hanged by Llywelyn ap Iorwerth in 1230. The stated reason for the hanging was the accusation that William had dallied with Llywelyn's wife Joan, bastard of King John. This does not withstand close scrutiny, and William was in all probability hung for the crimes against the Welsh committed by his grandfather, William de Braose lord of Bramber and Abergavenny (Edwards Cal. Wales 51-52, xi, 56a, 56b). Eve and William's daughters were: Maud/Matilda (d1301) who married Roger de Mortimer of Wigmore (d1282): Isabel (d after 1246) who married (1229) David (d1246), son of Llywelyn ap Iorwerth; Eve (d1255) who married William de Cantelou (d1254); and Eleanor (dc1250) who married Humphrey de Bohun earl of Hereford (d1265). It is worth noting that Eve's daughter, Isabel, was married to the son of the man who had hung her father. Her fate is not known except for the fact that she and David had no children and that she was alive at the time of her husband's death in 1246. There are records of letters between Isabel's uncle William, her mother Eve, and Llywelyn about her marriage contract to David after her father's death, which will be given under the history of her uncle William. Given the time period and known practices, it must be assumed that Isabel's uncle, William, decided that the marriage was necessary for the good of the feudal family.

The last daughter was Johanna/Joan (d after 1234) who married Warin de Munchensi of Swanscombe after 1220. They had three children: John (dsp1247); William (dsp1287); and Joan (d1307) who married William de Valence (d1296). Warin died in 1255 and the inheritance of Johanna and Warin passed through their daughter Joan to the de Hastings of Abergavenny.

XVI. William Marshal II

Turning from Marshal's daughters, though Eve and Isabel will reappear in the stories of the two older sons, the life of the first-born son, William the younger, continues the story. William had been with his father when the regent died, and he had seen that all the form and customs of a great noble's death and burial had been fulfilled with regard to William Marshal's exit from his world.

On the death of the regent in 1219 the regency government had to be re-organized. There was no single ruling voice and authority for the minor King Henry III. The papal legate, Pandulf, was the greatest power because he held the king and England as the representative of the pope, who was the feudal overlord of both. Peter des Roches was still Henry's tutor, and Hubert de Burgh was justiciar of all England. Because of the fact that there were now three voices involved in the governing of England and the fact that those three were often not in the same place at the same time, they could not make quick and decisive judgments and decisions. In June 1219 the three men with the consent and advice of a great council worked out an arrangement for governing the realm. Hubert de Burgh was given the office of attesting to the royal letters, responsibility for the king's seal, and the job of the day-to-day governing of the realm. Hubert sat often and presided over the Exchequer and was head of the judicial administration as justiciar of England. Peter des Roches had charge of the king's person and tutoring, but was also active in the government, sitting at the Exchequer, sealing, sending, and receiving letters jointly with de Burgh (Close R Henry III 401, 401b; Pat Rolls 1216-1225 204-5).

Pandulf was still in charge and above de Burgh and des Roches until his resignation in 1221. Since September 1218 the papal legate had full power from the pope who had ordered all ecclesiastical and lay men to carryout the legate's instructions as the pope's representative in England (Walt Cov 233). Pope Honorius was concerned about the king's rights and the recovery of the demesne, castles, wardships, and escheats. As a ward and a vassal of the pope, any loss of Henry III's rights was a reflection and loss of the papal rights (Close R Henry III 378).

Carpenter points out that Hubert de Burgh, rather than des Roches, had the authority and responsibility for the day-to-day governing of the realm because of a growing sense of nationalism in England (Minority of Henry III 135). Hubert was a native born Englishman; des Roches was a native of Touraine and a foreigner. The barons trusted de Burgh to be more moderate and reasonable in his governing of England. Peter des Roches was "John's man," who had antagonized the barons by his arrogance, his heavy-handed exaction of scutages and fines, and attempts to force the barons to abjectively submit to John's will (*Ann Mon* ii 281). Hubert, though he had served under John, had spent most of his time out of England and was therefore not closely allied to King John and his unpopular policies (*Coggeshall* 139-40, 146, 154-55). It is worth noting that King John had replaced des Roches as justiciar with de Burgh at Runnymede in 1215 as an act of conciliation to the rebelling barons who wanted the "foreigners" removed from royal offices (*Chron Maj* vi 65; ii 489, 629-30). As a result of the re-ordering of the rule of the realm after Marshal's death by Pandulf and the council, de Burgh would be responsible for upholding the king's rights and dispensing justice under the guidelines of the great Charter and the

Charter of the Forest. Hubert survived in his office for thirteen years because he managed to dispense justice while balancing the politics of restoring barons to their possessions and granting them concessions against protecting the rights of the crown. Since most of the fights over the king's manors and sheriffdoms were settled through the Exchequer, de Burgh managed to control them as he was *justiciar* of the realm and head of that office.

In June 1219 David earl of Huntingdon died, and as a former rebel, some of his lands had been granted to William Marshal the younger, including Fotheringay castle. Marshal had been ordered to restore the lands to David in 1218 but had refused and held Fotheringay and some of David's lands until 1220 (Close R Henry III 305b, 354b, 397, 428b). In the fall of 1219, Marshal had impleaded Falkes de Breaute at the King's Bench at Westminster for the manors of Luton in Berkshire and the manors of Brabourne, Sutton, and Kemsing in Kent claiming that Falkes held them only at Marshal's pleasure and not in perpetuity as Falkes claimed. Hubert saw that the case was postponed until the Easter term 1220 (*CRR* viii 248-52). In January 1220 Marshal was summoned to a meeting of the great council; the letter reached him at Cirencester as he was on his way to Chepstow to see his ill and dying mother. Marshal returned the writ of summons with the request that he be given the exact date of the council in order to appear on time (Chaplais Diplomatic Documents #71).

Isabel de Clare, wife of the regent, died March 9, 1220 (*Mon Ang v* 266). It is interesting to note that Isabel died almost exactly a year after her husband, the regent. Isabel would have been forty-nine to fifty-three years old, and she had borne ten children all of whom lived. Perhaps the two strangers who had met in the Tower of London in 1189 had forged a true and inseparable bond rather than simply a practical alliance. Isabel de Clare Marshal was buried at Tintern Abbey in Monmouth, but there are no known extant records of the cause of her death or of her funeral and burial. However, there is one additional record relating to Isabel de Clare Marshal. In an article by H. G. Leask from 1948, he notes the discovery of a cenotaph (an empty tomb or monument erected to one who is buried elsewhere) discovered in the churchyard of St. Mary's Church at New Ross, Ireland. The cenotaph carried the image of a lady's head with a high fillet and a barbette (hair-net) and the words "Isabel *Laegn*" (65). The *laegn* is the beginning of the Latin word for Leinster, and Isabel de Clare was the only Isabel of Leinster as the sole heir of her father Strongbow, lord of Leinster. Leask suggests that the cenotaph may have been more than simply that; it may have marked the burial of the heart of Isabel de Clare Marshal in the parish church of St. Mary's (Leaske "A Cenotaph" 65, 67, 67 f7).

In May 1220 the barons were summoned to London for the second coronation of Henry III (Shirley <u>Royal Letters</u> i lxxxv). The coronation was held at Westminster Abbey on May 17, 1220, where Henry III was crowned king of England before most of the greater magnates of England, including most of those who had been former rebels against the king's father. This was an important act as it established before most of the realm Henry III's legitimate position as king and resulted in a beginning acceptance of Henry's right to resume the royal castles, sheriffdoms, and escheats. Philip of Oldcoates surrendered the castle of Mitford, Marshal the castle of Fotheringay, the count of Aumale was removed from Rockingham, and Henry fitz Count from Cornwall. On May 18 the barons gathered

298

and swore before the king, legate, and primate that they would resign the royal castles and wards in their hands at the king's will and would render a faithful account for their farms at the exchequer (*Ann Mon* iii 57). Immediately after this ceremony, William Marshal did homage to the king for his mother's lands and paid the one hundred pounds relief for seisin of her lands. In May or June 1220, William issued a charter dated June 20, 1220, in which he confirmed to his brother Richard all of the Norman lands that had been held by his mother and father (*Rotuli Normanniae* ii cxxxviii)

The regency government faced two problems in May 1220, Llywelyn in Wales and Hugh de Lusignan in Poitou. In May Hubert, Pandulf, des Roches, and Stephen Langton had met Llywelyn at Shrewsbury before the coronation. They had agreed to recognize Llywelyn's son, Daffydd, as Llywelyn's sole heir to the exclusion of Llywelyn's bastard son Gruffydd. Llywelyn was given the right to re-open the case of Morgan of Caerleon against the earl of Pembroke for the return of his castle and lands. Llywelyn was supposed to return the king's castle Maelienydd in exchange for these concessions (Close R Henry III 436b, 418, 448b). A truce was arranged to last until Michaelmas and a second meeting was set for August 2, 1220, to hear disputes between Llywelyn and the Marcher barons (Davies Wales 249; Walker "Hubert de Burgh and Wales" 271).

In Poitou, Hugh de Lusignan had married Henry III's mother Isabella, though he was betrothed to Henry III's sister Joan and had her in his custody as well as her marriage portion of Saintes, the Saintange, and the Isle of Oleron. Hugh was now demanding Niort in Poitou, Exeter castle and Rockingham in England as Isabella's marriage portion. The regency government replied to Hugh's demand by inviting him to England for the translation of the body of Thomas Becket in Canterbury to be held on July 7, 1220, to discuss the issues (PR 1216-1225 232-33). Hugh did not accept the invitation, nor did he return Joan or her marriage portion lands.

Two disputes that involved Marshal, earl of Pembroke, were resolved under the skillful hands of de Burgh. The case between Marshal and Falkes was settled with Falkes buying out Marshal's rights to Lutton, Sutton, Brabourne and Kemsing for one thousand pounds, though Marshal regained them after the fall of Falkes (*CRR* ix 205; *Ann Mon* iii 92). In the case of the Berkeley inheritance, which the earl of Salisbury was holding against the heir of Robert Berkeley, Robert's brother Thomas, de Burgh found a solution. Marshal paid the earl of Salisbury the sixty pounds that Robert de Berkeley had owed Salisbury. Thomas did homage for his brother's lands and paid the one hundred pounds relief for seisin of his brother's lands, and the king held Berkeley castle until 1224 (Close R Henry III 630b).

In August 1220 Llywelyn attacked in Wales, taking the lordship of Kidwelly and Swansea castle, and the lordship of Gower. Llywelyn then invaded Pembrokeshire, razing Narberth castle, seizing Wiston, and burning Haverford up to the castle gates. The knights and men of Pembroke bought a truce with Llywelyn to last until May 1221 for one hundred pounds and an agreement not to rebuild the castles that Llywelyn had destroyed (*Brut* 97-98). Llywelyn gave Gower to John de Braose, nephew of Reginald de Braose and Gilbert de Clare, and married de Braose to his daughter Margaret (*Brut 99;* Close R Henry III 459b*)*. Marshal had been caught totally unprepared for Llywelyn's attack; he had spent part of the year in France and was currently dealing with settling the debts and establishing control of his mother's lands. The regency government could do no more than issue royal letters in October ordering the men of Pembroke to consider their agreement with Llywelyn null because Llywelyn was not acting for the king (PR 1216-1225 254-55).

In April 1221 Marshal returned to England from Wales and Ireland where he had been attending to the process of surveying and assuming control of the vast lands of his mother's inheritance. On his way to London, Marshal was met by Falkes, acting as a representative of de Burgh and Pandulf, who carried a message with the offer of Henry III's sister Eleanor as wife to Marshal (PR 1216-1225 287; Close R Henry III 454b; Shirley Royal Letters i clii). This is a puzzling act, and the extant sources that provide reasons for this proposal do not illuminate the issue. From a political viewpoint, de Burgh saw this as a political alliance that would aid him governing the realm. Hubert possibly saw this also as a means of getting the greater magnates approval of de Burgh's intention to marry Margaret, sister of Alexander king of Scotland. There was also the probability that de Burgh saw this as a way to get Marshal to turn over the royal castles of Marborough and Ludgershall, which Marshal still held and which Marshal might seek to claim in court as his by right of inheritance from the time of his grandfather John fitz Gilbert (*Ann Mon* iii 68; Close R Henry III 465b).

What is more difficult to understand is why Marshal would have taken this offer; it was against everything his father had believed and known. The regent had known, lived, and worked with the Plantagenets all his life; he knew their characteristics, abilities, and faults as well as any other person in that time. Of all the things he might have wished and hoped for his children, the very last thing would have been a marriage of one of his children to any of John's offspring. This was not just because of the taint of any child born of John, but because it would have upset the balance of king and baron. Marshal understood the primary principle of feudal England and the possibilities of the Magna Carta. The king could rule only with the cooperation and support of some of his feudal barons, and the only check against the will of the king was the force and power of those same greater barons. The baron retains his power to cooperate and also check the king only if he is not "owned" by the king. So the question of why William the younger would agree to marry one of John's children and weaken his own power as an independent baron and lord remains an unsolved question.

A crisis within the realm that threatened the minority began with a perceived threat of treachery within the realm itself. A rumor had reached the ears of de Burgh and Pandulf that Peter de Maulay, castellan of Corfe castle, was planning to free Eleanor of Brittany and send her to the king of France (*Ann Mon* iii 58; *Coggeshall* 190). Eleanor was the sister of Arthur of Brittany and the daughter of Constance of Brittany and Geoffrey Plantagenet. She was therefore a granddaughter of King Henry II, daughter of an older son of Henry II, and legally capable of claiming the crown of England. Was it an actual real threat or an excuse to remove some of the foreign castellans of royal castles? It was probably a little of one and more of the other. Peter de Maulay was seized, and Corfe was surrendered to the king's representative (Walt Cov 160; *Ann Mon* ii 68; *Coggeshall* 190).

In July 1221 Geoffrey de Marsh was replaced as justiciar of Ireland by Henry de London, archbishop of Dublin; Stephen Langton returned to England, and Pandulf resigned as papal legate (Close R Henry III 476b, 477; Walt Cov 250; *Ann Mon* iii 74; PR 1216-1225 510-11). On October 1, 1221, Henry III would be fourteen and by custom he would no longer need a tutor. Henry III would not come of age to rule until he reached the age of twenty-one, but the pope as overlord of England would make any and all decisions regarding the status of Henry III. When Pandulf resigned as papal legate, no one was appointed to take his place. Pandulf had accomplished much in his office as papal legate; he had helped to resume many individual royal manors, gained the royal castles of Marlborough and Ludgershall, Corfe, Bristol, and Devizes, and resumed the farms of Lancashire, Shropshire, and Staffordshire. That a new legate was not appointed was the result of the pope's decision that Henry III was old enough to not need one and the assurances of Langton that de Burgh, with Langton's aid, was capable enough and sufficiently supported enough to govern the realm without a papal legate.

In April 1223 Wales would become the focus of the royal government and William Marshal. Llywelyn had managed to isolate the Marshal family in Wales. Llywelyn had given Maelgwyn ap Rhys the royal castle of Carmarthen in 1216. On the death of Rhys Ieuanc in 1222, Llywelyn gave Maelgwyn the castles of Cemais, St Clears, and Laugharne, and the Marshal's lordships of Cilgerran and Emlyn. Rhys Gryg held Kidwelly, and John de Braose held Gower (*Brut* 99). Marshal had not forgotten Llywelyn; he had spent the winter in Ireland gathering an army of his knights and returning to Chepstow in March 1223 to gather more knights (*Brut* 99-100; *Ann Camb* 75-76; *Ann Mon* iii 82-83). In April 1223 Marshal struck in Wales taking Cardigan, and two days later taking Carmarthen. Marshal then headed for Kidwelly where he met Llywelyn's army under Llywelyn's son Gruffydd. After having fought all day, Gruffydd retired from the field, and Marshal withdrew to the north to repair the castle of Carmarthen and rebuild the castle of Cilgerran in stone. By the end of Marshal's campaign in Wales, he had gained control of Cardigan, Carmarthen, Cilgerrran, Emlyn and Cemais; he had destroyed Maelygywn ap Rhys' control, and the dominance of Llywelyn in south Wales. In May 1223 de Burgh sent Robert de Vaus to take custody of the king's lordships of Cardigan and Carmarthen (Close R Henry III 569b; PR 1216-1225 441). Marshal's campaign is described in the *Brut* (Red Hergest):

> On Easter Monday Marshal attacked Cardigan, and that day the castle
> was surrendered to him, and the following Wednesday he drew towards
> Carmarthen and took that castle also. Gruffudd, son of Llywelyn, came to
> meet Marshal at Kidwelly. After fighting all day, they both fell back, but
> because of lack of provisions, Gruffudd withdrew to his own land Marshal
> repaired the castle of Carmarthen and began to build a stone castle at
> Cilgerran. (223-35)

A meeting was arranged between Pembroke and Llywelyn at Ludlow on July 8-9, 1223, but Llywelyn would not cooperate. Stephen Langton, who had helped to arrange the meeting, excommunicated Llywelyn and placed his lands under interdict (*Brut* 100; Shirley Royal Letters i cxci; PR 1216-1225 376). Hubert de Burgh entered the battle and placed the weight of the full government behind Pembroke, placing Pembroke and Salisbury in command of an army that contained about one hundred forty knights, mostly supplied by six earls and the tenants-in-chief of the southwestern shires of England. William Marshal now had Cilgerran castle back in his hands, and he refortified this de Clare/Marshal castle using stone (Close R Henry III 596; PR 1216-1225 377, 406-07; *Brut* 225).

On July 14, 1223, King Philip of France died, and the government of England decided that they would send Stephen Langton, the bishop of London, and the bishop of Salisbury to France to try to persuade the Archbishop of Rheims to postpone Louis' coronation until he gave back the Angevin lands in Normandy as he had agreed to do in the unwritten portion of the Treaty of Lambeth in 1217 (PR 1216-1225 406; *Ann Mon* iii 81). This plan came to nothing as the barons of Anjou did not rise in support of Henry III, and Langton and his colleagues did not arrive in France until after Louis' coronation. Louis told Langton and the bishops that if the English made any hostile move toward Anjou, he would gather an army and invade England again (*Ann Mon* iii 81-82).

In September 1223 Llywelyn attacked Reginald de Braose's castle of Builth, and the government summoned all tenants-in-chief, except for the barons already involved in south Wales, to assemble at Gloucester. Builth was relieved on September 21-23, and then the army with de Burgh and the king moved to Montgomery (*Foedera* 170; *Chron Maj* ii 64). Here a new castle was constructed which would help secure the region from the Welsh, and thus royal power was established in Wales to check Llywelyn (Davies Wales 230-31, 233, 235). By October Llywelyn, Maelgwyn ap Rhys, and Rhys Gryg had come to the king at Montgomery and made their submission. Langton removed the excommunication from Llywelyn and the interdict on his lands. This agreement stated that Llywelyn and his allies could regain only those lands that they had held in fee from the time the war began (PR 1216-1225 386, 411-12, 481; *Ann Mon iii* 83). Llywelyn lost southern Powys and Montgomery; Maelygyn lost Carmarthen and Cardigan castles, which he had held as Llywelyn's constable. They lost Cemais, Cilgerran, Emlyn, St Clears, Laugharne, Llansteffan, and Kidwelly; these lands would be returned to their Marcher lords.

At Westminster on December 10, 1223, Langton and de Burgh decided to put into effect the papal order of April 1223 that the king would henceforth attest personally with his own seal all future royal letters (Close R Henry III 587). This did not mean that the king had come of age; he was still prohibited from making permanent alienations of fiefs, castles, and titles. This meant that the king would take personal responsibility for the issuing of royal letters and for the decisions that those letters might institute. Hubert de Burgh remained at the king's side to aid him along with the assistance of Jocelin of Wells, bishop of Bath, and Richard le Poore, bishop of Salisbury (*Foedera* 171). Langton, though not an actual part of the government, took an active role in the realm's political life. He greatly influenced the government's support of the Charters, supported the program of the resumption of royal rights, and fought to maintain the peace and order of the realm. Langton, who had helped shape the Magna Carta, was committed to the principle that the king proceed by judgment or by the law of the land, not by his will. Langton would participate in crucial decisions in this time that would aid to shape the political future of England (Holt Magna Carta and Government 188). In the serious political crisis approaching the realm, Langton supported de Burgh because he saw de Burgh as the keeper of the peace of the realm. Langton saw de Burgh's opponents, des Roches, de Maulay, William de Cantelupe, Ranulf earl of Chester, Gilbert earl of Gloucester, John de Lacy, Robert de Vieuxpont, Falkes, Brian de Lisle, and de Cigogne as disturbers of the peace and order of England. As early as the 1220s des Roches had determined to pull down Hubert de Burgh and replace de Burgh with himself as the ruling power in the king's minority. Peter des Roches had found an ally in Ranulf earl of Chester, who violently disliked de Burgh (Walt Cov 260). Since de Burgh was currently allied with Pembroke and since the earl of Chester's heir, John the Scot, was married to one of Llywelyn's daughters, this doubled the antipathy of Ranulf against de Burgh. One important element of this struggle was essentially a question of nationality. The core of the knightly class in early thirteenth century England was English in the sense of being a native-born Englishman or in considering England as their homeland. The great Anglo-Norman families who had helped to found feudal England considered their homeland where they had the most estates and spent the most time, England or Normandy. Though both foreigner and native had fought together during the war against Louis' invasion of England, the re-establishment of peace and order in England seemed to bring the issue of aliens to the forefront. Too many of the castellans and sheriffs appointed by King John and who still held castles and sheriffdoms that rightfully belonged to either the king or even former rebels were by birth and thought foreigners. Many of des Roches' allies were these very aliens who did not consider themselves English and who were in their positions because of the excessive actions and exactions of King John. In the eyes of many Englishmen these men were stained by both the brush of alienism and of the injustices of King John. They may have seen England as their greatest chance of a future at a higher level than mercenary, but they certainly did not think of themselves as Englishmen, nor did those who were actually Englishmen. Led by Peter des Roches, these men tried to seize the person of the king in London, attacked the Tower of London, and now were planning a gathering of their armed men at Northampton for Christmas 1223 (Close R Henry III 58; PR 1216-1225 481-82).

Both the schismatics and the royalists had sent envoys to Rome arguing in the first cause that de Burgh needed to be removed, Langton needed to be recalled, and a new papal legate needed to be appointed, and in the second cause that Langton and de Burgh had control of the peace of the realm and that neither England nor the minor king needed another papal legate. The king, most probably with the advice of de Burgh and Langton, announced that he intended to spend Christmas at Northampton, and the other side withdrew to the earl of Chester's borough of Leicester (*Ann Mon* iii 84).

When the king arrived at Northampton, he arrived with so many bishops, earls, barons, and armed knights that all the populace remarked on the unprecedented sight of such a holiday gathering. Pembroke, the earls of Salisbury, Surrey, Essex, Norfolk, Warwick, Hereford, and Derby were in the king's company, along with Robert fitz Walter, Robert de Ros, and William de Albini (*Foedera* 171; Close R Henry III 579b). One can safely assume that a show of force and support was not lost on those who wished to change the king's government. The day after Christmas, Langton and his suffragans excommunicated all disturbers of the realm, and the king summoned the earl of Chester and his supporters to his court at Northampton.

They appeared at Northampton on December 30, 1223, and were shown the papal letters ordering that all of the king's castles were to be returned to him. Langton promised excommunication if the barons did not obey, but he also promised that all would be treated equally and that those men of the king's party who held royal castles would also be surrendering them (Walt Cov 262; *Ann Mon* iii 84; *Chron Maj* iii 82-83). The Chancery rolls of December show that Chester resigned the castles of Shrewsbury, Bridgnorth, and Lancaster as well as their sheriffdoms. Falkes gave up the castle of Hertford and the castle and sheriffdom of Oxford and Northampton. The castles of Windsor and Odiham were given up by de Cigogne; Knaresborough, Bolsover, and the Peak were surrendered by de Lisle; the castle of Kenilworth and sherriffdoms of Warwickshire and Leicestershire were surrendered by de Cantilupe (PR 1216-1225 417-21). On January 7, 1224, des Roches was ordered to give up the castles of Winchester, Portchester, and Southhampton as well as the sherriffdom of Hampshire. Hubert de Burgh resigned the castles of Dover, Canterbury, Rochester, Norwich, Orford, and Hereford; Salisbury resigned Salisbury castle, and William Brewer resigned Devizes.

Langton placed many of the castles and counties in the hands of ecclesiastics; the bishops of Bath, Salisbury, London, Lincoln, and Hereford, and the archbishop of York received custody of some of the castles. Many of the royalists' supporters retained the castles and/or sherriffdoms that they had resigned, but this was due to the fact that Chester and de Roches had brought the country to the brink of war and even now were refusing to accept the king's right to resume his royal castles (PR 1216-1225 430). The rules governing sherriffdoms were also changed at this time.

Sherriffs were appointed as custodians who were answerable at the exchequer for all the revenues which they collected from their county farms, and these same terms applied to any and all who had retained their office's as sheriff (Carpenter <u>Minority of Henry III</u> 328-29, 329 f 17, f 18).

Hubert de Burgh survived this attempt to overthrow him because he exercised a moderate form of government and because he recognized and respected the inherent changes that the Charters had made to the form and policy of the government of the realm. The clause limiting the relief of a barony to one hundred pounds was strictly observed as well as the clauses regarding the administration of justice. The King's Bench was at Westminster for all to use, and the eyres of the counties were in action for justice to be available for the local populace. Any amercement of a baron was reserved to the king's council, and the king's judges visiting the counties once a year heard the assizes with knights from those counties. Hubert dealt with the debts owed to the crown with great latitude to avoid any reminder of the ruthlessness of King John. Hubert stressed and understood that the connection of the king's rights to the rights of his subjects was essential because if the king's rights were not protected, then the king could not protect the rights of his subjects. Two things that de Burgh possessed that des Roches did not; de Burgh understood the barons and magnates of England and the necessary balance between them for the realm to survive; even more important, de Burgh realized and recognized that the great Charter had changed the form and means of government and rule of England. Peter des Roches never understood the changes that the Magna Carta and the later versions of the Charter had brought to the governing of the realm and to the limits of the "king's will." Peter des Roches never grasped that he was no longer living in John's world; John's world had brought rebellion, war, and the Magna Carta. The one thing that had survived that world and changed it forever was the Magna Carta and the ideas of justice and rule it evinced.

On April 23, 1224, William Marshal married the sister of King Henry III, Eleanor (*Ann Mon* iii 83; PR 1216-1225 376, 481). She was only nine at the time of this marriage, and it seems that King Henry III married her to Marshal to keep Marshal from marrying into either a Normandy family and increasing his ties to his brother Richard, or into the de Brus family and strengthening his ties to Scotland (PR 1216-1225 156; Edwards Cal. Wales #109; Chaplais Diplomatic Documents #140). Henry III wrote to his representatives in Rome explaining this marriage:

> In order to counter malicious misrepresentations which may be
> made to the pope and cardinals, Henry III gives the reasons which led him,
> by counsel of his magnates, to give his younger sister in marriage to the Earl
> Marshal. (1) In order to avoid the inconvenience and danger of the earl's
> making a marriage alliance to either the sister of the Earl of Bruce or the
> daughter of the King of Scotland or the daughter of the Duke of Brabant, all
> of whom were foreigners. (2) Because of the faithful service given by the
> earl, especially in Wales, where the earl had recovered certain royal castles
> which Llywelyn, Prince of North Wales, had taken and which would have
> scarcely otherwise been recovered. (3) Because of the example of the kings
> of France who have married their daughters, sisters, nieces to their own
> nobles rather than to foreigners. (Shirley Royal Letters i 244-46)

This marriage of William to the sister of the king severely limited his ability to remain a baronial check against the possibility of royal abuse of law and power. It was also one of the greatest errors a king could make. For the Crown to enter into an alliance with one of the most powerful of the baronial families, especially an alliance by marriage, was to put into jeopardy the power of the king to restrain the barons' power. On February 5, 1224, Langton, de Burgh, and the bishops of Bath and Salisbury, and the king arranged for the approved marriage of Henry's nine-year-old sister, Eleanor, to William Marshal (PR 1216-1225 426). The marriage did not take place until April 23, 1224, according to Gervase of Canterbury (113).

Meanwhile, in March 1224 an agreement made before Langton, the bishops of Bath, Salisbury, and Ely, de Burgh, Pembroke, and the earl of Salisbury sent Walter de Lacy to Ireland to stop his brother Hugh and their half-brother William from pillaging and burning the king's lands and either killing or holding the king's men for ransom (PR 1216-1225 483). Hugh de Lacy, who had been aiding and abetting Llywelyn in his wars against Marshal in Wales, decided to attack Marshal's and the king's lands in Ireland (Shirley Royal Letters i 4, 174). When Walter failed to stop his brother Hugh in Ireland, William Marshal was appointed justiciar of Ireland on May 24, 1224, and ordered to take into the king's peace all but de Lacy and the other major rebellious barons (Sweetman Doc. Ireland i 185-87; Close R Henry III 600-03, 605b). In July 1224 Marshal took William de Lacy's castle of Trim and the crannog of O'Reilly and sent his cousin William le Gras to take Hugh's castle of Carrickfergus (Brooks Knights' Fees 71-74; Shirley Royal Letters i 500-02, 203-04). Hugh surrendered to the king in October 1224 and was sent to England. Marshal remained justiciar of Ireland until June 22, 1226, when he surrendered his office to the king at Winchester (Sweetman Doc. Ireland i 12, 13, 14; Shirley Royal

Letters i 500-02).

From 1228 William was mostly in England and high in the king's favor. On May 2, 1230, Llywelyn of Wales hung William de Braose the son and heir of Reginald de Braose and the husband of Eve Marshal (*Brut 229*). The alleged reason for the execution of William de Braose was that he had been caught with Llywelyn's wife Joan, bastard of King John, in Joan's bedchamber. This was all a manufactured lie to cover the reality of de Braose being executed for the sins of his grandfather. Llywelyn wrote two letters, one to Eva de Braose and one to William Marshal, soon after killing William de Braose. In both Llywelyn states:

> The magnates of Llywelyn's land would not forgo judgment on William de Braose, who had plotted treachery against Llywelyn, entering Llywelyn's chamber, and bringing upon Llywelyn opprobrium beyond measure. Llywelyn wishes to know if Eva and Marshal still wish to have the alliance between Eva's daughter Isabel and Llywelyn's son Dafydd. Llywelyn still desires it and wishes to be informed as to their intentions. (Shirley Royal Letters i 368, 369)

The marriage did take place between Isabel de Braose and Daffydd, and one can only imagine the justification William Marshal made to his sister and her daughter about why it was necessary for Isabel to marry the son of the man who had killed her own father.

In August 1230 William Marshal accompanied the king to Brittany. William stayed in Brittany with Ranulf of Chester until February 1231 when he returned to England (Sweetman Doc. Ireland #1680, #1789, #1812; *Ann Mon* i 78). In March, William arranged the marriage of his sister Isabel, widow of Gilbert de Clare, to

Richard, earl of Cornwall and brother to King Henry III (*Ann Mon* i 78). This is
the second act of William Marshal that raises questions. Marshal's own marriage to
John's daughter Eleanor would have greatly displeased his mother, Isabel de Clare,
who had a healthy antipathy for John and what he had done to her Irish lands. But
for Isabel's son to marry his own sister to another child of John would have enraged
her, especially as this daughter was Isabel's own namesake. The fact that Isabel
found this marriage to Richard of Cornwall highly distasteful and unwanted is
clearly revealed in Isabel's wish to be buried by her first husband Gilbert de Clare at
Tewkesbury Abbey.

William Marshal's reasons for subjecting his sister to such a marriage are
not known; what little contemporary information available regarding this marriage
does leave the distinct impression that it was not done by his sister's wish or with
her own welfare considered. Isabel had given Gilbert de Clare six children; she had
her dower rights of de Clare's lands, and she had five living brothers who could have
seen to her welfare and status as a noble widow. There was no reason for her to have
to marry again, and William Marshal's actions in this matter, as in the matter of his
niece's marriage to Llywelyn's son, are questionable to say the least. They seem to
be the actions of a man making power alliances which were not necessary. It seems
incomprehensible that the son of William Marshal would have not learned from his
father that the greatest mistake a baron or a king could make was to enter into an
alliance with each other. What makes the marriage of Isabel to Richard of Cornwall
so ironic is the fact that within less than a month after this marriage, William
Marshal the younger died on April 6, 1231, at about the age of forty (*Ann Mon* iii 76-

78).

Considering that William's father, the regent, had lived to well into his seventies and had a longer and much more physically active life than his son, it does seem somewhat puzzling that the son died at barely forty years of age leaving no children at all. There are no records of what and how William died, but Matthew Paris in his chronicles writes that later in King Henry III's reign Hubert de Burgh, justiciar of England, was accused of poisoning William Marshal (*Chron Maj* iii 223). There are no other sources that agree with this which makes this allegation not credible, and there are no other records or chronicles that give any additional information regarding William's death. William was buried near his father in the Temple Church in London on April 15, 1231.

XVII. Richard Marshal

When William died, his brother Richard, who was his heir, was in France. Richard had probably gone to Normandy to take charge of his mother's share of the Giffard lands in early 1219 when Richard would have been twenty-seven or twenty-eight years old. Richard did not arrive in England until the end of July 1231. Richard had been at the French court at the time of the death of his father in 1219. It is not known exactly when he went to Normandy, but it certainly would not have been before the Treaty of Lambeth had been signed. William Marshal senior had given Richard the Normandy lands as Richard's inheritance on William's death in 1219, and this had been confirmed when William the younger had deeded these lands to Richard in 1220 (*Rotuli Normanniae* cxxxviii; *Ann Mon* i 79). Isabel Marshal had gone to France soon after William's death in 1219 to secure her Norman lands for her sons William and Richard (*Layettes du Tresor* I #1354). On Isabel's death in 1220, both William and Richard had gone to the French court where Richard had done homage to King Philip against all men for his father's and mother's Norman lands. If Richard should die, William would do liege homage to the French king for only the lands on that side of the sea, as his father William had done (*Layettes du Tresor* I #1397).

Richard had been in England and Normandy and Ireland during the years that his brother William lived. He was lord of Long Crendon in England, a part of the Giffard inheritance, which may have been given to him by his brother William (*CRR* xiii #861, #1355, #1730, #2294, #2311; xiv #672, #1150, #1723). Richard had been in Ireland for he was a witness for at least two charters of his brother there between 1220 and 1230 (Cal. Ormond i p 23 #46, p 36 #76). So Richard Marshal did not come to England and to his parents' lands as a stranger; he had lived there for most of the first twenty-eight years of his life and had been there frequently during the past ten years of his older brother's time.

Roger of Wendover in his history wrote that when Richard came to England and to King Henry III at the castle of Matilda in Wales, Henry tried to deny Richard his right to *seisin* of his parents' and brother's lands, titles, and offices on the advice of Hubert de Burgh, justiciar (Giles ii 542). This story is surely a fabrication as all other contemporary chronicles state that Richard did homage and was granted investiture of all his lands on August 3, 1231. They record no delay by Henry III in granting Richard seisin of his brother's lands, castles, and titles (*Ann Mon* ii 127, iv 72: Sweetman Doc. Ireland i #1905).

Prior to 1224 Richard had married Gervaise, daughter of Alan de Dinan, and had become in her right lord of Dinan. Alan de Dinan was a magnate in Brittany, and his daughter and heir, Gervaise, had already been married twice. Her first husband was Juhel de Mayenne, whom she had married before 1198 and had given three daughters. The eldest daughter of this marriage, Isabel, had been married to Dreux de Mello by 1216. Her second husband had been Geoffrey viscout of Rohan, a Breton magnate who had died in 1221. Why Richard married such an older woman who had little chance of giving him children is not clear. Perhaps he did so at the behest of the king of France, or perhaps he did so presuming that he was not likely to inherit the patrimony of his father and mother because of his older brother

William. One chronicle wrote that Richard had received the best knightly and chivalric training in France and was the "marshal of the army of the King of France" (*Ann Mon* iv 72).

After receiving investiture of his lands, Richard spent the months of April to November 1231 visiting and assuming control of his parents' lands in England and Wales. In November Richard went to Ireland and stayed until June 1232 to take control of his mother's vast Irish lands. It is definitely worthy of note that on February 12, 1232, Pope Gregory IX sent a mandate to the bishop of Lisieux to determine what degree of affinity existed between Richard Marshal and his wife Gervaise de Dinan (Cal Papal 131). Was Henry III contemplating trying to marry another of his siblings to Richard Marshal so that he could eventually gain control of all of Marshal's vast lands and lordships? One needs to look at the marriages that occurred between King John's children and William Marshal's children. There are serious questions that arise from these new discoveries of Pope Gregory's inquiries and monitions regarding Isabel Marshal's marriage to Richard of Cornwall and Richard Marshal's marriage to Gervaise de Dinan. Whose purpose and what agenda was behind these letters regarding the marriage of these two children of William Marshal? Who may have wanted to acquire some of the vast lands held by William Marshal the elder? Henry III and some of his advisors worked to acquire substantial Marshal lands as dower for his sister Eleanor as the widow of William Marshal the younger even though Eleanor was only about sixteen when William Marshal died. Not until June 1232 did Richard Marshal meet King Henry III at Worcester and work out an arrangement in regard to the dower rights of Henry's sister Eleanor, widow of

William the younger (Sweetman Doc. Ireland i #1950; Brooks Knights' Fees 45).

Meanwhile, forces were at work in England that would eventually draw Richard Marshal into rebellion against Henry III's *curiales*. In July 1231 Peter des Roches returned to England from five years on crusade, and he went to Painscastle in Wales with de Brugh's old enemy Peter de Mauley to see Henry III (*Chron Maj* iii 211). In the redistribution of royal castles and sheriffdoms in 1222/1223, des Roches had lost the castle and sherriffdom of Hampshire and most of his power along with his allies in that power struggle. Peter had vowed to "remove de Brugh if it cost him all that he had" (*Ann Mon* iii 84). Now he was back to accomplish this and to put his nephew, Peter des Rivaux, back into power.

Hubert de Burgh had lost most of his supporters; William Marshal had died, Stephen Langton had died, and the archbishopric of Canterbury had been vacant since Richard Grant, Langton's successor, had died in 1231 (*Chron Maj* iii 205-06). Richard le Poore, bishop of Salisbury in the crisis of 1222/1223, was now bishop of Durham and removed from the court, and Joscelin of Wells was no longer influential at court (Walt Cov ii 268; Close R Henry III i 578). Hubert de Burgh had antagonized and created a great many enemies during his time as justiciar. Many of the men were old servants and allies of King John who had held their offices, castles, and sheriffdoms since the civil war of 1215-1217. Many were foreign mercenaries that had been put in office by King John and had been one of the major contributing causes to the baronial rebellion in 1215, but one was the powerful earl of Chester. Chester had lost the castles and sheriffdoms of Lancashire and Shropshire-Staffordshire in 1223 (Walt Cov ii 251). Hubert had opposed Richard of Cornwall in 1227 over a dispute about a manor that had ended with the earls of

Chester, Gloucester, Surrey, Hereford, Derby, Warwick, and Pembroke supporting

Richard of Cornwall instead of the king and de Burgh (Denholm-Young Richard

of Cornwall 10-12). Instead of supporting Richard Marshal in his succession to his

brother William, de Burgh had created difficulties for Marshal, which had earned

him Richard's distrust (*Chron Maj* iii 204-06; Close R Henry III 571b, 577, 580,

582, 540; PR1225-1232 435).

Hubert was a vulnerable man by 1232, and the pope had handed de Burgh's

worst enemy, Peter des Roches, one weapon that des Roches would use to the

fullest. There had been a series of riots against the Italian men who had been given

English benefices by the pope. The pope had written letters of complaint to Henry

III about them and appointed the abbot of Bury St Edmond's and Peter des Roches to

investigate these riots and discover and punish the men behind them (*Chron Maj* iii

217-18).

Henry III deprived de Burgh of all royal castles that he held in custody in

August 1232. Henry stated that only after the pope's letters of complaint were

received and after Henry was informed of de Burgh's involvement in the riots by

"men of good faith" (des Roches) had he removed de Burgh from office (*Foedera*

i 207; PR 1225-1232 496; Close R Henry III 93). Peter des Roches had the perfect

weapon to force a separation between de Burgh and Henry III. Henry III's ascribed

devotion to the papacy guaranteed that any injury to that office would result in

Henry's anger and action against the perpetrator. Henry III had appointed Peter des

Rivaux treasurer of the royal household for life with the office of keeper of the king's wardrobe and chamber (Chart. Roll 1227-1231 599; *Ann Mon* iii 265). Between

July 16 and September 18, Henry III had given des Rivaux the custodies of the

wards and escheats, of the Jews, the mint and exchange, the ports and navy, custody

of Marlborough and Ludgershall castles, and the treasureship and chamberlainship

of the Exchequer (Shirley Royal Letters i 517-19, #1, #2, #3, #4, #5, & #6). In

July, he was granted for life the king's forests and a large number of counties (PR

1225-1232 488, 489; *Ann Mon* iii 129). Henry's court included Peter des Roches,

Peter des Rivaux, Ranulf of Chester, Brian de Lisle, Stephen of Seagrave, Richard

of Cornwall, and Richard Marshal, though Cornwall and Marshal were only with

the king at Woodstock and not in Oxford (*Chron Maj* iii 229; PR 1225-1232 504;

Close R Henry III 576; CRR xiv, xvi). Peter des Roches' rise brought back many

of the men who had been absent since the rebellion of 1222-1223; Peter de Mauley,

Engelard de Cigogne, Matthias Becille, and John de Plescy were some of these men

(*Claus* 139b; *CRR* xv #1426; Chart Rolls 1231-1234 202, 250, 327).

The trials and tribulations of de Burgh during the fall of 1232 were such that

many English barons wondered at the king's actions. When word of de Burgh's

possible arrest appeared, de Burgh took refuge in the church at Merton, but the

king sent the mayor and the citizens of London to forcibly remove de Burgh from

his holy sanctuary. This action of the king was stopped by the advice of the earl of

Chester. Hubert de Burgh went to the bishop of Norwich for respite, and the king

sent the knight Godfrey de Craucombe to capture de Burgh and remove him to the

Tower of London. Godfrey did take de Burgh from a church near the house of the

bishop of Norwich and brought him to the Tower. Roger bishop of London went to the king and threatened to excommunicate all who had violated the sancitity of the holy church if de Burgh was not returned to the chapel from which he had been taken. Hubert was returned on September 27, 1232, but the king ordered the sheriffs of Hereford and Essex to blockade Hubert in the chapel so that he received no food or visitors. Hubert decided that he did not want to die of starvation and surrendered himself to the sheriffs and was confined in the Tower (Wendover, Giles ii 557-58).

Henry III lost the most level-headed and strongest English magnate he had on October 28, 1232. Ranulf earl of Chester died at Wallingford and was succeeded by his nephew John le Scot, son of Ranulf's sister and David earl of Huntingdon. The death of Ranulf meant that there was no English baron of sufficient power and status to serve as a check on the overweening ambition of des Roches.

In October 1232 Hubert de Burgh was attacked and accused of all manner of evils by Peter des Roches, his allies, and those who had long hated or envied de Burgh. Hubert was accused of poisoning William Longespee earl of Salisbury, William Marshal, and Falkes, of dissuading Henry III from attempting to recover Normandy, of seducing and then marrying the daughter of the king of the Scots, and of somehow persuading Llywelyn to kill William de Braose. All of these ridiculous charges were recognized at the time as false, but de Burgh was brought before a tribunal composed of Richard earl of Cornwall, William de Warenne earl of Surrey, Richard Marshal earl of Pembroke, and John de Lacy earl of Lincoln on November 10, 1232. Hubert made no attempt to defend himself but submitted to the judgment of Henry III. Henry granted de Burgh all the lands which he had held from his father and those that he had purchased, and de Burgh was sent as a prisoner on parole to the castle of Devizes with Richard of Cornwall, Richard Marshal, William de Warenne, and William de Ferrers standing surety for him (Sweetman Doc. Ireland i 408-10).

Peter des Roches had managed the fall of de Burgh, but his own inability to even try to understand the English barons, and the change that the Magna Carta had created in the men and kingdom of England led to his own downfall. Peter des Roches' contempt for English custom, the English barons, and his dangerous view of royal power as unlimited as John had employed it doomed him. Wendover wrote that des Roches had replaced all the native curiales with foreigners from Poitou was inaccurate in extent but correct in the contemporary view of the English reaction to des Roches. Wendover said that Henry III invited men from Poitou and Brittany, who were poor and covetous of wealth, to come to England. He wrote that some two thousand men did come, and some were given charge of royal castles, counties, and wardships (Giles ii 565-66). The numbers are exaggerated, but the attitude inherent in Wendover's writing is an accurate indication of how the English barons saw and reacted to the growing power of des Roches over Henry III (PR 1225-1232 137). Henry III like his father King John failed to learn from the actions of Richard I and King Henry II. Henry II and Richard had both primarily kept the Poitevins out of England and out of the English government knowing that they had no place there and that they would be greatly resented and opposed by the English barons and ecclesiastical officials (Heiser "Royal Familiares" 36).

Richard Marshal as marshal of the kingdom saw these injustices, and he, as well as some of the other barons, went to Henry III and reproached Henry for bringing in these men who were oppressing Henry's kingdom and his people. Tout says that Richard Marshal was a gallant warrior, handsome and eloquent, pious, upright, well educated, and the best of the Marshal's sons. Richard would stand as the leader of the opposition to des Roches and his allies for the rest of his short life (History of England 45).

The king summoned the barons to a meeting in Oxford on June 24, 1233, but they refused to come fearing the treachery of des Roches and being angry with the king for allowing the foreigners to rule their land. Henry III thought to force the barons to come, but the preaching of Robert Bacon, Dominican friar, before the court told Henry III that he would never have peace in his land if he did not get rid of des Roches and de Rivaux (Stevenson Robert Grosseteste 110). Peter des Roches then urged Henry to crush this rebellion, take their castles, and give them to the Poitevins. Gilbert Basset, an ally of Richard Marshal and an English baron of long standing, was deprived of a manor he had held since the reign of John, and an attempt was made to capture Basset's brother-in-law, Richard Siward, as a warning to the rebel barons. The lands of Basset and Siward were given to Peter de Rivaux according to Wendover (Giles ii 552). On July 18, 1233, Henry III ordered the bailiffs of Dover to search all messengers of Richard Marshal who were returning from abroad (Shirley Royal Letters i 417-18 #cccxlv).

Henry III called another council in London at Westminster for August the first. Richard Marshal, still hoping for a peaceful solution, stopped on his way to London to stay with his sister Isabel, wife of Richard of Cornwall. When she discovered that Richard was on his way to the conference in London, she warned him:

Know, my dear brother, they your enemies are plotting to take you prisoner

and they will give you up to the king and the bishop of Winchester, in

order that they may serve you the same as they did the earl of Kent.

(Wendover, Giles ii 569)

Richard did not believe his sister until she showed him proof of the manner and

the men who were planning to take him prisoner. That Isabel risked the ire of her

husband, who was the brother of Henry III, to acquire evidence and warn her brother

of the danger is proof of her courage, intelligence, and sense of honour. Marshal

took to his horse that very night and did not rest until he was back in Wales. The

conference in London did nothing to solve the issues destroying the kingdom, so

Henry summoned all military tenants to appear at Gloucester with horses and arms

on August 14, 1233. When Richard Marshal did not appear, Henry III declared him

a traitor and ordered his lands invaded. However, the king did not have the men

or resources to enable him to invade Marshal's Welsh lands at this time, so another

council was held at Westminster on October 9, 1233.

At this conference several bishops remonstrated with Henry III to make

peace with his barons whom he had condemned without any trial by their peers.

The barons demanded that any action against Richard Marshal must be in a court

trial by his peers. Peter des Roches informed all there that there were no peers in

England as there were in France and that the king alone had the power to condemn

any disloyal subject *per voluntatem Regis*. Peter des Roches' statement of such an

unacceptable doctrine of the king's right caused the bishops to join the magnates

and threaten to excommunicate des Roches, Rivaulx, Stephen of Seagrave, who had been appointed justiciar in de Burgh's place, and Robert Passelewe, treasurer of the king. During this chaotic council, messengers brought Henry III news that Richard Marshal had retaken his castle of Usk. Henry then demanded that the bishops excommunicate Richard Marshal by name then and there, but the bishops refused, saying that Marshal did not deserve to be excommunicated for taking back his own castle of Usk because the king had refused to return Usk to Marshal despite the king's own oath that he would (Wendover, Giles ii 572-73).

During October, de Burgh had escaped from Devizes castle fearing that des Roches would have him killed and fled to a church in the town. When des Roches had ordered that de Burgh be taken forcibly from the church and returned to Devizes castle, the bishop of London had demanded that Henry restore de Burgh to the sanctuary of the church. On October the thirtieth, de Burgh was rescued by Siward and Basset and taken to Richard Marshal's castle of Chepstow in Wales. Civil war had begun. Siward and Basset were harrying the lands of the Poitevins, and Richard Marshal formed an alliance with Llywelyn of Wales. Marshal and Llywelyn attacked the lands of Glamorgan which were part of the Gloucester inheritance of Marshal's sister, Isabel. Richard, son and heir of Isabel and Gilbert de Clare, was a minor and his wardship had been given to Peter des Roches on the fall of de Burgh despite custom that should have placed Richard and his lands in the custody of an English baron. Marshal and Llywelyn took Cardiff and most of the castles of Glamorgan as well as the castle of Abergavenny and other neighboring strongholds. Marshal's Permbrokeshire vassals were besieging the royal castle of Carmarthen.

On November 2, 1233, Henry III ordered the sheriff of Worcester to destroy

Richard Marshal's castle of Inceberg (Inkberrow) and its gardens and the holdings of Hamo le Gras, Marshal's cousin (Shirley Royal Letters i 428-29; Close R Henry III 18). Henry III summoned an army to Gloucester and led them in November toward Richard Marshal's castle of Chepstow, the center and caput of Marshal's vast lands in Gwent. The king had a powerful army; he had even purchased the support of his brother Richard of Cornwall. The new earl of Chester, John le Scot, nephew of Ranulf earl of Chester, John de Lacy, earl of Lincoln, and John de Monmouth were also some of the barons who joined Henry's army. It is of note that Richard of Cornwall was husband to Isabel, sister of Richard Marshal, and that John de Monmouth was the grandson of Rohese de Clare. When Henry and his army invaded Marshal's lands in Gwent, he discovered that Marshal was indeed a cautious and superb military tactician. Marshal had removed all cattle and provisions from his lands, and the king was unable to support his army and had to move his army away from Chepstow and up the Wye valley to the area of the castles of Grosmont, Monmouth, Skenfrith, and Whitecastle (*Ann Mon* i 90).

Henry withdrew his army to the castle of Grosmont and stayed there several days. On the night of November 11, 1233, in the castle of Grosmont with Henry were des Roches, Ralph bishop of Chichester, Stephen of Seagrave, de Rivaulx, Bigod earl of Norfolk, William earl of Salisbury, and William Beauchamp (Wendover, Giles ii 573). The army was encamped outside the castle walls, and on this night they were attacked by barons and Welsh allies of Richard Marshal, not however by Richard Marshal himself because he refused to personally attack the king. The surprised royal army fled into the castle or off in every direction, and the attackers took possession of all their horses, arms, provisions, and equipment. The attackers refrained from killing or capturing any of the fleeing army; they merely took all the booty they had acquired and retreated. Many of Henry's army went home citing their reason for leaving as having no equipment with which to fight, and Henry and his ministers withdrew to Gloucester having been completely defeated. Henry left his Poitevin mercenaries to defend the border castle under the charge of John de Monmouth and Ralph de Toeni (Giles ii 573).

On November 25, 1233, Richard Marshal was in the area of Monmouth castle on a foraging expedition. Richard ordered the bulk of his army to proceed while he took a small force and went to scout out the castle of Monmouth. Marshal was seen and recognized by Baldwin de Guisnes, custodian of the castle for Henry III. Baldwin immediately gathered his forces and charged forth from the castle with the intent of capturing Marshal. In the record of this engagement Marshal is seen as the superb knight and warrior that he was, his father's son. From Wendover the battle is described thus:

> Baldwin with twelve of his stoutest knights made an attack on the marshal in
> person, and endeavoured to take him prisoner and carry him off to the castle;
> he (Marshal) however kept them at a distance, brandishing his sword right
> and left, and struck down whoever came within reach, either killing them
> or stunning them by the force of his blows, and although engaged single-
> handed against twelve enemies, defended himself for a length of time. His
> enemies not daring to approach him, killed his horse with their lances, but
> the marshal who was well practiced in the French way of fighting, seized
> one of the knights who was attacking him by the feet, and dragged him to
> the ground, and then quickly mounting his adversary's horse, he renewed the

battle. The knight Baldwin was ashamed that the marshal defended himself single-handed against so many of his enemies for such a time, and made a desperate attack on him, and seizing his helmet, tore it from his head with such violence, that blood gushed forth from his mouth and nostrils; he then seized the marshal's horse by the bridle, and endeavoured to drag it with its rider toward the castle whilst others assisted him by impelling the marshal on from behind. The latter however, sweeping his sword behind him struck two of his enemies to the earth stunned, but could not then release himself from their grasp [. . .] a crossbowman amongst the marshal's company, seeing his lord in danger, discharged an arrow from his bow, which striking Baldwin, who was dragging the marshal away, in the breast, entered his body, notwithstanding his armour, and he fell to the earth believing himself mortally wounded; his companions on seeing this, left the marshal and went to raise Baldwin [. . .]. (Wendover, Giles ii 574-75)

The bulk of Marshal's army, having received word of this battle, hurried to his assistance, and they drove the enemy back and took the castle. Wendover's account of this battle has the detail that would be expected of an eye-witness, and gives a clear picture of the skill and the character of the knight who was William Marshal's second son.

A week or so before Christmas 1233 Marshal happened to be at Margam Abbey, and according to Wendover, a brother named Agnell came to speak with him as an attendant of King Henry III. This dialogue is probably part truth and part argument by Wendover of the wrongs that Henry III's foreign advisors were inflicting on the realm of England. Quoting parts of this passage gives an understanding of the way Richard Marshal viewed his actions in opposing King

Henry III:

> The marshal replied that he had not invaded the king's territory, that he had
> been always ready to abide by the law and the decisions of his peers in
> Henry's court, and often had asked the king by messengers to grant him this,
> but the king had always refused it to him, and the king himself had invaded
> Marshal's territory and attacked him contrary to all the laws of justice. [.
> . .] after the truce of fifteen days, before Marshal entered Wales, or took
> any measures for his own defence against any one, the king, without a trial,
> deprived Marshal of his office of marshal, which belonged to him, and which
> he held by hereditary right, nor would the king on any terms restore it to him
> when he asked [. . .]. (Giles ii 576-80)

The monk tried to reason with Richard Marshal and convince him that he would be
safe to throw himself on the mercy of Henry III, des Roches, and Stephen of
Seagrave. Though these words are most probably the words of Wendover; the
intent and the purpose of them are such that Richard Marshal would have been quite
capable of having spoken them.

Robert Grosseteste was a prelate and one of the most learned and respected
men of his time. Grosseteste was a rector at Oxford and the lector of the
Franciscans there by 1224. He became bishop of Lincoln in 1235. Grosseteste was
the friend and spiritual advisor of Richard Marshal, and apparently saw Marshal as
a fit instrument to defend the Magna Carta against the inroads made by Henry III
and his foreign advisors (Stephenson Robert Grosseteste 93). Grosseteste believed
that the continuing presence of des Roches and his allies in England would prevent

330

Henry III from ever having peace in his realm (Stephenson 100, 100 f 2). Like Stephen Langton, Grosseteste believed that the reform of the Church must be tied to the reform of the state, and that the Magna Carta and the rights initiated by it were the future of the English realm. All records of the type of man Richard Marshal was depict him as being a man intelligent, eloquent, pious and honourable. The fact that Richard Marshal was a close and respected friend to one of the most brilliant thinkers, theologians, and philosophers of his time is a more accurate portrait of the man, his ideals, and purposes than some of today's interpretations of his character. Marshal saw his cause as just and necessary, not only for his own preservation but also for the preservation of England under the laws and customs of its realm.

Henry III spent Christmas 1233 at Gloucester, but after Marshal's success at Monmouth, Henry left and went to Winchester with des Roches. Henry had placed John de Monmouth in charge of a large army. After Christmas, John decided to try to surprise Marshal with an attack. Richard, however, learned of the planned attack and placed his own forces in a wood through which Monmouth would have to pass with his army, and from here Marshal ambushed de Monmouth. Marshal's forces were completely successful and put to rout de Monmouth and his men. Marshal's men then proceeded to pillage and burn the villages and other properties of de Monmouth, returning with the captured goods to their own lands. During this same time, Richard Siward in alliance with other proscribed nobles attacked the lands and properties of Richard of Cornwall, of Stephen of Seagrave, and of des Roches, bishop of Winchester. According to Wendover, these actions were directed solely at the foreign advisors of the king who were responsible for the rebels being exiled.

Wendover wrote that when the king fled back to England from Gloucester, the lands from Gloucester south into Wales were left exposed to the ravages of the rebels and that the corpses of the slain lay exposed and unburied along the roads (Giles ii 580-81). The bishops with Henry III kept advising him to make peace with Marshal. Henry replied that he would never come to terms with Marshal unless Marshal came before him and begged for mercy with a halter around his neck and acknowledged that he, Marshal, was a traitor.

Since Richard Marshal had defeated the men that had been sent against him, des Roches, de Rivaulx, and others devised a plan to conquer him by treachery since he could not be defeated in honourable battle. They wrote letters, affixed with Henry III's seal as well as the seal of eleven others, and sent them to Ireland. Wendover wrote that the letters were sent to Maurice fitz Gerald, justiciar of Ireland, Walter and Hugh de Lacy, Richard de Burgh, nephew of Hubert, Geoffrey de Marisco, and others who were sworn allies of Marshal. The letters told these men that Marshal had been banished from England by decree of the king, that all of Richard Marshal's property and possessions had been burned or confiscated, and despite this Marshal was still perservering in his offenses against the king. The letters said:

> We therefore order you on your oath, as faithful subjects of our lord the king,
> to seize Marshal if he should happen to come to Ireland, and bring him, dead
> or alive, before the king. If you do this, all of Marshal's inheritance and
> possessions in the kingdom of Ireland, which are now at the disposal of our
> lord the king, will be granted to you to be divided amongst you, and to be
> held by you by hereditary right. For the faithful fulfillment of this promise
> to you by our lord the king, all of us, by whose advice the business of the
> king and kingdom is managed, will become securities if you bring the above

design to effect. (<u>Wendover</u>, Giles ii 582)

These men in Ireland then sent letters to the counselors of the king saying that if the promises in the letters sent to them were confirmed to them, they would attempt to carry out the proposed plan. The king's advisors by royal warrant granted the men in Ireland all the rights of Marshal to be divided between them, even detailing the places, possessions, and rights that would be granted to each individual.

Marvin Colker has discovered a copy of the Margam (Margan) Chronicle in a Dublin manuscript that contains information not found in any other version. This Dublin text states that the nobles of King Henry III had renounced their allegiance to the king in 1233 because of the abuses of the king's foreign advisors ("The Margam Chronicle in a Dublin Manuscript" 134-36 sec 17, 21). If true, this makes the betrayal and murder of Richard Marshal by the nobles in Ireland doubly heinous. No longer owing allegiance to King Henry III, they urged Marshal to come to Ireland, and then betrayed and killed Marshal because of their own greed.

The de Lacys of Meath, fitz Gerald, Marisco, and de Burgh then attacked Marshal's lands in Ireland taking what they could and burning what was left (Tout <u>History of England</u> 48-49). While in England on the day of the Purification of Mary (February 7, 1234), Henry III held a council at Westminster. Edmund Rich, archbishop elect of Canterbury, was there with several of his bishops, and he told the king of their sorrow at the desolation and unrest that was tearing at Henry's realm at this time (*Ann Mon* i 92). The words of Edmund are recorded in Wendover, and in this instance, due to Wendover being the scibe of St. Alban's, the words are in all probablility at least the main gist of what was said:

Lord king, we tell you in the Lord's name, that the counsel which you now receive and act upon, namely that of Peter bishop of Winchester, and Peter de Rivalux, is not wise or safe, but on the contrary is cruel and dangerous to yourselves and to the whole kingdom [. . .] they estrange your affections from your people, and those of your people from you, as is evident from the conduct of the Marshal, who is the best subject in your dominions, and by the wicked lies which they tell you about your people, they pervert all your people's words and deeds. It is by the acting on the advice of this same man that your father also lost first the affections of his people [. . .] and almost the sovereignty of England, and never enjoyed tranquility afterwards. It is because of this man's counsel that the kingdom was embroiled and laid under interdict [. . .] this insurrection which is now endangering your kingdom has been caused by the evil counsels of these two men; for if your people had been governed according to the rules of justice and the proper laws of the land, this disturbance would not have happened, you would not have had your possessions ravaged [. . .] these men, since they cannot increase their wealth by peace, endeavor to do so by embroiling the people of the kingdom and by depriving others of their inheritance [. . .] we advise you in the presence of God and man, and we beg of and warn you to dismiss such advisors [. . .] for we have to inform you that unless you correct these abuses in a short time, we shall proceed, by means of the censure of the church, against you and all other gainsayers,and we are only awaiting the consecration of our venerable father the archbishop elect of Canterbury.

(Giles ii 583-84)

Henry III asked for a respite as he could not dismiss his counselors without time for an accounting of all of the moneys and properties that had been entrusted to them. The council was ended with the hope that the king would do what was necessary to return peace to the kingdom.

Meanwhile, Richard Marshal on learning that his lands and castles in Ireland were being invaded and attacked set sail for there in February 1234. Marshal gathered an army of his vassals and proceeded to take back some of his own castles and lands and some of the royal castles, including Limerick. Due to Marshal's successes, the allies of des Roches sent brothers of the Templar order to him to seek a truce. They told Marshal that he was acting as a traitor to the king by attacking the king's possessions in Ireland and that they were acting as the king's representatives in Ireland defending his lands and rights. They asked for a truce in order that they, as representatives of the king, could seek an answer from their lord, the king, as to whether the king was going to aid them in defending Ireland or was going to leave Ireland to its fate. Marshal sent word by the Templar brothers that he would meet these barons on April 1, 1234, at the Curragh of Kildare to discuss a truce.

Marshal came to the meeting with only fifteen of his own knights, and the rest were those who were Marshal's supposed loyal vassals, including Geoffrey de Marisco. Richard Marshal was met by Maurice fitz Gerald, justiciar of Ireland, Richard de Burgh, and Hugh de Lacy of Meath and their knights, numbering over one hundred and forty. Notice three of these men: Maurice was nephew of William of Naas and Aline, Strongbow's natural daughter; Richard de Burgh was nephew of Hubert de Burgh, whose life Richard Marshal's vassals had saved by bringing him to Marshal's castle of Chepstow; and Hugh de Lacy was probably the grandson of Baderon de Monmouth and Rohese de Clare.

When Marshal wanted to grant the king's men terms that were acceptable, Marisco persuaded him that such a position was unacceptable and unworthy of a son of William Marshal. The moment Marshal refused terms, the opposition drew up their troops for battle, and de Marisco and his allies withdrew from the Marshal's side with the excuse that de Marisco was married to a daughter of de Lacy and could not fight against him. Richard Marshal, seeing that he had been betrayed and recognizing the impossibility of his plight, sent his brother Walter from the field with the words, "Take my brother to my castle near, and do not let the whole of my family perish in this battle; for I trust in his bravery, if he attain the age of maturity, to show himself a brave knight" (Wendover, Giles ii 589). Then Richard exhorted his own men to battle, acknowledging his own view of the reality of his situation by saying, "For I am well aware that I am doomed to die this day; but it is better for me to die with honour in the cause of justice, than to fly from the field and to endure the reproaches of my fellow knights forever" (Giles ii 589).

Wendover wrote that only Marshal's own personal retinue of fifteen knights charged forth to meet the enemy. According to the *Brut* Marshal was betrayed and deserted by his Irish vassal knights (234-35). The rest of his supposed men gave themselves up without force and without a single wound of lance or sword. Marshal slew six men attacking him, and when a giant of a man tried to seize Marshal by his helm, Marshal cut off his hands with a single blow of his sword. When another attacked Marshal, striking him a blow on the head, Marshal turned and cut the man

336

in half to his waist. Daunted by the skill of Marshal as a knight, the enemy then tried to kill his horse, and they were finally forced to cut off the feet of Marshal's horse with axes. With Marshal on the ground, the enemy rushed upon him, lifted his armour, and struck him in the back. They then took the badly wounded body of Marshal to his own castle of Kilkenny, which Maurice fitz Gerald had seized (*Brut* 233-34; *Ann Mon* i 92-93).

After a few days Marshal began to recover from his wounds. His enemies then showed him the warrants from the king that had ordered Marshal's capture dead or alive as a traitor and advised Marshal to surrender his Irish lands to the king. Wendover wrote that Marshal then sent letters ordering that his castles and lands in Ireland be surrendered to the king (Giles ii 591). Marshal's wounds apparently begin to swell, and he asked Maurice fitz Gerald, in whose custody Marshal was at the time, for a physician. The physician, whose purpose was definitely not to prolong life, probed Marshal's wounds with a long-heated instrument so deeply and so often that Marshal developed a fever and succumbed to this abuse on the fifteenth of April (*Mon Ang* v 266). Marshal was hurriedly buried in the oratory of the Franciscan church at Kilkenny.

While this chaos and treachery was flourishing in Ireland, a new archbishop of Canterbury was consecrated on April 2, 1234. Edmund Rich was consecrated as Archbishop of Canterbury in Christ Church by Roger bishop of London with the king and thirteen bishops in attendance. Edmund the Archbishop of Canterbury had seen enough of the self-destruction of England. At his consecration, Edmund with his suffragans upheld the good name and honour of Richard Marshal and told Henry

III that he must rid himself of his foreign advisors and send them out of England as they were destroying the country and the people (*Ann Mon* i 92). April 4, 1234, Pope Gregory IX sent a letter to Henry III stating that he knew of the improvident alienations by Henry III and that he had sent a letter to Edmund archbishop of Canterbury ordering him to enjoin the king to revoke these alienations as they were contrary to Henry III's coronation oath (Cal Papal 140). On April 9, 1234, Edmund declared that unless Henry III removed the Poitevins from power, Edmund would forthwith pronounce Henry III excommunicate. Henry sent Peter des Roches back to his diocese of Winchester and deprived Peter de Rivaux of all of his offices. Henry III then dispatched Edmund to Wales to make peace with Llywelyn and the Marshal, and Henry himself left for Gloucester in order to meet the archbishop on his return from Wales (Shirley <u>Royal Letters</u> i 433-34).

On his way to Gloucester, Henry III stopped for one night at Woodstock, and it was at Woodstock that messengers arrived from Ireland telling Henry of Richard Marshal's death. According to Wendover, to the astonishment of all those present, Henry III went into loud and visible lamentations "over the death of such a distinguished knight, declaring that Marshal had died leaving no equal to himself in the whole kingdom" (Giles ii 592). Henry then ordered a funeral service for the soul of Marshal and bestowed generous alms on the poor. So too did Brutus lament the death of Caesar. It was much too late for Richard Marshal for he had died by treachery while fighting for justice for himself and for the realm.

Henry then proceeded to Gloucester where he met Edmund and the bishops who had accompanied the archbishop into Wales. Edmund told the king that

Llywelyn would agree to peace only if the king first would receive into his peace all the nobles and allies of Llywelyn who had been proscribed and exiled due to Henry's evil advisors. On May 26, 1234, Henry III granted safe conduct to Gilbert Marshal and other rebels to come to him (Shirley Royal Letters i 438-39). On May 29, 1234, Henry met with these former rebels at Gloucester, and there they all received a full pardon. Hubert de Burgh, Gilbert Bassett and his brothers, Richard Siward, and all the others who had been banished with them and on their account were admitted to the king's peace and had all their rights restored to them. Gilbert Marshal, brother and heir to Richard Marshal, also came at this time and swore fealty and did homage to Henry III and was given the earldom, lands and castles of Richard Marshal in England and Ireland. On Whitsunday, Henry III knighted Gilbert and gave him the wand of the marshal of the court to be held as his father and his brothers had held it. Of the men who had connived at Richard Marshal's destruction and death, Stephen of Seagrave, forgetting his knighthood, retreated to a church in Leicester, and Peter de Rivaux, while protesting that his orders made him immune to arrest, was found to be wearing chain mail under his clerical garments and was put into a lay prison. Peter des Roches was ordered to return to his diocese of Winchester and to care for the soul of his flock and never again to intrude in the government of the realm.

At this conference in May 1234 Edmund archbishop of Canterbury read a copy of the letters that had been sent to the barons in Ireland regarding their charge to destroy Richard Marshal as a traitor of the king and reap the rewards of a division of Marshal's lands in Ireland. Henry III pleaded that he had been compelled to set his seal to some letters by des Roches and de Rivaux, but that he had not known the purpose of the letters. According to Wendover, Edmund then said to the king:

> Examine your conscience, my king, for all those who caused these letters
> to be sent and were aware of the treachery intended, are just as guilty of the
> murder of the Marshal, as if they had slain him with their own hands. (Giles
> ii 594)

In proof of Henry III's sense of outrage at his ministers' actions, Henry summoned
des Roches, de Rivaux, Stephen of Segrave, and Robert de Passelewe to meet him at
a conference and render him an account of of all money received and spent by them,
the misuse of Henry's seal by them, and to answer all charges against them. They
appeared at Westminster on July 14, 1234, under the safe conduct of the archbishop
of Canterbury and the bishops. As a result of this meeting, the above named
foreigners were reduced to their former status. From this point, the governing of the
realm was solely in the hands of Henry III. Henry would rule as his own justiciar,
as the office ceased to exist. The treasurership was held by a succession of short-
lived royal clerks, and the chancelorship, though occupied by Ralph de Neville, was
controlled by Henry who took the seal to himself in 1238 (Tout History of England
51-52).

Richard Marshal failed in his effort to gain support among the English
barons due to one of the quirks often found in history. Unlike his father and his
older brother, Richard did not find powerful, mature men among his contemporaries
in England. The most influential and powerful man of this time when it came to
checking the actions of the king and des Roches, Ranulf earl of Chester, had died
in 1232. Of Richard's brothers-in-law, Hugh Bigod had died in 1225, and Gilbert

de Clare had died in 1230. Hugh's son Roger was barely 21, if that, and Richard de Clare was still a child in the custody of des Roches. Robert fitz Walter of the cadet de Clares was an old man who died in 1235. William Longespee, earl of Salisbury and related by marriage to the Marshals, had died in 1226. William's son was perhaps just 21 at this time, and he and Roger Bigod were supposed supporters of the king. William de Warenne, second husband to Richard Marshal's sister Maud, also supported the king's side. Richard of Cornwall, brother to Henry III and second husband of Isabel Marshal de Clare, was bribed with money and lands to switch to the side of Henry III. William de Ferrers, earl of Derby and husband to Richard's sister Sibyl, and Warin de Mountchesney, husband to Richard's sister Joanna, apparently stayed out of the conflict. Richard's bastard uncle John Marshal stayed out of the entire conflict due to age and/or inclination. The best of William and Isabel's children found himself in a battle for justice with regard to the disseisen of barons without the due process of law (Gilbert Basset/Siward/Marshal) and the right of English barons to counsel the king in governing and not be replaced by "foreigners." Richard Marshal failed to achieve his goal because of at least two factors; first because many of the men who had fought against these same injustices during the reign of King John in 1216/1217 were dead, and second because those still alive from that time did not wish to see the country again in such turmoil. The greatest irony of all is that this same battle would be fought again in less than thirty years led by Richard Marshal's nephews, Roger Bigod and Richard de Clare (Morris The Bigod Earls 58-59).

Before leaving this section on Richard Marshal, it is essential to look at his murder, for murder it was. Henry III was twenty-five years old at the time of Richard Marshal's murder, he was a grown man who had been ruling England for a number of years and who had already displayed in his actions a lack of steadfastness of purpose and a propensity for being influenced by those around him. Henry had the same temper that characterized his father John, the same jealousy and mistrust of his English barons, and the same greed and acquisitivenss. Richard was the second son of the very man, William Marshal, who had saved the crown and realm of England and probably the very life of Henry III. Richard was one of the few greater barons of the English realm, and he was killed through treachery and hurriedly and secretly buried in Ireland. No notice or consideration was given to his family which was allied by blood and marriage to most of the greatest families of England. No chance was given to his family to bring his body home to be buried next to his father in The Temple Church which Richard Marshal had the right to expect. No matter how this event is viewed, there is a taint of deceit, secrecy, and betrayal about it that nothing will wash away. The writs were issued and sealed by Henry III's seal as king. Either one must ascribe mental deficiency to Henry III or one must ascribe the act of outright murder and then lying in order to protect his own conscience.

On the scales of justice is submitted the following writ sent by Henry III in 1246, after the death of all five of William Marshal's sons, to William de Cheeny, Henry's seneschal of Leinster:

> We desire to have in our kingdom of Ireland one chief justiciar, one
> treasurer, one chancellor, and that under the seal of the latter all writs
> shall issue, and that there shall be but one exchequer which shall sit at

Dublin. You and your sub-sheriffs are to answer for all receipts and issues of your bailiwicks in the same manner as our sheriffs. We prohibit you from issuing, and your sub-sheriffs from executing writs under your seal connected with matters pertaining to our royal rights, neither are you to hold assizes, but cause writs from our chancery to run and our justiciaries to proceed as before the late earls Marechal usurped royal liberties. (<u>Historic and Municipal Documents of Ireland 1172-1320</u> 106-07)

By the orders of this writ, Henry III is taking away the hereditary rights of the lordship of Leinster granted by King Henry II to Strongbow and by King John to William Marshal in right of his wife, Isabel de Clare. The lordship of Leinster had been granted special, specific privileges and rights by King Henry II to Strongbow and by King John to William Marshal. The lord of Leinster, like that of Meath, exercised the right to have his own courts of civil and criminal causes from which he could and did take part and/or all of the revenues. The lord could constitute his own judges, seneschals, sheriffs, coroners, and escheators; and the king's writ did not run in his lordship except with regard to ecclesiastical lands and to the four pleas of the crown of rape, arson, treasure-trove, and forestalling. A vassal of these lordships could appeal to the king's court in cases of default of justice or right in the lord's court, but otherwise the king had no power in the lordship of Leinster. With the above writ of Henry III and the clear intent of that writ can one honestly believe that Henry III was blind to the intent and purpose of the writs issued against Richard Marshal under his own seal?

As further proof of Henry III's illegal actions with regard to Richard Marshal, Ralph Turner has shown that in the summer of 1234 Hubert de Burgh initiated proceedings in the royal courts to regain the lands that Henry III had taken from him ("Royal Courts" 15-16). The judgment of the *magna curia Regis* was that Henry III had unlawfully outlawed his barons and seized their lands ("Royal Courts" 15). In essence this action was a reassertion of the principle of the Magna Carta that the king was subject to the law. Therefore the acts taken by Richard Marshal in his attempt to force the king to abide by those principles were done in a just and right cause against the illegal actions of Henry III and Peter des Roches.

Of all of Marshal's sons, Richard was the closest to equaling his father in honour, knightly skills, and nobility of character. Richard had not attacked the king; he had tried every means at his disposal to make the king see and do what was right according to English law, custom, and the clauses set down in the Magna Carta. Only when Richard was personally attacked did he try to defend himself and the justice and laws of England. Some recent works have defended des Roches and Henry III and their actions, but nothing can refute the truths of the contemporary chroniclers. Lydon states clearly in Cosgrove's <u>A New History of Ireland: II Medieval Ireland</u> that there is no doubt that Henry III was complicit in the attack and murder of Richard Marshal on the Curragh of Kildare April 1, 1234 (168). In the annals of Ireland the murder of Richard Marshal is seen for what it truly was, one of the worst deeds of that age (*Ann Hib* 1233.2; *Ann Conn* 30).

According to contemporary chronicles, "Richard was a man endowed with all honorable qualities, distinguished for his noble birth, well-endowed in liberal arts, most vigorous in the exercise of arms, and one who kept God before his eyes in all his works" (*Ann Mon* ii 313). The ghosts of Richard's parents must have wept and raged at the betrayal of their son by men who owed almost everything they possessed to the power, honour, and fealty of Richard Strongbow de Clare and William Marshal (d1219) earl of Pembroke. William Marshal must have deeply regretted that his wish for a short life for Henry III should he exhibit the worst qualitites of his father John had not come true. Richard Marshal had seen injustice, wrongs, and the abrogation of rights guaranteed by the Magna Carta and had taken up his sword, fought, and died trying to rectify them.

XVIII. Gilbert, Walter, and Anselm Marshal

On Richard's death, his brother Gilbert was his heir and successor. Gilbert
had been intended for an ecclesiastical career (*Foedera* i 212). He had taken
minor orders and received the livings of Orford in Suffolk on May 30, 1225, and
of Wigham in Kent on September 19, 1228. He was in Ireland when Richard
was killed, but after Richard's murder, Gilbert returned to Wales (Sweetman Doc.
Ireland #2109; *Ann Mon* iv 80). For taking part and supporting his brother Richard
in rebellion against the king's foreign advisors, Henry III pardoned Gilbert, along
with his brothers Walter and Anselm (Shirley Royal Letters i 438-39; Sweetman
Doc. Ireland #2120, #2151, #2175). On June 4, 1235, there is a decree addressed
to Gilbert and his brothers Walter and Anselm from Pope Gregory IX. It stated that
they had been deprived unjustly of their lands, castles, and tenements in Ireland and
forced by the king to take an oath to their prejudice. Since the king had released
them from this oath by letters patent, the pope declared that they were no longer
bound by this oath or obligation (Cal Papal 147). This decree was followed by a
grant of protection from Pope Gregory IX for Gilbert, Walter, and Anselm for all
of their lands in Ireland and Wales from anyone excommunicating them (Cal Papal
147). On June 11, 1235, Gilbert was knighted and invested with all his brother's
lands and offices by King Henry at Worcester (*Ann Mon* iii 137; *Brut* 235).

In 1238 Gilbert supported his brother-in-law, Richard of Cornwall, against
the king's foreign advisors. On November 12, 1239, Gilbert took the cross with his
brother-in-law Richard of Cornwall at Northampton. Gilbert took the cross with the

understanding that Richard would use his influence to return Gilbert to the king's favor which he had lost when he supported Richard in 1138 (*Chron Maj* iii 476). In July 1240 Gilbert was on the point of leaving England to go on crusade when the king recalled him and took him back into favor.

On June 27, 1241, Gilbert was taking part in an unauthorized tournament at Ware; he was thrown from his horse and dragged across the field. He died from his injuries that very day and was buried in the Temple Church in London near his father and his brother William Marshal (*Mon Ang* v 266).

In September 1230 Gilbert married Margaret de Lanvallei; she later died or was divorced because in August of 1235 Gilbert married Margaret, sister to Alexander II of Scotland (*Excerpta e Rot Fin i 202; Ann Mon* iii 143). Gilbert had no children by either marriage.

Walter succeeded his brother Gilbert as his heir; he had been with his brother Richard at the Curragh of Kildare but had been saved when his brother Richard sent him away from the battle. Walter had been pardoned by Henry III for his support of his brother Richard, along with his brothers Gilbert and Anselm, through the mediation of Archbishop Edmund Rich (Shirley <u>Royal Letters</u> i 438-39; Sweetman <u>Doc. Ireland</u> i #2120,# 2151, #2175). Because Henry III was still angry at Gilbert Marshal's death as a result of participating in an unauthorized tournament, he did not invest Walter with his lands, title, and offices until October 1241. Walter accompanied the king to Gascony in 1242. In 1244 Walter was elected a member of the Committee of Twelve at the Parliament at Westminster Hall. This committee was charged with drawing up articles that would regulate King Henry III's conduct and nominate the king's principal and responsible ministers, all of which would be agreed to by the entire assembly of barons and ecclesiastical respresentatives of that Parliament. Though the king tried to avoid this restriction on his power and activities, he was forced to agree that he would be granted the funds he requested from his subjects only on the conditions that he appoint the responsible ministers suggested, observe the laws of the land, and allow the Committee of Twelve to act as trustees in the expenditure of the funds granted (Stevenson Robert Grosseteste 220-22). This submission by Henry III did not last, and he would later again exclude the English barons from participation in the central government.

Walter was married January 2, 1242, to Margaret (d1266). Margaret was the widow of John de Lacy, earl of Lincoln and the daughter of Hawise, sister of Ranulf of Chester, and Robert de Quenci. Walter died November 24, 1245 at Goodrich castle and was buried at Tintern Abbey (*Chron Maj* iv 491). Walter and Margaret had no children; there are no known records of why and how he died.

Anselm was his brother's heir, but he apparently died before he was ever invested with the lands, titles and offices. He married Maud, daughter of Humphrey de Bohun, second earl of Hereford, but they had no children. Anselm died December 24, 1245, at Striguil, but there are no records of how he died (*Ann Mon* ii 266). Anselm, with his brother Walter, was buried near their mother, Isabel, at Tintern Abbey in Monmouthshire (Sweetman Doc. Ireland i 823, 825). The last two sons and heirs of William Marshal and Isabel de Clare died within thirty days of each other of unknown causes and with both only in their thirties.

Thus all five of William and Isabel Marshal sons died without any children, and the division of all the lands these two individuals inherited, acquired, and held would eventually be split among the children of their five daughters. There is no direct male lineal descent from William Marshal's line. Out of the ten children that Isabel and William Marshal had, two seem to be the most like their parents. Isabel Marshal had the courage and honour to warn her brother Richard of the trap laid by des Roches and Henry III for him and the boldness to ask that her body be buried by the man who held her affection. Richard Marshal had the honour and skill of his chivalric father. Like his father, Richard placed personal ambition second to his desire to see that the Plantagenet Crown, the English realm, and the essential clauses of the Magna Carta would survive the ineptitude and greed of King Henry III and des Roches. Of Marshal and Isabel's five sons, William the younger, Walter, and Anselm died in unexplained or undiscovered manner, Richard was murdered, and Gilbert died in a tournament. No known extant records show any children born to any of these five sons.

William Marshal and Isabel de Clare had ten children, and of their five sons none lived past forty-five years of age and none had children. This is amazing when their father lived well past the age of seventy, despite his hard and rigorous life as a knight and crusader, and produced ten healthy children.

XIX. William Marshal's Legacy

Earl William Marshal of Pembroke was a pivotal point in some of the major events in medieval history, and he has earned an acknowledged place in the medieval history of England, Wales, and Ireland. His life and actions as a medieval knight help define and clarify the position and importance warrior knights played in shaping the history of his time period. Marshal's role as baron and earl provide a living example of the value such men had in aiding and checking the rule of a king in feudalistic society. William Marshal was not like his contemporaries. Unlike Hubert de Burgh and Peter des Roches, Marshal did not crave power nor did he seek status and position. Marshal had achieved position by birth, blood, and marriage; his power and status was gained through his own abilities and actions throughout his life. Marshal understood that unless power is used judiciously and wisely it produced only fear and mistrust. Henry II was a master at using power in such a manner, and Richard I used it from his proven position as a skillful and successful warrior knight. John never understood that power used indiscriminately and as a weapon would result in nothing but distrust, disrespect, and fear.

Marshal never betrayed anyone nor did he betray his oath of fealty to the Plantagenet kings. As a knight and head of the *mesnie* household of the young Henry and one with no title or any royal blood, Marshal did his best to rein-in the excesses of the young king. When most of the young Henry's knights abandoned him during his last days, Marshal stayed, protected Henry's body, and delivered it to the cathedral of Rouen for burial. After his crusade in the Holy Land, Marshal returned to Henry II and served Henry as military commander, ambassador, and *familiaris Regis* faithfully and well. During the horrors of the war with Philip and with Henry's son Richard, Marshal was steadfast in his fealty to Henry. When Henry died, Marshal was one of those who tried to clothe the king in suitable garments when servants had stolen all, and he accompanied Henry's body to Fontrevault to see that he was properly buried. Marshal had no fear of Richard when Richard came to view Henry II's body at Fontrevault; Marshal knew that he had been right and honourable in supporting Henry II against Richard's rebellion. Richard recognized Marshal's faithful service to his king, Henry II, and bestowed the hand and lands of Isabel de Clare on Marshal. Richard knew that loyalty was the greatest virtue in their feudal society and giving the hand and lands of Isabel de Clare to William Marshal secured the safety and loyalty of that portion of Richard's kingdom to himself and his crown. During Richard's time on crusade and as a prisoner, Marshal helped Queen Eleanor and Walter de Coutance control and stabilize England against John's rebellion and attempt to steal the crown and Lonchamp's excessive zeal. On Richard's return to England, Marshal again served Richard as military commander, ambassador, and *familiaris Regis* in Normandy. With Richard's death and the war with the French in Normandy against King John, Marshal would again serve a king as military commander and ambassador. When John was at war with the pope over the election of Stephen Langton, Marshal gathered the Anglo barons of Ireland and issued letters of support for King John. During the rebellion of the English barons, William Marshal served as a trusted mediator and representative for both sides. He and Stephen Langton did their utmost to resolve the issues between King John and his barons without throwing the country into civil war. With the advent of civil war, Marshal served to protect and defend John's position as king against the threat of Louis of France taking the throne and kingdom of England. Even King John who harbored animosity toward Marshal recognized on his deathbed that unless Marshal supported and protected his heir Henry III, the Angevin Crown would be lost. These qualities of loyalty and honour gave Marshal his power; they are what engendered the respect and trust of his contemporaries, both allies and opponents.

William Marshal's reputation as a knight, commander of men, and ambassador for kings was earned through his own abilities and skills. William Marshal spent more than half of his life in the households and centers of power in Normandy, England, and France. He learned through experience the lessons of power and rule from some of the greater medieval lords, kings, and Eleanor of Aquitaine. Some have labeled Marshal as King John's man, but he was never John's man because Marshal could and would not be bought or owned by any man. Marshal respected his own sense of honour and fealty to the Angevin crown, but this did not mean that he did not question or challenge the man who held it. Marshal walked the fine edge of a sword when it came to King John, but he did not defy the office of the king. William Marshal did what he thought was right for himself, his family, his vassals, and England. Marshal went as close to that edge as one could go without breaking his oath of fealty. William Marshal was a man of his time and subject to the frailties of all men, but in his own carefully conceived idea of what constituted a man's honour and worth he was unique.

William Marshal has been presented as a phenomenal warrior knight and military commander accurately, but the intelligent and wise side of the man has been neglected. Recognition has not always been given to the shrewd and entrepreneurial aspect of Marshal. Once Marshal married Isabel de Clare, he became a greater magnate and baron; he was now lord of Chepstow, Leinster, and Longueville as well as earl of Pembroke. He took his responsibiblity and obligation as lord of these vast lands and as husband and father seriously. He enlarged his wife's holdings and saw that they had grants of freedom of tolls to make shipping of goods easier; he saw that they were granted markets and fairs within their boundaries to make each group of fiefs more profitable and self-sustainable. Marshal well understood that the primary obligation and duty of a medieval lord to his family and his vassals was to protect, preserve, and enrich all of his fiefs for the benefit of his descendants and of the vassals who held lands of him. Marshal's great success in his role as medieval lord can be found in the extant records of his vast fiefs.

William Marshal's skill and wisdom in regard to power and rule can easily be seen in his actions during and after the reign of King John. When John's actions against Marshal pushed him to the very edge of Marshal's fealty to the king, Marshal removed himself to Ireland and exercised patience and self-control. Historians agree that if Marshal had decided to join the barons rebelling against King John in 1215, John could have easily lost his throne. Marshal did not betray his oath of loyalty to the king; instead he did his very best to try to prevent the rebellion. When it came, Marshal rallied his knights and vassals and defended John against the rebels and the invading army of Louis of France. With John's death and Marshal's election as regent of England, Marshal used his knowledge and experience to secure the return and loyaty of the rebel barons to Henry III. Marshal had lived a long life, seen, and

been part of some of the most important events during the early 1200s. He knew

that the Magna Carta was an important document. Marshal saw that the Charter was

re-issued twice during his regency and that it was extended to include all of Ireland.

The ideas and concepts that all men, including the king, should be governed by and

answerable to laws were essential to the development of a country and its society.

Choices can have far reaching effects, and William Marshal's choices greatly

influenced his world and the course of medieval history.

The word *honour* has lost a great deal of its original meaning today,

and the quality of honour has become rare in much of mankind. Marshal took

the ideas of chivalric honour and loyalty and molded and defined both into his

own interpretation; he adopted those definitions and lived and died holding them

inviolate. Though William Marshal the man is dead, his spirit and example still cast

a light that can be seen by those who choose to look.

ABBREVIATIONS FOR NOTATION'S BIBLIOGRAPHY

Ann Camb	*Annales Cambriae.* Ed. J. Williams ab Ithel. London: Longman, Green, Longman, and Roberts, 1860.
Ann Conn	*Annala Connacht*: The Annals of Connaught. Ed. A. Martin Freeman. Dublin: Institute for Advanced Studies, 1944.
Ann Hib	*Annalium Hiberniae Chronicon*: The Annals of Ireland by Friar John Clyn,of the convent of Friars Minors, Kilkenny; and Thady Dowling Chancellor of Leighlin. Ed. Richard Butler. Dublin: Irish Archaeological Society, 1849.
Ann Mon	*Annales Monastici Vol. I: Annals de Margan: Annals de Theokesberia: Annals de Burton.* Ed. H. R. Luard. London: HMSO, 1864.
	Vol. II: Annals de Wintonia, Annals Monasterii de Waverlein. Ed. H. R. Luard. London: Longman, Green, Longman, Roberts and Green, 1865.
	Vol. III: Annals de Dunstable. Ed. H. R. Luard. London Longman, Green, Longman, Roberts, and Green, 1866-67.
	Vol. IV: Annals de Osney and Worcester. Ed. H. R. Luard. London: Longman, Green, Longman, Roberts,

and Green, 1868-69.

Brooks Knights' Fees   Brooks, Eric St John. _Knights Fees in Counties Wexford, Carlow and Kilkenny._ 3 vols. Dublin: Irish Manuscript Commission, 950.

Brut   _Brut y Tywysogyon_: Or The Chronicle of the Princes Peniarth MS 20 Version. Trans. Thomas Jones. Cardiff: U of Wales P, 1952.

Brut Red   _Brut y Tywysogyon_ or The Chronicles of the Princes, Red Book Hergest. Trans. T. Jones. Cardiff: U Wales P, 1955.

Cal. Doc. France   Calendar of Documents Preserved in France Illustrative of The History Of England and Ireland. Ed. J. Horace Round. London: G. Eyre and A. Spottiswoode, 1899.

Cal. Ormond   Calendar of Ormond Deeds Vol. I 1172-1350. Ed. Edmund Curtis.Dublin: Stationery Office, 1932. Vol II 1350-1413. Ed. Edmund Curtis. Dublin: Stationery Office, 1934. Vol. III 1413-1509. Ed. Edmund Curtis. Dublin: Stationery Office, 1935.

Cal Papal   Catholic Church. Calendar of Entries in the Papal Registers Relating To Great Britain and Ireland. Letters Vol. I 1198-1304. Eds. H. W. Bliss and C.

	Johnson. London: G. Eyre and A. Spottiswoode, 1893.
Cal. Pat. Rolls	Calendar of Patent Rolls Preserved in the Public Record Office: Henry III 1225-1247. 6 vols. London: HMSO, 1901-13. (noted by years)
Chart	*Rotuli Chartarum in turri londensi 1199-1216.* Ed. T. D. Hardy. London: G. Eyre and A. Spottiswoode, 1837.
Chart St Mary's	Chartularies of St Mary's Abbey Dublin: with the Register of Its House at Dunbrody. Ed. John T. Gilbert. 2 vols. London: Longman & Co.; Paternoster Row: Trubner & Co, Ludgate Hall, 1884.
Chron Maj	*Chronica Majora, Matthaei Parisiensis Monachi Sancti Albini; Chronica Majora.* Ed. H.R. Luard. 7 vols. London: Rolls Series, 1884-89.
Chron. Reign Richard I	Chronicles and Memoriales of the Reign of Richard I. Ed. William Stubbs. 2 vols. London: HMSO, 1864-65.
Claus	*Rotuli litterarum Clausaram in turri londensi Asservati.* 2 vols. London: G. Eyre and A. Spottiswoode, 1833-44.
Close R Henry III	Close Rolls of the Reign of Henry III Preserved in the Public Record Office. 14 Vols. London: HMSO, 1902-38.

Coggeshall   Randulphi de Coggeshall. *Chronicon*
                    Anglicanum. Ed. J. Stevenson. London:
                    Longman, 1875.

CRR   *Curia Regis Rolls* of the Reigns of Richard I, John, and
                    Henry III Preserved in the Public Record Office. 16
                    vols. London: Record Commission, 1922-79.

Diceto   Ralph of Diceto. *Radulphi de Diceto decani*
                    Lundoniensis. Ed. W. Stubbs. 2 vols. London:
                    Longman, 1876.

Edwards Cal. Wales Edwards, J. G. A Calendar of Ancient Correspondence
                    Concerning Wales. Cardiff: U Press Board of Wales,
                    1935.

Expugnatio   *Expugnatio Hibernica*: The Conquest of Ireland by
                    Giraldus Cambrensis. Eds. and trans. A. B. Scott and
                    F. X. Martin. Dublin:The Royal Irish Academy, 1978.

Eyton *Itin*   Eyton, Robert William. Court, Household, and
                    Itinerary of King Henry II. London: Taylor, 1878.

Farrer Itin Henry I Farrer, W. An Outline Itinerary of King Henry I.
                    Oxford: F. Hall, 1920.

Foedera   *Foedera, conventions, litterae et conjuscunque generis*
                    acta publica. Ed. T. Rymer. 4 vols. New ed. Vol.
                    I Part I. Eds. A. Clarke and F. Holbrook. London:
                    Record Commission, 1816-69.

Gervase   Gervase of Canterbury. <u>The Historical Works of Gervase of Canterbury.</u> Ed. W. Stubbs. 2 vols. London: Longman, Green, Longman and Roberts, 1884-89.

Gesta Regis Henrici Secundi   *Gesta Regis Henrici Secundi Benedicti Abbatis.* <u>The Chronicle of the Reigns of Henry II and Richard I Commonly known as Benedict of Peterborough.</u> Ed. W. Stubbs. 2 vols. London: Rolls Series, 1867.

Gesta Stephani   *Gesta Stephani Regis Anglorum.* <u>Chronicles and Memorials of the Reigns of Stephen, Henry II, and Richard I Vol. III.</u> Ed. Richard Howlett. London: Longman, 1884-89.

Giraldus   Giraldus Cambrensis. *Giraldi Cambrensis Opera.* Eds. J.S. Brewer, James F. Dimock, and George Warner. 8 vols. London: Longman, Green, Longman, and Roberts, 1861-91.

Hist   *L'histoire de Guillaume le Marechal, comte de Striguil et de Pembroke, Regent d'Angleterre de 1216-1219.* Ed. Paul Meyer. 3 vols. Paris: *Societe de l'histoire de France*, 1891-1901. (noted by line number)

Houedene   *Chronica Magistri Rogeri de Houedene.* Ed. W. Stubbs. 4 vols. London: Longmans, Green, Reader, and Dyer, 1868-71.

Layettes du Tresor	Archives Nationale France. <u>*Layettes du Tresor des Chartes*</u>. Alexandre Teulet. 5 vols. Paris: H. Plon, 1863-1909.
Liberate	<u>*Rotuli de Liberate ac de Misis et Praestitus, Regnante Johanne*</u>. Ed. T. D. Hardy. London: G. Eyre and A. Spottiswoode, 1844.
Liber Feodorum	<u>*Liber Feodorum*: The Book of Fees Commonly Called Testa de Nevill</u>. Ed. H.C. Maxwell Lyle. 3 vols. London: HMSO, 1921-31.
Matt Paris	Matthaei Parisiensis. <u>*Historia Anglorum.*</u> Ed. F. Madden. 3 vols. London: Rolls Series, 1866-69.
Mon Ang	<u>*Monasticon Anglicanum.*</u> Eds. Sir William Dugdale, Roger Dodsworth, and John Stevens. 6 vols. London: 1655-73, 1722-23. Rev. ed. Eds. John Caley, Henry Ellis, and B. Bandinel. London: Bohn, 1846.
Oblatis	<u>*Rotuli de Oblatis et finibus in turri londensi Asservati Tempore Regis Johannis*</u>. Ed. T. D. Hardy. London: G. Eyre and A. Spottiswoode, 1835.
Orderic	<u>Orderic Vitalis: The Ecclesiastical.</u> Ed. Marjorie Chibnall. 6 vols. Oxford: Clarendon,

1969-80.

Pat   *Rotuli litterarum patentium in Turri londensi Asservati*. Ed. T. D. Hardy. London: G. Eyre and A. Spottiswoode, 1835.

PR 1216-1225   Patent Rolls of the Reign of Henry III 1216-1225. London: HMSO, 1903.

PR 1225-1232   Patent Rolls of the Reign of Henry III 1225-1232. London: HMSO, 1906.

Reg Anglo-Norm   *Vol. I Regesta Regum Anglo-Normannorum.* Ed. H. C. Davis. Oxford: Clarendon, 1913.

---. Vol. II 1066-1154: Regesti Henrici Primi. Eds. C. Johnson and H. A. Cronne. Oxford: Clarendon, 1957.

---. Vol. III Regesta Stephani ac Mathildis Imperatricis et Gaufridi et Henrici Ducum Normannorum. Eds. H. A. Cronne and R. C. Davis. Oxford: Clarendon, 1968-69.

---. Vol. IV Facsimilies of Original Charters and Writs of King Stephen The Empress Mathilda and Dukes Geoffrey and Henry 1135-1154. Eds. H. A. Cronne and R. H. Davis. Oxford: Clarendon, 1969.

Rot Chart   *Rotuli Chartarum.* London: Record Commission, 1833, 1844. (Charters 1204-26)

Rotuli de Dominabus   *Rotuli de Dominabus et Pueris et Puellis de XII*

	*Comitatibus,*1185. Intro. J. H. Round. London: St. Catherine's P, 1913.
Rotuli Normanniae	*Rotuli Normanniae in turri Londinensi asservati, Johanne et Henrico quinto, Angliae Regibus.* London: G. Eyre and A. Spottiswoode, 1835.
Shirley <u>Royal Letters</u>	Shirley, Walter W., ed. <u>Royal and Other Historical Letters Illustrative of the Reign of Henry III.</u> <u>Vol. I 1216-1235.</u> London: Longman, Green, Longman, and Roberts, 1862. <u>Vol. II 1236-1272.</u> London: Longman, Green, Ruder, and Dyer, 1866.
Song	Conlon, Denis. <u>The Song of Dermot and Earl Richard FitzGilbert/ *Le Chansun de Dermot e li Quens Richard FizGilberti.*</u> NY: Peter Lang, 1992
Sweetman <u>Doc. Ireland</u>	Sweetman, H. S., ed. <u>Calendar of Documents Relating to Ireland 1171-1251.</u> 2 vols. London: HMSO, 1875-86.
Wendover	*Chronica Rogeri de Wendover liber qui dicitu flores historiarum.* Ed. H. G. Hewlett. 3 vols. London: Rolls Series, 1886-89.
Walt Cov	Walter of Coventry. *Memoriale fratis Walteri de Coventria.* Ed. W. Stubbs. 2 vols. London: Longman, 1872-73.

Wendover, Giles   <u>Roger of Wendover's Flowers of History.</u> Ed. and trans. J. A. Giles.2 vols. London: Henry G. Bohn, 1844-49.

William le Breton   William le Breton: *Gesta Philippi Augusti.* ed. H. F. Delaborde, in *Oeuvres de Rigord et Guillaume le Breton, historiens de Philippe Auguste.* 2 vols. Paris: *Societe de l'histoire de France*, 1882-85.

NOTATIONS BIBLIOGRAPHY

Addison, C. C. The Temple Church. London: Longman, Brown, Green, and
    Longmans, 1843.

Altschul, Michael. A Baronial Family: The Clares 1217-1314. Baltimore: Johns
    Hopkins P, 1965.

Anderson, A. O. and Marjorie Anderson, eds. The Chronicle of Melrose. London:
    Percy Lund Humphries & Co., 1936.

The Annals of Ireland Translated from the Original Four Masters. Trans. Owen
    Connellan. Dublin: B. Geraghty, 1846.

Barker, J. R. V. The Tournament in England 1100-1400. Woodbridge: Boydell,
    1986.

Barnard, Francis Pierrepont, ed. English History From Contemporary Writers:
    Strongbow's Conquest of Ireland. NY: G. P. Putnam's Sons, 1888.

Blakely, Ruth. The Brus Family in England and Scotland 1100-1295. Woodbridge:
    Boydell P, 2005.

Bracton's Note Book. Ed. F. W. Maitland. 3 vols. London: C. J. Clay, 1887.
    Buffalo: W. S. Hein, 1999.

Bradbury, J. Stephen and Matilda: The Civil Wars of 1139-53. Stroud,
    Gloucestershire: Alan Sutton, 1996.

Brooks, Eric St John. "Unpublished Charter of Raymond le Gros." Journal of the
    Royal Society of Antiquaries of Ireland 69 (1939): 167-69.

---. "Unpublished Charter Relating to Ireland 1177-82." Proceedings of the Royal

Irish Academy XLIII Section C (Dec. 1936): 313-65.

Brown, R. Allen. Castles From the Air. Cambridge: Cambridge UP, 1989.

---. English Castles. London: B.T. Batsford, 1974.

---. English Medieval Castles. London: Batsford, 1955.

---. "A List of Castles 1154-1216." EHR (April 1959): 249-80.

Calendar of Charter Rolls 1226-1257. Vol. 1 of 6 vols. London: HMSO, 1903-27.

    (noted by years).

Carpenter, David. The Minority of Henry III. London: Methuen, 1991.

Chaplais, Pierre, ed. Diplomatic Documents Preserved in the Public Record Office,

    1101-1272. London: J. W. Ruddock & Sons, Ltd., 1971.

Chartae, Privilegia et Immunitates. Dublin: Irish Record Commission, 1889.

"The Charters of the Cistercian Abbey of Duiske, County Kilkenny." Trans.

    Constance Butler. Ed. J. H. Bernard. Proceedings of the Royal Irish

    Academy XXXV Section C (1918-20): 1-189.

Chartes du prieure de Longueville de l'ordre de Cluny au diocese de Rouen

    anterieures a 1204. Ed. Paul le Cacheux. Rouen: Libraire de la Societe de

    l'Histoire de Normandie, 1934.

Cheney, M. "The Litigation Between John Marshal and Archbishop Thomas Becket

    in 1164." Law and Social Change: Papers Presented at the Bristol Legal

    History Conference, 14-17 July 1981. Royal Historical Society Studies in

    History 40 (1984): 9-26.

The Chronicle of Florence of Worcester with the Two Continuations. Trans. Thomas

    Forester. London: H. G. Bohn, 1854.

The Chronicle of Henry of Huntingdon. Trans. Thomas Forester. London: Henry

> G. Bohn, 1853. London: George Bell & Sons, 1876.

Chronicles of the Reigns of Stephen, Henry II, and Richard I. Ed. Richard Howlett.

> London: Longman, 1884-89.

> Vol I. *Historia rerum anglicarum* of Historia William of Newburgh.

> Vol II. *Historia rerum anglicarum v; Draco normannicus of Etienne de
> Rouen.*

> Vol III. *Gesta Stephani Regis Anglorum*; Chronicle of Richard of Hexham;
> *Relatio de standardo of St. Aelred*; Chronicle Jordan Fantosme; Chronicle
> Richard of Devizes.

> Vol IV. Chronicle of Robert of Torigni.

Chronicon Monasterii de Abingdon. Ed. J. Stevenson. 2 vols. London: Rolls

> Series, 1858.

The Church Historians of England. Trans. Joseph Stevenson. Vol. 2. "The

> Chronicle of Florence of Worcester." London: Seeleys, 1853.

Church, S. D., ed. King John: New Interpretations. Woodbridge: Boydell, 1999.

Clohosey, T. J. "Kilkenny Castle." Old Kilkenny Review 3 (1950): 50-53.

Colker, Marvin. "The 'Margam Chronicle' in a Dublin Manuscript." Haskins

> Society Journal 4 (1992): 123-48.

Cosgrove, Art and F.X. Martin, eds. A New History of Ireland: II Medieval Ireland

> Oxford: Clarendon, 1987.

Crede Mihi: The Most Ancient Register Book of the Archbishops of Dublin Before

> the Reformation. Ed. J. T. Gilbert. Dublin: Irish Manuscript Commission,

1897.

Crouch, David. The Beaumont Twins: The Roots and Branches of Power in

the 12th Century. Cambridge: Cambridge UP, 1996.

---. Image of Aristocracy in Britain 1000-1300. London: Routledge, 1982.

---. "Robert of Gloucester's Mother and Sexual Politics in Norman

Oxfordshire." Historical Research 72.179 (Oct.1999): 323-34.

 Davies, John. A History of Wales. London: Alan Lane, 1993.

Davis, H. W. C., ed. Mediaeval England: A New Edition of Barnard's

Companion to English History. Oxford: Clarendon P, 1924.

Denholm-Young, Neal. Richard of Cornwall. Oxford: Basil Blackwell,

1947.

Dingley, Thomas. History From Marble: Compiled in the Reign of Charles II. 2

vols. Intro. John G. Nichols. London: Camden Society, 1866-68.

Dolley, Michael. Anglo-Norman Ireland 1100-1310. Dublin: Gill & MacMillan,

1972.

Douglas, David C. and George Greenway, eds. English Historical Documents 1042-

1189. 2nd ed. London: Methuen, 1981..

Duffy, Sean. "John and Ireland: the Origins of England's Irish Problem." Church,

King John 221-45.

Empey, C.A. "A Case Study of the Primary Phase of Anglo-Norman Settlement: The

Lordship of Kells." Old Kilkenny Review 3.1 (1984): 32-40.

Evans, C. J. O. Monmouthshire: Its History and Topography. Cardiff: William

Lewis, 1954.

Excerpta e Rotulis Finium in turri Londinensi Asservatis 1216-1272. Ed. Charles
Roberts. 2 vols. London: Public Record Commission, 1835-36.

Farrer, William. Honors and Knights' Fees. Vol. I Bidun, Chokes, Visdelou, Wahull,
Curcy, Peverel of Nottingham. London: Spottiswoode, Ballantyne & Co.,
Ltd., 1923.

---. Vol. II Chester and Huntingdon. London: Spottiswoode, Ballantyne & Co.,
Ltd., 1924.

---. Vol. III Arundel, Eudes the Sewer, Warenne. London: Longman, Green and
Co., 1925.

Feet of Fines of the Reigns of Henry II and the First Seven Years of the Reign Of
Richard I. London: Pipe Rolls Society, 1894.

Flanagan, Marie T. Irish Society, Anglo-Norman Settlers, Angevin Kingship.
Oxford: Oxford UP, 1989.

Gillingham, John. "Love, Marriage, and Politics in the Twelfth Century." Forum for
Modern Language Studies 25 (1989): 292-303.

---. Richard Couer de Lion: Kingship, Chivalry and War in the Twelfth Century.
London: Hambledon, 1994.

---. Richard I. NY: Yale UP, 1999.

Given-Wilson, Chris and Alice Curteis. The Royal Bastards of Medieval England.
London: Routledge, 1984.

Guillaume le Breton: la chronique en prose. Ed. H. F. Delaborde. 2 vols. Paris: E.
Thorin, 1881-85.

Gwynn, A. "The Origins of St Mary's Abbey Dublin." The Journal of the Royal

Society Of Antiquaries of Ireland 79 (1949): 110-25.

Heiser, Richard. "The Royal *Familiares* of King Richard I." Medieval Prosopography 10 (1989): 25-50.

Henry of Huntingdon. *Historia Anglorum*: The History of the English People. Ed. and trans. Diana Greenway. Oxford: Clarendon, 1996.

Histoire de ducs de Normandie et des rois d'Angleterre. Ed. F. Michel. 3 vols. Paris: *Societe de l'histoire de France*, 1840.

Historic and Municipal Documents of Ireland AD 1172-1320. Ed. J. T. Gilbert. London: Longmans, Green, and Co., 1870.

The History and Antiquities of the Exchequer of the Kings of England. Ed. Thomas Madox. 2 vols. 2nd ed. 1769. NY: Augustus M. Kelley, 1969.

The History of English Law Before the Time of Edward I. Eds. F. Pollock and F. Maitland. 2nd ed. London: Cambridge UP, 1968.

Holden, Brock W. "King John, the Braoses and the Celtic Fringe." Albion 33.1 (Spring 2001): 1-23.

Hollister, C. Warren. "Henry I and the Anglo-Norman Magnates." Monarchy, Magnates, And Institutions in the Anglo-Norman World. London: Hambledon, 1986. 174-89.

Holt, James C. Magna Carta. 2nd ed. Cambridge: Cambridge UP, 1992.

---. Magna Carta and Medieval Government. London: Hambledon, 1985.

---. The Northerners: A Study in the Reign of King John. Oxford: Oxford UP, 1961.

Kaeuper, Richard W. Chivalry and Violence in Medieval Europe. Oxford: Oxford UP, 1999.

Keats-Rohan, K. S. B. <u>Domesday Descendants: A Prosopography of Persons</u>
<u>Occurring In English Document.</u> Vol. II. Woodbridge: Boydell, 2002.

---. <u>Domesday People: A Prosopography of Persons Occurring in English</u>
<u>Documents 1066-1166.</u> Vol. I. Woodbridge: Boydell, 1999.

Keefe, T. K. <u>Feudal Assessments and the Political Community Under Henry II and</u>
<u>his Sons.</u> Berkeley: U of California P, 1983.

King, Edmund. "King Stephen and the Anglo-Norman Aristocracy." <u>History</u> 59
(1974): 180-94.

---. <u>Medieval England 1066-1485.</u> Oxford: Phaidon, 1988.

Lalley, J.E. "Secular Patronage at the Court of King Henry II." <u>The Bulletin of the</u>
<u>Institute of Historical Research</u> 49 (1976): 159-84.

Landon, Lionel, ed. <u>The Itinerary of King Richard I.</u> London: J. W. Ruddock &
Sons, 1935.

---. <u>The *Cartae Antiquae* Rolls 1-10.</u> Lincoln: J. W. Ruddock & Sons, 1939.

Leaske, H. G. "A Cenotaph of Strongbow's Daughter at New Ross, County
Waterford." <u>Journal of the Royal Society of Antiquaries of Ireland</u>
LXXVIII pt. 1 (1948): 65-67.

Lees, Beatrice, ed. <u>Records of the Templars in England in the Twelfth Century:</u>
<u>The Inquest of 1185 with Illustrative Charters and Documents.</u> London:
Humphrey Milford, 1935.

Legge, M. Dominica. "William Marshal and Arthur of Brittany." <u>Bulletin of</u>
<u>the Institute of Historical Research</u> 55 (May 1982): 18-24.

Liber Primus Kilkenniensis. Ed. Charles McNeill. Dublin: Irish Record

Commission, 1931. Trans. J. Otway-Ruthven. Kilkenny, 1961.

Lloyd, J. E. A History of Wales from the Earliest Times to the Edwardian Conquest. 3rd ed. 2 vols. London: Longmans, Green, & Co., 1967.

Martindale, Jane. "Eleanor of Aquitaine: The Last Years." Church, King John 136-64.

Meade, Marion. Eleanor of Aquitaine. 1977. NY: E.P. Dutton, 1991.

"Miscellaneous Records of the Norman Exchequer 1199-1204." Ed. Sidney Packard. Smith College Studies in History XII (1928): 5-116.

Morris, Marc. The Bigod Earls of Norfolk in the Thirteenth Century. Woodbridge: Boydell P, 2005.

Muir's Historical Atlas. 10th ed. Eds. R. F. Treharne & Harold Fullard. London: George Philip & Son, Ltd., 1965.

Mullally, Evelyn. "The Portrayal of Women in the 'Histoire de Guillaume le Marechal.'" Peritia 10 (1996): 352-62.

Orpen, G. H. Ireland Under the Normans. 4 vols. London: Oxford, 1911.

---. The Song of Dermot and the Earl. Oxford: Clarendon, 1891.

Painter, Sidney. William Marshal Knight-Errant, Baron, and Regent of England. Baltimore: Johns Hopkins, 1982.

---. The Reign of King John. Baltimore: Johns Hopkins, 1949.

---. "The Rout of Winchester." Speculum 7.1 (Jan. 1932): 70-75.

Phelan, M. "William Marshal." Old Kilkenny Review n.s. 2.5 (1983): 497-505.

Power, Daniel. "The French Interests of the Marshal Earls of Striguil and

Pembroke, 1189-1214." Proceedings of the Battle Conference on

    Anglo-Norman Studies 25. Ed. John Gillingham. Woodbridge:

    Boydell, 2003. 199-225.

Powicke, F. M. The Loss of Normandy 1189-1204: Studies in the History of

    The Angevin Empire. 2nd ed. Manchester: Manchester UP, 1961.

---. Stephen Langton. London: Merlin, 1965.

Recueil des actes de Henri II roi d'Angleterre et duc de Normandie. Ed. Leopold

    Delisle. 3 vols. Rev. ed. Paris: Imprimeric Nationale Librairie C.

    Klincksieck, 1916.

Red Book of the Exchequer. Ed. Hubert Hall. 3 vols. London: G. Eyre & A.

    Spottiswoode, 1896.

Rees, William. "The Medieval Lordship of Brecon." Transactions of the

    Honourable Society of Cymmrodorion (1915-16): 165-224.

Register of the Abbey of St. Thomas, Dublin. Ed. John T. Gilbert. London: G. Eyre

    and A. Spottiswoode, 1889.

Richard of Devizes. Chronicon Ricardus divisiensis de rebus gestis Ricardi primi.

    Chronicles and Memorials of the Reigns of Stephen, Henry II and Richard I

    Vol. III. Ed. Richard Howlett. London: Longman, 1884-89.

Richardson, H. G. "The Letters and Charters of Eleanor of Aquitaine." EHR

    CCXCI (April 1959): 193-213.

Richardson, H.G. and G. O. Sayles, eds. The Administration of Ireland, 1172-1377.

    Dublin: Stationary Office, 1963.

Robert of Torigny. Chronique. Chronicles and Memorials of the Reigns of Stephen,

Henry II and Richard Vol. IV. Ed. Richard Howlett. London: Longman,
   1884-89.

Roche, Richard. "The Roches of Wexford." Journal of the Old Wexford Society 2
   (1969): 29-48.

Roderick, A. J. "Marriage and Politics in Wales 1066-1282." Welsh History Review
   4 (1968-69): 1-20.

Rotuli Cancellarii vel Antigraphum Magni Rotuli Pipae de Tertio Anno regni Regis
   Johannis. London: G. Eyre and A. Spottiswoode, 1833.

Round, J. H. Ancient Charters: Royal and Private Prior Prior to 1200 AD. London:
   Wyman & Sons, 1888.

---. ed. The Commune of London and Other Studies. Westminster: Archibald
   Constable & Co., 1899.

---. "The Family of Clare." The Archaeological Journal 56 (1899): 221-31.

Rowlands, I. W. "William de Braose and the Lordship of Brecon." The
   Bulletin of the Board of Celtic Studies 30 (1982-83): 122-33.

Salter, H. E., ed. Newington Longeville Charters. London: Oxford Record Society,
   1921.

Sanders, I. J. English Baronies: A Study in their Origin and Descent. Oxford:
   Clarendon, 1960.

Sayers, William. "Anglo-Norman Verse on New Ross and Its Founders." Irish
   Historical Studies XXVII.10 (Nov. 1992): 113-23.

Sheehy, Maurice P. "Diplomatica: Unpublished Medieval Charters and Letters
   Relating to Ireland." Irish Historical Records 25 (1962): 123-35.

---. *"The Registrum Novum*: A Manuscript of Holy Trinity Cathedral: The Medieval

     Charters." <u>Reportum Novum; Dublin Diocesan Historical Record</u> 3 (1963-4):

     249-81.

Smith, J. Beverly. "The Treaty of Lambeth." <u>EHR</u> xciv (1979): 562-79.

Somerset-Fry, Plantagenet. <u>British Medieval Castles.</u> London: David and Charles,

     1974.

Stevenson, Francis. <u>Robert Grosseteste: Bishop of Lincoln.</u> Dubuque, Iowa:

     Wm. C. Brown, 1967.

---. "Robert Grosseteste and his Correspondence: A Reappraisal." <u>Archives</u>

     16.7 (April 1984): 227-57.

Strickland, Matthew. <u>War and Chivalry: The Conduct and Perception of War in</u>

     <u>England and Normandy 1066-1217.</u> Cambridge: Cambridge UP, 1996.

Stubbs, William, ed. <u>Select Charters and other Illustrations of English Constitutional</u>

     <u>History from the Earliest Time to the Reign of Edward I.</u> 9th ed. Ed. H. W.

     C. Davis. Oxford: Clarendon, 1929.

Sweetman, David. <u>Medieval Castles of Ireland.</u> Woodbridge: Boydell, 1999.

Taylor, A. J. "Usk Castle and the Pipe Roll of 1185." *Archaeologia Cambrensis* 99

     (1946-7): 249-55.

Tout, T. F. <u>The History of England from the Accession of Henry III to the</u>

     <u>Death Of Edward III (1216-1377).</u> London: Longmans, Green, and

     Co., 1905.

Turner, Ralph V. "The *Miles Literatus* in 12th and 13th Century England."

     <u>American Historical Review</u> 83 (1978): 929-45.

---. "Royal Courts Treat Disseisin by the Kings: John and Henry III 1199-
1240." American Journal of Legal History XII (1968): 1-17.

Le Verdier, Pierre. *"Guillaume le Marechal, comte de Striguil et de
Pembroke, de Buckingham et de Longueville."* Bulletin de la Societe
de l'Histoire de Normandie 15 (1935): 161-70. (courtesy of his
grandson Antoine du Boullay)

Victoria County History. History of the County of Lancashire, Vol.II. Eds.
William Farrer and J. Brownbill. London: Constable, 1908.

Victoria County History. History of the County of Wiltshire. Vol. III. Eds. A.
B. Pugh and Elizabeth Crittall. London: Oxford UP, 1956.

Vincent, Nicholas. "A Roll of Knights Summoned to Campaign in 1213."
The Bulletin of the Institute of Historical Research 66 (1993): 89-97.

---. "William Marshal, King Henry II, and the Honour of Chateaurous."
Archives 25 (2000): 1-15.

Visitations by the Heralds in Wales. Transcribed and ed. Michael Powell
Siddons. Stroud, Gloucestershire: Alan Sutton, 1996.

Wagner, Anthony R. "A Seal of Strongbow in the Huntingdon Library." The
Antiquaries Journal 21 (1941): 128-32.

Walker, R. F. "Henry II's Charter to Pembroke." Bulletin of the Board of
Celtic Studies 36 (1989): 132-45.

---. "Hubert de Burgh and Wales 1218-1232." English Historical Review
87.344 (Jul. 1972): 465-94.

Walsh, F.R. "Castle Eve." Old Kilkenny Review 10 (1958): 42-46.

Walter Map. *De nugis curialium.* Ed. & trans. M. R. James. Oxford: Clarendon, 1983.

Ward, Jennifer. "The Medieval County of Kildare." <u>Irish Historical Studies Joint Journal of the Irish Historical Society and the Ulster Soceity for Irish Historical Studies.</u> 11(1959): 181-99.

---. "Royal Service and Reward: The Clare Family and the Crown 1066-1154." <u>Proceedings of the Battle Conference on Anglo-Norman Studies XI</u>. Ed. R. Allen Brown. Woodbridge: Boydell, 1989. 261-78.

Warren, H. L. <u>King John.</u> Berkeley: U California P, 1978.

Waugh, Scott L. <u>The Lordship of England: Royal Wardships and Marriage in English Society and Politics 1219-1327.</u> Princeton: Princeton UP, 1988.

Way, Albert. "A Letter to William Marshal, earl of Pembroke, c 1216, by Archbishops Of Tuam and Dublin." <u>Journal of Royal Society of Antiquaries of Ireland</u> VIII Vol. V (1864-66): 137-39.

West, F. J. <u>The Justiciarship in England 1066-1232.</u> Cambridge: Cambridge UP, 1966.

<u>William of Malmesbury</u>*: Historia Novella.* Ed. Edmund King. Trans. K. R. Potter. Oxford: Clarendon, 1998.

William of Newburg. *Historia Rerum Anglicarum.* <u>Chronicles and Memorials of the Reigns of Stephen, Henry II and Richard I Vols. I & II</u>. Ed. Richard Howlett. London: Longman, 1884-89.

Williamson, J. Bruce. <u>The History of the Temple, London.</u> London: John

Murray, 1924.

Wright, Thomas. Essays on Subjects Connected with Literature, Popular
      Superstitions and History of England in the Middle Ages. Vol. II London:
      John Russell Smith, 1856.

Pipe Rolls and Government Documents:

Leges Henrici Primi. Ed. and trans. L. J. Donnen. Oxford: Clarendon, 1972.

Normandy Exchequer. *Magni Rotuli Scaccarii Normanniae sub regibus Angliae*.
      Trans. T. Stapleton. 2 vols. London: Sumptibus Soc. Antiq. Londensi, 1840-
      44.

Pipe Roll 17 John. Ed. R. A. Brown. Praestitia Roll 14-18 John: Roll of
      Summonses 1214: Scutage Roll 16 John. Ed. J. C. Holt. Lincoln: J. W.
      Ruddock & Sons, 1964.

Recueil des actes de Philippe Auguste. Eds. H. F. Delaborde, E. Berger, and C.
      Brunel. 2 vols.   Paris: *Imprimeric Nationale*, 1916-27

Three Rolls of the King's Court in the Reign of King Richard I 1194-95. London:
      G. Eyre and A. Spottiswoode, 1899.

THE PIPE ROLLS (In order of the kings and their years.)

PR (year) (king) = all pipe rolls noted in this manner

Great Roll of the Pipe for the Thirty-first Year of the Reign of Henry I
      Michaelmas1129-1130. London: PRS, 1921.

Great Roll of the Pipe for the Second, Third, and Fourth Years of the Reign of Henry
      II, 1155-1158. Ed. J. Hunter. London: G. Eyre and A. Spottiswoode, 1844.

Great Roll of the Pipe for the Fifth Year of the Reign of King Henry II 1158-1159.

Vol. I. London: PRS, 1844.

Great Roll of the Pipe for the Sixth Year of the Reign of Henry II 1159-1160. Vol. II. London: PRS, 1884.

Great Roll of the Pipe for the Seventh Year of the Reign of Henry II 1160-1161. Vol. IV London: Wyman and Sons, 1885. Vaduz: Kraus Reprint, 1966.

Great Roll of the Pipe for the Eighth Year of the Reign of Henry II 1161-1162. Vol. V. London: PRS, 1885.

Great Roll of the Pipe for the Ninth Year of the Reign of Henry II 1162-1163. Vol. VI London: Wyman & Sons, 1886. Vaduz: Kraus Reprint, 1966.

Great Roll of the Pipe for the Tenth Year of the Reign of Henry II 1163-1164. Vol. VII. London: Wyman & Sons, 1886. Vaduz: Kraus Reprint, 1966.

Great Roll of the Pipe for the Eleventh Year of the Reign of Henry II 1164-1165. Vol. VIII. London: PRS, 1886-87.

Great Roll of the Pipe for the Twelfth Year of the Reign of Henry II 1165-1166. Vol. IX. London: PRS, 1887.

Great Roll of the Pipe for the Thirteenth Year of the Reign of Henry II 1166-1167. Vol. XI. London: Hansard Publishing Union, 1889. Vaduz: Kraus Reprint, 1966.

Great Roll of the Pipe for the Fourteenth Year of the Reign of King Henry II 1167-1168. Vol. XII. London: Hansard Publishers Union, 1890. Vaduz: Kraus Reprint, 1966.

Great Roll of the Pipe for the Fifteenth Year of the Reign of Henry II 1168-1169. Vol. XIII. London: Wyman & Sons, 1890. Vaduz: Kraus Reprint, 1966.

Great Roll of the Pipe for the Sixteenth Year of the Reign of King Henry II 1169-
1170. Vol. XV. London: Wyman & Sons, 1892. Vaduz: Kraus Reprint, 1966.

Great Roll of the Pipe for the Seventeenth Year of the Reign of King Henry II 1170-
1171. Vol. XVI. London: Wyman & Sons, 1893. Vaduz: Kraus Reprint,
1966.

Great Roll of the Pipe for the Eighteenth Year of the Reign of King Henry II 1171-
1172. Vol. XVIII. London: Wyman & Sons, 1894. Vaduz: Kraus Reprint,
1966.

Great Roll of the Pipe for the Nineteenth Year of the Reign of King Henry II 1172-
1173. Vol. XIX. London: Wyman & Sons, 1895. Vaduz: Kraus Reprint,
1966.

Great Roll of the Pipe for the Twentieth Year of the Reign of Henry II 1173-1174.
Vol. XXI. London: PRS, 1896.

Great Roll of the Pipe for the Twenty-First Year of the Reign of King Henry II 1174-
1175. Vol. XXII. London: PRS, 1897. London: Percy Lund, Humphries &
Co., 1929.

Great Roll of the Pipe for the Twenty-Second Year of the Reign Henry II 1175-1176.
Vol.XXV. London: Spottiswoode & Co., 1904. Vaduz: Kraus Reprint, 1966.

Great Roll of the Pipe for the Twenty-Third Year of the Reign of Henry II 1176-
1177. Vol.XXVI. London: Spottiswoode & Co., 1905. Vaduz: Kraus
Reprint, 1966.

Great Roll of the Pipe for the Twenty-Fourth year of the Reign of Henry II 1177-
1178. Vol. XXVII. London: PRS, 1905-06.

Great Roll of the Pipe for the Twenty-Fifth Year of the Reign of Henry II 1178-1179.
Vol. XXVIII. London: Arthur Doubleday, 1907. Vaduz: Kraus Reprint, 1966.

Great Roll of the Pipe for the Twenty-Sixth Year of the Reign of Henry II 1179-1180.
Vol. XXIX. London: St Catherine's Press, 1909. Vaduz: Kraus Reprint,
1966.

Great Roll of the Pipe for the Twenty-Seventh Year of the Reign of King Henry
II 1180-1181. Vol. XXX. London: St Catherine Press, 1909. Vaduz:
KrausReprint, 1966.

Great Roll of the Pipe for the Twenty-Eighth Year of the Reign of Henry II 1181-
1182. Vol. XXXI. London: St Catherine Press, 1910. Vaduz: Kraus Reprint,
1966.

Great Roll of the Pipe for the Twenty-Ninth Year of the Reign of Henry II 1182-
1183. Vol. XXXII. London: St Catherine Press, 1911. Vaduz:Kraus Reprint,
1966.

Great Roll of the Pipe for the Thirtieth Year of the Reign of Henry II 1183-1184.
Vol. XXXIII. London: St Catherine Press, 1912. Vaduz:Kraus Reprint, 1968.

Great Roll of the Pipe for the Thirty-First Year of the Reign of Henry II 1184-1185.
Vol. XXXIV. London: PRS, 1913. Vaduz: Kraus Reprint, 1966.

Great Roll of the Pipe for the Thirty-Second Year of the Reign of Henry II 1185-
1186. Vol. XXXVI. London: PRS, 1914. Vaduz: Kraus Reprint, 1966.

Great Roll of the Pipe for the Thirty-Third Year of the Reign of Henry II 1186-1187.
Vol. XXXVII. London: St Catherine's Press, 1913. Vaduz: Krause Reprint,
1966.

Great Roll of the Pipe for the Thirty-Fourth Year of the Reign of King Henry II, 1187-1188. Vol. XXXVIII. London: The Hereford Times, 1925. Vaduz: Kraus Reprint, 1966.

Great Roll of the Pipe for the First Year of the Reign of Richard I 1189-1190. ns I. Ed. J. Hunter. London: G. Eyre and A. Spottiswoode, 1844.

Great Roll of the Pipe for the Second Year of the Reign of Richard I Michaelmas 1190-1191. Vol. XXXIX. ns II. Ed. D. M. Stenton. London: St Catherine Press, 1925.

Great Roll of the Pipe for the Third, Fourth and Fifth Year of the Reign of Richard IMichaelmas 1191-Michaelmas 1192. Ed. Doris Stenton. London: J, W, Ruddock & Sons, 1926.

Great Roll of the Pipe for the Fifth Year of the Reign of Richard I Michaelmas 1193-1194. ns V. Ed. Doris Stenton. London: J. W. Ruddock & Sons, 1927.

Great Roll of the Pipe for the Sixth Year of the Reign of Richard I Michaelmas 1194-1195. ns VI. Ed. Doris Stenton. London: PRS, 1928.

Great Roll of the Pipe for the Seventh Year of the Reign of Richard I Michaelmas 1195-1196. ns VII. Ed. Doris Stenton. London: J. W. Ruddock & Sons, 1929.

Great Roll of the Pipe for the Ninth Year of the Reign of King Richard I Michaelmas1196-1197. ns VIII. Ed. Doris M. Stenton. London: J. W. Ruddock & Sons, 1931.

Feet of Fines of the Tenth Year of the Reign of Richard I AD 1198-1199 [Excepting the counties of Bedford, Berkshire, Buckingham, Cambridge, Devon and

Dorset] and A Roll of the King's Court. Vol. XXIV. London: Percy Lund, Humphries & Co., 1929.

Feet of Fines of the Reigns of Henry II and the First Seven Years of the Reign Of Richard I. London: Pipe Roll Society, 1894.

The Itinerary of King Richard I: With Studies on Certain Matters of Interest in His Reign.Vol. LI. nsXIII. Ed. Lionel Landon. London/Lincoln: J. W. Ruddock & Sons, 1935.

Three Rolls of the King's Court in the Reign of King Richard I 1194-1195. London: HMSO, 1891. Vaduz: Kraus Reprint, 1966.

Great Roll of the Pipe for the First Year of the Reign of King John Michaelmas 1198-1199. ns X. Ed. Doris M. Stenton. London: J. W. Ruddock & Sons, 1933.

Great Roll of the Pipe for the Second Year of the Reign of King John, Michalemas 1199-1200. Vol. L. ns XI. Ed. Doris M. Stenton. London: J. W. Ruddock & Sons, 1934.

Great Roll of the Pipe for the Fourth Year of the Reign of King John Michaelmas 1201-1202. Vol. LIII. ns XV. Ed. Doris M. Stenton. London: J.W. Ruddock & Sons, 1937.

Great Roll of the Pipe for the Fifth Year of the Reign of King John Michaelmas 1202-1203. Vol. LIV. ns XVI. Ed. Doris M. Stenton. London: J. W. Ruddock & Sons, 1938.

Great Roll of the Pipe for the Sixth Year of the Reign of King John Michaelmas 1203-1204. Vol. LVI. ns XVII. Ed. Doris M. Stenton. London: J. W. Ruddock & Sons, 1940.

Great Roll of the Pipe for the Seventh Year of the Reign of King John Michaelmas
1204-1205. Vol. LVII. ns XIX. Ed. Sidney Smith. London/Lincoln: J. W.
Ruddock & Sons, 1941.

Great Roll of the Pipe for the Ninth Year of the Reign of King John Michaelmas
1206-1207. ns XXII. Ed. Mary Kirkus. London: J. W. Ruddock & Sons,
1942.

Great Roll of the Pipe for the Tenth Year of the Reign of King John Michaelmas
1207-1208. ns XXIII. Ed. Doris M. Stenton. London: J. W. Ruddock &
Sons, 1947.

The Great Roll of the Pipe for the Twelfth Year of the Reign of King John,
Michaelmas 1209-1210. Vol. LXIV. ns XXVI. Ed. C. F. Slade. London: J.
W. Ruddock & Sons, 1951.

Great Roll of the Pipe Roll for the Thirteenth Year of the Reign of King John
Michaelmas 1210-1211. ns XXVIII. Ed. Doris M. Stenton. London: J. W.
Ruddock & Sons, 1953.

Great Roll of the Pipe for the Fourteenth Year of the Reign of King John Michaelmas
1212-1212 Vol. LXVIII. ns XXX. Ed. Patricia Barnes. London: J.
W.Ruddock & Sons, 1950.

Great Roll of the Pipe for the Sixteenth Year of the Reign of King John I Michaelmas
1214-1214. Ed. Patricia Barnes. London: J. W. Ruddock & Sons, 1962.

Great Roll of the Pipe for the Second Year of the Reign of King Henry III
Michaelmas 1218 ns XXXIX. Ed. P. Ebden. London: PRS, 1964.

Great Roll of the Pipe for the Third Year of the Reign of King Henry III Michaelmas

1219 ns XLII. Ed. B. E. Harris. London: PRS, 1969-70.

Great Roll of the Pipe for the Fourth Year of the Reign of King Henry III

   Michaelmas 1220 ns XLVII. Ed. B. E. Harris. London: PRS, 1981-83.

Great Roll of the Pipe for the Fifth Year of the Reign of King Henry III Michaelmas

   1221 ns XLVIII. Ed. D. Crook. London: PRS, 1984-86.

Great Roll of the Pipe for the Fourteenth Year of the Reign of King Henry III

   Michaelmas 1230. ns IV. London: PRS, 1927.

Interdict Documents. Vol. LXXII. ns Vol. XXXIV. Eds. Patricia M. Barnes and W.

   Raymond Powell. London: J. W. Ruddock & Sons, 1960.

Genealogy Tables

de Clare Family 1

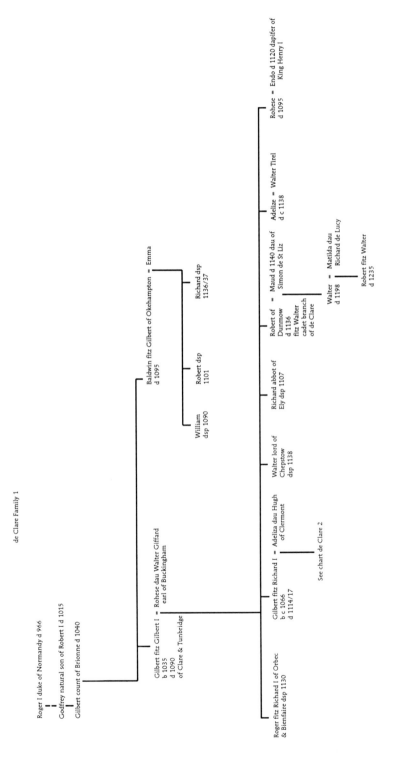

Roger I duke of Normandy d 966

Godfrey natural son of Robert I d 1015

Gilbert count of Brionne d 1040

Gilbert fitz Gilbert I = Rohese dau Walter Giffard
b 1035   earl of Buckingham
d 1090
of Clare & Tunbridge

Baldwin fitz Gilbert of Okehampton = Emma
d 1095

William   Robert dsp   Richard dsp
dsp 1090   1101   1136/37

Roger fitz Richard I of Orbec
& Bienfaire dsp 1130

Gilbert fitz Richard I = Adeliza dau Hugh
b c 1066   of Clermont
d 1114/17

See chart de Clare 2

Walter lord of
Chepstow
dsp 1138

Richard abbot of
Ely dsp 1107

Robert of   =   Maud d 1140 dau of
Dunmow   Simon de St Liz
d 1136
fitz Walter
cadet branch
of de Clare

Walter = Matilda dau
d 1198   Richard de Lucy

Robert fitz Walter
d 1235

Adelize = Walter Tirel
d c 1138

Rohese = Eudo d 1120 dapifer of
d 1095   King Henry I

387

de Clare Family 2

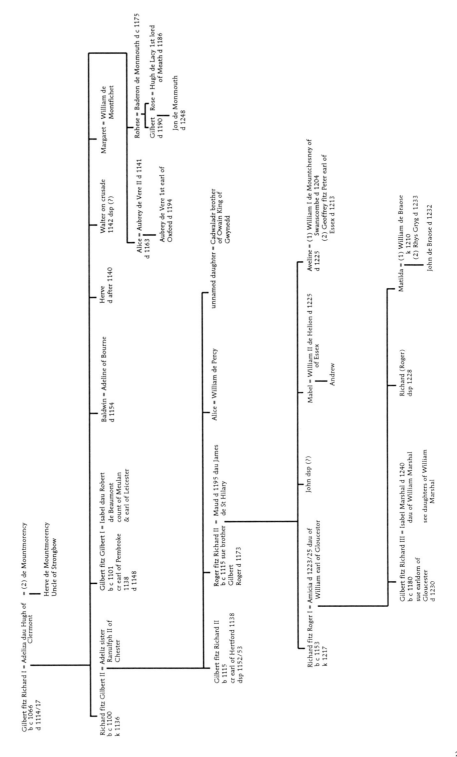

The de Clare Genealogy

Gilbert count of Brionne (d1040)

1. Richard fitz Gilbert I (bc1035 d1090) = Rohese dau. Walter Giffard earl of
Buckingham

    a. Roger fitz Richard I of Orbec & Bienfaite (dsp1130/31)

    b. Gilbert fitz Richard I of Tunbridge (bc1066 d1114/17) = Adeliza dau. Hugh
    (see page 2a)   of Clermont

    c. Walter fitz Richard lord of Netherwent/Chepstow (dsp1138)

    d. Richard fitz Richard abbot of Ely (dsp1107)

    e. Robert fitz Walter of Dunmow (d1136) = Matilda/Maud (d1140) dau.
    (founder fitz Walter cadet branch of de Clare's)   Simon de St Liz

        e1. Walter (d1198) = Matilda dau. Richard de Lucy

        e2. Maude = William de Albini "Brito"

    f. Adelize (dc1138) = Walter Tirel of Poix, Picardy

        f1. Hugh lord of Poix crusade 1147

    g. Rohese (d1121) = Eudo de Ria (d1120) *dapifer* of Henry I

        g1. Margaret = William de Mandeville (d1120/29)

2. Baldwin fitz Gilbert (d1095) of Okehampton = (1) Albreda
                                  = (2) Emma

    2a. William (dsp 1096)

    2b. Robert (dsp 1101/03)

    2c. Richard (dsp 1136/37)

    2d. Adeliza (d1142) = (?) Ranulph Avenel

2a The de Clare Genealogy

Gilbert fitz Richard I (bc1066 d1114/17) = Adeliza dau. Hugh of Clermont

    a. Richard fitz Gilbert II (bc1100 k1136) = Adeliz sis. Ranulph earl of

    (see below)   Chester

    b. Gilbert fitz Gilbert I (bc1101 d1148) = Isabel de Beaumont dau. Robert

    (see 1b Richard "Strongbow")   earl of Leicester (d1118)

    c. Baldwin (d1154) = Adeline of Bourne, Lincolnshire

        1c. Emma = Hugh Wake I (dc1176)

        2c. Rose = William de Bussey (d1166) of Old Wardon

    d. Hervey expedition Cardigan 1140 (d?)

    e. Walter on crusade 1147 (d?)

    f. Margaret = William de Montfichet lord of Stansted, Essex

    g. Alice/Adeliza (d1163) = Aubrey de Vere (k1141) lord of Hedingham,

                                                      Essex

        g1. Aubrey (d1194) 1st earl of Oxford

    h. Rohese = Baderon de Monmouth (d1170/76)

        h1. Gilbert (d1190)

        h1a. John de Monmouth (d1248)

Richard fitz Gilbert II (bc1100 k1136) = Adeliz sis. Ranulph II earl of Chester

    a. Gilbert fitz Richard II (b1115 dsp1152/53) cr. Earl of Hertford 1138

    b. Roger fitz Richard II (d1173) = Maud (d1195) dau. James de St Hilary

        (see page 3a)

    c. Alice = William de Percy

    d. unnamed daughter = Cadwaladr brother of Owain king of Gwynedd

3a The de Clare Genealogy

Roger fitz Richard II (d1173) = Maud (d1195) dau. James de St Hilary of
Succeeded his brother Gilbert (dsp1152/53)   Field Dalling, Norfolk

    a. Richard fitz Roger (bc1153 d1217) = Amica (d1225) dau. William earl of
    (see below)   Gloucester (d1183)

    b. John (dsp ?)

    c. Mabel = William de Helion II (d1225)

        c1. Andrew

    d. Aveline (dc1225) = (1) William de Mountchesney of Swanscombe (d1204)
                (2) Geoffrey fitz Peter (d1213) earl of Essex

Richard fitz Roger (bc1153 d1217) = Amica (d1225) dau. William earl of
                                      Gloucester

    a. Gilbert fitz Richard III (bc1180 d1230) = Isabel Marshal (d1240)
      Earl of Hertford & Gloucester

    b. Richard/Roger (dsp1228)

    c. Matilda = (1) William de Braose (k1210)
             (2) Rhys ap Gryg (d1233)

      1c. John de Braose (d1232)

Richard Strongbow de Clare & Dermot MacMurchada

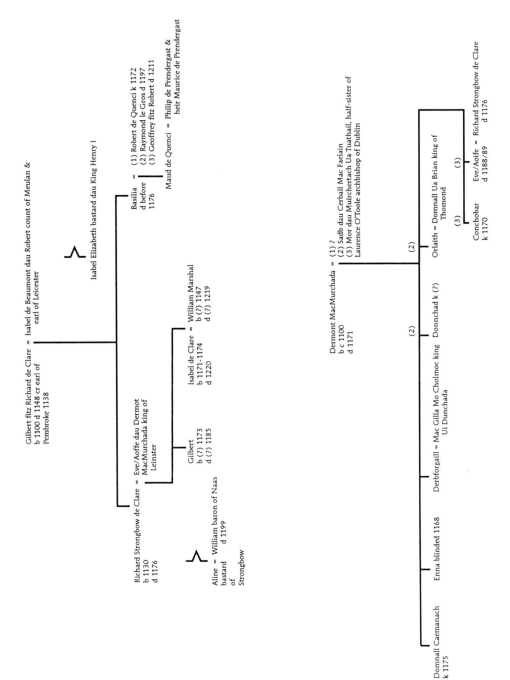

1b. Richard "Strongbow" de Clare and Dermot MacMurchada

Gilbert fitz Richard de Clare (b1100 d1148) = Isabel de Beaumont dau. Robert earl
created. Earl of Pembroke 1138   of Leicester

1. Richard "Strongbow" (b1130 d 1176) = Eve/Aoife MacMurchada dau. Dermot
                                              MacMurchada King of Leinster

        a. Gilbert (dsp before 1185)

        b. Isabel (b 1171/1174 d 1220) = William Marshal (d1219)

        Aline (bastard of Richard "Strongbow") = William baron of Naas

                                (d1199)

2. Basilia (d before 1203) = (1) Robert de Quenci (k1172)

    (see 2 e.)   (2) Raymond le Gros (d1186/88)

                         (3) Geoffrey fitz Robert (d1211)

Dermot MacMurchada (b c 1110 d 1171) = (1) unknown

                        (2) Sabd dau. Cerball Mac Faelain king
                                   of Faelain

                        (3) Mor dau. Muirchertach Ua Tuathail
                                King of Ui Muiredaig
                                Half-sister of Laurence
                                O'Toole
                                archbishop of Dublin

1a. Domnall Caemanach (k1175)

1b. Enna (blinded 1168)

1c. Derbforgaill = Mac Gilla Mo Cholmoc king of Ui Dunchada

2a. Donnchad (k ?)

2b. Orlaith = Domnall Ua Brian king of Thomond

3a. Conchobar (k1170)

3b. Eve/Aoife (d1188/89) = Richard "Strongbow" de Clare (d1176)

The Marshal Family

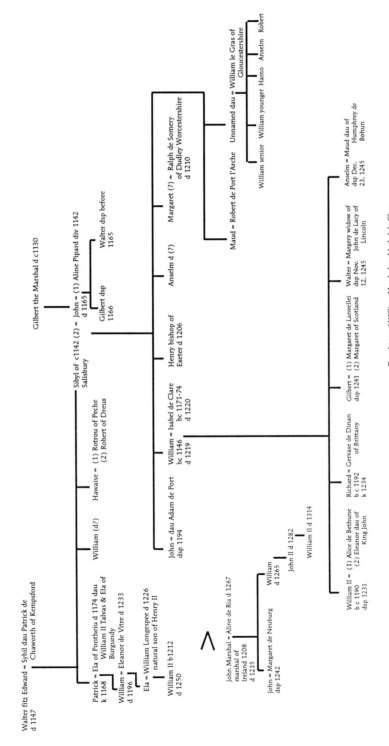

1c Family of William Marshal

Walter fitz Edward (d1147) = Sibyl dau. Patrick de Chaworth of Kempsford

    1. Patrick (k1168) earl of Salisbury = Ela of Pontheiu (d1174) dau. William II
                                   Talvas & Ela of Burgandy

        1a. William (d1196) = Eleanor de Vitre (d1233)

                1a1. Ela countess of Salisbury = William Longespee (d1226)

    2. William (d?)

    3. Hawaise = (1) Rotrou of Peche (d1144)

                (2) Robert of Dreux

    4. Sibyl = John fitz Gilbert the marshal (d1165)

        (see below)

John fitz Gilbert the marshal (d1165) = (1) Aline Pipard divorced 1242

                                (2) Sibyl of Salisbury

    1a. Gilbert (dsp1166)

    1b. Walter (dsp before 1165)

    2a. John (dsp1194) = dau Adam de Port

    2b. William (d1219) = Isabel de Clare (d1220)

        (see below 2c & 1d)

    2c. Henry bishop of Exeter (dsp 1206)

    2d. Anselm (d?)

    2e. Margaret (?) = Ralph de Somery (d1210)

    2f. Maud = Robert de Port l'Arche

    2g. unnamed dau. = William le Gras of Gloucestershire (sons went to Ireland
                            with William Marshal became the Grace's)

Bastard John Marshal who became marshal of Ireland in 1208

    John (d1235) = Aline de Ria (d1267) of Hockering, Norfolk

        1. John (dsp1242) = Margaret sis. & heir Thomas earl of Warwick

        2. William (d1265) = (?)

            2a. John II (d1282)

                2a1. William (d1314) at Bannockburn

Maud Marshal

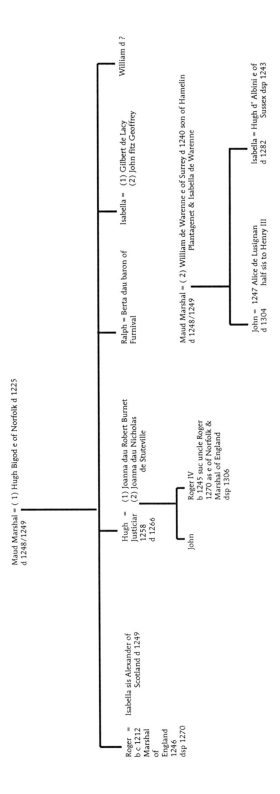

Maud Marshal = (1) Hugh Bigod e of Norfolk d 1225
d 1248/1249

Roger =
b c 1212
Marshal
of
England
1246
dsp 1270

Isabella sis Alexander of
Scotland d 1249

Hugh =
Justiciar
1258
d 1266

(1) Joanna dau Robert Burnet
(2) Joanna dau Nicholas
de Stuteville

John

Roger IV
b 1245 suc uncle Roger
1270 as e of Norfolk &
Marshal of England
dsp 1306

Ralph = Berta dau baron of
Furnival

Maud Marshal = ( ) William de Warenne e of Surrey d 1240 son of Hamelin
d 1248/1249   Plantagenet & Isabella de Warenne

John = 1247 Alice de Lusignan
d 1304   half sis to Henry III

Isabella = Hugh d' Albini e of
d 1282   Sussex dsp 1243

Isabella = (1) Gilbert de Lacy
             (2) John fitz Geoffrey

William d ?

Isabel Marshal

Isabel Marshal = Gilbert fitz Richard e Hertford &
d 1240   Gloucester b c 1180 d 1230

Richard = (1) Margaret d 1237 Hubert de Burgh
b 1222   (2) Maud d 1289 John de Lacy e of
d 1262   Lincoln

Gilbert = (1) Alice d 1290 dau Hugh de Lusignan
b 1222   (2) Joan of Acre d 1307 dau Edward I
d 1262

William b 1228
dsp 1258/59

Gilbert priest b 1229

Amicia = (1) Baldwin III de Reviers e Devon d 1245
b 1220   (2) Robert de Guines d 1283
d 1283

Isabel Marshal = (2) Richard of Cornwall d 1272 son of
d 1240   King John

John b Jan 1232
d Jan 1232

Isabel b 1233
d Oct 1234

Henry b Nov 1235
k March 1274

Nicholas b Jan 1240
d Jan 1240

Isabel = Robert de Brus
b 1226   of Ammandale
d 1254   d 1295

Robert VI = Marjorie of
b 1226   Carrick
d 1254

Robert I King of
Scots 1306-1329

Eve Marshal

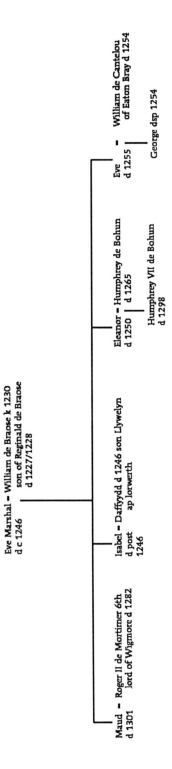

Eve Marshal – William de Braose k 1230
d c 1246   son of Reginald de Braose
              d 1227/1228

Maud – Roger II de Mortimer 6th
d 1301   lord of Wigmore d 1282

Isabel – Daffyydd d 1246 son Llywelyn
d post   ap Iorwerth
1246

Eleanor – Humphrey de Bohun
d 1250   d 1265

Humphrey VII de Bohun
d 1298

Eve –   William de Cantelou
d 1255   of Eaton Bray d 1254

George dsp 1254

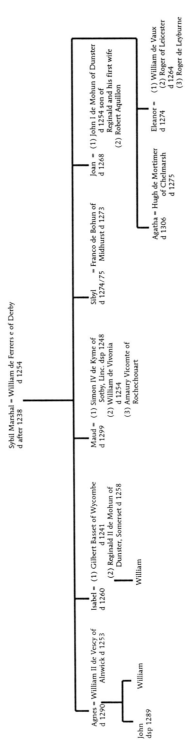

Sybil Marshal

Sybil Marshal = William de Ferrers e of Derby
d after 1238   d 1254

Agnes = William II de Vescy of
d 1290   Alnwick d 1253

John   William
dsp 1289

Isabel = (1) Gilbert Basset of Wycombe
d 1260   d 1241
         (2) Reginald II de Mohun of
             Dunster, Somerset d 1258

William

Maud = (1) Simon IV de Kyme of
d 1299   Sorby, Linc. dsp 1248
         (2) William de Vivonia
             d 1254
         (3) Amaury Vicomte of
             Rochechouart

Sibyl   = Franco de Bohun of
d 1274/75   Midhurst d 1273

Agatha = Hugh de Mortimer
d 1306   of Chelmarsh
              d 1275

Joan = (1) John I de Mohun of Dunster
d 1268   d 1254 son of
              Reginald and his first wife
         (2) Robert Aquillon

Eleanor = (1) William de Vaux
d 1274   (2) Roger of Leicester
                  d 1264
              (3) Roger de Leyburne

411

Joan Marshal

Joan Marshal = after 1219 Warin de
Muntchesney d 1255
d after 1234

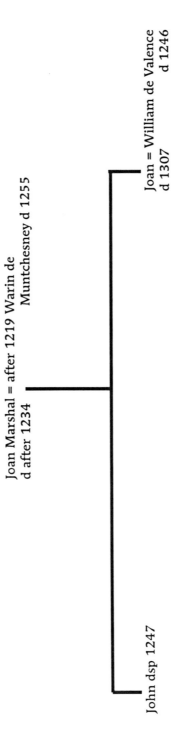

John dsp 1247

Joan = William de Valence
d 1307   d 1246

2c. William Marshal (bc1147 d1219) = Isabel de Clare (bc1171-74 d1220)

   1. William II (bc1190/91 dsp1231) = (1) Alice de Bethune

                                          (2) Eleanor dau. King John

   2. Richard (bc1192 k1234) = Gervase de Dinan of Brittany

   3. Gilbert (dsp1241) = (1) Margaret de Lanvellei

                            (2) Margaret of Scotland

   4. Walter (d Nov. 12, 1245) = Margery widow of John de Lacy of Lincoln

   5. Anselm (d Dec. 23, 1245) = Maud dau. Humphrey de Bohun

Not one of William Marshal's five sons had any children.

1d. Daughters of William Marshal and Isabel de Clare

1. Maud Marshal (d1248/49) = (1) Hugh Bigod earl of Norfolk (d1225)

   a. Roger (dsp1270) = Isabella sis. Alexander of Scotland

   (1246 Marshal of England)

   b. Hugh (d1266) = (1) Joanna dau. Robert Burnet

                   (2) Joanna dau. Nicholas de Stuteville

                     2a. Roger IV 5th earl of Norfolk (dsp1306)

   c. Ralph = Berta de Furnivall

   d. Isabella = (1) Gilbert de Lacy (d1230)

   e. William (d?)

1. Maud Marshal (d1248/49) = (2) William de Warenne earl of Surrey (d1240)

                   son of Hamelin Plantagenet & Isabella de Warenne

   a. John (d1304) = Alice de Lusignan half sister to Henry III

   b. Isabella (d1282) = Hugh d' Albini earl of Sussex (d1243)

2d. Daughters of William Marshal and Isabel de Clare

2. Isabel Marshal (d1240) = (1) Gilbert fitz Richard de Clare earl of Gloucester
(bc1180 d1230)

    a. Richard (b1222 d1262) = (1) Margaret (d1237) dau. Hubert de Burgh
(d1243)

        (2) Maud (d1289) dau. John de Lacy earl of
Lincoln

        2a. Gilbert (b1243 d1295)

    b. William (b1228 dsp1258)

    c. Gilbert a priest (bc1229)

    d. Amicia (b1220 d1283) = (1) Baldwin III de Reviers (d1245) earl of Devon
(2) Robert de Guines (d1283)

    e. Isabel (b1226 d1254) = Robert de Brus of Annandale (d1295)

        e1. Robert de Brus VI= Marjorie countess of Carrick

            e1a. Robert I king of Scots 1309-1329

2. Isabel Marshal (d1240) = (2) Richard earl of Cornwall (d1272) son of King John

    a. John (b Jan.1232 d Jan.1232)

    b. Isabel (b1233 d Oct.1234)

    c. Henry (b Nov.1235 k March 1274)

    d. Nicholas (b Jan.1240 d Jan.1240)

3. Sibyl Marshal (d after 1238) = William de Ferrers earl of Derby (d1254)

    a. Agnes = William II de Vescy (d1253) of Alnwick

        a1. John (dsp1289)

        a2. William

    b. Isabel (d1260) = (1) Gilbert Basset of Wycombe (d1241)

                (2) Reginald II de Mohun of Dunster ((d1258)

    c. Maud (d1299) = (1) Simon IV de Kyme of Sotby (dsp1248)

                (2) William de Vivonia of Curry Malet (d1254)

                (3) Amaury Vicomte Rochechouart

    d. Sibyl (d1274/75) = Franco de Bohun of Midhurst (d1273)

    e. Joan (d1268) = (1) John de Mohun of Dunster (d1253/54)

                (2) Robert Aquillon

    f. Agatha (d1306) = Hugh de Mortimer of Chelmarsh (dc1275)

    g. Eleanor (d1274) = (1) William de Vaux

                (2) Roger of Leicester (d1264)

4. Eve Marshal (dc1246) = William de Braose (k1230) son of Reginald (d1227/28)

    a. Maud (d1301) = (1) Roger II de Mortimer 6th lord of Wigmore (d1282)

        a1. Edmund (d1304)

    b Isabel (d after 1246) = Daffydd (d1246) son of Llywelyn ap Iorwerth

    c. Eleanor (dc1250) = Humphrey de Bohun (d1265)

        c1. Humphrey VII de Bohun (d1298)

    d. Eve (d1255) = William de Cantelou of Eaton Bray (d1254)

        d1. George (dsp1273)

5. Joan Marshal (d after 1234) = Warin de Muntchesney (d1255)

    a. John (dsp1247)

    b. Joan (d1307) = William de Valence (d1246)

Anglo-Normans in Ireland 1

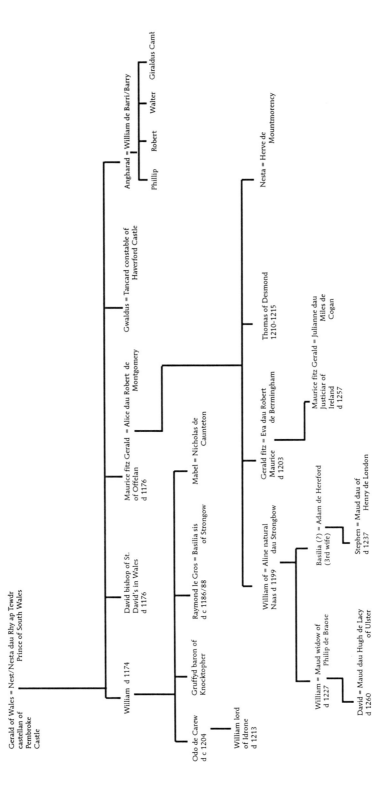

Anglo- Normans in Ireland 2

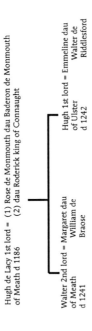
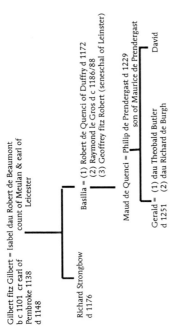

Gilbert fitz Gilbert = Isabel dau Robert de Beaumont
b c 1101 cr earl of   count of Meulan & earl of
Pembroke 1138   Leicester
d 1148

Richard Strongbow
d 1176

Basilia = (1) Robert de Quenci of Duffry d 1172
         (2) Raymond le Gros d c 1186/88
         (3) Geoffrey fitz Robert (seneschal of Leinster)

Maud de Quenci = Philip de Prendergast d 1229
                 son of Maurice de Prendergast

Gerald = (1) dau Theobald Butler   David
d 1251   (2) dau Richard de Burgh

Hugh de Lacy 1st lord = (1) Rose de Monmouth dau Baderon de Monmouth
of Meath d 1186   (2) dau Roderick king of Connaught

Walter 2nd lord = Margaret dau
of Meath   William de
d 1241   Braose

Hugh 1st lord = Emmeline dau
of Ulster   Walter de
d 1242   Riddlesford

Natural children of Nest wife of Gerald castellan of Pembroke castle

Nest -- Stephen constable of Cardiff   Nest -- King Henry I
        castle

Robert fitz Stephen k 1182   Henry fitz Roy k 1157
castellan Cardiff castle

                                            Meiler fitz Henry Justiciar
                                            of Ireland 1200-1208

1e. Anglo-Normans Ireland

Gerald of Wales = Nest/Nesta dau. Rys ap Tewdr Prince of South Wales
- 1. William (d1174)
    - a. Odo de Carew (dc1204)
        - a1. William lord of Idrone (d1213)
    - b. Gruffyd baron of Knocktopher
    - c. Raymond le Gros (dc1186/88) = Basilia sis. of Strongbow
    - d. Mabel = Nicholas de Caunteton
- 2. David Bishop of St David's (d1176)
- 3. Maurice fitz Gerald of Offelan (d1176) = Alice dau. Robert de
    - (see below)   Montgomery
- 4. Gwaldus = Tancard constable of Haverford castle
- 5. Angharad = William de Barri
    - a. Phillip
    - b. Robert
    - c. Walter
    - d. Giraldus Cambrensis (Gerald of Wales)

Maurice fitz Gerald of Offelan (d1176) = Alice dau. Robert de Montgomery
- 1. William of Naas (d1199) = Aline bastard of Strongbow
    - a. William (d1227) = Maud widow of Philip de Braose
        - a1. David = Maud dau. Hugh de Lacy of Ulster
    - b. Basilia (?) = 3rd wife of Adam de Hereford
- 2. Gerald fitz Maurice (d1202) = Eva dau. Robert de Bermingham
    - a. Maurice fitz Gerald (d1257) = Julianne dau. Miles de Cogan
        - (*justiciar* of Ireland)
- 3. Thomas of Desmond (1210-1215)
- 4. Nesta = Herve de Mountmorency (uncle of Richard "Strongbow")

2e. Anglo-Normans in Ireland

Hugh de Lacy 1st lord of Meath (d1186) = (1) Rose de Monmouth dau. of Baderon

    1. Walter de Lacy 2nd lord of Meath (d1241) = Margaret dau. William de Braose (d1211)

    2. Hugh de Lacy 1st lord of Ulster (d1242) = Emmeline dau. Walter de Riddlesford

Gilbert fitz Gilbert de Clare (d1148) = Isabel de Beaumont dau. Robert earl of Leicester

    1. Richard "Strongbow" de Clare (d1176) = Eve/Aoife MacMurchada dau. Dermot king of Leinster
    (see 1b)

    2. Basilia = (1) Robert de Quenci of the Duffry (d1172)
        (2) Raymond le Gros (d1186/88)
        (3) Geoffrey fitz Robert (seneschal of Leinster)
        1a. Maud de Quenci = Phillip de Prendergast (d1229) son of Maurice
            1a1. Gerald de Prendergast (d1251) = (1) dau. Theobald Butler
                (2) dau. Richard de Burgh

Bastards of Nest/Nesta

Stephen constable of Cardiff

    Robert fitz Stephen (k1182) castellan of Cardiff

King Henry I

    Henry fitz Roy (k1157) = (?)

        1. Meiler fitz Henry *justiciar* of Ireland 1200-1208

William de Braose   Llywelyn ap Iorwerth

William de Braose = Maud k 1210 dau Bernard de St Valery
d 1211 lord of
Bramber &
Abergavenny

Giles bishop of
Hereford dsp 1215

Reginald de Braose = (1) Graecia dau William I Briwerre d 1226
d 1227/28   (2) Gwaldus dau Llywelyn ap Iorwerth

William de Braose = Eve Marshal dau William
k 1230   Marshal

Margaret = Walter de Lacy d 1241 of Meath

Annora = Hugh de
              Mortimer

Llywelyn ap Iorwerth = John bastard dau King John
d 1240

William IV = Matilda de Clare
k 1210

John de Braose = Margaret dau Llywelyn
d 1232   ap Iorwerth

William
d 1290

Daffydd = Isabel de Braose
d 1246   d post 1246

Helen = (1) John le Scot d 1237 earl of
              Chester
           (2) Robert de Quenci

Gwaldus = (1) Reginald de Braose
                   d 1227/28
               (2) Ralph de Mortimer

Margaret = (1) John de Braose d 1232
               (2) Walter Clifford

429

1f. William de Braose and Llywelyn ap Iorwerth

William de Braose (d1211) = Maud (k1210) dau. Bernard de St Valery

    1. William IV (k1210) = Matilda de Clare

        1a. John de Braose (d1232) = Margaret dau. Llywelyn ap Iorwerth

            1a1. William (d1290)

    2. Giles Bishop of Hereford (dsp1215)

    3. Reginald (d1227/28) = (1) Graecia dau. William I Briwerre

                        (2) Gwaldus dau. Llywelyn ap Iorwerth

        1a. William (k1230) = Eve Marshal

    4. Margaret = Walter de Lacy (d1241) 2nd lord of Meath

    5. Annora = Hugh de Mortimer

Llywelyn ap Iorwerth (d1240) = Joan bastard of King John

    1. Daffyydd (d1246) = Isabel de Braose (d after 1246)

    2. Helen = (1) John le Scot (d1237) earl of Chester

          (2) Robert de Quenci

    3. Gwaldus= (1) Reginald de Braose (d1227/28)

              (2) Ralph de Mortimer who succeeded his brother Hugh of

                                          Wigmore

    4. Margaret = (1) John de Braose (d1232)

          (2) Walter Clifford

GLOSSARY

Adulterine castles: Castles and strongholds that had been built without authorization by the king. During the wars between Stephen and the Empress Matilda a great many of these castles had been built and became one of the main objectives of Henry II when he was crowned. Henry determined to either get control of them or to destroy them.

Advowson: The customary right of a lord/baron, king, or ecclesiastic as a feudal land holder to appoint a clergyman of his choice to a benefice (a church post) within that lord's holdings. This position provided income as well as rights that went with the office and was a valuable asset that combined spiritual as well as worldly power. The patronage of an ecclesiastical office was the manifestation of the power and status of a feudal lord.

Affinity: The connection between a person (usually a knight) and a magnate based upon that magnate's personal standing rather than tenure of land.

Aid: Payment that was customary and due to King or lord on specific occasions; i.e.,for knighting of lord's heir, marriage of his eldest daughter, or ransom of lord, or a payment that was granted for a special emergency. The one hundred thousand marks demanded by Henry of Hohenstaufen as ransom for Richard I was an aid collected by Queen Eleanor from all of Richard's lords and vassals.

Alienation: The transference of one man's property to another; the act of transferring ownership of land from one to another.

Amercement: A financial penalty levied at "the mercy" of the king or his justices; the payment made by an offender to obtain "mercy" of the king or of the court.

Angevin: The name of two medieval dynasties that originated in France. Fulk count of Anjou in 10th century was the original source; Fulk V count of Anjou was the father of Geoffrey IV who married the Empress Matilda, daughter of King Henry I of England. Their son Henry II became the first Angevin or Plantagenet king of England. Fulk V at the age of forty left Anjou and married Melisende, heiress of Jerusalem, and became king of Jerusalem.

Assart: Woodland or waste that has been made arable or pastureland. To assart in the royal forest without a licence was a serious offense. William I on conquering England had designated the forests as "Rex Anglae" (lands held by and/or of the king). Since the main source of fresh meat in winter and spring was wild game taken from the forests and the right to hunt in the forest was a valuable asset, to assart in those forests without a licence was a serious offence.

Assize: Literally it means "an assessment" and was orginally a rule, regulation, or law that was enforced by the authority of the Crown with the assent of the barons that modified or changed the customary law. Later it was the term applied to the procedures to establish an individual's possession of land, etc.; or an itinerant court that was originally designed for the purpose of establishing who had possession of land and by what right.

Assize of Arms 1181: The attempt to reorganize the military obligations under feudalism on the basis of wealth rather than land. The English military force was divided into four categories. (1) The holder of each knight's fee (roughly equated with an estate providing at least sixteen marks or more in movables and rents) was to have a shirt of mail (a hauberk extending to the knee), a helmet, shield, lance, sword, and warhorse. (2) Every freeman who had movable possessions (chattels) and rents from land of sixteen marks or more was to have a shirt of mail, a helmet, a shield, and a lance. (3) Every freeman who had movable goods and rents of ten marks or more was to have a mail shirt (hauberk), an iron cap, and a lance. (4) All freemen with movables and rents of less than ten marks were to have a quilted coat, an iron cap, and a lance. All four of these groups were to swear fealty to Henry II and bear arms in his service according to Henry's command.

Assize of Clarendon 1166 and Assize of Northampton 1176: Henry II ordered thatinquest juries of twelve men from each hundred and four men from each town meet periodically and swear an oath to be truthful and to do justice (*jureur* originally meant a person who swears an oath) and report the names of notorious criminals to the king's sheriff or itinerant justice. The criminals were then forced to submit to trial by ordeal, and punished if they failed the trial. These juries were created to supply information and were composed of people from that district who would know the facts. They were more indictment juries than trial juries as are understood in modern times since modern trial juries are supposed to know nothing of the facts and are to rely solely upon the evidence given at a hearing.

Attainder, Attaint: The deprivation of rights [which could include office, titles, lands, castles, chattel, etc., including those of heirs] that was the consequence of the conviction of treason or felony.

Bachelor: A knight who was a resident of lord's or king's household but did not hold land of that lord or king.

Banneret: A senior knight who was entitled to display a banner on the tournament or battle field, and one who commanded (held in service to himself) other knights.

Barony: A feudal estate which was held in chief of the king or of another lord and which could include subinfeudated knights' fees and a baronial court.

Benefice: An ecclesiastical preferment held for life that could be a lay or church position, especially a living held by a rector or vicar of a parish church for the care of souls. The right to appoint such a church position was called an advowson.

Burgess: A holder of land or a house in a borough/town who had special judicial privileges and who played a part in running the borough.

Capias: A writ ordering a sheriff or other officer to arrest an individual or individuals, from the Latin *capias* meaning to take.

Capias in manum: A writ ordering seizure of lands or goods into the king's hands; its literal meaning in Latin is "to take in hand."

Cartae Baronum of 1166: An inquest that required all tenants-in-chief toanswer to the king on three points. (1) How many knights they had enfeoffed prior to Henry I's death in 1135. (2) How many knights they had enfeoffed between 1135 and 1166 and if that enfeoffment was less than the required knights' military quota the monarchy had imposed on them. (3) They were to identify by name all the knights they had enfeoffed. Both lay and ecclesiastical tenants-in-chief were required to answer these questions. It was an inquest by Henry II to determine who held what lands, castles, etc. and the number of knights that individual was responsible for providing to the king's army in case of need.

Castellan: A man or woman who held a castle for someone else, an office.

Castellany: A lordship that contained a castle and its surrounding lands.

Chancery: The principal royal office which issued formal letters, grants, commissions, pardons, writs, etc. under the king's great seal. This office was headed by the king's Chancellor.

Chattel: Personal property that could be transported, moved. This was personal property as opposed to real property.

Charter Rolls: The registers of royal grants of lands, honours, dignities, hereditary offices, liberties, and other estates of inheritance to the nobility and the commonality. These are the contemporaneous registers of royal grants which included royal grants to cities and boroughs, grants of fairs and markets and free warrens.

Chartulare: A cartulary is a register of charters.

Clausarum {**Letters closed**}: Letters closed and sealed, issued to individuals at the personal direction of the king.

Coat-of-arms: A system of colors and symbols borne on a medieval shield as a means of personal identification which could be recognized from a distance on the battle or tournament field. They first appeared during the twelfth century, and as armorial bearings they were handed down from one generation to the next. To blazon a coat-of-arms is to give a verbal description of those arms in heraldric terms.

Common law: Law based upon custom and precedent and administered in the king's common law courts of Common Pleas and King's Bench; most were initiated by writ.

Common Pleas: The royal court of common law that sat at Westminster and was primarily concerned with civil suits involving land and debt.

Co-parceners: Tenants (usually sisters) who inherit jointly.

Custodia commissa de: A writ committing control of lands, castles, etc. of a minor to a specified guardian or keeper.

Dapifer: An office in the household of the king or lord who was responsible for the administration of the king's or lord's hall, a steward of the household.

Darrein presentment: Legal process to determine if a benefice was ecclesiastical or lay.

Decessit sine prole {dsp}: Means that the individual died without issue [children].

Decessit sine prole mascule {dspm}: Means the individual died without male issue.

Decessit sine prole supersita {dsps}: Means the individual died without surviving issue.

Demesne: Land held by a feudal or manorial lord for his own use, though it may be "worked" by tenants/vassals.

Demesne, Ancient: Land held in demesne by the Crown in the time of Edward the Confessor.

Demise: A grant of estate, usually for a limited term; for example, a lease of land or rights pertaining to land.

Devise: A gift or disposition especially by a will.

Disentailment: The removal of entail restricting the power to dispose of one's estate.

Disseisin: The act of wrongfully dispossessing a man of his lands, castles, and goods.

Dower: The right of the widow of a landholder to one-third of that landholder's land for her lifetime.

Novel disseisin, **Assize of:** Novel disseissin meant new or recent dispossession from the Latin writ that refers to *nova disseisina.* It was a writ or legal action that a person who was recently dispossessed of land could bring to recover possession of that land. This possessory assize provided that a landholder who claimed that he had been violently disposed could purchase a royal writ ordering the local sheriff to summon a jury and inquire into whether or not the plaintiff had been driven from his land unjustly. The novel disseisin jury in effect testified to the facts regarding a man being dispossessed of his lands. It was limited to *novel* or recent dispossession to make clear that the King's Courts were not going to deal with claims for dispossession that occurred during the civil wars of Stephen and the Empress where land would have been seized and then lost many times. It is the basis of the common law approach which does not recognize absolute ownership of land but simply decided between two claimants as to who has the better claim. Before Novel Disseisin, the issue of possession of land was dealt with by a Writ of Right issued from the King's Court which usually involved arranging a trial by combat with the victor in the battle being the winner of the case. Novel disseisin had to be applied for in a very limited time, and after that time period it was not available. Because of the time limit on this procedure, a man who was on crusade or pilgrimage and was disseised of lands could find his family in great peril of losing all that they held to a land-grabbing knight.

Distraint: The seizure of chattels and/or goods and/or lands to enforce payment of debt or appearance in court.

Earl: The highest rank of nobility until the rank of duke was created in 1337.

Enfeoffment: The most important of feudal ceremonies by which a lord would create a feudal tenancy. It usually involved the standing upon the lands in question and giving to the tenant a clod of earth or a twig to symbolize the giving of rights over the land. In return for the land, the tenant would give homage to the lord by declaring himself to be that lord's "man."

Entail: A term of feudal tenancy (*feudum talliatum*) that restricted the tenant's rights to dispose of his estate by sale or will. The most common was an entail male which restricted the inheritance of the entailed estate to only male issue or male relatives of the holder of the estate. In the feudal society where the holding of land was primarily for the purpose of providing well equipped men at arms, this was a practical and useful restriction.

Escheat: The reversion of land to a feudal lord or king for default of heir or for treason or felony.

Escheator: The official of the Crown who deals with revenues that are derived from escheat, wardship of minors, and other feudal incidents.

Essoin: The official excuse for the non-appearance in the king's or the lord's court by reason of illness or infirmity.

Exchequer: The king's financial office and court which heard pleas affecting the financial interests of the Crown.

Eyre: The visitation by the king or by the itinerant justices acting in the king's name which occurred periodically throughout the shires/counties. Eyre means literally "one who runs his eye over things." A member of the eyre was both a royal civil servant and a judge who was able to deal with any business that involved the King's rights.

Familiaris: The men who were close associates of either the king or a greater baron/ earl who were his advisors and close confidantes

Farm: A fixed sum or rent paid annually, usually. A sheriff's farm was the fixed sum paid annually by the sheriff based on the royal revenues coming in from a specific shire. The amount was contracted in advance of the appointment as sheriff, and whatever the sheriff collected above that fixed amount was his profit.

Fealty: An oath of fidelity/loyalty, not to be confused with homage, though both oaths were commonly performed together when a vassal received a fief from a lord. An oath of fealty could be given to a person from whom the oath-giver held no land, as William Marshal gave to the young Henry when he was appointed head of the young king's *mesnie* household. Fealty could be given by a woman.

Fee: The fief, the hereditary lands held by a feudal tenant; it is also the payment due to the Crown on each "knight's fee" held by a feudal tenant.

Felonie, **felony:** The criminal offense of violating one's oath of fealty to one's lord subject to forfeiture of lands, titles, offices, goods, and/or life. It was considered the greatest of crimes in medieval time.

Feudal Incidents: Obligations of a vassal to his lord that were inherent to holding land by feudal service; i.e., payments of aids, reliefs for succession to lands, wardships of minor heirs.

Feudal Tenure: The system of land-holding by which all properties were held of a lord and subject to the feudal services and incidents due from that tenure such as military service, incidents, scutage, fealty, and homage.

Fief: A landed estate, normally heritable, that was held on the condition of homage and on the performance of services to a superior lord, by whom it had been granted. The services were primarily military aid, which consisted of the provision of fully equipped men at arms or military supplies or equipment. Later this actual physical military service could be substituted by the payment of scutage (a fixed amount of money). (See "fee" above.)

Fine: (1) Payment to the Crown, especially payment by the offender. (2) Payment to one's feudal lord. (3) A final concord used as a mode of conveyance.

Fine Rolls: The records of payments to the king and a source of great wealth. They were records of payments for wardships, marriages, lands, liberties, privileges, safe conduct,and other marks of great favor from the king. They were called *oblata* rolls. (See *oblata.)*

Forfeiture: The loss of land and/or goods of an individual as a result of misdeeds. The lands and/or goods forfeited would go to the Crown or one's lord.

Frankalmoign: The tenure of lands or tenements granted to persons who had devoted themselves to the service of God. The grantee's service to the grantor was the service of prayer, primarily for the souls of the grantor and his family and ancestors.

Homage: A ceremonial acknowledgement of a feudal tenant to his "lord" of thefealty and homage due that lord for the right to hold the land granted to the feudal tenant by the lord. The word comes from the French *Homme* meaning man, and it is the ceremony whereby a feudal tenant declares himself to be his lord's man. Homage given before Magna Carta meant a willingness and ability to fight as a knight. Therefore, a woman could not give homage to men, but she could receive it from men. If the woman was an heiress, all of her vassals would and did give her homage as recognition of her status as their lord, meaning that they would fight for her. When and if a woman inherited lands, her husband would do homage for her lands to her immediate lord, be he another baron or the king.

Honour: A large geographically dispersed fief held by a great lord which usually included many knights' fees, several manors, and an honorial court.

Hundred: A subdivision of a county/shire and contains several vills and has its own court and bailiff; the men of a given hundred would owe suit to their court, usually at regular intervals.

In right of his wife: This phrase was used when a knight or noble married an heiress. The lands, castles, vassals, knights, and title were the wife's by birth, blood, and inheritance. They were all hers, not her husband's; they could not be claimed or inherited by her husband, but only by any children her husband had by that wife. Therefore, the husband gave homage in right of his wife to the lord from whom the wife held all of her inheritance whether that lord was another baron or the king. Since women could not provide knight service to their lord, their husbands would give homage in their stead. If the wife died before her husband, their oldest male son if of age, or if no son, their daughter/daughters would inherit their mother's property providing they were of age and married. The husband was allowed to hold his deceased wife's dowry/maritagium until his own death. If there were no children born to such a couple, the lands, castles, vassals, knights, and title would revert back to the father of the wife or to his heirs.

King's Bench: The royal court of common law which was held at Westminster; it was the senior criminal court and handled civil and criminal cases.

Knight's fee: An estate which usually contained at least one manor, and it was granted on the basis that one knight's fee would equal the service of one knight. A knight's fee was equal to 2 to 10 hides in land, and a hide was roughly equal to 120 acres of land. The land must provide enough surplus revenue to cover the cost of a warhorse, a palfrey, hauberk, helmet, shield, lance, and sword, the essential equipment necessary for a fighting knight.

Laws of Breteuil: Breteuil was a small town near the border of Maine and Blois, and was held by William Fitz Osbern, one of William the Conqueror's vassals. This borough was given specific rights which came to be the model for towns created and/or absorbed by the Normans. The burgesses were allotted specific building sites within the borough and small amounts of agricultural land outside the walls/limits of the borough. They were allowed to sublet or rent parts of their lots and to engage in trade within the borough. For these privileges they were charged a maximum of twelve pence, and their annual rent was not allowed to exceed this. The burgesses were free to give up their place and to leave without any penalty. If their lord was forced to borrow money from one of the burgesses, there was a set limit on the amount of time he had before he had to repay the loan. The burgesses could not be forced to serve or stand trial in any court but that of the borough. They could not be amerced a fine greater than their rent, with the exception of certain royal offenses, and if they were imprisoned they were allowed to meet their own bail. These were very liberal laws, and are found to have been granted to many of new boroughs that were created by the Anglo-Norman lords.

Liberate: The records of writs from the Court of the Chancery to the Chancellor of the Exchequer to pay out or to deliver sums of money due individuals for debts, pensions, gifts, and/or regular disbursements.

Liberty: A royal privilege given by royal grant or prescription to a man for a specific area of land.

Livery: The delivery of lands, estates, castles, etc, delivery of *seisin* (possession), or an allowance made to a servant for his or her maintenance.

Magnate: The name used to describe a great man; one who was among the wealthiest and most powerful of the nobility.

Man: To be described as "someone's man" meant that the person owed some obligation to that lord. A woman could also be someone's man.

Manor: A small estate which was usually a compact estate with demesne, tenants, and a manorial court.

Mark: A unit of money equal to two-thirds of today's pound sterling. One gold mark in medieval times would be roughly equivalent to six pounds today.

Mesne: An intermediate with reference to legal processes or to feudal tenure. For example, William Marshal as earl of Pembroke held his lands directly from the king as tenant-in chief, but the men who held their lands as tenants of Marshal as earl of Pembroke were *mesne tenants.*

Mort d' ancestor: Legal process that determines if an heir was wrongfully kept out of his inheritance, his lands. This required a sheriff to ask a jury if the plaintiff's father had held the land in question when it last passed to an heir. If so, and the plaintiff was the eldest son, then he was to be given the land. This was a crucial stage in the acceptance of the concept of hereditary rights, especially regarding lands/fiefs. It was a possessory assize as well which meant that the plaintiff was not obligated to risk engaging in trial by combat which is what he would have had to do under the old Writ of Right.

Mortmain: A grant of land or tithes or churches to a religious house which "inalienation" exempts the grantee from any incidents due on the death of the feudal tenant who granted them.

Nova conventions: The voluntary or quasi-voluntary payments made to recover the king's favor or to escape his wrath. These included fines or reliefs paid on succession to estates held in chief of the king.

Oblata: Obligations/payments offered to the Crown, usually in the form of gold or silver in marks or pounds; palfreys, hunters, chargers, falcons, hawks, and hunting birds could also constitute payments. These were "fines" offered to the king to obtain honours, offices, lands, liberties, wardships, custodies, marriages, and/or privileges. In many instances these payments are what would be defined as bribery today.

Palatinate: An area of land/fief in which an earl or baron or ecclesiastic exercised the judicial and administrative rights that were elsewhere reserved to the Crown. Palatine lords exercised power almost equal to the king in the lands of a palatine lordship.

Patent, letters patent: A sealed open letter of a grant by a lord or the Crown of estate, right, liberty, monies, castles, and other "original" grants. All charters or deeds are a species of letters patent. The letters patent were often letters of safe conduct, of credence, of protection, of pardon, of grace, of acquittance, of remission, of favor, of armistice, of licence, of summons, of warranty, of presentation, and of prohibition.

Brevia patentis: Letters patent that relate to judicial affairs, treaties, truces, correspondence, and negotiations with foreign powers or states.

Plea: An action in law.

Pleas of the Crown: The more serious crimes such as breaches of the king's peace, concealment of treasure trove (which always belonged to the king), and treason or rebellion against the king. No one but officers of the Crown had jurisdiction over these offenses.

Pipe Roll: The name given to the records of the Exchequer because of their appearance when rolled up. These were the annual audit of the accounts of sheriffs and other debtors owing money to the Crown.

Plantagenet: Not a real surname but a nickname for the count of Anjou who had a habit of wearing in his helmet a yellow blossom from the broom plant, the *planta genesta*. This is the origin of the name.

***Praestita* Roll:** The roll for the twelfth year of the reign of King John and records many advances of accommodation and monies that King John granted in that year.

***Pre breve*:** The Latin phrase that means that instructions were given by letter. It is the record of an action ordered by a written notice/letter.

Privilege: A grant made to an individual, church, or group of people of a right or an immunity not usually enjoyed; i.e., the privilege given by the king to a baron or an ecclesiastic to take certain game from the royal forests.

Purprestures: The act of converting forest land to arable land and enclosing it within hedges and ditches.

Purveyance: The supply or exaction of provisions such as in time of war.

Quo titulo clamat: A writ that directs the tenant of an estate to show by what title he claims that estate/lands.

Quo Warranto: Legal procedure found in writs directing the claimant to land or liberty, etc. to show by what right or warrant he claims such.

Reeve: A royal official or a manorial official appointed by a lord or chosen by the villien tenants.

Relief: The payment the heir/heirs of a feudal tenant owes and pays his lord on that tenant's succession to a feudal tenure. It is the feudal equivalent of key money.

Remembrancer: The official concerned with making or acting upon remembrances, memoranda, or reminders.

Rex Anglae: When William the Conqueror took England by force of arms, he became unique among European feudal kings as he by right of conquest owned the entire kingdom. This made him *Rex Anglae*, king of England, as opposed to *Rex Anglorum*, king of the English. This meant that the English king was the ultimate feudal lord of any land holder in the kingdom. He had more fundamentalauthority over the holding of land in England than the King of France held as a feudal lord over William the Conqueror as duke of Normandy. Henry II inherited this theoretical but fundamentally important position. This meant that no one in England could deny that Henry II was their ultimate feudal lord. This gave Henry II the position and power to impose a law that no one had to answer for his freehold in England without a writ from the King.

Scutage: The feudal payment a man holding land by knight's service owes to his lord in lieu of the actual physical presence of that knight in the lord's service. It means literally "shield money."

Seisin: The actual possession or occupation of lands.

Serjeanty: The feudal tenure of land by some service to the Crown other than normal military or knight service; land held by serjeanty. Serjeanty could be Grand Serjeanty or Petty Serjeanty. Grand Serjeantys were held in chief of the Crown and involved the provision of major military services. Petty Serjeantys could involve a service as small as providing upon demand a bow or performing a small personal sevice. The word *serjeant* means literally servant.

Servitium debitum: The service of a specific number of knights due from a feudal lord in time of war.

Sheriff: The "shire-reeve"who was the principal man of the Crown in the counties/ shires for administrative, judicial, and financial purposes.

Sub-infeudation: The feudal process of granting land to lesser men by a lord in return for military service.

Tenant-in-chief: The feudal tenant who holds his lands directly from the Crown.

Treason: The betrayal of one's lord, of one's oath of fealty, especially one's oath to the king; it was considered the most heinous offense in medieval feudal society.

Venison: Classified as the flesh of beasts protected by game laws, especially the deer and other large game. These animals were usually the sole right of the king to hunt and kill.

Vill: A local community that is smaller than a town, and sometimes coinciding with a parish. It was the smallest administrative unit of the realm.

Ward: A minor in the keeping of a guardian who may be lord or king; it is also the duty owed by a feudal tenant in defense of his lord's castles and was known as "castle-ward".

Wardrobe: The storage and expenditure department of the royal household.

Wardship: When a vassal died leaving a minor male heir or an unmarried female heir/heirs, the lord of that vassal had custody of the fief/lands after he had given the widow her dower rights/lands/monies. The revenues of those lands/fiefs were to provide for the support of the minor heirs. After providing for the heir/heirs, whatever revenues were left over could be used by the lord as he saw fit. The lord was supposed to conserve the capital of the fief/fiefs, maintain the number and quality of the stock on the manors, keep the buildings/castles in good repair, conserve the woods and other resources of the fief/fiefs, and refrain from extorting money from the tenants of all classes. Henry II had wardship of Isabel de Clare as the sole heir of Richard Strongbow de Clare until Isabel was married.

Prerogative Wardship: The ordinary lord held in custody only the lands/fiefs held directly from him when a vassal died, but the king claimed custody of all lands/fiefs held by a tenant-in-chief, no matter where they were located. Richard "Strongbow" de Clare acquired his lands in Ireland by conquest and by marriage to Aoife, daughter of Dermot king of Leinster, but Henry II insisted that de Clare hold those Irish lands as grants of Henry II and therefore as tenant-in-chief of Henry II as king. John extended this claim to all fiefs held in chief by serjeanty. The king claimed the right to marry any unmarried heir/heiress of a tenant-in-chief as he chose, and John extended this to the heirs/heiresses of royal serjeanties.

Warrant: A document that serves as the authority for payment, grant, appointment or other act.

Warhorse, *destrier, destrarius*: Special breeds of horse raised and trained to fight and defend the knight that they carried; these were the most valuable horses and were similar to draft horses such as the Belgian, Shire, or Percheron and stood at least sixteen hands (over 64 inches) at the withers. By 1200 a good destrier cost 40 to 80 pounds.

Warren: The right of a liberty of preserving and hunting small game within a specified area.

Waste: Uncultivated land or lands destroyed in battles and/or war.

Widow: Widows were considered a feudal incident when they were the widows of feudal vassals. A widow was entitled to her dower for her life, and this was usually 1/3 of her husband's lands/fiefs, as well as any property she had brought to her marriage and/or any inheritance that she possessed in her own right as an heiress. Widows were supposed to be allowed to remain single if they chose, or to choose their next husband with the approval of the widow's lord.

Writ (breve): A sealed document that conveys a formal command of the Crown or of the court.

Writ of Right: Before Novel Disseisin the issue of possession of land was dealt with by a Writ of Right (*brevo de recto*) issuing from the King's Court. The procedure usually involved arranging a trial by combat with the victor being the winner of the case. As a result of the legal reforms by Henry II, the person in possession of the land had the option of trial by Grand Assize, which was the procedure whereby four knights of the district were tasked to select twelve other knights of the district who had knowledge of the rights of conflicting parties and who would declare those rights of their own knowledge. These knights did not constitute a jury as we understand one, but were neighboring landowners who would know, and were required to declare of their own knowledge who was in the right in the dispute.

BIBLIOGRAPHY

Government Documents, Chronicles, and Annals

Abbreviatio Placitorum Richard-Edward II. Eds. G. Rose and W. Illingworth. London: G. Eyre, 1811.

Aelred of Rievaulx. *De bello Standardii.* Vol. III. Chronicles and Memorials of the Reigns of Stephen, Henry II, and Richard I. Ed. Richard Howlett. London: Longman, 1884-89.

Ancient Deeds series A (E.40/13673-115068) Calendar. Vol.151. London: HMSO Swift Printers, 1978.

Borand, Paul, ed. Curia Regis Rolls XVIII 27 Henry III to 30 Henry III, 1243-1245. Woodbridge: Boydell, 1999.

Calendar of Inquisitions Miscellaneous. London: HMSO, 1916.

Calendar of Inquisitions Post Mortem and Other Analagous Documents Preserved in The Public Record Office. 3 vols. London: G. Eyre and A. Spottiswoode, 1904.

Catholic Church. Diocese of Salisbury. Sarum Charters and Documents: Charters And Documents Illustrating the History of the Cathedral, City, and Diocese Of Salisbury in the Twelfth and Thirteenth Centuries. Ed. W. Dunn Macray. London: G. Eyre and A. Spotiswoode, 1891.

The Chronicle of John of Worcester 1118-1140. Ed. J. R. Weaver. Oxford: Clarendon, 1958.

Church, S.D. "The Earliest English Muster Roll, 18/19 December 1215." The

Bulletin of the Institute of Historical Research 67 (1994): 1-17.

Corner, David. "The *Gesta Regis Henrici Secunda and Chronica* of Roger, Parson of Howden." Bulletin of the Institute of Historical Research LVI (1983): 126-44.

Curia Regis Rolls Vol. 5-8. 1207-1219: Vol. 6. 11 and 14 King John: Vol. 7, 15-16 John, Appendix, 7 Richard I. Ed. C. T. Flowers. London: HMSO, 1935.

Dillange, Michael. *Les Comtes de Poitoui ducs d'Aquitaine (778-1204).* Moagon: *Geste* Editions, 1995.

Eley, Penny. "History and Romance in the *Chronique des Ducs du Normandie.*" *Medium Aevum* 68.1 (1999): 81-95.

Etienne de Rouen. *Draco Normannicus.* Vol. III. Chronicles and Memorials of the Reigns of Stephen, Henry II, and Richard I. Ed. Richard Howlett. London: Longman, 1884-89.

Feudal Documents from the Abbey of Bury St. Edmund's. Ed. D. C. Douglas. London: Humphrey Milford, Oxford UP, 1932.

Flowers, C. T., ed. Introduction to the Curia Regis Rolls 1199-1230 A.D. London: Quaritch, 1944. London: Professional Books, 1972.

The Gesta Normannorum Ducum of William Jumieges, Orderic Vitalis, and Robert of Torigni. Vol. I. Ed. and trans. Elizabeth Van Houts. Oxford: Clarendon, 1992.

Gesta Stephani. Ed. and trans. K. R. Potter. Oxford: Clarendon, 1973.

Green, Judith. *"Praeclarum et magnificum antiquifatis monumentum*: The EarliestSurviving Pipe Roll." Bulletin of the Institute of Historical Research

(1982): 1-16.

Harper-Bill, Christopher. The Cartulary of the Augustine Friars of Clare. Woodbridge: Boydell, 1991.

Index to the Records Called the Originalia and Memoranda on the Lord Treasurer's Remembrancer's side of the Exchequer. Ed. Edward Jones. 2 vols. London: Printed for the editor, 1795.

Ireland. High Court of the Chancery. Calendar of Patent and Close Rolls of Chancery in Ireland. Ed. James Morrin. 3 vols. Dublin: Thom, 1861-63.

"The Irish Pipe Roll of 14 John 1211-1212." Eds. Oliver Davies and David Quinn. Ulster Journal of Archaeology 3rd ser 4.2 (July 1941): Supplement: 1-76.

Irish Record Commission. *Rotularum Patentium et Clausarum Cancellariae Hiberniae Calendarium.* Dublin: Irish Record Commission, 1928.

Jordan Fantosme's Chronicle. Ed. and trans. R. C. Johnston. Oxford: Clarendon, 1981.

The Life and Letters of Thomas a Becket: Gathered from the Contemporary Historians. Ed. J. A. Giles. 2 vols. London: Whittaker, 1846.

Magnum Rotulum Scaccarri vel Magnum Rotulum Pipae de Anno Tricesimo Primo Regni Henrici Primi (ut videtue) quem plurimi hactenus Laudarunt pro Rotulo Quinti anni Stephani Regis. Ed. J. Hunter. London: Public Record Office, 1833.

Matthew Paris. Chronicles of Matthew Paris. Ed. and trans. Richard Vaughan. NY: St Martin's, 1984.

Memoranda Rolls 16-17 Henry III. Ed. R. Allen Brown. London: HMSO, 1991.

Richard of Hexham. *De gestis Regis Stephen et bello Standardii*. Chronicles and
    Memorials of the Reigns of Stephen, Henry II and Richard I Vol III. Ed.
    Richard Howlett. London: Longman, 1884-89.

Rolls of Divers Accounts for the Early Years of the Reign of Henry III. Ed. Fred
    Cazel. Lincoln: J. W. Ruddock and Sons, 1982.

Rotuli Curia Regis: Rolls and Records of the Court Held before the King's Justiciars.
    Vol. I. The Sixth Year of King Richard I to the Accession of King John. Ed.
    Sir Francis Palgrave. London: Record Commission, 1835.

---. Vol. II. The First Year of King John. Ed. Sir Francis Palgrave. London:Public
    Record Commission, 1835.

Rotuli Selecti ad Rec Anglicas et Hibernicas. Ed. Joseph Hunter. London: HMSO,
    1834.

*Rotuli selectic ad rec Anglicas et Hibernicas Spectantes ex Archivis in Doma
    capitulari: west Monasteriensi deprompt.* London: G. Eyre and A.
    Spottiswoode, 1834.

Selected Letters of Pope Innocent III Concerning England 1198-1216. Eds. C.R.
    Cheney and W. H. Semple. London: T. Nelson, 1953.

Stoke by Clare Cartulary: Part One. Eds. Christopher Harper-Bill and
    Richard Mortimer. Woodbridge: Boydell, 1982.

Stoke by Clare Cartulary: Part Two. Eds. Christopher Harper-Bill and
    Richard Mortimer. Woodbridge: Boydell, 1983.

Stoke by Clare Cartulary: Part Three. Eds. Christopher Harper-Bill and
    Richard Mortimer. Woodbridge: Boydell, 1984.

KINGS

Amt, Emilie. <u>The Accession of Henry II in England: Royal Government Restored 1149-59</u>. Woodbridge: Boydell, 1993.

Anderson, Carolyn. "Narrating Matilda 'Lady of the English' in the *Historia Novella*, the *Gesta Stephani*, and Wace's *Roman de Rou*." <u>Clio</u> 29.1 (Fall 1999): 47-67.

Appleby, John T. <u>John, King of England.</u> New York: Knopf, 1959.

Bachrach, Bernard. "Henry II and the Angevin Tradition of Family Hostility." <u>Albion</u> 16.2 (Summer 1984): 111-30.

Baldwin, J. W. <u>The Government of Philip Augustus: Foundations of French Royal Power in the Middle Ages.</u> Berkley: U of California P, 1986.

Barlow, Frank. <u>William Rufus.</u> Berkeley: U of California P, 1987.

Barratt, Nick. "The English Revenues of Richard I." <u>EHR</u> 116 (2001): 635-56.

---. "The Revenues of John and Philip Augustus Revisited." Church, <u>King John.</u> 75-99.

Bartlett, Robert. <u>England Under the Norman and Angevin Kings, 1075-1225.</u> Oxford: Clarendon, 2000.

Bazeley, M. L. "The Forest of Dean and its Relations with the Crown during the 12th and 13th Centuries." <u>Transactions of the Bristol and Gloucester Archaeological Society</u> xxiii (1910): 153-282.

Beeler, J. H. <u>Warfare in England 1066-1189.</u> Ithaca, NY: Cornell UP, 1961.

Bishop, T. A. M. and Pierre Chablais, eds. <u>Facsimilies of English Royal Writs to 1100.</u> Oxford: Oxford UP, 1957.

Blair, C. H. "Amorials on English Seals From the Twelfth to the Sixteenth

    Centuries." *Archaeologia* LXXXIX (1943): 1-26.

Bradbury, J. "Philip Augustus and King John: Personality and History." Church,

    King John 347-61.

---. Philip Augustus King of France 1180-1223. London: Longman, 1998.

Callahan, Thomas. "The Arrest of the Bishops at Stephen's Court: A Reassessment."

    Haskins Society Journal 4 (1992): 97-108.

Carpenter, David. "Abbot Ralph of Coggeshall's Account of the Last Years of

    Richard I." EHR 113 (1998): 1210-30.

---. "Kings, Magnates and Society: The Personal Rule of Henry III, 1234-1258."

    Speculum LX (1985): 39-70.

Chibnall, M. "Mercenaries and the *Familia Regis* under Henry I." History 62

    (1977): 15-25.

Church, S. D. "The Earliest English Muster Roll 18/19 December 1215." Historical

    Research 67 (1994): 1-17.

---. "The Rewards of Royal Service in the Households of King John: A Dissenting

    Opinion." EHR 110 (April 1995): 277-302.

Christlelow, Stephanie Mooers. "A Movable Feast? Itineration and the

    Centralization of Government under Henry I." Albion 28 (1996): 229-50.

---. "The Royal Love in Anglo-Norman England: Fiscal or Courtly Concept?"

    Haskins Society Journal 8 (1996): 27-42.

Clanchy, M. T. "Did Henry III have a Policy?" History LIII (1968): 203-16.

Colvin, H. M. and R. Allen Brown, eds. The History of the Kings' Works. Vol. I &

II. London: HMSO, 1963.

Crispin, M. J. and L. McCary. <u>Falaise Roll Recording Prominent Companions of William Duke of Normandy at the Conquest of England.</u> Reprint Baltimore: Genealogical Publishing, 1994.

Critchley, J. S. "Summonses to Military Service Early in the Reign of Henry III." <u>EHR</u> 86.388 (Jan 1971): 79-95.

Davies, Rees. "Keeping the Natives in Order: The English King and the Celtic Rulers 1066-1216." <u>Peritia</u> 10 (1996): 212-24.

Davis, R.H.C. <u>King Stephen 1135-1154.</u> 3rd ed. London: Longman, 1990.

---. "What Happened in Stephen's Reign 1135-54?" <u>History</u> 49 (1964): 1-12.

Duggan, Anne. "*Ne in dubium*: The Official Record of Henry II's Reconciliation at Avranches, 21 May 1172." <u>EHR</u> (June 2000): 643-58.

Duncan, A. M. "John King of England and the Kings of the Scots." Church, <u>King John.</u> 247-71.

Everard, J. A. <u>Brittany and the Angevins: Province and Empire, 1158-1203.</u> Cambridge: Cambridge UP, 2000.

---. "The Justiciarship in Brittany and Ireland under Henry II." <u>The Proceedings ofthe Battle Conference on Anglo-Norman Studies XX.</u> Ed. Christopher Harper-Bill. Woodbridge: Boydell, 1998. 87-106.

Fryde, Natalie. "King John and the Empire." Church, <u>King John</u> 335-46.

Galbraith, V. H. "Seven Charters of Henry II at Lincoln Cathedral." <u>Antiquaries Journal</u> (1932): 269-78.

---. <u>Kings, and Chroniclers: Essays in English Medieval History.</u> London:

Hambledon, 1982.

Harper-Bill, Christopher. "John and the Church of Rome." Church, King John 289-
315.

Harris, B. E. "King John and the Sheriff's Farm." EHR LXXIX (1964): 532-42.

Heiser, Richard. "Households of the Justiciars of King Richard I." Haskins Society
Journal 2 (1990): 223-35.

---. "Richard I and His Appointments to English Shrievalties." EHR CXII (1997):
1-19.

Helm, Lauren. "English Ecclesiastical Vacancies During the Reigns of William II
And Henry I." Journal of Ecclesiastical History 42 (July 1991): 363-93.

Helmerichs, Robert. "King Stephen's Norman Itinerary 1137." Haskins Society
Journal 5 (1993): 89-98.

Heslin, A. "The Coronation of the Young King in 1170." Studies in Church History
2 (1965): 165-78.

History of the Revenues of the Kings of England 1066-1399. Ed. James Ramsey.
Oxford: Clarendon, 1925.

Holden, Brock W. "The Balance of Patronage: King John and the Earl of Salisbury."
Haskins Society Journal 8 (1996): 79-89.

Hollister, C Warren. "Stephen's Anarchy." Albion 6 (1974): 233-39.

Holt, J. C. and Richard Mortimer, eds. *ACTA* of Henry II and Richard I. London:
Paradigm Print, 1986.

Jared, Lauren Helm. "English Ecclesiastical Vacancies During the Reigns of
William II and Henry I with Appendix." Journal of Ecclesiastical History 42

(July 1991): 362-93.

Joliffe, J. E. A. <u>Angevin Kingship.</u> London: Adam and Charles Black, 1955.

Jones, Thomas M. <u>War of the Generations: The Revolt of 1173-74.</u> Ann Arbor, MI:
U of Michigan P, 1980.

Keefe, T. K. "Counting Those Who Count: A Computer Assisted Analysis of
Charter Witnesses List and Itinerant Court of King Richard." <u>Haskins
Society</u> <u>Journal</u> 1 (1989): 135-46.

---. "King Henry II and the Earls: The Pipe Roll Evidence." <u>Albion</u> 13.3 (Fall
1981): 191-222.

---. "Place-date Distribution of Royal Charters and Historical Geography and
Patronage Strategies and the Court of King Henry II." <u>Haskins Society
Journal</u> 2 (1990); 180-94.

King, Edmund. "Stephen of Blois, Count of Mortain and Boulogne." <u>EHR</u> 115
(2000): 271-96.

La Patourel, John. <u>Feudal Empires: Norman and Plantagenet.</u> London: Hambledon,
1984.

Latimer, Paul. "Henry II's Campaign Against the Welsh in 1165." <u>Welsh History
Review</u> 14 (1989): 523-52.

Lawlar, H. J. "An Unnoticed Charter of Henry III in 1217." <u>EHR</u> XXII (1970);
515-18.

Lydon, J. F. "The Exchequer Documents from the Reign of Henry III." <u>Proceedings
of the Royal Irish Academy</u> Vol. 65 Section C (1966-67): 1-27.

Mooers, Stephanie. "A Reevaluation of Royal Justice Under Henry I of England."

American Historical Review 93.2 (April 1988): 340-58.

Moss, V. D. "The Norman Exchequer Rolls of King John." Church, King John. 101-16.

Newman, Charlotte A. The Anglo-Norman Nobility in the Reign of Henry I: The Second Generation. Philadelphia: U Pennsylvania, 1988.

Owen, D.D. Eleanor of Aquitaine: Queen and Legend. Oxford: Blackwell, 1993.

Pafford, J. H. P. "King John's Tomb in Worcester Cathedral." Transactions of the Worcestershire Archaeological Society 35 (1958): 58-60.

Power, Daniel. "The End of Angevin Normandy: The Revolt of Alencon (1203)." Historical Research 186 (2001): 444-64.

---. "King John and the Norman Aristocracy." Church, King John 117-36.

Powicke, F. M. "The Angevin Administration of Normandy." EHR 22.85 (Jan 1907): 15-42.

Prestwich, J. O. "The Military Household of the Norman Kings." EHR XCVI (1981): 1-35.

Ramsay, Jane H. The Angevin Empire: The Reigns of Henry II, Richard I and John. London: Swann, Sonnenschein, 1903. New York: AMS, 1978.

Round, J. H. "King Stephen and the Earl of Chester." EHR 10 (1895): 87-91.

Rowlands, Ifor W. "King John and Wales." Church, King John 273-87.

Sheppard, Walter L. "The Bastards of Henry II." The Genealogists Magazine 14.11 (Sept. 1964): 361-68.

Smith, R. J. "Henry II's Heir: The *Acta* and Seal of Henry the Young King 1170-1183." EHR 116 (2001): 297-326.

Stringer, Keith J. The Reign of King Stephen: Kingship, Warfare, and Government in Twelfth Century England. London: Routledge, 1993.

Turner, Hilary L. Town Defenses in England and Wales. London: John Baker, 1970.

Turner, R.V. "John and Justice." Church, King John 317-33.

---. King John. London: Longman, 1994.

---. "King John's Concept of Royal Authority." History of Political Thought 17 (1996): 157-78.

---. The King and His Courts: The Rule of John and Henry III in the Administration of Justice 1199-1240. Ithaca: Cornell UP, 1968.

---. "The Problem of Survival for the Angevin Empire: Henry II and His Sons Vision Versus Late 12th Century Realities." American Historical Review 100 (Feb 1995): 78-96.

---. "Religious Patronage of Angevin Royal Administrators." Albion 18 (1986): 1-22.

Turton, Lt. Col. W.H. The Plantagenet Ancestry. 1928. Reprint. Baltimore: Genealogy Publishing, 1993.

Warmington, A. "Some Knights of the Household of King John." Transactions of the Bristol and Gloucestershire Archaeological Society. 104 (1986): 175-82.

White, G. H. "King Stephen's Earldoms." Transactions of the Royal Historical Society 4.13 (1930): 51-82.

---. "The Constitutio Domus Regis and The King's Sport." The Antiquaries Journal 30 (1950): 52-63.

LAW

Adams, George Burton. Council and Courts in Anglo-Norman England. New
    Haven: Yale UP, 1926.

The Antiquities and Curiosities of the Exchequer. Ed. Hubert Hall. 1893. NY: Burt
    Franklin, 1968.

The Antient Kalendars and Inventories of the Treasury of His Majesty's Exchequer
    Together with Other Documents Illustrating the History of that Repository.
    Ed. Sir Francis Plagrave. 3 vols. London: Public Records Commission,
    1836.

Barrington, Boyd C. The Magna Carta and Other Great Charters of England.
    Philadelphia: W. J. Campbell, 1900. Littleton, CO: F. B Rothman, 1993.

Biancalana, J. "Widows and Common Law: The Development of Common Law
    Dowry." The Irish Jurist ns 33 (1988): 255-329.

---. "For Want of Justice: The Legal Reforms of Henry II." Columbia Law Review
    88 (1988): 433-536.

Brooke, Christopher N. The Medieval Idea of Marriage. Oxford: Oxford UP, 1989.

Bullough, D. A. and R. L. Storey, eds. The Study of Medieval Records: Essays in
    Honour of Kathleen Major. Oxford: Clarendon, 1971.

Cam, Helen M. Magna Carta-An Event or Document? Selden Society Lecture, July
    7, 1965. London: Quaritch, 1965.

Cheney, C. R. The Papacy and England 12th through 14th Centuries. London:
    Variorum Reprints, 1982.

Cole, H., ed. Documents of English History Illustrative of English History in the

13ᵗʰ and 14ᵗʰ Centuries. London: Record Commission, 1844.

The Course of the Exchequer by Richard, son of Nigel. Trans. Charles Johnson.
London: Thomas Nelson & Sons, 1950.

Crook, David. "Early Remembrances of the Exchequer." Bulletin of the Institute of
Historical Research LIII (May 1980): 11-23.

Davies, J. C., ed. The Cartae Antiquae Rolls 11-20. Lincoln: J. W. Ruddock and
Sons, 1960.

Davies, R. R. The British Isles 1100-1500: Comparisons, Contrast, and
Connections. Edinburgh: John Donal, 1988.

---. Domination and Conquest: The Experience of Ireland, Scotland and Wales.
Cambridge: Cambridge UP, 1990.

DeAragon, Ra Gena. "The Growth of Secure Inheritance in Anglo-Norman
England." Journal of Medieval History 8 (1982): 381-91.

---. "In Pursuit of Aristocratic Women: A Key to Success in Anglo-Norman
England." Albion 14 (1982): 258-67.

DeHaas, Elsa, ed. Early Registers of Writs. London: Spottiswoode, Ballantyne &
Co., 1970.

Douglas, David C. and George Greenway, eds. English Historical Documents 1042-
1198. London: G. Eyre and A. Spottiswoode, 1975.

English Historical Documents 1189-1327. Ed. H. Rothwell. NY: Oxford UP, 1975.

Fleming, D. "Milites as Attestors to Charters in England 1101-1300." Albion 22.2
(1990): 185-98.

Fleming, Robin. Domesday Book and the Law: Society and Legal Custom in Early

Medieval England. Cambridge: Cambridge UP, 1998.

---. Kings and Lords in Conquest England. Cambridge: Cambridge UP, 1991

Galbraith, V. H. "Monastic Foundation Charters of the Eleventh and Twelfth
Centuries." Cambridge Historical Journal 4.3 (1934): 205-22.

---. "Runnymede Revisited." Proceedings of the American Philosophical Society
110 (1966): 307-17.

Garnet, George and John Hudson, eds. Law and Government in Medieval England
and Normandy: Essays in Honour of Sir James Holt. Cambridge: Cambridge
UP, 1994.

Gillingham, John and J.C. Holt, eds. War and Government in the Middle Ages:
Essays in Honour of J. O. Prestwich. Woodbridge: Boydell, 1984.

Goldberg, P. J., ed. Woman is a Worthy Wight: Women in English Society 1200-
1500. NY: Alan Sutton, 1992.

Great Britain. Public Record Office. Syllabus of the Documents Relating to
England and Other Kingdoms Contained in Rhymer's 'Foedera'. Ed. T. D.
Hardy. London: Longmans, Green and Co., 1869.

Groot, Roger. "The Crime of Rape Temp. Richard I and John." Journal of Legal
History 9 (1988): 324-34.

Hall, Hubert. Studies in English Official Historical Documents. Cambridge:
Cambridge UP, 1908.

Hanawalt, Barbara. "Good Governance in the Medieval and Early Modern
Context." Journal of Medieval Studies 37.3 (July1998): 246-57.

---. The Ties That Bound. NY: Oxford UP, 1986.

Harfield, C. G. "A Hand-list of Castles Recorded in the Domesday Book." <u>EHR</u>
106 (1991): 371-90.

Helmholz, R. H. <u>Marriage Litigation in Medieval England.</u> Cambridge: Cambridge
UP, 1975.

Hollister, W.C. "Anglo-Norman Succession Debate of 1126." <u>Journal of Medieval
History</u> 1 (1975): 19-41.

---. <u>Anglo-Norman Political Culture and the Twelfth Century Renaissance.</u>
Woodbridge: Boydell, 1997.

Holt, James C. "The Barons and the Great Charter." <u>EHR</u> 70.274 (Jan 1955): 1-24.

---. "The 'Casus Regis' The Law and Politics of Succession in the Plantagenet
Dominions 1185-1247." <u>Law in Medieval Life and Thought</u> 5 (1990): 21-42.

---. <u>The Making of the Magna Carta.</u> Charlottesville,VA: UP Viriginia, 1965.

---. <u>Magna Carta and Medieval England.</u> London: Hambledon, 1962.

Hoyt, R. J. <u>The Royal Demesne in English Constitutional History 1066-1272.</u> NY:
Greenwood, 1968.

Hudson, J. <u>The Formation of English Common Law.</u> London: Longman, 1996.

---. <u>Land, Law, and Lordship in Anglo-Norman England.</u> Oxford: Clarendon, 1994

---. "Life Grants of Land and the Development of Inheritance in Anglo-Norman
England." <u>Proceedings of the Battle Conference on Anglo-Norman Studies
12.</u> Ed. Marjorie Chibnall. Woodbridge: Boydell, 1990. 67-80.

---. "Medieval Charters: The Last Witness." <u>Journal of the Society of Archivists</u> 5
(1974): 71-89.

<u>Inquisitions and Assessments Relating to Feudal Aids, 1284-1431.</u> Eds. S. A.

Maskelyne, C. Johnson, and J. V. Lyle. 6 vols. London: HMSO, 1899-1920.

Nendeln, Liechtenstein: Kraus Reprint, 1973.

Kaeuper, Richard. W. War, Justice, and Public Order. Oxford: Clarendon, 1987.

Keats-Rohan, K. S. B. Domesday Names: An Index of Latin Names and Place

Names. Woodbridge: Boydell, 1997.

Keefe, Thomas K. "Proffers for Heirs and Heiresses in the Pipe Rolls: Some

Observations on Indebtedness in the Years before Magna Carta, 1180-1212."

Haskins Society Journal 5 (1993): 99-110.

Latimer, P. "Grants of 'Totus Comitatus' in 12th Century England: Their Origins and

Meanings." Bulletin of the Institute of Historical Research 59 (1986): 137-

45.

Lists of Sheriffs for England and Wales. London: Lists and Indexes IX, 1898.

Loengard, Janet. "Legal History and the Medieval Woman." Law and

History Review 4 (1986): 161-88.

Lyon, Bryce. "Medieval Restrictions on Royal Authority." The High Middle Ages

1000-1300. Glencoe, NY: The Free Press, 1964. 250-73.

Maddicott, J. "Magna Carta and Local Community 1215-1259." Past and Present

102 (Feb. 1984): 25-65.

Martindale, Jane. "An Agreement Between Count William V of Aquitaine and Hugh

IV of Lusignan." EHR 84 (1969): 541-48.

---. Status, Authority, and Regional Power: Aquitaine and France Ninth to the

Twelfth Century. Aldershot: Variorum, 1997.

McCash, June Hall. The Cultural Patronage of Medieval Women. Athens: U of

Georgia P, 1996.

Menupe, Noel James, ed. Medieval Women and the Law. Woodbridge: Boydell,
2000.

Miller, E. "Background of Magna Carta." Past and Present 23 (1962): 72-82.

Nicholls, K. W. "Inquisitions of 1224 from the *Miscellanea* of the Exchequer."
Analecta Hibernica 27 (1972): 103-12.

Painter, Sidney. "Magna Carta." American Historical Review 53.1 (Oct. 1947): 42-
49.

Palmer, Robert C. The County Courts of Medieval England 1150-1350. Princeton:
Princeton UP, 1982.

Poole, A. L. Domesday to Magna Carta. Oxford: Clarendon, 1966.

---. Obligations of Society in the 11th and 12th Centuries. Oxford: Clarendon, 1946.

Richardson, H.G. The Governance of Mediaeval England from the Conquest to
Magna Carta. Edinburgh: UP, 1963.

Round, J. Horace. Peerage and Pedigree: Studies in Peerage Law and Family
History. 2 Vols. London: James Nisbet, 1910.

Rousseau, Constance and J. T. Rosenthal, eds. Women, Marriage, and Family
in Medieval Christendom: Essays in Memory of Michael M. Sheehan.
Kalamazoo: Medieval Institute, 1998.

Sanders, I. J. Feudal Military Service in England: A Study in Constitutional and
Military Powers of the "Barones' in Medieval England. London: Oxford UP,
1956.

Sayers, Jane E., ed. Original Papal Documents in England and Wales From the

Accession of Pope Innocent III to Pope Bendict XI, 1198-1304. Oxford: Oxford UP, 1999.

Sheehan, Michael. The Will in Medieval England. Toronto: Pontifical Institute of Medieval Studies, 1963.

---. "A List of the 13th Century English Wills." The Geneaologist's Magazine 13 (1961): 259-65.

Stenton, Doris M. After Runnymede: Magna Carta in the Middle Ages. Charlottesville, VA: U Virginia P, 1965.

---. English Justice Between the Norman Conquest and the Great Charter, 1066-1215. Philadelphia: American Philosophical Society, 1964.

Stewart-Brown, Ronald. The Serjeants of the Peace in Mediaeval England and Wales. Manchester: Manchester UP, 1936.

Stubbs, William. Historical Introductions to the Rolls Series. Ed. Arthur Hassall. NY: Kaskell House, 1968.

Summerson, H.R.T. "Structure of Law Enforcement in Thirteenth Century England." American Journal of Legal History XXIII (1979): 313-43.

Thorne, Samuel. "English Feudalism and Estates in Land." The Cambridge Law Journal 23 (1959): 193-209.

Turner, Ralph V. "Changing Perceptions of the New Administrative Class in Anglo-Norman and Angevin England: The Curiales and their Conservative Critics." Journal of British Studies 29 (April 1990): 93-117.

Van Caenagen, R. C., ed. English Law Suits from William I to Richard I. 2 vols. London: Selden Society, 1990-91.

Walker, Sue. "The Feudal Family and the Common Law Courts." Journal of
    Medieval History 14 (1988): 13-31.

---. "Free Consent and Marriage of Feudal Wards in Medieval England."
    Journal of Medieval History 8 (1982): 123-34.

---. "Proof of Age of Feudal Wards in Medieval England." Mediaeval
    Studies 35 (1973): 306-23.

---. "Punishing Convicted Ravishers: Statutory Strictures and Actual
    Practice." Journal of Medieval History 13 (1987): 237-50.

---. "Violence and the Exercise of Feudal Guardianship." The American
    Journal of Legal History 16 (1972): 320-33.

---, ed. Wife and Widow in Medieval England. Ann Arbor: U of Michigan P, 1993.

Waugh, Scott L. "Marriage, Class and Royal Lordship in England." Viator 16
    (1985): 181-207.

---. "Non-Alienation Clauses in 13th Century English Charters." Albion 17 (1985):
    1-14.

Warren, W. L. The Governance of Norman and Angevin England 1084-1272.
    Stanford: Stanford UP, 1987.

INDIVIDUALS

Alexander, J. W. Ranulf of Chester: A Relic of the Conquest. Athens: U of Georgia
    P, 1983.

Barlow, Frank. Thomas Becket. London: Weidenfeld & Nicholson, 1986.

Bartlett, Robert. Gerald of Wales 1146-1223. Oxford: Clarendon, 1982.

Bearman, Robert. "Baldwin de Redvers: Some Aspects of a Baronial Career in the

Reign of King Stephen." <u>Proceedings of the Battle Conference on Anglo-Norman Studies XVIII</u>. Ed. Christopher Harper-Bill. Woodbridge: Boydell, 1996. 19-46.

Blaauw, W. H. "Letters to Ralph de Nevill: Bishop of Chichester (1222-1224) and Chancellor to King Henry III." <u>Sussex Archaeological Collections Relating to the History and Antiquities of the County</u> 3 (1850): 35-76.

Brooks, Eric St John. "Archbishop Henry of London and His Irish Connections." <u>JRSAI</u> ser.6. 20 Part I (1920): 1-22.

---. "The de Ridelesfords." <u>JRSAI</u> LXXXI Part I (1951): 115-38.

---. "The de Ridelesfords." <u>JRSAI</u> LXXXII Part I (1952): 45-61

Brown, R. Allen. "Framlingham Castle and Bigod." <u>Proceedings of the Suffolk Institute of Archaeology</u> XXV.2 (1950): 127-48.

Carpenter, David. "The Fall of Hubert de Burgh." <u>The Journal of British Studies</u> XIX (1980): 1-17.

Cazel. F.A., ed. <u>Feudalism and Liberty: Articles and Addresses of Sidney Painter.</u> Baltimore: Johns Hopkins P, 1964.

---. "Intertwined Careers: Hubert de Burgh and Peter des Roches." <u>The Haskins Society Journal</u> 1 (1989): 173-81.

---. "The Last Years of Stephen Langton." <u>EHR</u> LXXIX (Oct 1964): 673-97.

<u>Collection de Sceaux.</u> Ed. M. Douet D'Arcq. Paris, Henri Plon, 1868.

Colvin, H. "A List of the Archbishop of Canterbury's Tenants-in-chief by Knight Service in the Reign of Henry II." <u>Kent Records</u> 18 (1964): 1-40.

Crouch, David. "Earl William of Gloucester and the End of the Anarchy: New

Evidence Relating to the Honour of Eudo Dapifer." EHR 103(1988): 69-75.

---. William Marshal, Court, Career and Chivalry in the Angevin Empire. London: Longman, 1990.

Crump, J. J. "Repercussions of the Execution of William de Braose." Historical Research 73 (2000): 197-212.

Dalton, Paul. "Eustace fitz John and the Politics of Anglo-Norman England: The Rise and Survival of a 12th Century Royal Servant." Speculum 71 (April 1996): 358-83.

Delisle, Leopold. *"Le Sceau de Guillaume le Marechal." Bibliotheque de l'Ecole des Chartes* 69 (1908); 346-51.

Dictionary of National Biography. Eds. Leslie Stephen & Sidney Lee. 22 vols. Oxford: Oxford UP, 1937-60.

Duby, Georges. *L'Historie le Guillaume le Marechal*: William Marshal The Flower of Chivalry. Trans. Richard Howard. NY: Pantheon, 1986.

English, Barbara. The Lords of Holderness 1086-1260. Oxford: Oxford UP, 1979.

Fairbank, F. Royston. "The Last Earl of Warenne and Surrey and the Distribution of his Possessions." The Yorkshire Archaeological Journal 19 (1907): 193-264.

FitzMaurice, Mrs. S. H. "Hervey de Montmorency." Journal of the Old Wexford Society 2 (1969): 19-25.

Fox, L. "The Honor and Earldom of Leicester Origin and Descent, 1066-1399."EHR 54 (1939): 385-402.

Gillingham, John. Angevin Empire. London: Oxford UP, 1984.

---. "Conquering the Barbarians: War and Chivalry in Twelfth Century Britain."
Haskins Society Journal 4 (1992):67-84.

---. The English in the Twelfth Century: Imperialism, National Identity, and
Political Values. Woodbridge: Boydell, 2000.

---. "Historians Without Hindsight: Coggeshall, Diceto, and Howden on the Early
Years of John's Reign." Crouch, King John 1-26.

---. "The Introduction of Knight Service into England." Proccedings of the Battle
Conference on Anglo-Norman Studies. WoodBridge: Boydell, 1990. 53-64.

---. "War and Chivalry in the History of William Marshal." Thirteenth Century
England II: Proceedings of the Newcastle upon Tyne Conference 1987. Eds.
Peter Coss & S. D. Lloyd. Woodbridge: Boydell, 1988. 1-13.

Harris, B.E. "Ranulf III Earl of Chester." Journal of the Chester Archaeological
Society (1975): 99-114.

Harvey, Ruth. "Cross-Channel Gossip in the Twelfth Century." Harlaxton Medieval
Studies VIII (2000): 48-59.

Hudson, B. T. "The Destruction of Gruffydd ap Llwelyn." Welsh History Review
15 (1990/91): 331-50.

Johns, Susan. "The Wives and Widows of the Earls of Chester, 1100-1252: The
Charter Evidence." Haskins Society Journal 7 (1995): 117-32.

Johnston, S. H. F. "The Lands of Hubert de Burgh." EHR 1 (1935): 418-32.

Keats-Rohan, K. S. P., et. al. "Continental Origins of English Landholders."
Medieval Prosopography 17(1996): 223-62.

Kightly, Charles, ed. A Mirror of Wales: Gerald of Wales and His Journey of

1188. Ed. David M. Robinson. Cardiff: CADW, 1988.

LeBarge, Margaret Wade. A Baronial Household of the 13th Century. NY: Barnes & Noble, 1965.

Lewis, C. P. "The Early Earls of Norman England." Proceedings of the Battle Conference on Anglo-Norman Studies XIII. Ed. Marjorie Chibnall. Woodbridge: Boydell, 1991. 207-23.

Lloyd, J. E. "Who was Gwenllian de Lacy?" Archaeologia Cambrensis 6th ser. (1919): 292-99.

Lloyd, L. C. "Origin of the Family of Warenne." Yorkshire Archaeological Journal 31(1934): 97-113.

Materials for the History of Thomas Becket, Archbishop of Canterbury. Eds. J. C. Robertson and J. B. Sheppard. 7 vols. London: Rolls Series, 1875-85.

Meisel, J. Barons of the Welsh Frontier: the Corbets, Pandulf and Fitz Warrin Families 1066-1217. Lincoln, Nebraska: U Nebraska P, 1980.

Mortimer, R. "Beginning of the Honour of Clare." Proceedings of the Battle Conference on Anglo-Norman Studies 3. Ed. R. Allen Brown. Woodbridge: Boydell, 1981. 119-41.

---. "The Family of Ranulph de Glanville." Bulletin of the Institute of Historical Research 54 (May 1981): 1-16.

---. "Land and Service: The Tenants of the Honour of Clare." Proceedings of the Battle Conference on Anglo-Norman Studies VIII. Ed. R. Allen Brown. Woodbridge: Boydell, 1986. 177-97.

Orpen, G. et. al. "Charters of Earl Richard Marshal of the Forests of Ross and Taghman." JRSAI 63 (1934): 54-63.

Page. Mark. "Cornwall, Earl Richard and the Barons' War." EHR 115 (2000): 21-38.

Patterson, R. B., ed. Earldom of Gloucester Charters to A.D. 1217. Oxford: Clarendon, 1973.

---. "Robert fitz Harding of Bristol: Profile of an Early Angevin Burgess-Baron Patrician and his Family's Urban Involvement." Haskins Society Journal 1 (1989): 109-22.

Prendergast, Richard. "The Faithful Norman." Old Kilkenny Review 22 (1970): 34-41.

Power, Daniel. The Norman Frontier in the 12th and early 13th Centuries. Cambridge: Cambridge UP, 2004.

Pryce, Frederick R. "Anglo-Norman Barons and their European Relations." Genealogists' Magazine 19.2 (June 1977): 55-58.

Revell, Elizabeth, ed. The Later Letters of Peter of Blois. Oxford: Oxford UP, 1993.

Richardson, H. "Letters of the Legate Gualo." The English Historical Society XLVIII (1933): 250-59.

Round, J. H. "The Countess of Ireland." The Geneaologist 18 (1901): 166-67.

---. "A Great Marriage Settlement." The Ancestor (1904): 153-57.

---. Geoffrey de Mandeville: A Study of Anarchy. London: Longman, Green & Co., 1892.

Rowlands, I. W. "William Marshal and the Pembroke Inheritance." Chateau

Gaillard 17 (1994): 152-55.

Sayers, J. E. _Papal Government and England During the Pontificate of Honorius III_
   _1216-1227._ Cambridge: Cambridge UP, 1984.

Smith, David. "The Rolls of Hugh of Wells, bishop of Lincoln, 1209-35." _Bulletin_
   of the Institute of Historical Research 43 (192): 155-95.

Sparks, May. "The Graces." _Old Kilkenny Review_ 19 (1967): 26-28

Stephen Langton: The Ford Lectures. F. M. Powicke. NY: Barnes & Noble, 1930.

Stones, Jeanne & Lionel. "Bishop Ralph Neville, Chamberlain to King
   Henry III and His Correspondence: A Reappraisal." _Archives_ XVI.71
   (April 1984): 227-57.

Stringer, K. J. _Earl David of Scotland 1152-1219._ Edinburgh: Edinburgh
   UP, 1985.

---, ed. _Essays of the Nobility of Medieval Scotland_. Edinburgh: Edinburgh
   UP, 1985.

Studies in Medieval History Presented to F. Maurice Powicke. Eds. R.W.
   Hunt, W.A. Pantin, & R.W. Southern. Oxford: Clarendon, 1948.

Turner, R. V. "The Mandeville Inheritance 1189-1236." _The Haskins_
   Society Journal 1 (1989): 147-72.

---. _Men Raised From the Dust: Administrative Service and Upward_
   Mobility in Angevin England. Philadelphia: U of Pennsylvania P,
   1988.

Vincent, Nicholas. "Isabella of Angouleme: John's Jezebel." Church, _King_
   John 165-219.

---. Ed. <u>The Letters and Charters of Cardinal Guala Bicchieri Papal Legate in England 1216-1218.</u> Woodbridge: Boydell, 1997.

---. <u>Peter des Roches An Alien in English Politics 1205-1238.</u> Cambridge: Cambridge UP, 1996.

---. "Warin and Henry Fitz Gerald, the King's Chamberlains." <u>Proccedings of Battle Conference on Anglo-Norman Studies</u> 21 (1999): 233-60.

Vine, M. J. "Two Yorkshire Rebels: Peter de Brus and Richard de Percy."<u>The Yorkshire Archaeological Journal</u> 47 (1975): 67-79.

Walker, D. ed. "Charters of the Earldom of Hereford 1095-1201." <u>Camden Miscellanea 22</u> Camden Society 4th ser. I (1964): 1-75.

Walker, R. F. "The Supporters of Richard Marshal Earl of Pembroke in the Rebellion of 1233-1234." <u>Welsh History Review</u> 17 (1994): 41-65.

Ward, Jennifer. "The Estates of the Clare Family." <u>Bulletin of the Institute of Historical Research</u> 37 (1964): 114-16.

---. "Fashions in Monastic Endowments: The Foundations of the Clare Family, 1061-1314." <u>Journal of Ecclesiastical History</u> 32 (1981): 427-51.

---. "The Lowy of Tonbridge and the Lands of the Clare Family in Kent, 1066-1217." <u>*Archaeologia Cantiana*</u> 96 (1980): 119-13.

Wareham, A. "Motives and Politics of the Bigod Family." <u>Proceedings of Battle Conference on Anglo-Norman Studies XVII.</u> Ed. Christopher Harper-Bill. Woodbridge: Boydell, 1995. 223-42

Weiss, M. "The Castellan: The Early Career of Hubert de Burgh." <u>Viator</u>

(1974): 235-42.

White, G. "King Stephen, Duke Henry and Ranulf de Gernons, Earl of
Chester." <u>EHR</u> 91 (1976): 555-65.

Wrightman, W. E. <u>The Lacy Family in England and Normandy 1066-1194.</u>
Oxford: Clarendon, 1968.

---. "The Palatinate Earldom of William fitz Osbern in Gloucestershire and
Worcestershire." <u>EHR</u> 77 (1962): 6-17.

FEUDALISM, KNIGHTS, AND SOCIETY

Ailes, Adrian. "Heraldry in Twelfth Century England." <u>England in the Twelfth
Century</u> <u>Proceeding of the 1988 Harlaxton Symposium.</u> Ed. D. Williams.
Woodbridge: Boydell, 1990. 1-16.

---. "Heraldry in Medieval England: Symbols of Politics and Propaganda."
<u>Heraldry</u> <u>Pageantry and Social Display</u> 83-104.

---. "The Knight, Heraldry and Armor: The Role of Recognition and the Origins
of Heraldry." <u>Medieval Knighthood IV: Papers from the Fifth Strawberry
Hill Conference.</u> Eds. C. Harper-Bill and R. Harvey. Woodbridge: Boydell,
1992. 1-21

---. <u>The Origins of the Royal Arms of England: Their Development to 1199.</u>
Reading: Graduate Center for Medieval Studies, 1982.

Archer, Lucy. <u>Architecture in Britain and Ireland 600-1500.</u> London: Harvill, 1999.

Barber, R. <u>The Knight and Chivalry.</u> Rev. ed. Woodbridge: Boydell, 1995.

Barraclough, Geoffrey, ed. <u>Social Life in Early England.</u> NY: Barnes & Noble,
1960.

Bateson, Mary. <u>Medieval England, 1066-1350.</u> NY: Books for Libraries, 1971.

Beattie, William. <u>The Castles and Abbeys of England.</u> 2 vols. London: J. S. Virtue
    & Co., 1884-85.

Beeler, J. H. "Castles and Strategy in Norman and Early Angevin England."
    <u>Speculum</u> 31 (1956): 581-601.

---. "The Composition of Anglo-Norman Armies." <u>Speculum</u> 39 (1965): 398-414.

---. <u>Warfare in England 1061-1189.</u> Ithaca: Cornell UP, 1961.

Bell, David N. <u>An Index of Cistercian Authors and Works in Medieval
    Library Catalogues in Great Britian.</u> Kalamazoo, MI: Cistercian
    Publications, 1999

Bellot, Hugh. <u>The Inner and Middle Temple: Legal, Literary, and Historical
    Associations.</u> London: Methuen, 1902.

Beresford, Maurice. <u>New Towns of the Middle Ages.</u> NY: Frederick
    Praeger, 1967.

"Bernard of Clairvaux's Letter to Hugh de Payens on Knights Templar." <u>The
    Cistercians Fathers Series: No. 19: The Works of Bernard of Clairvaux.</u>
    Vol. 7. Treatises III. Trans. Conrad Greenia. Kalamazoo: Cistercian
    Publications, 1977.

Binns, Alison. <u>Dedication of Monastic Houses in England and Wales 1066-
    1216.</u> Woodbridge: Boydell, 1982.

Bisson, Thomas. "Medieval Lordship." <u>Speculum</u> 70 (1995): 743-59.

Blair, C. H. Hunter. "Armorials on English Seals from the Twelfth to the Sixteenth
    Centuries." <u>*Archaeologia* or Miscellaneous Tracts Relating to Antiquity</u>

LXXXIX (1943): 1-26.

Blashill, Thomas. "The Architectural History of Tintern Abbey." <u>Bristol and Gloucestershire Archaeological Society</u> 6 (1881): 88-106.

Blore, Edward. <u>The Monumental Remains of Noble and Eminent Persons Comprising the Sepuchral Antiquities of Great Britain.</u> London: Harding, Lepord, 1826.

Bonney, T. G., ed. <u>Abbeys and Churches of England and Wales.</u> London: Cassell, 1887.

Bottomley, Frank. <u>The Castle Explorer's Guide.</u> NY: Avenel, 1979.

<u>Boutell's Heraldry Revised.</u> Rev. by J. B. Brooke-Little, Richmond Herald of Arms. London: Frederick Warne, 1978.

Boutell, Rev. Charles. <u>Monumental Brasses and Slabs; An Historical and Descriptive Notice of the Incised Monumental Memorials of the Middle Ages.</u> London: G. Bell, 1858.

Bradley, Edith. <u>The Story of the English Abbeys Told in Counties.</u> Vol. I & II.London: Robert Hale, 1938.

Brakspear, Harold. <u>Tintern Abbey.</u> 2nd ed. London: HMSO, 1921.

Brault, Gerard J. <u>Early Blazon: Heraldic Terminology in the 12th and 13th Centuries.</u> Oxford: Clarendon, 1972.

Brown, R. Allen. "An Historian's Approach to the Origins of the Castle in England." <u>The Archaeological Journal</u> CXXVI (1969): 131-48.

---. <u>The Architecture of Castles: A Visual Guide.</u> NY: Facts on File, 1984.

---. <u>Castles, Conquest and Charters: The Papers of R. Allen Brown.</u> Woodbridge:

Boydell, 1989.

---. English Castles. London: B.T. Batsford, 1974.

---. The Norman Conquest: Documents of Medieval History. London: Edward
    Arnold, 1984.

---. The Normans and the Norman Conquest. London: Thomas Y Crowell, 1968.

---. The Origins of English Feudalism. London: George Allen and Unwin, 1973.

---, ed. Proceedings of the Battle Conference on Anglo-Norman Studies II.
    Woodbridge: Boydell, 1980.

---. ed. Proceedings of the Battle Conference on Anglo-Norman Studies IV.
    Woodbridge: Boydell, 1982.

---. ed. Proceedings of the Battle Conference on Anglo-Norman Studies VIII.
    Woodbridge: Boydell, 1986

---. "Royal Castle Building in England 1154-1216." EHR 70.276 (July 1955): 353-
    98.

---. "The Status of the Norman Knight." Castles, Conquest, and Charters.
    Woodbridge: Boydell (1989): 290-304.

Brown, S. D. "Leavetaking: Lordship and Mobility in England and Normandy in the
    Twelfth Century." History 79.256 (1990): 199-205.

Butler, Lawrence. "The Origins of the Honour of Richmond and Its Castles."
    Liddiard, Anglo-Norman Castles 91-104.

Cairns, Trevor. Medieval Knights. Cambridge: Cambridge UP, 1992.

Campbell, Louise and Francis Steer, eds. A Catalogue of Manuscripts in the
    College of Arms Collections. Vol. I. London: College of Arms, 1988.

Carpenter, D. "The Second Century of English Feudalism." Past and Present 168 (2000): 30-71.

Cazel, F. A. "The Fifteenth of 1225." Bulletin of the Institute of Historical Research XXXIV (1961): 67-81.

Chandler, Victoria. "Family Histories: An Aid in the Study of the Anglo-Norman Aristocracy." Medieval Prosopography 6 (1985): 1-74.

Chibnall, Marjorie. Anglo-Norman England 1066-1166. Oxford: Basil Blackwell, 1986.

---. "Orderic Vitalis on Castles." Liddiard, Anglo-Norman Castles 119-32.

---. Piety, Power and History in Medieval England and Normandy. Aldershot: Ashgate/Variorum, 2000.

Sir Christopher Hatton's Book of Seals. Eds. Lewis C. Loyd & Doris Mary Stenton. Oxford: Clarendon, 1950.

Church, Stephen and Ruth Harvey. eds. Papers from the Sixth Strawberry Hill Conference. Woodbridge: Boydell, 1995.

Cooke, Alice. "Settlement of the Cistercians in England." EHR 8 (1893): 627-76.

Coss, Peter. "Aspects of Cultural Diffusion in Medieval England." Past and Present 108 (Aug. 1985): 35-79.

---. "Bastard Feudalism Revisited." Past and Present 125 (Nov. 1989): 27-64

---. The Knight in Medieval England 1000-1400. Dover, NH: Alan Sutton, 1993.

---. The Lady in Medieval England 1000-1500. Mechanicsburg, PA: Stackpole, 1998.

Coss, Peter and S. D. Lloyd, eds. Thirteenth Century England I: Proceedings of The

Newcastle-on-Tyne Conference. Woodbridge: Boydell, 1985-86.

---. eds. Thirteenth Century England II: Proceedings of The Newcastle-on-Tyne Conference. Woodbridge: Boydell, 1987-88.

---. eds. Thirteenth Century England III: Proceedings of the Newcastle-on-Tyne Conference. Woodbridge: Boydell, 1989-90.

---. eds. Thirteenth Century England V: Proceedings of the Newcastle-on-Tyne Conference. Woodbridge: Boydell, 1995.

Coulson, Charles. "Castles and the Anarchy." Liddiard, Anglo-Norman Castles 174-202.

Crossley, Fred H. English Church Monuments AD 1150-1550: An Introduction to the Study of Tombs and Effigies of the Mediaeval Period. London: B.T. Batsford, 1921-22.

Cowley, F. G. The Monastic Order in South Wales 1066-1349. Cardiff: U of Wales P, 1977.

Cownie, Emma. Religious Patronage in Anglo-Norman England, 1066-1135. Woodbridge: Boydell, 1998.

Crouch, David. "The Hidden History of the Twelfth Century." Haskins Society Journal 5 (1993): 111-30.

---. "The Histories, Lineage, and Heraldry 1050-1250." Heraldry, Pageantry and Social Display in Medieval England 17-38.

Denholm-Young, Neal. Collected Papers on Medieval Subjects. Oxford: Basil Blackwell, 1946.

Dennys, Rodney. Heralds and Heraldry. London: Jonathan Cape, 1982.

Dickinson, P. L. "The Heralds and Genealogy." The Genealogists' Magazine 21.5
    (1984): 289-98.

Duby, Georges. The Chivalrous Society. Trans. Cynthia Postan. Berkeley: U of
    California P, 1977.

Eales, Richard. "Castles and Politics in England 1215-1224." England Thirteenth
    Century II: Proceedings of the Newcastle-on-Tyne Conference 1987. Eds.
    Peter Coss and S.D. Floyd. Woodbridge: Boydell, 1988. 23-43.

---. "Royal Power and Castles in Norman England." Liddiard, Anglo-Norman
    Castles 41-68.

Eight Thirteenth Century Rolls of Arms in French and Anglo-Norman Blazon. Ed.
    Gerard J. Brault. University Park, PA: Pennsylvania State UP, 1913.

Eley, Perry. "History: Romance in the Chronique des Ducs de Normandie."
    Medium Aevuum 68.1 (1999): 81-95.

Esdaile, Mrs. Arundell. Temple Church Monuments: Being a Report to the
    Two Honourable Societies of The Temple. London: George Barber &
    Son, 1933.

Faulkner, Kathryn. "The Transformation of Knighthood in early Thirteenth century
    England." EHR 440 (Feb. 1996): 1-23.

Foster, Joseph. Some Feudal Coats of Arms From the Heraldic Rolls 1298-1418.
    London: James Parker, 1902.

Galbraith, V. H. "Monastic Foundation Charters of the Eleventh and Twelfth
    Centuries." The Cambridge Historical Journal 4.3 (1934): 205-98.

---. Studies in the Public Records. London: T. Nelson, 1948.

Giles, Adrian. "Heraldry in Twelfth Century England." Williams, <u>England in the 12<u>th</u> Century</u> 1-16.

---. "The Knight, Heraldry, and Armour: The Role of Recognition and the Origins of Heraldry." <u>Ideals and Practices of Medieval Knighthood II</u> Eds. Christopher Harper-Bill and S. Harvey. Woodbridge: Boydell, 1988 1-22.

Godfrey, W. H. "Recent Discoveries at The Temple, London, and Notes on the Topography of the Site." <u>*Archaeologia*</u> XCV (1953): 123-40.

Grandsden, Anotonia. <u>Historical Writing in England c550-1307.</u> London: Hambledon, 1974.

---. "Prologues on the Historiography of Twelfth Century England." <u>England in the Twelfth Century: Proceedings of the 1988 Harlaxton Symposium.</u> Ed. Daniel Williams. Woodbridge: Boydell, 1990. 55-81.

Green, Judith. <u>The Aristocracy of Norman England.</u> Cambridge: Cambridge UP, 1997.

---. "Aristocratic Loyalties on the Northern Frontier of England c 1110-1174." Williams, <u>England in the 12<u>th</u> Century</u> 83-100.

---. "Aristocratic Women in Early Twelfth Century England." Hollister, <u>Anglo-Norman Political Culture</u> 59-82.

---. "Family Matters: Family and the Formation of the Empress' Party in Southwest England." Keats-Rohan, <u>Family Trees and the Roots of Politics.</u> 147-64.

---. "Unity and Disunity in the Anglo-Norman State." <u>Bulletin of the Institute of</u>

Historical Research 62 (1989): 115-34.

Gwynn, Aubrey and R. Neville Hadcock. Medieval Religious Houses: Ireland.

London: Longman, 1990.

Haida, R. "Castles and Castellans and the Structure of Politics in Poitou,

1152-1271." Journal of Medieval History 4 (1978): 27-53.

---. "Family and Feudal Ties in Poitou, 1100-1300." Journal of

Interdisciplinary History 8 (1977): 117-39.

Harding, Alan. England in the Thirteenth Century. Cambridge: Cambridge

UP, 1992.

Harfield, C.G. "A Hand List of Castles Recorded in the Domesday Book."

EHR 106 (1991): 371-90.

Harper-Bill, Christopher. "The Piety of the Anglo-Norman Knightly Class" Brown,

ed., Proceedings of the Battle Conference on Anglo-Norman Studies II 63-

77.

Harper-Bill, Christopher, ed. Proceedings of the Battle Conference on Anglo-

Norman Studies XVIII. Woodbridge: Boydell, 1996.

Harper-Bill, Christopher, Christopher Holdsworth and Janet L. Nelson. eds. Studies

in Medieval History Presented to R.A. Brown.   Woodbridge: Boydell, 1989.

Harper-Bill, Christopher and S. Harvey, eds. The Ideals and Practices of Medieval

Knighthood III. Woodbridge: Boydell, 1990.

---. eds. The Ideals and Practices of Medieval Knighthood IV. WoodbBoydell,

1991.

Harvey, Barbara, ed. Twelfth and Thirteenth Centuries. Oxford: Oxford UP, 2001.

Harvey, S. "Knight and the Knight's Fee in England." <u>Past and Present</u> 49 (1970): 3-43.

Heiser, Richard. "Castles, Constables, and Politics in Late 12th Century English Governance." <u>Albion</u> 32 (2000): 19-36.

<u>Heraldry in Historic Houses of Great Britain.</u> Eds. Thomas Woodcock and John Robinson. New York: Harry N. Abrams, 2000.

<u>Heraldry, Pageantry and Social Display in Medieval England.</u> Eds. Peter Coss and Maurice Keen. Woodbridge: Boydell, 2002.

Hicks, Michael. <u>Bastard Feudalism.</u> NY: Longman, 1995.

Hill, Bennett D. <u>English Cistercian Monasteries and Their Patrons in the Twelfth Century.</u> Urbana: U of Illinois P, 1968.

Hollister, Warren, ed. <u>Anglo-Norman Political Culture and the Twelfth Century Renaissance.</u> Woodbridge: Boydell, 1966.

---. <u>Monarch, Magnates, and Institutions in the Anglo-Norman World.</u> London: Hambledon, 1986.

Holt, J. C. <u>Colonial England 1066-1215.</u> London: Hambledon, 1997.

---. "Feudal Society and the Family in Early Medieval England I: The Revolution of 1066." <u>TRHS</u> 32 (1982): 193-212.

---. "II Notions of Patrimony." <u>TRHS</u> 33 (1983): 193-220.

---. "III Patronage and Politics." <u>TRHS</u> 34 (1984): 1-25.

---. "IV The Heiress and the Alien." <u>TRHS</u> 35 (1985): 1-28.

---. "Politics and Property in Early Medieval England." <u>Past and Present</u> 57 (1972): 3-52.

Hooten, John Camden. <u>A Hand-Book to the Topography and Family History of England and Wales.</u> London: John Camden Hooten, 1883.

Hopkins, Andrea. <u>Knights.</u> NY: Abbeville, 1990.

Hyams, P. <u>Kings, Lords, and Peasants in Medieval England.</u> NY; Clarendon, 1980.

---. "Warranty and Good Lordship in 12th Century England." <u>Law and History Review</u> 5 (1987): 437-503._

Inner Temple London. <u>Catalogue of Manuscripts in the Library of the Honourable Society of the Inner Temple.</u> Ed. J. Conway Davies. 3 vols. London: Oxford UP, 1972.

Johnson, Paul. <u>Castles of England, Scotland, and Wales.</u> NY: Harper & Row, 1989.

Keats-Rohan, K. S. B. <u>Family Trees and the Roots of Politics.</u> Woodbridge: Boydell, 1997.

Keen, Maurice. <u>Chivalry.</u> New Haven, CT: Yale UP, 1984.

Kenyon, John R. "Fluctuating Frontiers: Normanno-Welsh Castle Warfare." Liddiard, <u>Anglo-Norman Castles</u> 247-58.

King, D. J. Cathcart. <u>The Castle in England and Wales: An Interpretative History.</u> London: Croom Helm, 1988.

Lawrance, Henry. <u>Heraldry From Military Monuments Before 1350.</u> Harleian Society Publications, Vol. XCVIII. London: John Whitehead, 1946.

Lewer, David. <u>The Temple Church.</u> London: Pitkin Pictorials, 1953(?).

Liddiard, Robert, ed. <u>Anglo-Norman Castles.</u> Woodbridge: Boydell, 2003

Lundwall, Sten. "The Knights with the Crossed-Legs." <u>*Formae*</u> (1960): 94-102.

Martindale, Jane. "The French Aristocracy in the Early Middle Ages; A

Reappraisal." <u>Past and Present</u> 75 (1977): 5-45.

Mason, Emma. "In the 1200's, Rising Population Brought Movement:
    Politically, Geographically, and Socially." <u>History Today</u> 50.5 (May
    2000): 39-45.

---. "Magnates, *Curiales* and the Wheel of Fortune." Brown, ed.,
    <u>Proceedings of the Battle</u> Conference on Anglo-Norman Studies II
    118-40.

Mason, J. F. A. "Barons and Their Officials in the 11th Century."
    <u>Proceedings of the Battle Conference on Anglo-Norman Studies XIII</u>
    Ed. Marjorie Chibnall. Woodbridge: Boydell, 1991. 243-62.

Meddings, John. "Friendship Among the Aristocracy in Anglo-Norman
    England." <u>Proceedings of the Battle Conference on Anglo-Norman
    Studies XXII</u>. Ed. Christopher Harper-Bill. Woodbridge: Boydell,
    2000. 187-204.

<u>Medieval Knighthood V: Papers From the Sixth Strawberry Hill Conference 1994</u>.
    Eds. Stephen Church and Ruth Harvey. Woodbridge: Boydell, 1995.

Mooers, Stephanie. "Familial Clout and Financial Gain in Henry I's Later
    Reign." <u>Albion</u> 14 (1982): 268-91.

---. "Networks of Power in Anglo-Norman England." <u>Medieval
    Prosopography</u> (1986): 25-54.

Moore, J. S. "Anglo-Norman Family Size and Structure." <u>Proceedings
    of Battle Conference on Anglo-Norman Studies 14</u>. Ed. Marjorie
    Chibnall. Woodbridge: Boydell, 1992. 155-96.

Mortimer, Richard. <u>Angevin England 1154-1258.</u> London: Blackwell, 1994.

O'Neil, Brian and Hugh St. John. <u>Castles: An Introduction to the Castles of England and Wales</u>. 2nd ed. London: HMSO, 1973.

Orme, N. <u>From Childhood to Chivalry:The Education of the English Kings And Aristocracy 1066-1530.</u> London: Methuen, 1984

Painter, Sidney. <u>Studies in the History of English Feudal Baronies.</u> Baltimore: Johns Hopkins, 1968.

---. "Castle Guard." Liddiard, <u>Anglo-Norman Castles</u> 203-10.

---. "English Castles in the Early Middle Ages: Their Number, Location, and Legal Position." <u>Speculum</u> 10.3 (July 1935): 321-32.

Partner, Nancy. "Introduction to Studying Medieval Women: Sex, Gender, and Feminism." <u>Speculum</u> 68 (1993): 305-404.

---. "No Sex, No Gender." <u>Speculum</u> 68 (1993): 419-44.

---. <u>Serious Entertainments: The Writing of History in Twelfth Century England.</u> Chicago: U of Chicago P, 1977.

Pierce, I. "The Knight, His Arms and Armor c.1150-1250." <u>Proceedings of the Battle Conference on Anglo-Norman Studies XV</u>. Ed. Marjorie Chibnall. Woodbridge: Boydell, 1993. 251-74.

Platt, Colin. <u>The Architecture of Medieval Britain.</u> New Haven, CT: Yale UP, 1990.

Poole, Austin L. <u>Obligations of Society in the XII and XIII Centuries.</u> Oxford: Clarendon, 1945.

Pounds, Norman. <u>The Medieval Castle in England and Wales.</u> Cambridge:

Cambridge UP, 1990.

Purser, T. S. "The Origins of English Feudalism? An Episcopal Land-Grant
Revisited." <u>The Bulletin of Historical Research</u> 73.180 (Feb. 2000): 80-92.

Quick, J. "The Number and Distribution of Knights in Thirteenth Century England:
The Evidence of the Grand Assize Lists." <u>Thirteenth Century England I:</u>
<u>Proceedings of the Newcastle upon Tyne Conference 1985</u>. Eds. Peter Coss
and S.D.Lloyd. Woodbridge: Boydell, 1986. 114-23.

Reuther, Timothy, ed. <u>Warriors and Churchmen in the High Middle Ages: Essays</u>
<u>Presented to Karl Leyser.</u> London: Hambledon, 1992.

Reynolds, Susan. <u>Fiefs and Vassals: The Medieval Evidence Re-interpreted.</u>
Oxford: Oxford UP, 1994.

Riley-Smith, Jonathan. <u>The First Crusaders, 1095-1131.</u> Cambridge: Cambridge
UP, 1997.

Ross, Frederick. <u>The Ruined Abbeys of Britain.</u> 2 vols. Illustrated by A. F.
Lydon. London: William Mackenzie, 1882.

Round, J. Horace. <u>Feudal England: Historical Studies in the Eleventh and Twelfth</u>
<u>Centuries.</u> Reprint. London: G. Allen & Unwin, 1964.

Rous, John. <u>The Rous Roll.</u> Intro. Charles Ross. Gloucestershire: Alan Sutton,
1980.

Smail, R.C. <u>Crusading Warfare 1073-1193.</u> Cambridge: Cambridge UP, 1956.
Reprint 1967.

Strickland, Matthew. "Against the Lord's Anointed: Aspects of Warfare and
Baronial Rebellion in England and Normandy 1066-1265." Garnet and

Hudson 41-59.

---. Anglo-Norman Warfare. Woodbridge: Boydell, 1992.

---. "Arms and the Men: War, Loyalty, and Lordship in Jordan Fantosme's
  Chronicle." Medieval Knighthood IV. Eds. Christopher Harper-Bill and
  Ruth Harvey. Woodbridge: Boydell P, 1991. 187-220

Thirteenth Century England VI: Proceedings of the Durham Conference 1995. Eds.
  Michael Prestwich, R. Britnell, and Robin Frame. Woodbridge: Boydell,
  1997.

Thirteenth Century England VII: Proceedings of the Durham Conference 1997. Eds.
  Michael Prestwich, R. Britnell, and Robin Frame. Woodbridge: Boydell,
  1999.

Thompson, Michael. Medieval Bishops' Houses in England and Wales. Aldershot:
  Ashgate, 1998.

Timbs, John. Abbeys, Castles, and Ancient Halls of England and Wales. Rev. & ed.
  Alexander Gunn. 3 vols. London: Frederick Warne, 1872.

Tummers, H. A. Early Secular Effigies in England: The Thirteenth Century.
  Leiden: E. J. Brill, 1980.

Turner, Hilary. Town Defenses in England and Wales, 900-1500. London: John
  Baker, 1970.

Upton-Ward, J. M. The Rule of the Templars: The French Text of the Rule of the
  Order of the Knights Templar. Woodbridge: Boydell, 1992.

Van Houts, E. M. C. History and Family Traditions in England and The Continent
  1000-1200. Aldershsot: Ashgate/Variorum, 1999.

---. Medieval Memories: Men, Women and the Past in Europe 700-1300. London: Longman, 2000.

Victoria County History of the County of Sussex. Vol. IV. Ed. L. F. Salzman. London: Oxford UP.

Wagner, Anthony Richard. Heralds and Heraldry in the Middle Ages: An Inquiry into the Growth Of the Armorial Function of Heralds. Oxford: Oxford UP, 1936, 1960.

---. Historic Heraldry of Britain: An Illustrated Series of British Historical Arms. London: Oxford UP, 1939.

---. The Records and Collections of the College of Arms. London: Metchim & Son, 1862.

Walker, David. The Normans in Britain. Oxford: Blackwell, 1993.

Ward, Jennifer. ed. and trans. Women of the English Nobility and Gentry. Manchester: Manchester UP, 1995.

Warren, Michelle R. History on the Edge: Excalibur and the Borders of Britain 1100-1300. Medieval Cultures Vol. 22. Minneapolis: U of Minnesota P, 2000.

White, H. L. "Monumental Inscriptions." The Genealogists' Magazine 16.9 (June 1971): 470-74.

Williams, Daniel, ed. England in the Twelfth Century: Proceedings of the 1988 Harlaxton Symposium. Woodbridge: Boydell, 1990.

Wood, Susan. English Monasteries and Their Patrons in the Thirteenth Century. London: Oxford UP, 1955.

Woolgar, C. M. The Great Households in Late Medieval England. New

    Haven: Yale UP, 1999

Wright, C. E. English Heraldric Manuscripts in the British Museum. London:

    British Museum Publications, 1977.

IRELAND

Anglo-Norman Studies XX: Proceedings of the Battle Conference in Dublin, 1997.

    Ed. Christopher Harper-Bill. Woodbridge: Boydell, 1998.

Barry, J. "A Guide to Records of the Genealogical Office, Dublin." *Analecta*

    Hibernica 26 (1971): 3-43.

---. "The Norman Invasion of Ireland: A New Approach." Cork History Journal

    LXXV (1970): 105-24.

Barry, T. B., Robin Frame and Katherine Simms, eds. Colony and Frontier in

    Medieval Ireland: Essays Presented to J. F. Lydon. London: Hambledon,

    1995.

Bernard, J. H. "The Foundation of Tintern Abbey, County Wexford."Proceedings of

    The Royal Irish Academy XXXIII Sect. C 17 (March 1917): 527-29.

The Book of Leinster: Formerly Lebra Na Nuachongbala. Vol. I. Eds. R. I. Best,

    Osborn Bergin, and M.A. O'Brien. Dublin: Institute for Advanced Studies,

    1954.

Bradley, John. "Some New and Neglected Medieval Tomb Slabs and Fragments

    From Kilkenny." Old Kilkenny Review ns 2.2 (1983): 5-21.

Brooks, Eric St John. "Sources for Medieval Anglo-Irish History." Historical

    Studies I (1958): 86-92.

Calendar of Ancient Records of Dublin. Vol. I. Ed. John T. Gilbert. Dublin: Joseph

   Dollard, 1889.

Cunningham, George. The Anglo-Norman Advance into the Southwest Midlands of

   Ireland 1185-1221. Rosecrea: Parkmore, 1987.

Curtis, E. and R. A. McDowell, eds. Irish Historical Documents 1172-1922.

   London: Methuen & Co., Ltd., 1943.

Doyle, Gerard. "County Kilkenny M.S.S. in British Museum." Old Kilkenny

   Review 17 (1965): 70-78.

Duffy, Sean. "The 1169 Invasions as a Turning Point in Irish-Welsh Relations."

   Smith, ed. Britain and Ireland 900-1300 98-113.

Empey, C. A. "The Cantreds of the Medieval County of Kildare." JRSAI 101 Part

   II (1971): 128-34.

Flanagan, Marie T. "Henry II and the Council of Cashel and Irish Bishops." Peritia

   10(1996): 184-211.

---. "Irish and Anglo-Norman Warfare in the Twelfth Century." A Military History

   of Ireland. Cambridge: Cambridge UP, 1996. 52-75.

---. "John de Courcy: The First Plantation and Church men." Smith, ed. Britain and

   Ireland 900-1300 154-78.

---. "Strategies of Lordship in Pre-Norman and Post-Norman Leinster."

   Proceedings Battle Conference on Anglo-Norman Studies XX. Woodbridge:

   Boydell, 1998: 107-26.

---. "Strongbow, Henry II and Anglo-Norman Intervention in Ireland." Essays in

   Honour of J. O. Prestwich. Woodbridge: Boydell, 1984. 62-77.

Frame, Robin. <u>Colonial Ireland 1169-1369.</u> Dublin: Helicon, 1981.

---. "The English Political Identity in Medieval Ireland." <u>TRHS</u> 6 ser. III (1993): 83-
104.

Gillingham, John. "Killing and Mutilating Political Enemies in the British Isles
from The late 12th to the early 14th Centuries." Smith, ed. <u>Britain and Ireland
900-1300</u> 114-34.

Graham, B. "Urbanization in Medieval Ireland c900 to 1300." <u>Journal of Urban
History</u> 13 (Feb. 1987): 169-96.

Greaney, Michael D. "Last of the Norman Invasions." <u>Military History</u> 15.5 (Dec.
1998): 42-49.

Grotty, Gerard. "Six Coats of Arms of St. Mary's, Ireland." <u>Old Kilkenny Review</u>
ns 1.5 (1978): 306-13.

Hand, G. J. "English Law in Ireland 1171-1351." <u>The Northern Ireland Legal
Quarterly</u> 23.4 (Winter 1972): 393-420.

Hays, L. and E. D. Jones. "Policy on the Run: Henry II and Irish Sea Diplomacy."
<u>Journal of British Studies</u> 29 (Oct. 1990): 293-316.

Hennig, John. "Medieval Ireland in Cistercian Records." <u>Irish Ecclesiastical
Record</u> 5th ser. LXXIII (1950): 226-42.

Hughes, Edward. "Duiske Abbey Graignamanagh: Abbey Triumphant." <u>Old
Kilkenny Review</u> ns 1.4 (1977): 254-60.

<u>Irish Pedigrees: The Origin and Stem of the Irish Nation.</u> Ed. John O'Hart. 5th ed. 2
vols. Baltimore: Genealogical Publishing, 1976-86

Long, Joseph. "Dermot and the Earl: Who Wrote 'the Song'?" <u>Proceedings Of the</u>

Royal Irish Academy 75 Sect. C (1975): 263-72.

Lydon, James, ed. The English in Medieval Ireland: Proceedings of the First Joint Meeting of the Royal Irish Academy and the British Academy. Dublin: Royal Irish Academy, 1984.

---. "The Expansion and Consolidation of the Colony, 1215-54." Cosgrove & Martin, eds. A New History of Ireland: Medieval Ireland II. Oxford: Clarendon, 1987. 156-75.

---. "Ireland and the English Crown 1171-1541." Irish Historical Studies XXIX. 115 (May 1995): 281-94.

MacAirt, Sean, ed. and trans. The Annals of Inisfallen [MS Rawlinson B503]. Dublin: Alex. Thom, 1951.

MacNiocaill, G., ed. The Red Book of the Earls of Kildare. Dublin: Irish Manuscript Commission, 1969.

McNeill, Tom. Castles in Ireland: Feudal Power in a Gaelic World. London: Routledge, 1997.

---. "Hibernia pacata et Castellata." Liddiard, Anglo-Norman Castles 259-72.

Mills, James. "The Norman Settlement in Leinster: the Cantreds near Dublin." JRSAI XXIV ser.5.4 (1894): 160-75.

Nichols, K. "The Charter of John, Lord of Ireland, in Favor of the Cistercian Abbey of Baltinglass." Peritia 4 (1985): 187-206.

Nugent, W. F. "Carlow in the Middles Ages." The Journal of the Royal Society Of Antiquaries of Ireland LXXXV (1955): 62-76.

O'Conbhui, Rev. C. O. "The Lands of St. Mary's, Dublin." Proceedings of The

Royal Irish Academy 62 Sect C. (1961-63): 21-84.

O'Keefe, Tadgh. "Diarmait MacMurchada and Romanesque Leinster: Four 12th
Century Churches in Context." Journal of the Royal Society of Antiquaries
Of Ireland 127 (1997): 57-79.

Otway-Ruthven, Jocelyn. "The Chief Governors of Medieval Ireland." Journal of
the Royal Society of Antiquaries of Ireland XCV (1965): 227-36.

---. A History of Medieval Ireland. 4 vols.   London: Benn, 1968

---. "Knight Service in Ireland." The Journal of the Royal Society of Antiquaries of
Ireland LXXXIX (1959): 1-15.

---. "Knights' Fees in Kildare, Leix, and Offaly." Journal of the Royal Society of
Antiquaries of Ireland XCI. pt. I (1961): 189-92.

 ---. "The Medieval County of Kildare." Irish Historical Studies 11 (1959): 181-99.

Prendergast, John. "An Ancient Record Relating to the Families into Which Were
Married the Co-Heiresses of Thomas fitz Anthony." Journal of the Royal
Society of Antiquaries of Ireland 8 (1864-66): 139-53.

Richardson, H. G. "Norman Ireland in 1212." Irish Historical Studies 3.10 (1942):
144-58.

Roche, Richard. The Norman Invasion of Ireland. 3rd ed. Dublin: Anvil, 1995.

Round, J. H. "Conquest of Ireland." The Commune of London and Other Studies.
Westminster: A Constable, 1899: 137-70.

---. "Foundation of Tintern Abbey, Co. Wexford." Proceedings of the Royal Irish
Academy 33 Sect. C (1916-17): 527-29.

Smith, Brendan, ed. Britain and Ireland 900-1300: Insular Responses and Medieval

European Change. Cambridge: Cambridge UP, 1999.

---. "Tenure and Locality in North Leinster in the Early 13th Century." Barry,

Frame and Simms, eds. Colony and Frontier in Medieval Ireland 140-58.

Stringer, Keith. "Nobility and Identity in Medieval Britain and Ireland: the de Vescy

Family, 1210-1314." Smith, ed. Britain and Ireland 900-1300 199-234.

Warren, W. L. "Church and State in Angevin Ireland." Peritia 13 (1999): 276-91.

Webster, Charles. "Diocese of Ross and Its Ancient Churches." Proceedings Of the

Royal Irish Academy XL Sect. C (1932): 255-95.

Wood, Herbert. "The Public Records of Ireland Before and After 1922."

Transactions of the Royal Historical Society 4th ser. 8 (1930): 17-49.

WALES

Adam of Usk. Chronicle of Adam Usk 1377-1421. Trans. C. Given-Wilson.

Oxford: Clarendon, 1997.

Annals and Antiquities of the Counties and County Families of Wales. Ed. Thomas

Nicholas. 2nd ed. 2 vols. Baltimore: Genealogical Publishing Co., 1991.

Blashill, Thomas. "The Architectural History of Tintern Abbey."

Transactions of the Bristol and Gloucestershire Society 6 (1881): 88-

106.

Bartrum, P. C., ed. Early Welsh Genealogical Tracts. Cardiff: U of Wales P,

1966.

Brakespeare, Harold. Tintern Abbey Monmouthshire. 2nd ed. London: HMSO,

1921.

A Calendar of the Public Records Relating to Pembrokeshire. Vol. I: the Lordship

Castle and town of Haverford. Ed. Henry Owen. London: The Honourable

    Society of Cymmrodorion, 1911.

A Calendar of the Public Records Relating to Pembrokeshire. Vol. II: The Castles,

    Towns, and Lordship of Cilgerran and Narberth. Ed. Henry Owen. London:

    The Honourable Society of Cymmrodorion, 1914.

A Calendar of the Public Records Relating to Pembrokeshire. Vol. III: the Earldom

    of Pembroke and Its members. Ed. Henry Owen. London: the Honourable

    Society Of Cymmrodorion, 1918.

A Catalogue of the Manuscripts Relating to Wales in the British Museum. Ed.

    Edward Owen. London: The Honourable Society of Cymmrodorion, 1900.

Carr, Anthony. Medieval Wales. NY: St Martin's, 1995.

"Chronicle of the Thirteenth Century, 1066-1298." *Archaeologia Cambrensis*

    (1862): 272-83.

Cowley, F. G. The Monastic Order in South Wales 1066-1349. Cardiff: U of Wales

    P, 1977.

David, H. E. "Margam Abbey, Glamorgan."*Archaeologia Cambrensis* 84

    (1929): 317-24.

Davies, R. R. "Kings, Lords and Liberties in the March of Wales 1066-1272."

    TRHS 29 (1979): 41-61.

---. "The Law of the March." Welsh History Review 5 (1971): 1-30.

---. "Race Relations in Post-Conquest Wales." The Transactions of the Honourable

    Society of Cymmrodorion (1974-75): 451-62.

Dillon, Myles. "The Irish Settlement in Wales." *Celtica* 12 (1977): 1-11.

Edwards, J. G. "The Normans and The Welsh March." Proceedings of the British

    Academy (6 June 1956): 157-77.

Edwards, Nancy. Landscape and Settlement in Medieval Wales. Oxford: Oxbow,

    1997.

Edwards, T. Charles. Early Irish and Welsh Kinship. Oxford: Clarendon, 1990.

Evans, A. Leslie. Margam Abbey. Port Talbot: Remploy, 1958.

Gillingham, John. "Henry II, Richard I and the Lord Rhys." *Peritia* 10 (1996): 225-

    36.

Given, J. B. State and Society in Medieval Europe: Gwynedd and Lonquedoc Under

    Outside Rule. Ithaca, NY: Cornell UP, 1990.

Griffiths, Ralph A. Conquerors and Conquered in Medieval Wales. NY: St Martin's,

    1994.

Harrison, Julian. "A Note on Gerald of Wales and *Annales Cambriae*." Welsh

    History Review 17 (1994/95): 252-312.

Higham, N. J. "Medieval Overkingship in Wales: The Earliest Evidence." Welsh

    History Review 16 (1992/93): 145-59.

Hogg, A. H. A. and D. J. Cathcart-King. "Masonry Castles in Wales." *Archaeologia*

    Cambrensis 110 (1970): 119-24.

Holden, Brock. "The Making of the Middle March of Wales1066-1250." Welsh

    History Review 20.2 (Dec. 2000): 207-26.

Howell, M. "Regalian Right in Wales and the March." Welsh History Review 7

    (1974-75): 269-88.

Huws, Daniel. Medieval Welsh Manuscripts. Cardiff: U of Wales Press & National

Library of Wales, 2000.

The Irish Cartularies of Llanthony Prima and Secunda. Ed. Eric St John Brooks. Dublin: The Stationary Office, 1953.

Jenkins, Daffydd. "Kings, Lords and Princes: The Nomenclature of 13th Century Wales." The Bulletin of the Board of Celtic Studies 26 (1974-76): 451-62.

Kenyon, John R. "Fluctuating Frontiers: Normanno-Welsh Castle Warfare." Liddiard, Anglo-Norman Castles 247-58.

Kenyon, John and Richard Avent, eds. Castles in Wales and the Marches; Essays in Honour of D. J. Cathcart King. Cardiff: U of Wales P, 1987.

King, D. J. Cathcart. "Castles and the Administrative Divisions of Wales." Welsh History Review 10(1980/81): 92-5

---. "Pembroke Castle." *Achaeologia Cambrensis* 127 (1978): 75-121.

Lewis, E. A., ed. An Inventory of the Early Chancery Proceedings Concerning Wales. Cardiff: Cardiff U Press Board, 1937.

Lewis, F. "A History of the Lordship of Gower from the Neath Cartulary." The Bulletin of the Board of Celtic Studies 9.2 (May 1938): 149-54.

Little, A. C. Medieval Wales Chiefly in the 12th and 13th Centuries. London: T. Fisher Unwin, 1902.

Nelson, Lynn H. The Normans in South Wales 1070-1171. Austin: U of Texas P, 1966.

O'Sullivan, Jeremiah. Cistercian Settlements in Wales and Monmouthshire, 1140-1540. NY: Declan McMullen, 1947.

Owen, Edward. "The Spoils of the Welsh Religious Houses." *Archaeologia*

Cambrensis 5 ser. 14 (1897): 285-92.

Patterson, Robert. "The Author of the 'Margam Annals': Early 13th Century Margam
    Abbey's Compleat Scribe." <u>Battle Conference on Anglo-Norman Studies</u>
    <u>XIV</u>. Ed. Marjorie Chibnall. Woodbridge: Boydell, 1992. 197-210.

Perks, John. "The Architectural History of Chepstow Castle During the Middle
    Ages." <u>Transactions of the Bristol and Gloucester Archaeological Society</u> 67
    (1946/47): 307-46.

Pettifer, Adrian. <u>Welsh Castles: A Guide by Counties.</u> Woodbridge: Boydell, 2000.

Pickering, W. "Chronicle of the Thirteenth Century: MS Exchequer Domesday."
    Archaeologia Cambrensis VIII. ns 3 (1862): 272-83.

Pryce, Huw. "In Search of Medieval Society: Deheubarth in the Writing of Gerald
    of Wales." <u>Welsh History Review</u> 13 (1986/87): 265-81.

Pugh, T. B., ed. <u>The Marcher Lordships of South Wales 1415-1536.</u> Cardiff: U of
    Wales P, 1963.

---. <u>Glamorgan County History III: The Middle Ages.</u> Cardiff: U of Wales P, 1971.

Rees, William. <u>An Historical Atlas of Wales From Early to Modern Times.</u> London:
    Faber & Faber, 1961.

---. Ed. <u>Calendar of Ancient Petitions Relating to Wales.</u> Cardiff: U Wales P, 1973.

---. <u>A History of the Order of St John of Jerusalem in Wales and the Welsh Border.</u>
    NY: AMS, 1947.

---. "The Possessions of Tewkesbury Abbey." <u>South Wales and Monmouthshire</u>
    <u>Record Society</u> ii (1950): 139-64.

Richter, Michael. "David ap Llywelyn: The First Prince of Wales." <u>Welsh History</u>

Review 5 (1971): 205-19.

Robinson, David M. Tintern Abbey. 3rd ed. Cardiff: CADW, 1995

Scott, J. L. "Some Original Documents Relating to the South Part of
　　Pembrokeshire." Journal of the British Archaeological Association XLI
　　(1885): 153-75.

Smith, J. B. "Dynastic Succession in Medieval Wales." The Bulletin of the Board
　　of Celtic Studies 33 (1986): 199-232.

---. Llywelyn ap Gruffudd Prince of Wales. Cardiff: Cardiff UP, 1998.

---. "The Lordship of Glamorgan." Morgannwg 2 (1958): 9-37.

---. "Magna Carta and the Charters of the Welsh Princes." EHR 99 (April 1984):
　　344-62.

---. "Middle March in the Thirteenth Century." Bulletin of the Board of Celtic
　　Studies XXIV (1970-72): 77-93.

Smith, J. Beverley, ed. Medieval Welsh Society: Selected Essays by Thomas Jones
　　Pierce. Cardiff: U of Wales P, 1972.

Smith, L. B. "Death of Llywelyn ap Gruffydd: The Narratives Reconsidered."
　　Welsh History Review 11 (1982-83): 200-13.

Soulsby, Ian. The Towns of Medieval Wales. Chichester, UK: Phillimore, 1983.

Suppe, Frederick C. "Castleguard and the Castlery of Clun." Liddiard, Anglo-
　　Norman Castles 211-22.

---. Military Institutions on the Welsh Marches: Shropshire, 1066-1300.
　　Woodbridge: Boydell, 1994.

Taylor, John. Tintern Abbey and Its Founders. London: Houlston & Wright, 1869

Walker, David. <u>Medieval Wales.</u> Cambridge: Cambridge UP, 1990.

---. "The Lordship of Builth in the Middle Ages." <u>*Brycheiniog*</u> 20 (1982-83): 23-33.

Williams, A. G. "Norman Lordship in South East Wales During the Reign of
William I." <u>Welsh History Review</u> 16 (1992/3): 445-66.

Williams, D. H. <u>Atlas of the Cistercian Lands in Wales.</u> Cardiff: U Wales P, 1990.

---. "Catalogue of Seals in Wales." <u>*Archaeologia Cambrensis*</u> 134 (1985): 162-89.

INDEX

Adeliza Pipard, first wife John fitz Gilbert, 27, 38-39

Aline/Alina, bastard daughter of Strongbow, 75,76

Aoife/Eve MacMurchada, wife of Strongbow, 36, 37-38, 77-78
    135-36

Angulo, William de, 64, 81

Arrouaise, order of, 283

Aumale, count of. See Bethune, Baldwin de

Bacon, Robert, 324

Bardolf, Hugh, 231

Barres, William de, 93, 97, 100, 111, 114, 174

Basset, Gilbert, 293, 324, 326, 339
  Thomas 180

Basilia, sister of Strongbow, 74, 76-77, 80

Beaumont, Robert de, 54

Beaumont, viscount of, 54
    Robert. See Leicester
    Waleran, 29, 41, 54

Becket, Thomas, 44-46

Bethune, Baldwin de, 91, 117-18, 121-22, 186-87
    226

Bigod, Hugh, earl of Norfolk, 64-95, 96, 288-89
    Roger, 226, 289

Blanche of Castile, wife of Louis VIII, 256

Bloet, Walter, 64
      Ralph 64, 136

Blois, Theobald, 100, 111, 115

Boisrohard, Gilbert de, 64

Bouvines, battle of, 227-28

Bradenstoke, priory of, 283

Braose, Giles de, bishop of Hereford, 237
    John de, son of William IV, 265, 300, 303
    Reginald, son of William III, 237, 255
    William III, 177-78, 179, 188, 206-08, 211-12,
      213, 216-18
    William IV, son of William, 214-15, 216-17
    William, son of Reginald, 265, 313

Breaute, Falkes de, 245, 251, 297-300

Breteuil, 74

Burgh, Hubert de, 176-77, 244, 245, 256, 272-90,
        295, 296-97, 301-05, 306-07, 310-11, 319-20,
        322-23, 326-339

Burgh, Richard de, 332, 335

Cardigan, 52, 65, 226, 236, 304

Carlow, 204

Carmarthen, 55, 226, 236, 304

Cartmel, 143

Cartmel, priory of, 143

Castles, 11-14

Caversham, 283

Champagne, Henry count of, 115

Chateau Gaillard, 179-80

Chepstow/Striguil, 55, 56

Chester, Ranulf, earl of, 41, 166, 226, 244, 245,
        250-51, 254, 266, 277, 307-08, 322

Cilgerran (Kilgerran), 142, 304

Clahull, John de, 79, 81, 194

Clahull, Hugh de, 79

Clare, de (earls of Clare & Hertford), history, 50-53, 55

Clare, Gilbert fitz Richard, earl Hertford & Gloucester, 227, 290-341

Clare, Gilbert fitz Gilbert, 1st earl of Pembroke, 53-55, 56-57

Clare, Isabel, countess of Pembroke: early, 76-77;
        marriage, 133-34, 136-39; lands, 139-42; Irish, 140,195-96,
        202-03; developed, 203-05; Marshal's death, 275, 277-78,
        286-87; her death, 297-98

Clare, Richard fitz Gilbert, "Strongbow": origins, 53-55, 56-57;
        name "Strongbow," 57-58; Henry II, 58-60;
        Dermot of Leinster, 60-62; men who went to Ireland, 62-65;
        in Ireland, 65-67; Henry II, 69-72; Henry II in Ireland, 72-74;
        "Strongbow" in Normandy, 74; England, 76; his death, 76-77;
        custody of Irish lands, 78; grants by "Strongbow," 80-81;
        summation, 82

Clare, Walter fitz Richard, lord of Chepstow/Striguil, 51, 53

Clarendon, Constitution of, 42-44

Cogan, Miles de, 63, 68

Cogan, Richard de, 68

Cornwall, Richard, 290-92
Coutances, Walter de, archbishop of Rouen, 148-49
Crendon, 272

Derby, earl of, William de Ferrers, 166, 226, 231, 244, 266
Dermot MacMurchada, king of Leinster, 60-62, 65, 66-67, 68
Devizes, 34-35
Dreux, count of, Robert I, 100, 115, 227
Drincourt (Seine Inferieure), battle of, 84-85
Dublin, archbishop. See Henry de London
        Lawrence O'Toole, 67, 79
Duiske Abbey, 204, 279
Dunamase, castle of, 204
Dunbrody Abbey, 279

Eleanor of Aquitaine: 19, 87-88; prisoner, 95-96, 126; free,
        134; England for Richard, 153-56; tries to save Normandy,
        167, 168-70; death, 180-81
Eleanor of Brittany, daughter of Geoffrey Plantagenet, 75,
        181, 302-03
Empress Matilda, daughter of Henry I, 27-29, 30-31, 35
England, king of: **Henry I**, 51, 54-55
        Henry II: 41-42; Becket, 42-46; Strongbow, 58-60, 67-70,
        71-72; Treaty Windsor, 76; young Henry, 74-75; rebellion,
        92, 94-95, 97; Eleanor, 95-96; death young Henry, 121-22;
        Gisors, 127-28; Le Mans, 129-30; death, 130-31
        young Henry:90-62; rebellion, 92, 94-97; tournaments,
        109-16; Marshal, 117-19; death, 121-22
        Henry III: 241-43, 247, 254-55, 257-58, 265, 267-68,
        272-73, 275-76, 295, 298, 301-02, 306, 308-09, 311, 313,
        317, 319, 320-21, 323, 324, 328, 331-33, 334-35, 338-40
        John: 98; marriage, 144; rebellion, 153-56, 164-65;
        coronation, 167; Mirabeau 173-76; Arthur, 176-78; French,
        172-73, 178-79; de Braose, 206-08, 211-12, 216-18; pope,
        219-20, 222-24; Normandy, 226-27; rebellion, 228-30, 236-39;
        Magna Carta, 232-34; death, 240-42
        hard I: tournaments 102; rebellion, 125-26; Le Mans, 129-32;
        ation, 144-45; crusade, 145; England, 146-51; captured,
        land, 156-57; Normandy, 160-63; death, 163-64

Stephen: crown, 27-29, 30, 35; Henry II, 41-42

Erley, John de, 126, 158, 197, 198, 202, 204, 215, 267, 279-80, 283-84

Essex, earl of: Geoffrey fitz Peter, 166, 225
      William de Mandeville, 85, 127, 253, 284
      Geoffrey de Mandeville, 226, 232

d'Evreux, Stephen, 195, 197, 198

eyre, 273-74

Ferns, Bishop of, 268-69

Ferrers, William de, 195, 204, 237, 244

fitz Anthony, Thomas, 195, 204, 237

fitz Audelin, William de, 72, 78

fitz Count, Brian, 36

fitz David, Miles, son of David fitz Gerald, 63, 81

fitz Gerald, David, bishop of St David's, 63
      Maurice of Llansteffan, 62, 63
      Maurice fitz Gerald, 68, 332, 335
      William of Carew, 63, 81

fitz Gerold, Henry, 282

fitz Harding, Robert, of Bristol, 61-62

fitz Henry, Meiler, 63, 81, 190, 193, 198-99, 200, 203, 269

fitz Robert, Geoffrey, 192, 195, 204, 215

fitz Stephen, Robert, castellan of Cardigan, 62-63, 65, 69

fitz Walter, Robert, 51-52, 179, 220, 249, 253

Flanders, count of, Philip, 84, 64-65, 96, 100, 109-110 115, 119-20, 127, 226

France, king of, **Louis VII**: 19, 92-97
     Philip Augustus: 115, 125-28, 146, 151-52, 167, 169-71, 181, 223-24, 305
     Louis VIII, son of Philip: 170-71, 238-245, 254-55, 305

Geoffrey Plantagenet, son of Henry II, 112, 115, 125-26

Geoffrey, bastard son Henry II, 149

Glanville, Ranulf de, 134-35

Gloucester, constable of, Miles, 29-30

Gloucester, earl of, Robert, 18, 29, 37, 39

Gras (Grassus, Crassus), William le, 48, 326-27

Gray, John de, bishop of Norwich, 209, 211-12, 220-21
Gregory IX, pope, 291, 318, 346
Gros, Raymond le, 60, 66, 68
Grosseteste, Robert, 330-31
Gualo, legate, 243-44, 249

Hamelin Plantagenet, bastard of Geoffrey of Anjou, 18
Henry of Blois. See bishop of Winchester
Hereford, Adam de, 81, 193
Huntingdon, earl of, David, brother of William of Scotland, 94,
        166, 226, 297

Inkberrow, (Worcestershire), 42
Innocent III, pope, 209, 219-224

Joan, bastard of King John, 220

Kilkenny, castle of, 279
Kilmainham, Knights' Hospitallers, 79
Knights, equipment, 104-06
Knights' Templar, 122-24

Lacy, Hugh de, lord of Meath, 72, 73, 78
        Hugh de, lord of Ulster, 188, 194, 198, 214, 312,
          332, 335
        Walter de, lord of Meath, 188, 194, 214, 236, 312,332
Lacy, John de, constable of Chester, 231, 253, 266
Lacy, Roger de, 166, 179
Lambeth, treaty of, 257-58
Langton, Stephen, archbishop of Canterbury, 209-10, 219-20,
        223, 228-30, 235, 303, 305-09
Leicester, earl of, Robert, 94, 95, 97, 181-82
ncoln, battle of (1141), 35; (1217), 250-53
    velyn ap Iorwerth of Wales, 219, 237, 245, 255-56,
        265, 268, 279-80, 293, 299, 300, 303, 305-06, 313, 338
        Henry de, 302-03
        , William, 146-49, 150-51, 158-59
        'illiam. See Salisbury
        '5

Louis VII. See France, king of

Lugershall, castle of, 31

Lusignan, Aimery de, 88
       Geoffrey de, 88, 227
       Guy de, 88
       Hugh de, count of Le Marche, 88, 227, 299-300
       Ralph de, count of Eu, 88

Marisco, Geoffrey, justiciar Ireland, 286, 333, 336

Marlborough, castle of, 31, 33, 270

Marshal: Anselm, 6th son of John, 48
       Eve, 4th daughter of William, 278, 293
       Gilbert, grandfather of William, 26-27
       Gilbert, eldest son of John, 48
       Henry, 5th son of John, 48, 146
       Isabel, 2nd daughter of William, 259, 278, 290-92, 324-25
       Joan/Jeanne, 5th daughter of William, 278, 294
       John fitz Gilbert, the marshal: origins, 26-27; office of marshal, 26-27;
       Henry I, 27; Stephen, 27-30, 32; Empress Matilda, 27, 30, 35-36;
       Devizes, 34-35; battle Winchester, 36-37; Patrick of Salisbury,
       37-38; son William as hostage, 39-41; end of civil war, 41;
       Henry II, 41-42; dispute with Thomas Becket, 43-46; legacy, 47-48
       John, 3rd son of John fitz Gilbert, 48, 146, 147-48, 156-57
       John, bastard nephew of William, 146, 193, 197, 226, 259, 267
       Margaret, daughter of John fitz Gilbert, 48
       Maud, daughter of John fitz Gilbert, 48
       Matilda/Maud, eldest daughter of William, 259, 278, 288-89
       Sibyl/Sibilla, 3rd daughter of William, 278, 292-93
       Walter, 2nd son of John, 48
       William, brother of John fitz Gilbert, 41

Marshal, earl of Pembroke: William:
          Chapt. IV: fostered, 83; knighted first battle at Drincourt,
          84-85; first tournament, 85-86; murder of uncle Patrick earl
          of Salisbury, 87;hostage and debt to Eleanor of
          Aquitaine, 88-89; head of young Henry's household,
          91-92; knighting young Henry, 92-93; rebellion
          1173/74, 93-97; peace with Henry II, 97-98
          Chapt. V: Normandy and tournaments, 100; definition
          of tournaments, 101-08; laws of Richard I, 102;

prudhomme, 108-09; tournaments, 109-16; accusation against Marshal, 117-19; return to young Henry, 120-21; death of young Henry, 120-21; crusader, 122; Knight Templar, 122-24

Chapt. VI: first fief at Cartmel, 125; *familiaris Regis,* 125; war with Philip of France, 125-26; battle of champions, 127-28; promised Isabel de Clare as wife, 128-29; battle at Le Mans, 129-30; treaty with Philip, 130-31; death of Henry II, 131-32

Chapt. VII: given Isabel de Clare to be wife, 133-34; Isabel de Clare, 133-39; greater magnate, 139-42; Richard's coronation, 144-45; Marshal's acquisitions, 146; Longchamp's problems, 146-50; *justiciar* 148; problem of Geoffrey of York, 149; rebellion Wales, 152-53; Marshal helps Queen Eleanor against prince John, 153-56; brother John Marshal dies, 156-57; Ireland, 158-59; Normandy, 160-62; Milli, 161-62; Longueville, 163; Richard I's death, 163-64

Chapt. VIII: John king, 167; created earl of Pembroke, 167; Eleanor protects Aquitaine, 168-70; war with Philip of France, 172-73; Mirabeau, 173-74; Arthur, 178-79; Eleanor dies, 180; Marshal's Norman lands, 181-83; estrangement, 186-88

Chapt. IX: Ireland, 189-90; loss of grants, 190-91; seneschal Ireland, 193; betrayal, 193; in Ireland, 193-96; in England, 196-97; John bribes vassals, 197-98; peace and new charter, 200-02; development Irish lands, 203-04

Chapt. X: problems of de Braose, 206-08; Stephen Langton, 209-10; de Braose in Ireland, 211-12; John in Ireland/revenge, 212; explanation of de Braose destruction, 216-18

Chapt. XI: John excommunicated, 219-20; threats to John, 220; Pope, 222-24; grants to Marshal, 225-26; John's expedition to Poitou, 226-27; English barons rebel, 228-30; Magna Carta, 232-34; Marshal's role, 234-35

Chapt XII: rebellion, 236; in Wales, 236-37; William II rebel, 238-39; Louis of France in England, 239; Marshal in Wales, 240; John's last days, 240-42

Chapt. XIII: Henry III, 243; choice of regent, 244; regent, 244-46; Magna Carta, 247-48; Louis, 248; William II

returns, 248-49; battle of Lincoln, 250-53; Wales and
Scotland, 255-56, 264-65; Treaty of Lambeth, 257-58;
governing as regent, 260-64; benefits to Marshal's
familares, 264-66; Marshal's gains, 267-72
Chapt. XIV: retires, 275-76; family, 277-78; ecclesiastical
grants, 278-79; Knight Templar, 280-82; last days, 283-84;
burial, 284-85; Isabel, 286-87
Chapt. XIX: William Marshal's legacy, 350-54
Marshal, earl of Pembroke, William II:
Chapt. XVI: 238-39, 248-49, 250, 267, 278; death of
regent/re-organization, 295; Isabel dies, 297-98;
2nd coronation of Henry III, 298-99; Wales,
300, 303-06; crisis, 302, 306-09; Eleanor 2nd wife,
301-02, 311-12; Ireland and Hugh de Lacy, 312-13;
Llywelyn and 2nd marriage of sister Isabel,
313-14; dies, 314-15
Marshal, earl of Pembroke, Richard:
Chapt. XVII: history, 227, 278, 316-17; question of
marriage, 317-18; de Burgh's troubles, 319-22; des Roches,
323; against foreigners, 323-24; vassals attacked, 324;
warned of treachery, 324-25; declared a traitor, lands attacked,
325-27; de Burgh rescued, 326; Llywelyn, 326-27; war
with king, 326-27, 328-31; Monmouth castle, 328-29;
Richard' view, 329-30; Robert Grosseteste, 330-31; heinous
acts, 332-33; rebuke of king, 333-35; attacks on Irish lands,
333,335; betrayed, trapped, 335-37; fall of des Roches,
338; peace, 339-40; summation, 340-45
Marshal, earl of Pembroke, Gilbert:
Chapt XVIII: Gilbert, 3rd son: history, 278;
Ireland, 339, 346; marriage and death, 347
Walter, 4th son: history, 278; Ireland,
336, 347; Committee of Twelve and death, 347-48
Anselm, 5th son: history, 278; marriage and death, 348
Milli, castle of, 160-62
Monmouth, Baderon de,52, 73
Monmouth, John de, 236, 331
Monmouth, battle of, 328-29
Montmorency, Herve de, 62, 69
Muntchesney, Warin de, 294

Naas, lord of, William fitz William, 194
Nest/Nesta, daughter of Rhys ap Tewdr, 62-63
Neufchatel-en-Bray. See Drincourt
New Ross, 192, 203-04, 238, 270
Newbury, castle of, 39-40
Norfolk. See Bigod, earl of
Nutley Abbey, 282-83

O'Toole, Lawrence, See Dublin
Oxford. See de Vere

Pandulf, papal legate, 219, 222-23, 275, 295, 296
Pembroke, Earldom of, See de Clare, Richard and Marshal, William
Perche, count of, 271-72
Plantagenet, Hamelin. See Warenne
Preaux, Peter de, 91, 117, 182
Prendergast, Maurice de, 62, 63-64, 81
     Philip de, 194, 197, 202

Quenci/Quency, Saher de, 91, 179, 226, 249-53
Quenci, Robert de, 64, 68, 73, 74
     Maud, dau of Robert, 74, 80

Rhys ap Gruffydd, 62, 65
Rhys ap Tewdr, 62
Rhys Gryg, 255-56, 265
Rich, Edmund, archbishop of Canterbury, 333-35, 337-40
Ridelsford, Walter de, 64, 81
Rivaux, Peter des, 321, 324, 325, 338-39
Roche, David de la, 197, 202, 215
     Richard de la, 64
   ιches, Peter des, 238, 243-44, 251-52, 268-69, 275-76,
     295-96, 307-08, 319, 320-21, 325-26, 338-39
     ς, William de, 174-75, 227
       Osbert de, 127, 182

       ·dan de, 197, 198, 267
         ν de, 238, 280-81

Salisbury, earls of:
   Patrick, uncle of William Marshal, 87-88, 90
   Sibyl, mother of William Marshal, 38-39
   William, cousin of William Marshal, 103
   William Longespee, natural son of Henry II, 18, 174, 226, 227,
      230, 248-49, 252-54, 271-72
Sanford, Hugh de, 190, 215
Sanford, Thomas de, 243
Scotland, king of: Alexander, 18, 245;
     William the Lion, 86, 94, 96, 211
Siward, Richard, 324, 326, 331, 339
Stephen. See England, king of
Striguil, lordship of. See de Clare, Richard and Marshal, William
Stuteville, Nicholas de, 249
Surrey, earl of: Hamelin Plantagenet, 18, 103;
     William II de Warenne, 226, 284, 289

Tancarville, lord of, William de, 44, 49, 83-85, 86, 87, 90,
     118-19
Tintern Abbey, 51
Tintern Minor, 193, 204
Tournaments: patrons of, 100; descriptions of, 101-02, 103-08;
     Anet-Sorel, 110; Eu, 111-12; Eure, 113-14; Joigny, 112-13;
     Lagni, 114-16; Pleurs, 110-11; Richard I, rules of, 102

Usk, castle of, 55

Vere, Aubrey de, 52
     Robert de, earl of Oxford, 284
Vescy/Vesci, Eustace de, 220

Walter, Hubert, 166, 181, 208
Warenne. See Surrey, earl of
Wexcombe, 42
Wherwell, abbey of, 36-37
Wigan, 42
William of Ypres, 36-37
William the Lion. See Scotland
Winchester, battle of, 36-37

Winchester, bishop of, Henry of Blois, 35-36
        See Peter des Roches
Winchester, earl of. See Saher de Quenci